The Best
Poor Man's Country

The Best
Poor Man's Country

A GEOGRAPHICAL STUDY

OF EARLY SOUTHEASTERN

PENNSYLVANIA

JAMES T. LEMON

THE JOHNS HOPKINS PRESS, BALTIMORE AND LONDON

The Johns Hopkins Press, Baltimore, Maryland 21218
The Johns Hopkins Press Ltd., London

Library of Congress Catalog Card Number 77-165352
ISBN 0-8018-1189-9

For Carolyn

Contents

List of Tables

List of Figures

Preface

Early Pennsylvania was, in many respects, the prototype of North American development. Its style of life presaged the mainstream of nineteenth-century America; its conservative defense of liberal individualism, its population of mixed national and religious origins, its dispersed farms, county seats, and farm-service villages, and its mixed crop and livestock agriculture served as models for much of the rural Middle West.

To many western Europeans of the late seventeenth and eighteenth centuries Pennsylvania was a veritable paradise and refuge from oppression. Indeed, many commentators referred to it as "the best poor man's country in the world."[1] Without doubt the area was one of the most affluent agricultural societies anywhere. For these reasons as well as for its contribution to the American style of life that followed, early Pennsylvania deserves a great deal more scrutiny than it has hitherto received.

This study in historical geography considers a number of issues bearing on the interplay of society and land in early Pennsylvania and centering on the Pennsylvanians' attachment to the land. The chief questions are: What factors determined where the first settlers occupied sites? How much spatial mobility was there in the area, and why did people move? Why did the settlers and their descendants organize the space into dispersed farms and open-country neighborhoods rather than agricultural villages? How did the urban pattern develop? What factors contributed to the mixed farming system, the diversity of livestock and crops but with emphasis on wheat? Why did the regionalization of types of agri-

xiii

culture, defined by specialization and intensity of land use, develop only slightly?

These core questions are geographic in focus. Like historical sociologists, folklife specialists, anthropologists, and demographers, historical geographers have shown that they have a valuable and distinctive role to play within the general framework of social and economic history.[2] With their emphasis on man-land relations, on spatial connections, and on regions, geographers can supply types of analysis not usually undertaken by historians.

One central conceptual matter needs to be mentioned: the interpretation. In this study a wide range of variables is used to explain the material. Traditionally, students of rural America have tended to present either the cultural background of settlers, or the natural environment, or the frontier as the key to understanding what people did. In Pennsylvania's case the emphasis has been on national or ethnic traditions.

In particular, the "Pennsylvania Dutch" (Germans) have been lauded since Benjamin Franklin's time as better farmers than those from the British Isles. Poor Richard admired the "habitual industry and frugality" of the Germans.[3] Dr. Benjamin Rush, another influential Philadelphian, asserted that German farms could be distinguished "by the fertility of their Fields; the luxuriance of their meadows, and a general appearance of plenty and neatness in everything that belongs to them."[4] Later commentators elaborated the theme until it became a commonplace in the literature.[5] A parallel assertion has been that Ulstermen (usually called Scotch-Irish), though poor farmers, were the "toughest, most adventurous pioneers" on the frontier.[6]

Such a stance accentuates the habitual behavior and the persistence of presumed customs and virtues of these groups. Proponents of national cultural traditions have, therefore, underplayed other cultural, environmental, and social factors.[7] They have not recognized that western Europeans generally shared, for example, a diet emphasizing pork, beef, and small grains. They have not recognized the importance of the new environment.

As is well known, others have used the frontier, or climate, or topography to explain the course of American development. I suspect that some historians think that geographers should talk about the role of, say, mountains in determining the course of settlement, as did Ellen Churchill Semple in her *American History and Its Geographic Conditions*, published in 1903.[8] That is not the perspective taken in this study because it does not give enough due to the people. If cultural determinists made people into preprogrammed automatons who followed custom, then environmentalists imagine people like Pavlovian dogs able only to react to external stimuli.

This study does not deny the power of tradition and environment; but it considers more centrally the decisions of the people and their more immediate social situation. The many decisions that shaped life on the land in early Pennsylvania were the result of how people perceived their situation. Inputs did come from the environment and cultural traditions, but they were interpreted in the light of what people expected to do and what they were able to do. In other words, their ideology (or less strongly, their goals) and their practices determined their actions. So we have to consider the political and economic structures they operated in, the constraints of population growth, developments in western Europe and the Atlantic world, and the status and beliefs of the people who came to the region.

A basic stress in these essays is on the "liberal" middle-class orientation of many of the settlers who elected to leave their European communities.[9] "Liberal" I use in the classic sense, meaning placing individual freedom and material gain over that of public interest. Put another way, the people planned for themselves much more than they did for their communities. Communities, like governments, were necessary evils to support individual fulfillment.[10] This is not to say that the settlers were "economic men," single-minded maximizing materialists. Few could be, or even wanted to be. Nevertheless, they defended their liberal propensities in a tenacious manner. The conservative supporters of individualism were not only the more affluent citizens but also those who moved elsewhere to seek better opportunities for themselves and their families. Undoubtedly their view was fostered by a sense that the environment was "open." As individualists, they were ready in spirit to conquer the limitless continent, to subdue the land. As we now struggle in a "closed" system to find commu-

nity and to learn to live with a finite nature, we must look at our
ancestors to learn how they operated in their environment. We can
see the early signs of liberal North America in Pennsylvania as
much as anywhere. The interpretation presented here leads us
closer, I believe, to an understanding of what the people were
doing than either the cultural or the environmental or the economic deterministic perspectives can alone.

A final question that might occur to readers has to do with
scale. The area in which I study the action of people is southeastern Pennsylvania, lying south and east of Blue or North Mountain, the northern margin of the Great Valley (Cumberland,
Lebanon, and Lehigh valleys; see the general location map, figure
1). Within this area, Chester and Lancaster counties, which included Delaware, Dauphin, and Lebanon counties before 1785
(figures 2 and 3), receive greater attention than others because of
the availability of data and the variety of social groups and environmental conditions there. But the area is not rigidly isolated; I
have used information relevant to the study from adjacent parts of
Pennsylvania, Delaware, Maryland, and New Jersey.

In light of the current emphasis on local community studies in
social history, particularly in New England, this area may appear
to be vast. But unlike early seventeenth-century Massachusetts, the
chief level of local government in Pennsylvania was the county. A
full range of records of small areas such as townships is not generally available. Of course, if a wide range of data for one township
were to come to light, then that place could be studied. Undoubtedly, depending on the problems investigated, research can
be undertaken at a variety of levels. Scale in itself is not the final
arbiter of what we do.

*More so
than JL
seems to
realize*

* * *

I am indebted to a great number of persons who have given
much of their labor in this study. Andrew Clark, Joseph Ernst,
Cole Harris, Joseph Illick, Roy Merrens, Gary Nash, Russell Nelson, David Ward, and John Walzer contributed the most through
their long discussions and arguments and through their reading of
the text. Clark Akatiff, Whitfield Bell, Charles Bennett, William

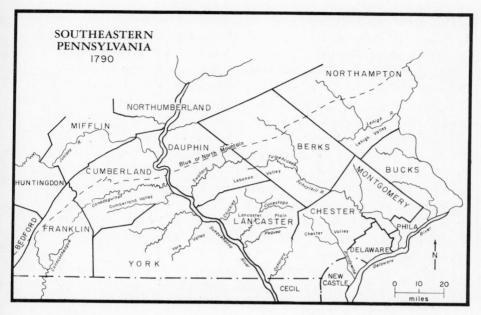

Figure 1

Bucher, Jack Bumsted, Henry Castner, Ronald Cooke, William Denevan, Joseph Glass, Gerry Hale, Lay Gibson, Lawrence Harper, Richard Hartshorne, Ronald Horvath, Merrill Jensen, Clarence Kulp, Placido LaValle, Howard Miller, Howard Nelson, Clarence Olmstead, William Pattison, John Rainbolt, Hunter Rineer, Hannah Roach, Morton Rothstein, Richard Shryock, Marga Stone, Norman Thrower, and Clifford Tiedemann, among others, at various times read parts of the manuscript, discussed various issues, or provided data. Elizabeth Kieffer, the Reverend Ira Landis, and Dorothy Lapp kindly aided in genealogical matters. I also thank local historians who sent me information on their towns, many of which recently have celebrated bicentennials. Mary Hamilton Coward, Peter Ennals, Mary Etzel, James Fitzpatrick, Barbara Gimla, Keith Harries, John Mannion, Conrad Moore, Nancy Danaher O'Hara, and Graeme Wynn worked long hours, many of them boring, as underpaid assistants. I am indebted to Barbara Muthig for typing the final draft of the manuscript.

The work could not have been done without the cooperation of the staffs of several libraries and depositories: the Historical Society of Pennsylvania, the historical societies of Chester, Lancaster, Berks, Bucks, Dauphin, and York counties, the American Philosophical Society, the Library Company of Philadelphia, the University of Pennsylvania, the Register of Wills and Recorder of Deeds offices in West Chester and Lancaster, the county clerk's offices in the various counties, the Division of Public Records in Harrisburg, the Historical Society of Wisconsin, the University of Wisconsin, the Henry E. Huntington Library, the University of Toronto, and the University of California, Los Angeles.

Financial aid to undertake research, draw maps, and type revisions, for which I am grateful, was contributed by the University of Toronto, the University of California, the University of Wisconsin, and the Canada Council.

Finally, it is now perfectly obvious why most authors reserve their highest praise for their families. For sustaining me I thank my daughters, Margaret, Janet, and Catherine, and above all my wife, Carolyn.

* * *

Portions of this study have appeared in *Agricultural History*, the *Geographical Review*, the *Journal of Social History*, and the *William and Mary Quarterly*. I wish to thank the editors of these journals for permission to reprint material.

The Best
Poor Man's Country

CHAPTER ONE

Society and Environment of Early Pennsylvania

Frederick Brown was a typical (if hypothetical) early Pennsylvanian.[1] Brown came from the Rhineland in 1725 as a boy of ten. With his parents and siblings he settled in Lancaster County near people from Germany and the British Isles. Brown's family was Lutheran; they shared the township with a wide variety of Protestant groups—Quakers, Mennonites, Scotch-Irish Presbyterians, and others. Brown's father established a reasonably successful farm that produced most of the materials needed for a comfortable if not affluent life. When his father retired in 1750 Frederick was married. He took over part of the family farm, carrying on much as his father had, but with increasing economic dependence on the Atlantic world through Lancaster and Philadelphia. As his own sons matured all but one left home, one to a nearby township, the others to the west. Eventually Brown, too, retired from farming in 1780 and became dependent on the support of his eldest son. In 1790 he was buried in the cemetery by the church.

Frederick Brown's life was quite ordinary—ordinary in the sense that he did the sorts of things that many rural Americans did in the eighteenth and nineteenth centuries. But the commonplace qualities of his life and the lives of his fellow Pennsylvanians should not keep us from trying to understand their structure and rhythm, for they stood as a model for later Americans.

The activities of Brown and others grew out of a range of factors including western European cultural traditions, the social

characteristics of Pennsylvania life, and the natural qualities of the
area. Pennsylvania was a part of western European society, and
many of its traditions—the patriarchial family and Christian doc-
trines, for example—were carried across the Atlantic. Yet the
migrants did not represent a cross section of western European
life. They were neither the richest nor the poorest Europeans,
most were skilled, and, perhaps most importantly, most were the
kind of people who sought individual satisfaction. To some extent
they were entrepreneurs, though not maximizing materialists.
Their descendants shared this concern and so imprinted Pennsylvania with a "liberal" image. Pennsylvanians nevertheless were
marked by different origins and belonged to different religious
groups that helped shape their style of life. The rate of population
growth exerted an influence. In their government, they erected
structures based on English precedents. They participated in an
economic system marked by a strong subsistence component but
also by Atlantic trading patterns. Their preindustrial technology
used animal and human rather than inanimate sources of energy.
These structures affected them all. Moreover, the people had to
deal with the Indians and a distinctive set of resources—the climate, the terrain, soil, and forests—that encouraged new methods
of land utilization.

These characteristics of tradition, society, and environment
combined to create the distinctive Pennsylvanian modes of life.
They will be utilized in varying degrees to explain the processes on
the land's surface.

* * *

While migrants were leaving for Pennsylvania, their western
European homelands were experiencing changes from medieval
attitudes and practices toward nineteenth century industrialization.[2] Some medieval ways were slow to change. The landed
gentry remained the most influential group in society. Agricultural
villages continued to be widespread along with open-field systems
in which farmers' holdings were divided into strips. Urbanization
was slight by modern standards. Yet in rural life strong new cur-
rents were running to encourage entrepreneurialism and new tech-

niques. The market system of exchange, which by this time embraced most of western Europe, fostered commercial agriculture. Farmers responded to changing market conditions with the "agricultural revolution," before 1650 in Flanders, possibly by then in parts of England, and during the eighteenth century in other areas of western Europe. While pork, beef, dairy products, and small grains remained the chief ingredients of the human diet, potatoes, a migrant from the New World, eventually became a boon for the poor folk of Europe. Farmers adopted clover, turnips, and potatoes for livestock consumption. Together with rational rotation schemes and applications of manure and other fertilizers, these new crops contributed to more clearly integrated systems of mixed crops and livestock agriculture. Land productivity increased as a result of these innovations.

Accompanying these improvements in agriculture were changes in tenure, industry, and population. By 1700 feudal dues in kind had largely been commuted to money payments. An unmistakable trend toward operation of farms by nuclear families arose, even where tenancy and open fields remained widespread. Cottage industry on a commercial basis appeared in certain rural areas, and by the middle of the eighteenth century new techniques leading to the factory system were clearly apparent in England. Population growth accelerated throughout western Europe in the late seventeenth and eighteenth centuries, though at varying rates. Greater social mobility loosened family ties and encouraged more and earlier marriages. Men and women formerly consigned to single life were now free to move from their home villages. These larger movements were signs of an increased individual pursuit of the good life. Protestantism may have contributed importantly to this change, and most migrants to Pennsylvania were dissenters from Rome.

Pennsylvanians came chiefly from England, Ulster, and the Protestant states of southwestern Germany, but also from Wales, Scotland, France, the Netherlands, and Switzerland. Swedes were the first to settle in the Delaware Valley. Changes in all of these Protestant areas encouraged movement. They were probably most marked in the regions of greatest emigration, but they were at work, at different rates, in all of these areas.

In England, the agricultural revolution early fostered the enclosing of open fields, the bringing together of strips into contiguous fields, and some scattering of villagers to dwellings on their farms. These alterations reinforced a shift toward operation of farms by nuclear families, even though a large number of farmers were tenants. This tendency antedated 1680, for in 1660 the Statute of Tenures confirmed the individual rights of tenants and owners of small farms. Widespread mobility and enclosure in Tudor times indicate that changes had long been under way.

In Ulster there was little opportunity for improved agriculture. Farming was commercialized, but the political power of English landowners and merchants forced the Irish after 1700 into less progressive directions, notably from livestock to flax and linen. Some enclosure occurred, but dispersion from the small villages, or clachans, did not take place in the main until the nineteenth century. While landlords in England granted their tenants the right to make improvements and provided capital to foster them, in colonial Ireland English landowners were less inclined to recognize such tenant rights and so hindered agricultural change.

In southwestern Germany the people in power clung tenaciously to many aspects of feudalism. Princes, while protecting peasant rights, retarded transformation by restricting the freedom of landlords to enclose lands, in contrast to England, and contacts between town and country were less frequent and less tightly integrated than they were in England. Individual operation of farms, however, was common even within open-field systems. In the eighteenth century many German farmers sowed clover on their own plots without the consent of others.

Pennsylvanians were moving out of these societies. Despite regional differences, they shared Protestantism, agricultural techniques, and long-standing dietary preferences, and they carried over ideas for experimentation in the new environment. Even though some of the changes did not occur in the same fashion in Pennsylvania, it became an outlier of western European culture.

* * *

Most migrants to Pennsylvania undoubtedly came from the upwardly mobile part of the population. Few landed aristocrats and successful merchants were willing to chance the hazardous voyage across the Atlantic to seek at best a marginally better life. Those at the other end of the social scale, the destitute without hope, also did not move because, as a Scottish settler in Pennsylvania observed, they knew "by long experience, that by their labors they can make no profit to themselves."[3] The migrants therefore were largely from the middle stratum of western European society.

Because they came from the middle class, these settlers brought with them certain characteristics that came to mark Pennsylvania's society and its geographical configuration. These migrants sought a better life, possessed certain skills, and were neither wealthy nor poverty stricken, at least when they left their homeland. Though modified, these qualities continued in Pennsylvania, which for nearly a century after 1680 possessed a reputation for providing the best chance in the western world for an improved standard of living and a life free of external restraint.[4]

As pursuers of an improved life in material, social, and spiritual senses, the emigrants were dissatisfied with their lot at home. In some instances they reacted, as in Ulster, to the termination of easy leases or as in England, if they were holders of small farms, to price squeezes.[5] By 1680 religious persecutions were on the wane, and during the period of greatest migration, 1725 to 1755, life in western Europe was generally tolerant and peaceful. Emphasis should therefore be placed as much on dissatisfaction and rising expectations as on unsatisfactory external conditions. This underlines the essential fact about a large proportion of the settlers, their desire for a better life.

Not surprisingly, settlers and their descendants supported an attitude of initiative and the virtues of hard work. In the 1680s the German sectarian Francis Daniel Pastorius clearly spoke for others when he wrote, "William Penn will coin money and agriculture will be better managed."[6] The attitude displayed in this statement persisted throughout the next century. During the American Revolution, the supply debacle at Valley Forge and the marketing of produce to the British who occupied Philadelphia brought anguished cries that "many disaffected persons are willing to be flogged" if they can make money, "for British currency may prove more attractive to the farmer than our Continental monies and it remains whether patriotism will conquer greed."[7] At the same time in York County, generals foresaw a bread shortage because distillers were paying more for wheat than was the army. The "complicated demon of Avarice" was abroad.[8]

Romantic notions of the subsistent and the self-sufficient farmer must be rejected. The golden age of noncommercial sim- plicity presented by scholars in the early twentieth century did not exist in rural or even in frontier Pennsylvania.[9] Many settlers and their descendants were filled with the Protestant (or, perhaps more accurately, the secularized middle-class Protestant) spirit of hard work and success, which is well expressed in the prayer of the Reverend Nathaniel R. Snowden:

> Quickly improve your time while in your power
> And carefully do husband every hour,
> For time will come when you will sore lament
> The unhappy minutes that you have misspent
> Despair of nothing that you would attain
> Unwearied diligence your point will gain.
>
> Oh my Lord and my God may I attend to these lines I desire to serve thee. . . .[10]

Profit maximizing, however, was not as rampant among early Pennsylvanians as some of the above examples might imply. Though wealth was becoming the chief criterion of social standing in both Europe and America, most people probably were reason- ably content with their lot once they had reached a certain material level.[11] In an area now well known for its rural conserva- tism, the well-to-do were not to flaunt their successes in an un- seemly fashion.[12] Other values, notably religious and political, moved settlers and their descendants in Pennsylvania to goals besides material ones. A majority of western Europeans and Penn- sylvanians probably pursued individual success more vigorously than their medieval forebears, and most certainly more than mem- bers of primitive societies, yet they did so with less intensity than the average nineteenth century American. The balance was shifting away from the community toward the individual, and this bour- geois or middle class (or whatever fitting term we may choose) tendency led to significant results in early Pennsylvania. Most people sought sites on good land or as near as possible to Phila- delphia, the focus of trade; most organized family farms rather than cooperative or manorial farms; and most responded to the demands of the market, which was reflected in the use of the land.

The occupations of immigrants varied, but most were probably skilled craftsmen and farmers, befitting their middle class attitude of seeking a degree of material success. Relatively few appeared to be unskilled laborers. The data are scattered, however, and do not provide a completely satisfactory answer, and besides many migrants may have lied to ship captains about their skills. In the late seventeenth century, ship lists suggest that laborers sailing from English ports to America were outnumbered five to one by craftsmen and farmers.[13] Immediately before the Revolution only 11 per cent of new arrivals were laborers, even though two-thirds of the sailings departed from London, a great pool of unskilled labor.[14] The occupations of Germans and Ulstermen corresponded to those of the English, and Arthur Young was undoubtedly overstating the case in the early 1700s when he said that only the "idle and the dissolute" set out from Belfast.[15] Except for a small number of Quaker merchants among the "First Purchasers" of land in Pennsylvania, very few of the squirearchy or of the wealthy merchant class emigrated.[16] The proportions of emigrant farmers and craftsmen varied, and the ratios of these two groups are not easy to determine from available information.[17] Yet even if we had complete data, the significance of previous skills to activities in Pennsylvania would not be clear. In this period farmers did much of their own manufacturing and craftsmen often worked some land. What is important is that few laborers apparently traveled among the migrants and that most newcomers were relatively skilled persons able to adjust to changing circumstances.

In Pennsylvania the number of settlers who pursued their Old World occupations is not certain. The traditional view is that most men became farmers; Benjamin Franklin asserted that only one in ten was a craftsman.[18] But tax lists from rural areas suggest that while a majority were farmers, their numbers were not as great as Franklin suggested. Tax returns of several townships in Chester and Lancaster countries from about 1760 indicate that farmers constituted one-third to two-thirds of the taxable heads of households.[19] More precisely, in Little Britain Township in Lancaster (figure 3), for example, 97 of 195 individuals were listed as

8   THE BEST POOR MAN'S COUNTRY

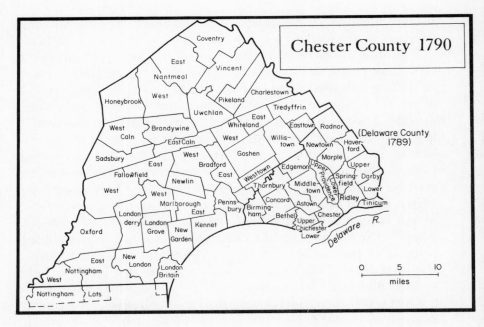

Figure 2

farmers and another 15 as part-time farmers. In Leacock Township
115 of 177 were full-time farmers and 15 others part-time. Those
townships with villages, mines, or forges held fewer farmers; in
Warwick Township only 30 per cent of 202 taxables were farmers.
Adjacent Elizabeth, and Coventry and East Nantmeal in Chester
County (figure 2), contained about the same proportion of
farmers. The most to be said is that in the rural counties of
Chester and Lancaster a majority of men were farmers and the
remainder artisans and laborers, many of whom tilled some land
and pastured some cows. In urban places, which by the end of the
eighteenth century held a fifth or more of the population of the
area, the ratio of laborers was higher (15 to 20 per cent) than in
the typical countryside.[20] The substantial number of laborers
probably meant that opportunities were fewer than Pennsylvania's
reputation in Europe led migrants to expect. Nevertheless, their
presence does not dispel the impression one gathers from a wide

range of data that a large share of Pennsylvanians held to a middle class ideal of material success and were skilled in crafts and farming.

Income and wealth can also be used as indicators of social and economic status; but because data are scarce, comparisons between western Europe and Pennsylvania must be extremely impressionistic. Although most immigrants were neither very poor nor very rich, their material circumstances did vary. Many who

Figure 3

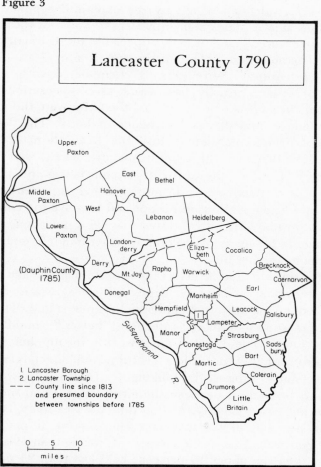

came in the earliest years, notably Mennonites and Quakers, had been self-supporting small farmers. Yet many persons came as indentured servants who sold their services for several years to pay for their passage.[21] After 1700 there were complaints that too many persons were coming without goods. In 1713 James Logan, the provincial secretary, regretfully said: "Great numbers of people are crowded in upon us from Europe, but they are mostly servants, and very few of estates."[22] Between 1725 and 1755, the period of greatest immigration, most settlers apparently were poor on arrival. Around 1750 societies were formed to take care of immigrants rendered indigent by the exploitative policies of unscrupulous ship captains and promoters.[23] Some of these servants were "indentured" and others, especially the German-speaking, were "redemptioners." The distinction is not clear, but those called "indentured" were persons encumbered with a definite period of service, usually four years, as compensation to those who paid their costs of passage, and the latter were those released from bondage immediately by friends or kin.[24] The flow of encumbered persons continued until the Revolution; in the early 1770s three-fifths of the English migrants had to serve time as servants.[25] Despite the difficult circumstances of perhaps a majority of settlers on arrival, most had had sufficient capital to break out of their stations in Europe and to move to Pennsylvania. More important, the drive toward success overcame financial impediments for many. Everyone, whether bonded or not, by and large sought a richer life.

In stressing the middle class origins of immigrants and character of Pennsylvania society, the degree of social stratification that developed in the region should not be understated. The inhabitants were conscious of the categories "better," "middling," and "poorer sorts." The distribution of wealth, the number of landless people toward the end of the century, and direct references to poverty tend to support this ranking. By 1800 a fairly wide spread in wealth had arisen between the most affluent and those at the bottom in Chester County. At that time the wealthiest 10 per cent paid 38 per cent of the taxes and the poorest 30 per cent paid only 4 per cent. This was a sharper difference than existed in the 1690s, when the upper 10 per cent held less than 24 per cent of the wealth (table 1).[26] Considering that the richer were probably undertaxed, the stratification was probably more marked than the tax lists suggest. In one of the few extant quantitative references to stratification, the assessor of relatively backward and predominantly German Brecknock Township in Lancaster County in 1750 recorded 27 per cent of the people "poor," compared with 40 per cent "middling" and 33 per cent "able," in their capacity to pay taxes.[27] But this is not altogether helpful. The various categories of wealth suggest that probably only three or four per-

Table 1

Vertical Distribution of Economic Status: Percentage of Taxes Paid by Taxpayers Ranked by Amount of Taxes Paid, Chester and Lancaster Counties, 1693-1802

County and Year	Taxpayer Group				Number of Taxpayers[a]
	Lowest 30%	Lower middle 30%	Upper middle 30%	Upper 10%	
Chester					
1693	17.4	21.1	37.7	23.8	257
1715	13.1	22.9	38.1	25.9	670
1730	9.8	21.7	39.8	28.6	1,791
1748	13.1	21.7	36.4	28.7	2,998
Lancaster					
1758-59	4.2	16.9	45.0	33.9	3,459[b]
Chester					
1760	6.3	20.5	43.3	29.9	4,290
1782	4.7	17.3	44.5	33.6	5,291
1800-2[c]	3.9	13.7	44.2	38.3	7,247

Source: MSS tax assessments: 1693, Chester Co. Miscellaneous Papers, Hist. Soc. Pa.; 1715, 1730, 1748, 1760, 1782, 1800, Chester Co. Hist. Soc.; 1758-59, Lanc. Co. Hist. Soc.; 1802, Delaware Co. Court House, Media. See nn. 19, 26, chap. 1.

Note: Some columns do not add to 100 because of rounding.

[a]Single freemen excluded from calculations.
[b]Present-day Lancaster Co. only; Lebanon Valley excluded. Data for Little Britain Tp. lacking.
[c]1800—Present-day Chester; 1802—Delaware Co. tps. that separated from Chester in 1789.

sons could be classed as "better sort"; most of 73 per cent called
"middling" and "able" were probably "middling." It seems
unlikely that most of the "poor" were destitute, but their circumstances are harder to determine. In 1782 nonlandowners in
Chester and Lancaster counties totaled about 30 per cent of the
population. This category included tenant farmers and "inmates,"
a designation that might refer to indentured and apprenticed persons, many of whom were born in Pennsylvania and some of
whom were married. The most that can be said with certainty,
however, is that inmates lived in someone else's house and were
craftsmen and laborers rather than farmers.[28] Whatever the facts,
the number of landless persons in Lancaster and Chester counties
seems to have been high if we presume, as did some in the
eighteenth century and later, that land was freely available and
that America was a nation of freeholders.[29]

In Pennsylvania, according to reports, poverty was not uncommon, at least in times of recession. In 1747 an observer in Philadelphia noted: "It is remarkable what an increase of the number
of Beggars there is about this town this winter, many more than I
have before observed."[30] Soon after this, when conditions were
quite good, an item in the Lancaster County Commissioners' Book
stated that the poor were suffering because the appropriation for
squirrel bounties had been curtailed.[31] In the early 1760s redemptioners were little in demand, and money was given to paupers.[32]
Agents of the Hamilton family, which owned the town of Lancaster, reported that quitrents could never be collected from the
poor of the town, who were idle "for want of employment,"
except during harvest time.[33] Mortgages were foreclosed on poorer
farmers during difficult times.[34] Toward the end of the century,
an Englishman who had expected to see few beggars reported a
"great" many in Pennsylvania, and about that time poor houses
were established, suggesting either that an endemic situation had
finally been recognized or that conditions had recently become
worse.[35]

Despite these references to poverty and the acceptance of a
tripartite division of society by early Pennsylvanians, we can still
affirm that Pennsylvanians were predominantly middle class. Except during times of depression, wages were probably higher

throughout the century than in Europe.[36] Even at the end of the century, few tax lists record destitute persons. "Poor tax" records have few entries.[37] If the "holy experiment" did not bring bounty for all, it allowed many to improve their material lot—and if not here, then somewhere to the west or southwest. Most important, even if there were many needy, as there were in Pennsylvania in recent years when about 25 per cent of the population could be classed as poor,[38] Pennsylvanians believed that hard work would bring success. In the last analysis, the middle class faith in the right to seek success was the hallmark of Pennsylvania society and distinguished it somewhat from western Europe, where the landed aristocracy still remained powerful and the many peasants had extremely limited aspirations. Yet it was from western Europe that this liberal philosophy had been carried to fulfillment in America, perhaps most clearly in Pennsylvania.

* * *

If the settlers and their descendants were similar in social and economic status, they were varied in language, national origin, and religion. These have contributed to the impression of the society as a pluralistic "mosaic." Many commentators on life in early Pennsylvania have stressed language and national origin, but, as will become clear in subsequent chapters, these were less relevant to people's action on the land than was previously thought.[39] Religious distinctions, however, were of considerable importance.

On the basis of surname analysis (admittedly an uncertain technique) and other data, the proportions of persons in national groups in 1790 can be estimated (table 2).[40] The major groups were Germans and German-speaking Swiss, Englishmen, and Ulstermen, the last called "Irish" by contemporaries and "Scotch-Irish" since the nineteenth century. Even though the distinctiveness of the Scotch-Irish as a cultural group can be questioned, as can that of any English-speaking Celts, in this study I have tried to separate them from the English largely for the sake of argument, because most writers have believed in the reality of the distinction. The presumably few southern Irish and Scots are included with the Scotch-Irish. The Welsh are sometimes discussed separately

Table 2

Population by Presumed National Origin, 1790

Origin	Pennsylvania		Southeastern Pennsylvania	
English	150,000	35%	92,000	29%
Welsh	. . .a		10,000	3
Scotch-Irish, Scots, South Irish	98,000	23	57,500	18
German-speaking	141,000	33	128,000	40
Other and unassigned	35,000	9	32,500	10
Total	424,000	100%	320,000	100%

Source: Modified from Howard F. Barker, "National Stocks in the Population of the United States as Indicated in Surnames in the Census of 1790," *American Historical Association Report 1931* (Washington: Government Printing Office, 1932), 2: 327, and others. See nn. 40, 71, chap. 1.

aIncluded with English.

from the English. Uncertain British names are included with the English. The small number of persons of Swedish, French, and Dutch ancestry are occasionally distinguished but generally are in the "Other" category with persons of uncertain origin, such as the Smiths.

In 1790 persons of German and Swiss background constituted a larger proportion of the population in southeastern Pennsylvania (40 per cent) than in the state as a whole (33 per cent). The English were more numerous in the state than in the region (35 per cent as compared with less than 30), as were the Scotch-Irish and Scots (23 per cent compared with 18 per cent). These proportions can be attributed to continued immigration from the British Isles after 1755, particularly in the early 1770s, and to a dearth of German-speaking migrants after 1755. Estimates of numbers in national groups earlier than 1790 are speculative. Before 1725 the "English" predominated and the Welsh and Swedes were considerably more numerous than they were later. In 1750 the proportion of Germans was probably higher than in 1790.[41]

Language is valid only to distinguish German-speaking from English-speaking persons. Yet many Germans Anglicized themselves. Excepting some Welsh, Highland Scots, and southern Irish, almost all the "Celtic" persons were English-speaking. Undoubtedly mixed with southern Irish, the Scotch-Irish were primarily descendants of English-speaking lowland Scots. In Pennsylvania the German language continued in use beyond 1800, perhaps in part perpetuated by the great number of German newspapers published in county towns after the Revolution.[42] Earlier attempts by provincial authorities to Anglicize Germans had failed. Even so,[43] at least the leading Germans in rural areas and towns used English with ease, as is shown by the Anglicized tax returns from predominantly German townships in Lancaster County. Surprisingly, German names with English cognates almost invariably appear in English; Brown, Smith, and Miller appeared on lists, but never Braun, Schmidt, or Mueller. Moreover, the returns were usually in English and English script, despite the overwhelming number of German assessors in many townships. Some Germans, including Mennonites, anxious to have their children learn English, set up schools with English teachers.[44] Although a differentiating characteristic, language was less significant as an influence on social and especially economic processes than has often been stated.

Differences in customs and practices associated with national groups have also been misstated or exaggerated far out of proportion to their significance. Two sets of material can be used here to examine supposed differences: economic status and the comments of contemporaries. The economic status of various national groups did not diverge greatly, as is indicated by tables 3, 4, and 5. A sample of estate inventories, excluding land values, in Lancaster

Table 3

Inventory Valuations by National Groups, 1713-90

Group	Sample	Value (£)[a]
German-speaking	160	254
English and undifferentiated		
British	130	270
Scotch-Irish, Scots	83	254
Welsh	23	261
Other and uncertain	51	325

Source: Register of Wills Offices, Lancaster and Chester counties.

[a]Excludes land.

Table 4

Average Assessment of National Groups in a Sample of Ethnically Mixed Townships[a]

Township	1758–59						1782					
	German	English	Scotch-Irish	Welsh	Other	Total	German	English	Scotch-Irish	Welsh	Other	Total
Lancaster Co.												
Bart	14.5s.	10.8s.	13.0s.	...	15.7s.	12.9s.	£9.7	£6.8	£6.2	...	£7.2	£7.4
Donegal	12.9	18.0	17.2	...	10.1	14.9	9.2	12.9	11.6	...	8.8	10.0
Leacock	15.8	17.5	15.9	...	14.1	16.1	10.1	12.2	11.9	...	12.9	11.3
Martic	18.0	12.7	11.6	...	10.9	13.3	7.6	3.0	4.2	...	5.1	5.9
Salisbury	...	13.5	17.9	...	...	16.4	10.3	12.7	14.4	...	10.8	13.0
Hanover	...	...	not available	...	...	...	5.8	6.5	6.2	...	6.2	6.1
Paxton	...	...	not available	...	...	...	6.8	7.8	7.4	...	5.9	7.0
Chester Co.												
Charlestown	11.7	18.1	15.6	15.9	15.4	16.3	6.7	9.6	7.0	7.9	7.3	7.9
E. Nantmeal	5.7	13.1	10.5	14.3	9.6	10.7	3.2	6.5	8.3	7.5	6.2	6.0
Vincent	12.2	15.1	11.7	14.4	8.3	12.8	7.1	6.2	9.2	9.9	11.1	7.8

Source: MSS tax assessments for Lanc. Co., 1758–59; for Ches. Co., 1759, 1782; for Lanc. Co., 1782, *Pa. Arch.*, 3d ser., 17: 689–97, 722–25, 732–39, 812–17, 823–28, 833–36, 856–60.

[a]Excludes single freemen. In locales with fewer than six Welsh heads of household, they are included with the English.

Table 5

Members of National Groups Paying over £40 Tax,
Lancaster County, 1782

Group	Number	Per Cent	Percentage of National Groups in Population
German	60	67	68
English	6	7	10
Scotch-Irish	11	12	13
Welsh	6	7	1
Other and uncertain	7	8	9

Source: Tax assessments, *Pa. Arch.*, 3d ser., 17: 687–898.

Note: Percentage columns do not add to 100 because of rounding.

and Chester counties between 1713 and 1790, though an imprecise measure, suggests that differences were not great (table 3). The average assessment within a number of townships with substantial numbers in each national group, probably a better yardstick than inventories, shows that in half of eighteen townships the "English" had the edge, but distinctions were not sharp (table 4). In 1782 (table 5) the most affluent were divided among national groups in Lancaster County; only the few Welsh were proportionately more wealthy.[45] In lower income levels differences were not great. Economic status, then, appears to have been much the same among national groups.

At the risk of applying *ad hominem* argumentation, the comments of contemporary observers can be quoted. They suggest little distinction among groups. Some persons disliked Scotch-Irish servants, others Germans.[46] The traveler Johann Schoepf found lazy Germans in northern Chester County and across Blue Mountain on the frontier.[47] Positive statements were made about the Scotch-Irish; for example, in Cumberland County their wives were found to "do all the Drugery [sic] of a family as well as any German woman you ever saw."[48] An illuminating comment comes from a correspondent to the York newspaper in 1792, who criticized political exploitation of stereotypes by Benjamin Rush and others and implied that differences in the style of life of Pennsylvanians derived from national origins were superficial:

[I] offer some observations on a dangerous prejudice, which has been actually fomented by a few designing men—I mean the distinction of *Dutch* and *Irish*—a distinction calculated to convulse our County—to raise and perpetuate national reflections, and to separate in interests and sentiments the nearest neighbors.

What is it to me, when I am about to vote, whether the great grandmother of the candidate came from Germany or from Ireland—from the banks of the Rhine, or the Lake of Calarney—whether he and his ancestors have dined oftenest on cabbage or potatoes? . . . I don't think one of those vegetables more calculated to make an honest man or a rogue than the other. All national prejudices are the growth of a contracted mind or silly head—it raises a distinction which destroys all enquiry into the merit of a candidate.[49]

Certainly in the manner in which they occupied, organized, and used the land, members of national groups did not behave very differently from one another.

Most Pennsylvanians were Protestants, or at least non-Catholic (table 6).[50] But denominational affiliations divided the people

Table 6

Estimated Numbers in Denominations,
Southeastern Pennsylvania, 1790

Denomination	Number	Percentage of Population
"Sects"		
Quakers	30,000	9
Mennonites	20,000	6
German "Baptists" (Dunkers, etc.)	5,000	2
Moravians	1,500	< 1
"Churches"		
Presbyterians	60,000	19
German Lutherans	45,000	14
German Reformed (including some French Huguenots and Dutch)	40,000	12
Anglican	7,500	2
"English" Baptist	5,000	2
Roman Catholic	8,000	2
Other	6,000	2
Not assigned	95,000?	29?
Total	323,000	100

Source: Various. See n. 50, chap. 1.

into groups, and this pluralism was a distinctive mark of the society. Although use of the word "denomination" implies tolerance and an easing of sharp theological conflicts,[51] and although it is clear that groups experienced varying degrees of doctrinal and social metamorphosis throughout the period, some differences remained clear enough to have a significant effect. The critical distinction was between "sects" and "churches."[52] Sectarian "plain folk," notably Friends and Mennonites, were much more prominent than in Europe. Because their values and organizations favored cooperation and discipline, these groups acted on the land in a somewhat different fashion than did Lutheran, Reformed, Anglican, and Presbyterian members. A substantial number of persons were not related to any denomination.

The Friends (mostly from the west of England, the London area, and Wales) and Mennonites (mostly from the lower and middle Rhine Valley and Switzerland) were the most important "sects." During the first forty years of the province these groups, especially the Quakers, were in the majority. In 1790, when Quakers and Mennonites were easily outnumbered by others, they remained substantial minorities in some counties, including Chester, Lancaster, Bucks, and Montgomery.[53] Although the term "sect" is not fully adequate for describing these "plain folk" or others such as the Dunkers, Schwenkfelders, and Moravians, who lived communally for a generation, certain social values set them apart from "church" groups.[54] The Quakers at first stressed the goal of perfecting rather than ignoring the world and encouraged other groups to share in the wealth of the land. But rural Friends and the Mennonites were markedly selective in membership, and as the century passed they relied more on "birthright" than voluntary confession to define membership. This exclusiveness was fostered by a strong sense of self-righteousness, and among the Quakers the notion of perfectibility shifted from the "holy experiment" and society at large to the group. This desire for perfection encouraged a drive for material well-being, possibly to prove their salvation to the world. Paradoxically, then, worldly success for individual members of the group became a goal for those who officially eschewed worldliness. To this end strong local leaders, especially in rural areas, exhorted members to purity of doctrine,

sobriety, domestic responsibility, hard work, and mutual help.
Thus for the sake of gain, both material and social, Mennonites
and Quakers formed societies of discipline, emulation, and mutual
aid.[55]

Because of these characteristics, reinforced by their early
arrival and their somewhat greater initial affluence,[56] Quakers and
Mennonites possessed throughout the period a higher average
economic status than members of other denominational groups. In
1782 in Lancaster County, among the sixty Germans paying taxes
of £40 or more, thirty-five were Mennonites, a proportion of 58
per cent compared with a Mennonite share of 37 per cent of
the German population (table 5).[57] In Chester County Quakers
headed many tax lists.[58] The tax data are corroborated by contemporary comments. For example, the Anglican clergyman
William Smith considered the Mennonites "the most considerable
and wealthy sect among the Germans," and another observer
asserted, "almost all the Quakers are wealthy people, who never
let anyone belonging to their sect be reduced to poverty."[59]
Although some poor Quakers and Mennonites lived in the area and
members of other groups acquired wealth, the sectarians were
generally the most affluent people in rural Pennsylvania.[60]

In spite of the sectarian views held by Quakers and Mennonites,
William Penn welcomed other Protestants to Pennsylvania, and
Roman Catholics were admitted. This permissive attitude even-
tually undercut the goal of a clearly structured society based on
Quaker principles; but far from making Pennsylvania a failure, as
Penn finally felt it might have, this policy resulted in the immigra-
tion of many persons who contributed to the growth of the
region.

The prominent "church" groups were Presbyterian, Lutheran,
Reformed, and Anglican, and to a lesser degree Baptist, Roman
Catholic, and eventually Methodist. Their members submitted to
looser disciplines and were less inclined to mutual help than the
sectarians, partly because they relied on an uncertain supply of
ministers from Europe or at least from other communities. In rural
areas their average economic status was lower despite the affluence
of some.

These "church" groups varied in size and prestige. Presbyterians became the largest group, especially after the "new side-old side" schism of the Great Awakening was healed in 1758. The rigorous Calvinistic order whose "pastoral staff is well tipped with steel" was modified and individual salvation was recognized more fully— a corollary of liberalism. Their general support of the Revolution gave the Presbyterians increased social prestige.[61] Most of the Scotch-Irish and Scots were Presbyterian, and the church included many "English." The Lutheran and Reformed churches were more strictly German throughout the period, though some French Huguenots and Dutch were Reformed. They had more organizational problems in early years than the Presbyterians, but they were as individualistic as the latter, if not more so.[62] The Anglicans were chiefly urban Philadelphians, many of whom had defected from the Friends for reasons of theological comfort and social prestige. Some Anglican farmers, too, became prosperous. The Revolution cut into the numerical strength of the Anglicans when several of their influential leaders remained loyal to the crown.[63] Only a few persons, mostly German and Welsh, identified themselves as Baptists before 1755, and they and the Methodists were becoming prominent only at the end of the century. Even in 1800 they were less numerous in southeastern Pennsylvania than elsewhere in America.[64] Roman Catholics were apparently excluded from Pennsylvania at first, but in the tolerant pluralistic society that emerged quite a number were able to live peacefully in certain areas.

Because these "church" people, especially the larger Presbyterian, Lutheran, and Reformed memberships, mainly arrived between 1725 and 1755, their influence on the initial patterns of action on the land was less marked than that of Quakers and Mennonites. Without doubt the "church" groups markedly influenced life during the third and subsequent generations. As first arrivals, Quakers and Mennonites were free to choose sites near Philadelphia or on the best soils. Even though substantial numbers of Quakers lived in towns, the many rural Quakers and the Mennonites were more tightly clustered geographically and were less mobile than "church" people. The greater wealth of Quakers and

Mennonites and other data suggest that on the whole they were better farmers than others. Unlike the communitarian Moravians, however, Quakers and Mennonites lived on family farms rather than in agricultural villages, and most "church" people followed this practice.

Pennsylvanians thus were divided in varying degrees by nationality and language and denomination as well as somewhat by economic status. The divisions varied in importance. Antagonisms among groups and also within groups led to such times of trouble as the debates over the Great Awakening, the controversy over defense against the French and Indians, and the Revolution. Expressing the thoughts of many others at the time was the English clergyman, Andrew Burnaby, who in 1759 remarked that different peoples in America "have a mutual jealousy of each other fomented by considerations of interest, power, and ascendancy."[65] During the Revolution, when a Scotch-Irish lieutenant from Lancaster County confronted some German-speaking persons in Northampton and upper Philadelphia counties, he reacted:

> I was looked upon as a barbarian . . . and they appeared to me like to many human beings scarcely endowed with the qualifications equal to that of the brute species. . . . I therefore concluded that they were devoid of any qualification calculated to complete happiness unless when blended with others equally ignorant with themselves.[66]

After the Revolution, the appearance of German newspapers in the back-country county seats may indicate minority dissatisfaction with the society.

Yet polemics, jealousy, and German newspapers were not necessarily signs of deep social divisions in this society. Distinctions in wealth did not follow national lines. Interaction among members of groups was common in rural areas. The journals of Henry M. Muhlenberg, the Lutheran patriarch, reveal little antagonism among denominations, and the surveyor-farmer David Shultze, a Schwenkfelder, wrote only praise of his Reformed, Mennonite, and Roman Catholic neighbors.[67] In 1737 Durs Thommen wrote to Switzerland that *"sind all Nationen frundtlich und dienstbhar* [sic] *gegen Einander."*[68] A wedding in Lancaster of a Reformed man and a Mennonite girl performed by a Lutheran minister was attended by some old Quakers who were so pleased that they removed their hats![69] Without subscribing to either the "melting pot" or the "mosaic" views of American settlement,[70] we can see that despite certain conflicts these people with a common western European background and similar goals were able to cooperate with one another most of the time regardless of denominational and national differences. Social unity contributed to a prosperous society.

Extremely insensitive to ethnic divisions

* * *

Not only the people's characteristics but their numbers were important in directing their actions on the land. Given limitations in the economic system and backward technologies in agriculture and transportation, the density of population and the rate of growth exerted considerable influence on availability of land and thus on farming opportunities in the areas of initial and later settlement. The population of the region expanded from about 9,000 in 1690 to more than 300,000 a century later (table 7).[71]

Table 7

Rates of Population Growth by Decade,
Southeastern Pennsylvania

Year	Population	Mean Annual Rate of Increase[a]
1690	8,800	9.0%
1700	21,000	2.9
1710	28,000	2.8
1720	37,000	2.8
1730	49,000	4.1
1740	73,000	4.0
1750	108,000	5.0
1760	175,000	1.6
1770	205,000	2.6
1780	265,000	1.5
1790	308,000	

Source: Various. See nn. 71, 72, chap. 1.

[a]On the formula $\dfrac{\log P_1 - \log P_0}{10}$.

The rate of growth was most rapid before 1700 and was quite marked between 1730 and 1760, a time of substantial immigration. Considerably slower increases occurred in the last third of the century, when fewer immigrants arrived, the birth rate probably was lower,[72] and the region had virtually been occupied, so that many people moved beyond rather than within southeastern Pennsylvania.[73]

* * *

The laws and the various levels of government influenced inhabitants as they operated on the land: the king and Parliament and the provincial and state, county, township, and municipal governments were based chiefly on English models. Although the crown and Parliament exercised some control over the economy, the structures of the provincial and county governments were of greatest relevance. On the whole, the general form of the provincial government was liberal for the time and encouraged immigration and the development of the area. On some specific matters the proprietor had little direct influence. Local activities were focused on county seats, some of which were founded by the sons of William Penn, rather than on local communities.[74]

Charles II granted William Penn a charter with only a few reservations on powers. As proprietor Penn became the governor with the right during his lifetime to appoint a lieutenant governor, judges, and magistrates. With the "Advice, Assent, and Approbation" of the freemen of the province, the governor could make laws, provided they were "consonant to reason, and not repugnant" to English law. The king was the final arbiter over all court decisions in Pennsylvania, but he could tax only with the approval of the proprietor, the people, or Parliament. The province had to adhere to the Navigation Acts aimed at giving Britain maritime supremacy on penalty of seizure of goods by the crown.[75]

Within the broad limits of the charter, Penn and the Quaker settlers worked out a structure of government and a charter of rights, even though during the first twenty years four frames of government were devised in attempts to resolve basic differences.

The frame of 1701 survived until 1776, when a new constitution was adopted, which was in turn replaced in 1790. The chief points of contention in the early years concerned the distribution of power between the proprietor and his council on one hand and the assembly on the other. The outcome was the acquisition of considerable power by the assembly.[76] Its members were elected from the counties and the city of Philadelphia, and had the power to create new counties and to designate the number of county representatives. It also determined the qualifications for voting; it granted broad suffrage for the time, based on property qualifications. As the assembly grew in strength, the executive council lost its powers of initiative and became only advisory to the governor, who continued to suggest legislation though not to initiate it. Although the proprietor, as the absolute owner of the area, continued to hold official power over the disposition of land through the surveyor-general and the Land Office, the people rather than the proprietor had the greater influence. These developments were of considerable importance in the lives of rural Pennsylvanians.[77]

The counties were of far greater administrative significance than townships and municipalities.[78] Except for judicial and some administrative offices, county government gradually came to be controlled by the county freeholders, who elected assessors, sheriffs, coroners, and (after 1722) commissioners, who became the most important officials. Justices of the peace in townships were appointed by the proprietary, but by 1725 their administrative powers were weakened through the rise of the commissioners.[79]

Townships, with no elected officials, were of little consequence; constables and overseers of roads and of the poor, all of whom had few powers, were appointed by the county commissioners. Despite the importance of townships in the Delaware valley area under the Duke of York before 1680 and their prominence in William Penn's plans for communities,[80] in Pennsylvania they served only as convenient assessment units, most noticeably after 1725.

Why counties came to have most of the local power is not clear. Before the Revolution few urban municipalities were legally constituted; Philadelphia was a city and a few other places were boroughs. In most of the larger towns urban problems were the responsibility of the county commissioners. In the 1780s most of these large places became boroughs (table 22).

The governmental structures at the imperial, provincial, and local levels had some bearing on decision-making by the people and consequently on the ways they occupied, organized, and used the land. The crown and Parliament influenced the direction of Pennsylvania's economy to some extent, not so much through the enforcement of the formal system under the Navigation Acts as indirectly through policies permitting London merchants to operate more effectively in Atlantic trading patterns.[81] The contributions of king and Parliament to events leading to the Revolution cannot be underestimated, but rural life was only temporarily and even minimally affected by that disturbance.

The proprietary and the assembly influenced the choices of sites by settlers, though the Penns and their agents were much more limited in actual power than the official position of the proprietor might indicate. Particularly between 1700 and 1732 the strength of the assembly, problems within the Penn family, the lack of proprietary machinery, confusion in various agencies, notably the Land Office, and speculation by public officials contributed to virtual sovereignty by the people. Even after 1732, when Thomas Penn took tighter hold on the proprietary reins, the people, especially those with capital, controlled the disposition of land. The significant achievements of Penn and his sons were the founding of Philadelphia and the establishment of several county towns that became the chief points of political, economic, and social interaction in the region. Although the assembly did not clearly represent all people because it was identified with the Quakers, particularly before 1756,[82] as a check on proprietary power it helped to throw much of the decision-making regarding occupation of the land and its development into the hands of the people, or more precisely into the hands of local elected officials and religious and economic leaders.

The structure of subregional and local governments, with the ascendancy of the county, exerted considerable influence on the kinds of local communities that developed and contributed to the importance of county seats as centers of activity. Municipal (city and borough) officials and provincial officials enacted regulations that guided to some extent the marketing activities of urban and rural dwellers.[83]

* * *

Pennsylvanians were involved in two economic systems, the subsistence economy and the Atlantic trading empire centered in London. Few persons were completely self-reliant; few depended entirely on others. Many townsmen kept gardens, orchards, and a cow or two, and remote frontiersmen and laborers bought and sold goods and services in the market. The eighteenth century witnessed an elaboration of the commercial network within the area and with other provinces, Great Britain, and foreign areas, so that Pennsylvania economically was well developed for the time and compared with most areas in Europe. By the third generation, after 1740, farmers of "middling" status sold between a third and a half or more of their production, at least during peacetime.[84] The pattern was preindustrial, however, and farmers did not specialize to the degree they would after 1820 or 1830 when manufacturing and urbanization increased demands for farm products.

The credit and marketing system in the Atlantic world involved many links that gave rise to urban places and a degree of commercial agricultural production.[85] Rural Pennsylvanians were connected by a chain of credit through Philadelphia and Baltimore and through merchants, millers, and shopkeepers in smaller places with London merchants. Although the Atlantic world's economic center was in London and Pennsylvania exported mostly unprocessed or little-processed agricultural and forest products, Pennsylvania was not locked into a bilateral and dependent pattern to the degree the "staple"-producing southern colonies were. Autonomous connections with other mainland colonies, the West Indies, and southern Europe provided income that helped to compensate for the persistent adverse balance of trade with England (figure 4). Success in trading encouraged even longer extensions of credit by London merchants confident of Pennsylvania's future growth.[86]

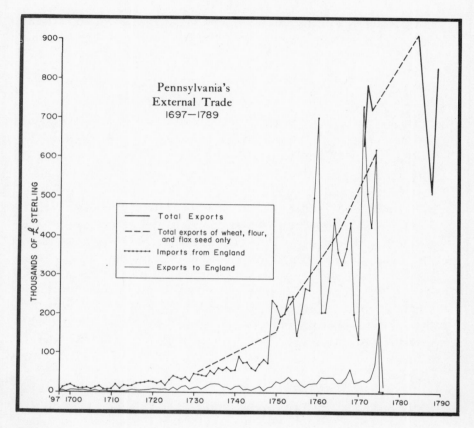

Figure 4

Rural Pennsylvanians, especially those west of the Susquehanna River, had the option of dealing with Maryland as well as Philadelphia.[87] In both cases farmers received goods from back-country shopkeepers and merchants, delivered or had delivered their products to Philadelphia or other points, and requested the buyers to credit their dealers' accounts with importers. Even though cash was scarce and banks did not appear until 1783, business was not on a barter level. All commodities carried monetary value, and merchants and other wealthy persons acted as bankers. These structures contributed to the development of urban places as the centers of regional activity. Philadelphia, Baltimore, and county seats especially became important.

Pennsylvania's customers were responsible for the kinds of commodities that entered its export trade. The West Indies, New England, southern Europe, Ireland, and ship provisioners demanded flour, bread, and wheat, and to a lesser extent corn, lumber, flaxseed, and many other goods.[88] Because the West Indies opened as a market at about the time Pennsylvania was founded, the Quaker colony was spared the limitations placed on southern colonies by the demands of England for tobacco, rice, and indigo. From the outset it was able to trade outside this bilateral system. Although Pennsylvania supplied England with iron after 1750 and wheat after 1765, encouragement of hemp and silk production as "staples" failed partly because of Pennsylvania's success with other commodities.[89] External markets had a significant bearing on shaping the agricultural system and regional patterns of land use.

Despite the complex commercial connections, internal and external markets were limited by later standards, communication and transport facilities were inadequate, processing operations were unsophisticated, and agricultural tools were primitive. These deficiencies contributed to a continuation of the subsistence aspect of the economy, to a limited specialization of agriculture, and to the existence of the family farm as the chief unit of production.

Information on market conditions outside Pennsylvania was vital for profitable decisions. But four weeks was the minimum travel time from London, so that when prices changed rapidly in Europe and elsewhere Pennsylvanians often could not react as quickly as they might have wished. Within the colonies, even in the late eighteenth century, the overland stage trip between Philadelphia and New York took a minimum of one day.[90] Horse-drawn wagons, the chief means of transporting goods, were slow and costly. Thirty miles was the maximum distance a loaded wagon could cover in a day under favorable weather conditions.[91] Ferriage was also expensive, especially across the Susquehanna.[92] Water transport complemented wagon transportation only to a small extent in Pennsylvania. By 1770 some Pennsylvanians were

displeased with their transportation facilities. Yet it appears that
more were satisfied with the rate of return from the economy, and
therefore not until the early 1790s did the legislature finance the
construction of the Lancaster Turnpike. Canals were built even
later than this.

The preindustrial character of the economy was nowhere more
apparent than in the manufacturing sector. It lacked diversifi-
cation, corporate enterprise, and concentration.[93] Many more
craftsmen lived in rural areas than scholars have recognized, and
Pennsylvania at the time did not trail many parts of Europe in
implementing new processing methods. Still, many goods were
fabricated by farmers, and most industrial organizations were
small and owned by proprietors. Only ironmaking and, toward the
end of the century, flour milling and cotton milling foreshadowed
nineteenth century corporate structures. Craftsmen and farmers
who integrated many operations were the chief manufacturers.
The British policy of restrictive laws and government subsidies in
the wrong areas, such as hemp and silk production, contributed to
this state of affairs. But more fundamental factors were the attractions of land investment and of agriculture and other primary
production.[94] Investors in England and Pennsylvania were attracted by the certain or higher rates of return in these sectors.
The slow development of textile manufacturing in the eighteenth
century and well into the nineteenth resulted basically from the
diversion of energies and capital to primary production, notably
farming, and speculation in land.

Finally, the tools of agriculture limited productivity and
encouraged reliance upon the family farm as the basic unit of
production. Relatively few innovations—such as the Dutch fan for
blowing away chaff—appeared in harvesting and threshing equipment despite recurrent labor shortages and higher labor costs than
in Europe.[95] Reformers tried to inform farmers of English
methods of improving yields, but aside from perhaps the more
affluent sectarians concerned with status, new ideas were not
welcomed. Not until the nineteenth century did the agricultural
technological revolution occur that has led to the highly capitalized corporate farming of today in many areas. In the eighteenth
century, technical limitations both on and off the farm restrained

commercialization and caused a large share of production to be consumed at home. Combined with the desire of most settlers to be captains of their own destiny and with the kinds of markets farmers sold to outside the region, these technical constraints encouraged the family farm to thrive as the cornerstone of this agrarian economy.

* * *

Indians, through their presence in the region and their material culture, affected the life of the interlopers on their land and so contributed another set of factors needed to understand the geography of the area. In 1680 few Indians inhabited southeastern Pennsylvania; smallpox and measles probably had already taken a heavy toll, and most of the Iroquoian-speaking Susquehannocks had been dispersed by the Iroquois Confederacy. Some Algonquian-speaking Delawares remained, and during the early eighteenth century the Iroquois Confederacy permitted some Conoys, Nanticokes, Shawnees, and Tuscaroras to occupy sites with the remaining Susquehannocks, by then called the Conestogas, in the Susquehanna Valley. But like the Delawares, they were controlled by the Iroquois. Despite relatively small numbers, the Indians, especially the Iroquois, had to be confronted. At first white men encountered them in fur trading activities, and as white settlement advanced William Penn sought to maintain peace by prohibiting settlement beyond the bounds of carefully negotiated purchases of land. Unfortunately less care was exercised in later decades, so that relationships gradually deteriorated to the point of conflict in the mid-1750s. The presence of the Indians exerted considerable influence on the rate of occupation of the land by the settlers.[96]

But more important in the long run were the Indians' few contributions to the technology of the settlers. The Delawares and the Iroquoian-speaking groups who lived in villages practiced agriculture. They grew maize, beans, and squash of different varieties on the same fields, as other Indians did in other regions. Corn (*Zea mays*), particularly of the flint and dent types and eventually their hybrids, came to be integrated into the diets of Europeans and their livestock. This crop became of paramount importance in American life. Various techniques of the Indians, such as corn hills and preparations of corn, were adopted by Europeans. Although Europeans might have been familiar with fallowing fields for long periods to regenerate the soil, they might have learned this from the Indians. Settlers sought "old fields" of the Indians, probably to save the labor of clearing large trees. Some Indian paths, modified for wagon traffic, became roads; the original route west from Philadelphia to Lancaster County was one of these.[97] Much of the rest of Indian culture, such as villages, matrilineal descent, and communal ownership, was ignored or rejected. Needless to say, the cultural gap between Europeans and Indians remained wide.

* * *

Immigrants and visitors who praised Pennsylvania as a place where "poor servants have become very rich" laid considerable stress on the bounty of nature as a contributing force.[98] Undoubtedly these publicists were impressed by the temperate climate, the rolling plains, the richness of the soils, the adequacy of the water supply, and the flora and fauna, which contributed to the economic well-being of the colony and state. Conditions were generally similar to those in western Europe, so that settlers on the whole adapted to the land with little difficulty.

The climate favored production of a wide variety of crops and livestock.[99] The settlers, especially those from the British Isles, were not accustomed to the wider seasonal range of temperatures; the average temperature in Harrisburg is ten degrees higher than in London in July and is ten degrees colder in January (table 8). Late spring and early fall frosts sometimes created hardships. Summer temperatures higher than those in western Europe restricted the production of root crops and sheep. Occasional excessively cold winters killed cattle and winter wheat. From time to time droughts or harvest-time rains affected yields. But on the whole Europeans had little trouble adapting to the generally benevolent climate with a growing season of between 165 and 200 days.[100]

The surface of the land, too, was favorable. The face of southeastern Pennsylvania, roughly 160 by 80 miles in its maximum

Table 8

Climatic Data, Pennsylvania and Europe

(Mean Monthly and Yearly Temperatures in Degrees Fahrenheit and Precipitation in Inches)

City		J	F	M	A	M	J	J	A	S	O	N	D	Yr.
Harrisburg	t.	29	30	39	51	62	70	74	72	65	55	43	33	52
	ppt.	3.0	3.2	3.0	2.7	3.4	3.6	3.7	4.0	3.1	2.9	2.2	3.0	37.8
London (Greenwich)	t.	39	39	43	50	54	60	64	64	59	52	45	42	51
	ppt.	2.1	1.6	1.5	1.5	1.9	1.7	2.0	2.3	1.6	2.0	2.3	2.0	22.5
Belfast	t.	40	41	42	46	51	56	59	58	55	49	43	41	48
	ppt.	3.2	2.8	2.8	2.8	2.7	3.5	3.8	4.4	3.1	4.0	3.4	4.4	40.9
Frankfurt-am-Main	t.	31	35	43	52	59	64	68	66	60	51	41	35	50
	ppt.	2.1	2.0	1.4	1.5	2.3	3.0	2.7	2.9	1.7	1.2	2.5	2.3	25.6

Source: For Harrisburg: Robert DeC. Ward et al., "The Climates of North America," in W. Köppen and R. Geiger, comp., Handbuch der Klimatologie, 2, pt. J. (Berlin: Gebrüder Borntraeger, 1936): 203; for Greenwich and Frankfurt: U.S. Department of Commerce, Weather Bureau, World Weather Records, 1941–1950 (Washington, 1959), pp. 779, 679–80; for Belfast: Dr. Buchan, "Mean Atmospheric Pressure and Temperatures of the British Islands," Journal of the Scottish Meteorological Society, 3d ser., vol. 11, nos. 13–14 (1895–96), plates 7–14, and G. J. Symons, H. Sowerby Wallis, and Hugh Robert Mill, comps., British Rainfall: On the Distribution of Rain in Space and Time over the British Isles . . . with Articles upon Various Branches of Rainfall Work . . . (London, 1892–1902), passim.

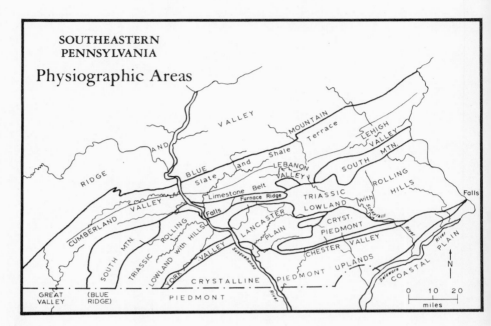

Figure 5

dimensions, was an amply wooded rolling plain with deep, well-drained loamy soils derived from limestone, shales, and crystalline rocks (figures 5 and 6).[101] But variations were distinct enough to divide the area into physiographic regions: the Great Valley of three parts (the Cumberland, Lebanon, and Lehigh valleys), marked off on its northern and western sides by Blue or North Mountain; the hill lands associated with the continuation of Virginia's Blue Ridge, known generally as South Mountain; the Piedmont, with three subregions: the Crystalline Piedmont Uplands, the Triassic Lowlands, and the Limestone Plains; and the Coastal Plain.

The Great Valley, the first in the "ridge and valley" country that extends to the north and west, is underlain by gray shales and slates on its northern side and by limestone on the south. The former is more rolling and has greater local relief than the gently sloping limestone belt. South Mountain and parts such as Furnace Ridge are composed of rocks more resistant to erosion that have

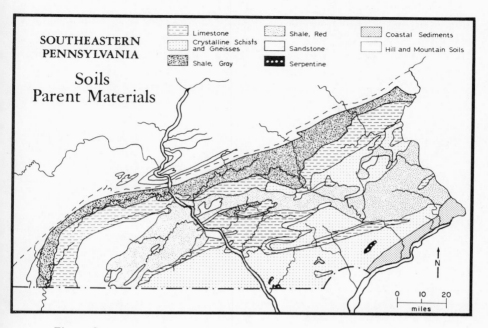

SOUTHEASTERN PENNSYLVANIA

Soils
Parent Materials

Limestone
Crystalline Schists and Gneisses
Shale, Gray
Shale, Red
Sandstone
Serpentine
Coastal Sediments
Hill and Mountain Soils

N

0 10 20
miles

Figure 6

created greater local relief and steeper slopes. Unlike the Great Valley, these ridges have been unsuitable for agriculture, except for commercial orchards here and there in recent times. In the eighteenth century several deposits of iron, copper, and lead were exploited.

On the Piedmont, substantial areas are underlain by limestone and similar but harder dolomite. These areas include the Lancaster Plain, composing half of Lancaster County, and the Chester and York valleys, both of which extend more than thirty miles in length. These limestone plains are useful for agriculture, having a high proportion of slopes with inclinations of less than 3 per cent, which are not so subject to erosion.[102] Adjacent to the Susquehanna River, however, are some deeply incised valleys. The Piedmont Lowland, underlain chiefly by soft red shales of Triassic age, and the Piedmont Uplands, mostly of much older metamorphosed crystalline schists and gneisses, have more extensive areas of greater relief and are more rolling than the limestone plains, but the slopes are generally under 10 per cent. The Lowland is a minor part of Lancaster and Chester counties but covers large parts of Bucks, Montgomery, and York. The Uplands cover most of Chester County and the southern parts of Lancaster and York counties. The latter have much of their gentle slope on the upper levels of their profiles, that is, on the interfluves (between the streams) rather than in valley bottoms. Despite the name Uplands, most of the area is of rolling plains and is suitable for most types of agricultural production. The term has arisen in part because steep slopes mark them from the limestone plains. Nowhere is this more apparent than on both sides of the narrow limestone-based Chester Valley. Scattered areas of sandstones and serpentine exist. The Coastal Plain is composed mostly of silt and sand sediments.

Of the two counties studied more intensively, Chester and Lancaster, the latter is somewhat better endowed from a topographical standpoint because of the large area of gentle slope on the Lancaster Plain (table 9). But the most widespread slope category in Chester, 3 to 8 or 10 per cent, was not a serious obstacle to farming, considering that technology was primitive. Although

Table 9

Categories of Slope as Percentages of Total Area[a]

Chester Co.[b]		Lancaster Co.[b]	
Slope (%)	*Area (%)*	*Slope (%)*	*Area (%)*
0–3	13	0–5	47
3–8	52	5–10	35
8–15	22	10–20	12
15–25	7	Over 20	6
Over 25	4		

Source: Ches. Co. Planning Comm., "Chester County: Slope," map (West Chester, 1963); Lanc. Co. Planning Comm., *A Report on the Physical Features and Natural Resources of Lancaster County, Pennsylvania* (Lancaster, 1960), p. 12.

Note: Percentages may not add to 100 because of rounding.

[a]Categories vary because of source material.
[b]Present-day areas only; excludes Delaware, Dauphin, and Lebanon counties.

generally speaking the steeper the slope, the more susceptible it is to erosion, data on erosion in the 1930s indicate that most of the land, even the Lancaster Plain with slopes of less than 3 per cent has been moderately eroded.[103] Unfortunately no information on erosion from the eighteenth century is available.

The drainage pattern both helped and hindered the activities of the people (figure 1). There are three major rivers, the Delaware, the Susquehanna, and the Schuylkill. The Delaware has always permitted easy entry from the Atlantic, and Philadelphia has remained one of the chief seaports of North America even though it is nearly a hundred miles from the open sea and its harbor in earlier years was frozen for a short period each winter. The Delaware was easily navigable to the falls at Trenton, where it bends from a northeasterly to northwesterly direction. The Susquehanna, on the other hand, was more of a hindrance than a help to movement and trade, mainly because of a series of rapids below Middletown where Swatara Creek enters it. From the standpoint of trade, the fact that the Susquehanna flows southward into Chesapeake Bay rather than eastward into the Delaware was important. Trade in Pennsylvania was oriented east and west rather than north and south, and so the Susquehanna—treacherous, rocky, and a mile wide at many ferry points—was a major obstacle. It thus served to strengthen trade connections between Maryland and the Pennsylvanians west of the river.[104] The Schuylkill was navigable only during spring freshets. Some lumber and grain was moved at this period, but the river had only potential importance before canals were dug along its route after 1800. A few other streams were navigable for short distances near their mouths, notably the Brandywine near Wilmington in Delaware, but were not significant upstream.

Many small, permanent, but unnavigable streams contributed to the activities of the inhabitants. With flows regulated by dams, they provided the chief source of energy for mills that processed grain, lumber, hemp, and seeds. The streams permitted entrepreneurs to turn this region, including adjacent Delaware, into the most important flour-milling area on the continent. The first settlers in most places sought small streams and springs on which to settle so as to ensure green meadows and a constant water

Table 10

Quality of Soils, Lancaster County, 1952-56

Series	Type	Parent Material	Slope (%)	Erosion	Index of Relative Productivity[a]					
					Corn	Wheat	Clover and Timothy	Bluegrass-Clover Pasture	Potatoes	Orchard
Hagerstown-Duffield	Silt loam[b]	Limestone	0–3	Little	100	100	100	100	100	100
			0–3	Moderate	98	98	98	98	98	98
			3–6	Moderate	98	98	98	98	98	98
Conestoga	Silt loam	Micaceous limestone	3–6	Moderate	98	98	100	98	90	100
			6–12	Moderate	90	90	95	90	90	95
Chester	Silt loam (deep)	Schists, gneisses	0–3	Little	98	100	100	97	100	100
			3–6	Moderate	95	95	95	95	95	100
			6–12	Moderate	88	90	94	87	90	100
Glenelg	Channery[c] silt loam (moderate depth)	Schists, gneisses	3–6	Moderate	75	87	87	80	85	85
Manor	Channery silt loam (shallow)	Schists, gneisses	15–25	Moderate	50	60	65	50	...	70
			25–40	Moderate	...	...	...	45	...	...
Berks	Silt loam	Gray shale	3–8	Moderate	55	80	80	65	60	78
			8–15	Moderate	50	75	75	60	50	75
Penn	Gravelly and silt loam	Red shale	3–8	Moderate	57	75	75	65	73	85

Source: John B. Carey, Soil Survey of Lancaster County, Pennsylvania, U.S. Department of Agriculture, Soil Conservation Service, Soil Survey, ser. 1956, no. 4 (Washington, 1959), pp. 8, 85.

[a]100 = average yields per acre on Duffield silt loam, 0–3% slopes: 80 bu. corn, 38 bu. winter wheat, 2.5 tons clover and timothy, 90 cows (1 cow equivalent to 1 steer, 1 horse, 5 hogs, 7 sheep) per day on bluegrass-clover pasture, and 300 bu. potatoes. No information on orchard productivity.

[b]Silt grains are larger than clay but smaller than sand. Silt loam contains little clay, ½ or more silt, and ¼–½ sand.

[c]Channery soils contain thin, flat fragments of rock up to 6 inches in length.

supply. Those who settled between streams, particularly in some excessively drained limestone "drylands" such as Northampton County between Bethlehem and Nazareth (figures 34 and 35), the Cumberland Valley between Carlisle and Shippensburg (figure 34), and Earl Township in Lancaster County (figure 3) had more difficulties than those along streams.[105]

Because the fertility of soils was of critical concern to people when they chose sites and cultivated the land and because many commentators have discussed these connections, a careful assessment of their qualities is necessary. In the eighteenth century the limestone lands and the alluvial bottom lands along the main rivers were thought to be the most fertile.[106] Recent soil surveys of both Lancaster and Chester tend to support these contentions, but the relative merits of different types of soil are not clear-cut.[107] Some of the supposedly inferior soils are almost as productive today as limestone lands. Application of humus and fertilizers in recent years may have reduced earlier differences among soil types. But more fundamentally, the relatively uniform climate and vegetation patterns over long centuries tended to reduce soils of different parent materials to a similar loamy, friable character.[108]

In the 1950s, soil scientists determined the productivity of various soils in prosperous Lancaster County (table 10). The silt loam soils on some limestones (Hagerstown-Duffield) with slopes of less than 3 per cent and little erosion had the highest average yields per acre of corn, wheat, hay, potatoes, and orchard crops. The pedologists compared all other soils with the productivity of this type. Conestoga limestone soils were a little less productive; wheat, for example, returned yields of thirty-seven bushels, or 98 per cent of the yield on Hagerstown-Duffield. Chester soils formed from crystalline rocks with slopes of between 3 and 6 per cent were rated at 95 per cent. Even with slopes between 6 and 12 per cent, these soils where protected against erosion could produce crops at a level of 87 per cent. Soils from shales in the Great Valley and red Triassic types were considered "pretty good" by eighteenth century commentators.[109] Recent data indicated that they produced from 50 to 85 per cent as well as the best limestone soils, depending on the crop. The areas developed from sandstone and serpentines were quite poor, and fortunately for settlers they were quite small. In general, the current capabilities of the land are high; southeastern Pennsylvania, particularly Lancaster and Chester counties, is one of the most productive areas in the United States, indeed in the world. If most eighteenth century farmers, whatever their European origins, achieved lower yields than they might have, this resulted from the agricultural practices of the time and not from the inherent fertility of most soils.

The vegetative cover at the time of settlement and subsequently is not easily determined. Although much of the area was in hard-wood forest, open areas occurred and the forest was composed of trees of varying ages. The widely used term "barrens" sometimes referred to open places but often meant land unsuitable for agri-culture, including steep wooded slopes and serpentine soils.[110] Nevertheless, contemporary reports and a continuing tradition support the view that the term referred to scrubby, partially open lands and grasslands. Besides natural marshy land adjacent to large rivers and some smaller creeks, the Indians had left old fields in various stages of successional growth. Sapling and *gruben* land were common terms.[111] Both the Indians and the settlers burned the forest and grasslands to drive out game and to provide succulent forage for animals, and settlers sought open areas.[112] Species composition of the forest was roughly that recorded on surveyors' drafts.[113] Black and white oaks and hickories predominated, and chestnuts grew prominently on drier slopes. The soft yellow tulip poplar was an important successional type. The forests con-tributed building materials and fuel to farmers and to ironmakers, who used enormous quantities of hardwood charcoal for reducing ore.

Animal life seems to have been abundant, at least in early years. Indians trapped beavers and sold their pelts to traders. The fur trade opened the back country for land speculation. Although the bison may have disappeared from the area before the advance of settlement, deer, turkeys, and fish were important contributors to the food supply and were a boon to the poor.[114] Squirrels and bears were pests to agriculture, and bounties were placed on their heads and on those of wolves and foxes.[115] In general, plants and animals were abundant enough in the early years to supplement agriculture and to support a bounteous rural life. Of course, as the century passed the flora and fauna changed dramatically.

Distance helped to determine activities. The availability of land
and the location of previous settlements were factors considered
by settlers. Later they and their descendants had to deal with
population pressure on the land in assessing their opportunities.
Accessibility to various parts of the area, especially to Philadelphia, during a time when transportation was limited and slow
was of considerable importance to the way the people organized
the region around towns and to their agricultural activities. Within
a 30-mile radius of Philadelphia the city's dominance stifled the
development of other towns. The back country beyond this line
was the area where urban developers were most active, particularly
between 1730 and 1765. Within the 160-by-80-mile area as a
whole, distances from one place to another were short enough to
permit most people to participate in commerce.

* * *

As citizens of a modern urban society we are inclined to consider Frederick Brown's life and his society and environment to be
very simple. Given his liberal philosophy, one suspects that Brown,
too, thought life was relatively easy. His ties to his neighbors were
not nearly as complex as ours are today; certainly the relatively
open spatial and social environments permitted looser connections
and less specialization of work. Yet his situation presented him
with many decisions, both perplexing and complex,[116] as we will
see in considering how the various aspects of society and environment influenced the people as they occupied the area, organized
the territory, and used the land.

CHAPTER TWO

Occupying the Land, 1681-1760

Most of the Europeans who crossed the Atlantic sought opportunity on the land. So their first task was to look for sites to
occupy. Many decided where to settle soon after their arrival,
though if indentured they had to wait for four years or more
before they were free to act independently. The settlers' decisions
on where to locate grew out of three sets of factors—their own
values, the social situation they found in their new home, and the
natural environment. Two powerful shapers of values, nationality
and religion, played a part in determining where they went, but
not in the way that is commonly understood; for example, the
Germans, rather than seeking already settled areas, went to the
frontier as frequently as the Scotch-Irish. Land policies of the
proprietors, including those relating to Indians, were a major element of the social situation. They affected the settlers' choice,
though less directly than Penn had intended. The quality of the
land was, of course, an important environmental factor for most
people. But other conditions were just as important, or more so—
proximity to markets, availability of land for sale or lease, the
time of entry into the region, and the material circumstances of
the settlers.

Settlers occupied most of southeastern Pennsylvania between
1681 and 1760. Although some Swedes had held land along the
Delaware River since 1638, their colonies had not grown. After
1681, with the new influx of settlers, the occupation spread
rapidly and progressively from Philadelphia and other points along
the Delaware to the west and north (figures 7-10).[1] After the

42

turn of the century and through the next few decades some groups settled in outliers, and speculators purchased land beyond the fringe of settlement. By 1740, after more than a decade of heavy immigration, settlers had taken up some land in all of southeastern Pennsylvania's more fertile areas, and many people coming through Philadelphia were now passing through to the back country of Maryland, Virginia, and Carolina, though some immigrants were able to take up land behind the line of occupation. Soon after, others spilled over the Blue Mountain into valleys beyond. But in 1755 immigration virtually ceased for more than a decade, and after 1760 the population growth of southeastern Pennsylvania began to slacken, most noticeably in the oldest and predominantly rural counties of Bucks and Chester (figure 11).

* * *

The distributional patterns of nationalities and religious denominations (figures 12, 13, and 14)[2] seem to indicate that settlers were strongly attracted by their own cultural groups. Extensive areas were occupied exclusively by people from one country, and religious groups as well showed some clustering. In 1760 Germans monopolized a larger area than did any other national group, occupying much of Berks, upper Philadelphia, Northampton, and York counties and the Lebanon Valley in Lancaster County. In several of these areas they represented the frontier. The Scotch-Irish were the overwhelming majority in the Cumberland Valley and in western York County (the Gettysburg area), and the English and Welsh held some parts of Chester and Bucks exclusively. Some religious groups were nearly coterminous with nationality and so do not appear in figure 14; the Lutheran and Reformed sections coincided with German areas and Presbyterian strength lay in Scotch-Irish areas.[3] Quaker and Mennonite expansion strongly tended toward areas next to those they already occupied.

Areal segregation was a consequence of nationalistic feeling, language, kinship, denominational adherence, and the arrival of immigrants in groups. Language was of greatest importance in the case of the Germans and influenced the Welsh to a minor extent in

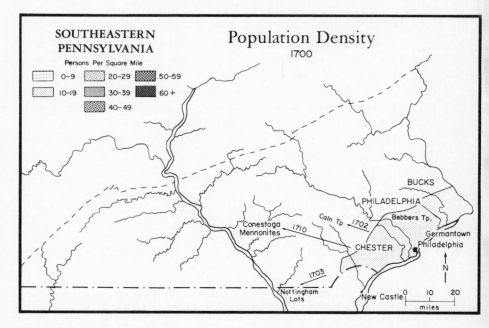

Figure 7

the early years.[4] Language reinforced feelings of national identification so that Germans often considered themselves separate. The
"Dutch" accent persists even today in some areas. Much of German exclusiveness, however, was simply the result of their large
numbers and their tendency to arrive in large parties. Even though
villages or congregations rarely (if at all) moved en masse, relatives
or people from the same state frequently traveled together. People
may have established strong ties during the ocean voyage, leading
them to settle as neighbors if they were not separated and sold as
indentured servants.[5] It is more difficult to explain how the
Scotch-Irish came to occupy areas exclusively. Antagonistic attitudes toward Ulstermen by the English and the Germans probably
contributed, but we do not know for certain. Scotch-Irish immigration apparently was heavier than that of the English in most
years after 1725, and so they went to areas that they might have
shared with the English at another time. Time of arrival, availability of land, and the poverty of most Scotch-Irish and Germans

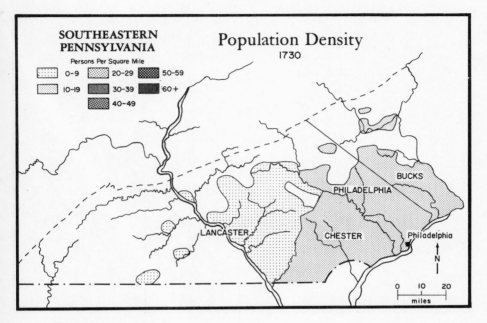

Figure 8

also helped to encourage separation.[6] For the Mennonites and, to a lesser extent, the Quakers, a sense of group cohesiveness probably led to a strong pattern of contiguity. In 1735, for example, William Pim of Caln Township in Chester Valley asserted that he "proposed to sell to none but Friends."[7]

We cannot easily understand why different groups occupied the areas they did—why, for example, Germans settled in the north and Scotch-Irish in the west. One factor may have been the requirement after 1725 that Germans debark at Philadelphia to take the loyalty oath before a judge or the mayor, whereas many Scotch-Irish landed farther south at New Castle.[8] Initial focuses of settlement also exerted a pull. Germantown and a derivative center, Bebber's Township near Skippack, influenced the location of one ingathering of German Mennonites east of the Schuylkill River and possibly attracted other Germans toward the north (figures 7–10). Reformed and Lutheran clusters started in upper Philadelphia County (later Montgomery) and at the Tulpehocken

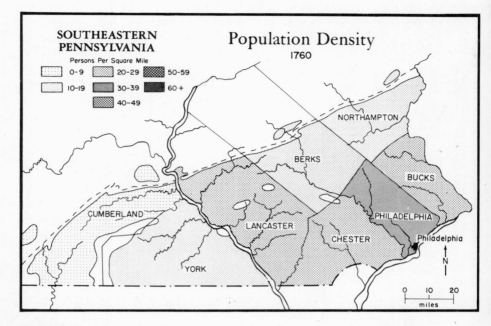

Figure 9

settlement in the Lebanon Valley.[9] All these settlements began
before the period of greatest immigration. In 1710 another assem-
blage of Mennonites quite separate from the one east of the
Schuylkill settled on the plain south of the site of Lancaster.[10]
This area served as a center of expansion for Mennonites and other
Germans who arrived later and spread across the Susquehanna into
the York Valley.[11] The first Scotch-Irish settled in New Castle
County, Delaware, and their later settlement extended into
southern Chester, southern and western York, and the Lancaster
Plain. Donegal Township in the latter area became a center for
expansion into the Cumberland Valley, the Valley of Virginia, and
western Pennsylvania.[12] Thus settlement proceeded outward
mostly in contiguous thrusts from a few focal points.

The overlap of various groups in many areas suggests that cultural segregation provides only a partial explanation of the location of settlers. Although Germans and adherents of religious sects

seemed to show a greater tendency toward unshared positions,
many of them initially settled with members of other groups.
Besides zones of coalescence between exclusive areas and several
spots where single congregations of one group settled within larger
assemblages (figures 12, 13, and 14), there were some very mixed
areas. The Lancaster Plain (figure 13) contained the richest med-
ley; all national groups and, at the outset, all religious groups were
found there. Reformed Huguenots, German Dunkers, Welsh Anglicans, and Scotch-Irish and Scottish Anglicans were among the
minority groups, not shown clearly on the maps. Although many
of these groups were alone at first, others came in soon afterward.
Chester County was less mixed, but Scotch-Irish and Welsh often
settled among the English and even among the Quakers, who were
the largest group in that county. Philadelphia City was also a place
of mingling; Lutheran and Reformed churches were founded soon
after 1725 and by 1790 Lutherans made up perhaps 20 per cent of

[handwritten marginalia: But did they actually mix on local level]

Figure 10

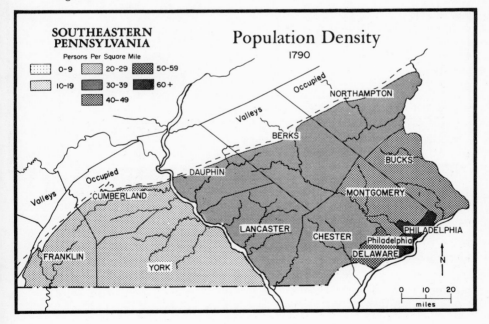

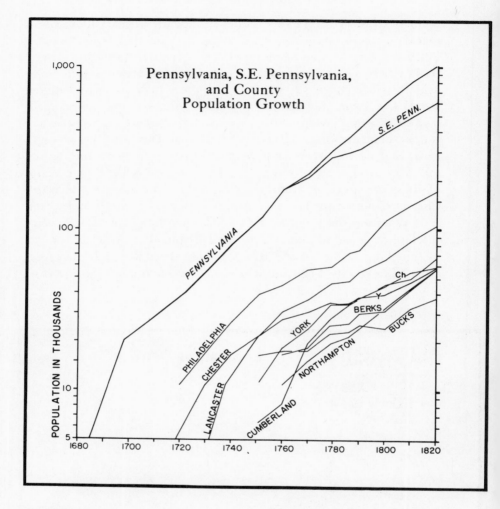

Figure 11

the city's population.[13] One other combination of groups was
German Lutheran with Reformed. Although usually spatially
separated in Europe, throughout southeastern Pennsylvania their
parishes were almost always coterminous; indeed, they often used
the same churches. Thus mixtures of groups were not unusual in

the early settlements. Because of this we have to consider noncultural factors to comprehend the distribution of people.

* * *

An examination of the policies and practices of the government and especially of the proprietors as the owners of the land can yield insights into Pennsylvania settlement patterns. On their face, these policies were largely ineffectual, especially in later years, in guiding and restricting the location of settlers. In fact, they crumbled and took new form under the pressures of settlement and speculation by various interests, including the proprietors and their agents themselves. As John Armstrong of Cumberland County asserted, proprietary agents carried "no more weight than the East Wind" in controlling settlement.[14] This speculative interest itself exerted an indirect influence, however, as did policies in

Figure 12

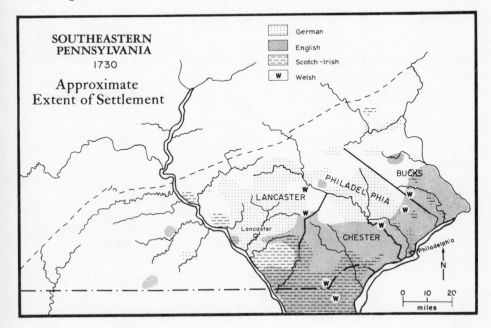

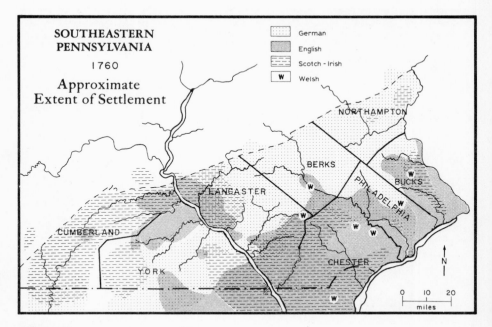

Figure 13

such matters as the boundary dispute with Maryland and transactions with the Indians.

William Penn, imbued with the idea of a structured society
based on religion as well as the desire for revenue, laid down an
orderly plan of occupation. He thought people should establish
themselves in contiguous tiers of townships, regularly laid out
and surveyed prior to settlement, with the Delaware River as the
base line.[15] To implement his plans he eventually sold about
860,000 acres to "First Purchasers" in England, most of them
Quakers who he thought would carry out his ideas.[16] To ensure
orderliness, a land office, under which surveyors in the field
served, was set up by the Board of Property and run by the surveyor-general.[17]

Operations were partly successful during the first twenty years.
The map of population density (figure 7), Thomas Holme's map
showing holdings about 1696 (figure 15),[18] and the map of minor
civil divisions in Chester County (figure 2) indicate contiguity and

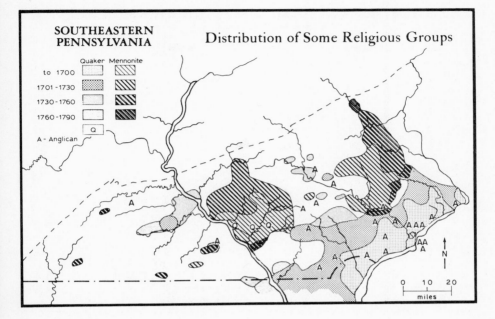

Figure 14

regularity in the eastern part of the county.[19] In most of these townships surveys preceded occupation and the Quakers were kept within the established bounds.

In 1690 a second major attempt at settlement was promoted by Penn and was supported by Quakers. Surveyors were to lay out 100,000 acres and a city on the east side of the Susquehanna to encourage progressive settlement eastward to meet the westward movement and to be the focus of fur trading activities to the north and west. Although a substantial number subscribed to the plan, the project failed.[20]

This failure was an early indication that Penn's plans would eventually falter. Other portents were his sale of land to speculators, reversing an earlier policy because of his need for revenue, and the organization of outlying "townships" that were unrelated to the Susquehanna plan. From 1681 to 1685 he granted land to individuals and companies among the "First Purchasers," but usually these speculators were obliged to settle people within three

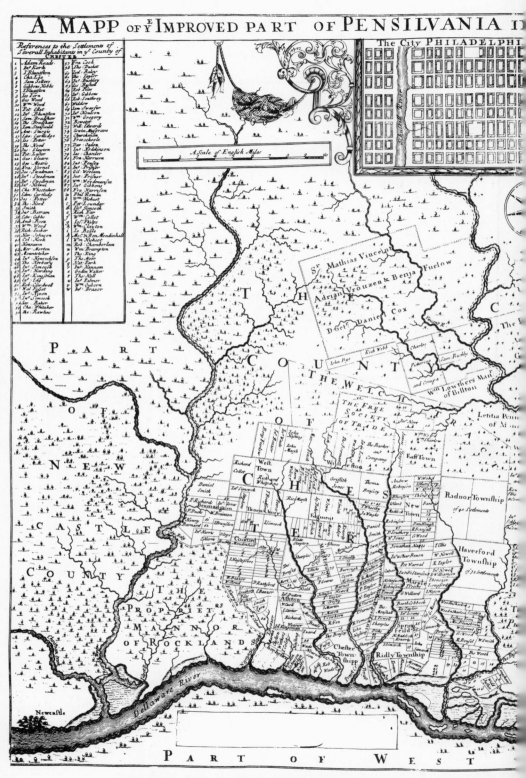

Figure 15. Thomas Holme's Map of Pennsylvania. Photo of original map

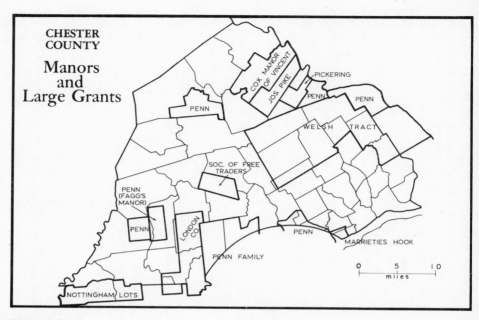

CHESTER COUNTY

Manors and Large Grants

Figure 16

years or lose their rights.[21] But even as early as 1684 and very clearly in 1699, when the Pennsylvania Company of London was granted nearly 60,000 acres, he waived this stipulation.[22] A third of the London Company's land was laid out in various parts of southern Chester County (figure 16) and the rest in other counties, including 5,553 acres on the Lancaster Plain east of the site of Lancaster town.[23] Other speculators, such as Amos Strettle and James Logan, the provincial secretary and merchant in the fur trade who used his public office for private gain, received land in the same area. Logan probably exerted more control over his own land than he did over the proprietor's.[24]

Groups of contiguous lots, sometimes called "townships," were laid out beyond the line of settlement. In 1702 the Nottingham Lots, straddling what became the Mason-Dixon Line (figures 7 and 16), and Bebber's Township at Skippack in Philadelphia County (figure 7) were surveyed for Quakers and Mennonites respectively.[25] In 1710 Swiss Mennonites went twenty miles beyond

other settlements into what became Lancaster County (figure 7). *all acting as cohesive groups*
Shortly thereafter, nearby Strasburg was settled by Huguenots,
and a group of Anglican Welsh obtained lots in what became
Caernarvon Township at the eastern end of the Lancaster Plain.[26]

Penn, his agents, and eventually his sons also directly contributed to settlement beyond contiguously occupied areas by the
way in which they laid out their own private lands. He and his
sons laid out "manors," which were ostensibly for conserving
woodland but were actually reserves for later speculation.[27] By
charter, the Penns were entitled to one-tenth of all townships laid
out. But instead they usually took large blocks, holding, for
example, 20 per cent of Chester County and 11 per cent of Philadelphia and Bucks. After 1730 and particularly before 1740,
Penn's sons set up extremely large tracts, such as Springettsbury
Manor in York (64,520 acres), Maske in the Gettysburg area of
York (43,500), and Conestoga in Lancaster County (16,000).
Although the Penns did not retain 10 per cent in these back-
country counties, altogether they held at various times 550,000
acres in seventy-eight tracts.[28] These speculative practices under-
mined the program of orderly contiguous settlements and also led
proprietary agents and surveyors to succumb to their own speculative desires and to the whims of affluent settlers who wanted land
regardless of the configuration of other lots.[29]

After the turn of the eighteenth century the practices of "indiscriminate location" and squatting were widespread, and the warrant and survey system came into use. In the back country
especially, settlement now preceded survey, and settlers marked
out their own land before applying for survey warrants. Technically this meant that all such people were squatters for a time.
Fortunately for the Penns, settlers usually sought survey warrants
for their own security, and in most areas the time between settlement and survey was not long. Acquiring a deed took much
longer, however, usually between five and twenty years and sometimes as long as seventy-five years.[30] Although this delay limited
the Penns' incomes, warrants provided certainty of tenure for settlers and so order in the society.

In table 11 a partial view of the pattern of holdings by deed,
warrant, and possession without any legal rights appears.[31] In

Table 11

Percentages of Land Held by Deed, Warrant, and Possession

Area	Deeded	Warranted and/or Surveyed	Unwarranted
1759 Lancaster Co.			
Caernarvon Tp.	69	31	Very little;
Earl	82	18	included with
Elizabeth	11	89	warranted
Manor	64	36	and surveyed
Salisbury	77	23	
1763 Cumberland Co.			
Upper Tyrone (beyond Blue Mtn.)	0	19	81
Hopewell (astride Great Valley, Shippensburg area)	14	42	44
Antrim (Great Valley, on Md. line)	26	72	2

Source: Lanc. Co. MSS tax returns; and Cumberland MSS returns, Lamberton Scotch-Irish Coll., 1: 41, Hist. Soc. Pa.

newly settled areas, such as Upper Tyrone Township beyond Blue Mountain (now in Perry County), squatters held most of the land, but in older areas, such as Antrim in the Cumberland Valley and the Lancaster Plain, more land was surveyed and deeded. But surprisingly, land was still undeeded after fifty years of settlement on the plain and thirty years in the Cumberland Valley. Clearly many people were in no hurry to pay the full purchase price. In 1732 the land office sharply dunned even the respected Mennonite leaders in Lancaster, Martin Kendig and Hans Herr, for payments on land warranted in 1717.[32]

The Penns disliked indiscriminate location because it made administration difficult. But their failure to recognize the facts contributed to loss of income and popular support. By 1710 William Penn was complaining bitterly about his "land enter'd upon without any regular Method, my Mannors invaded (under pretence that I had not duly survey'd them)."[33] After 1718 the land office virtually closed for fourteen years, and the lack of administrative machinery led to increased squatting by members of all national groups. Even after 1732, when Thomas Penn arrived, it was clear that people would not conform to such an inadequate system.[34] Thomas Penn said that 130,000 of 400,000 acres taken up between 1732 and 1740 had not been warranted by the latter date.[35] Coercive attempts to control settlers were met with defiant "claims clubs," as in Donegal Township in the early 1730s.[36] The ire of settlers rose further when Penn lifted the price of land from £10 to £15 10s. and quitrents from 1s. to 2s. 6d. per hundred acres.[37] Attempts to rent land were not very successful.[38] Thus by 1750 the situation had not improved. "Profligate fellows" and even those of the "better sort" invaded manors; surveyors, sheriffs, "rangers," and "overseers" were unable to fend them off.[39] Incomes were low. Richard Peters wrote ruefully to Thomas Penn: "Your quit rents are shamefully in arrears—Your Ferrys wrested out of your hands—Your Manor Lands and Appropriated Tracts are settled as other parts of the Province promiscuously by good and bad people. . . ."[40]

Not until the early 1760s did the Penns change land policies. Some of their agents had long been trying to reform the system; possession was tacitly recognized as early as the 1740s, when some squatters were permitted to purchase manor lands.[41] But the legal character of possession was ill defined. Peters said that the lawyers disagreed over the meaning of warrant rights.[42] In 1761 the legal question of "possession," generally defined as seven years' residence, came to court. One German, a tenant on London Company land in Lampeter Township, Lancaster County, had his case brought before the Privy Council. In the printed dossier, his lawyers argued that he held preemptive rights because the custom of possession was well established in America, "for that in new-settled Colonies Possession and Improvement is the best Title any man can have."[43] Whether he won the case or not is uncertain; but in 1765 the Penns officially recognized preemption by the "Application System" through which possessors had the first rights to take out warrants even though they might take their own time about it.[44] The price of land was also lowered to £5 per 100 acres. Owing to these more sensible policies and to prosperity in the early 1770s, the Penns' incomes rose to their highest levels.[45] For nearly a century the people had defied an uncompromising but ineffectual family and by 1765 had settled the area and won legal rights.

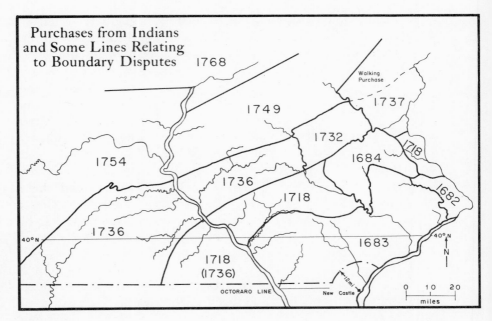

Figure 17

Some particular issues relating to occupation of the area engaged the government's attention. The boundary dispute with Maryland was partly responsible for the relaxation of Penn's rigorous plan for order since he and his agents encouraged settlement in the contested area, a broad strip between forty degrees north latitude and an east-west line through the mouth of Octoraro Creek (figure 17).[46] Also involved was the line between Maryland and the three counties of Delaware owned by the Penn family. The controversy began with the conflicting areal stipulations in the charters granted to the Calverts and the Penns. Attempts to reach a compromise failed in 1681, and almost a century of discord ensued before the final resolution. Feeling ran high over this dispute, especially in the 1730s. In 1701 and 1732 agreements were reached between Maryland and Delaware, and in 1738 a temporary line was drawn between Maryland and Pennsylvania.[47] By the mid-1760s Mason and Dixon fixed the final line, and in 1774 it achieved legal status.[48]

William Penn moved very early to strengthen his claim against Maryland's. The Nottingham Lots, now mostly south of the Mason-Dixon Line, were laid out in 1702 and settled by Quakers. London Company lands also extended south of the final boundary in Chester County (figure 16). Perhaps one of Penn's reasons for the second large settlement on the Susquehanna and for the permission he granted Mennonites in 1710 to settle south of the fortieth parallel on the Lancaster Plain was to lay claim by possession. Many Scotch-Irish and Quakers moved into the southern part of Lancaster and York counties and were not immediately pressed for payment by the proprietor's agents.[49] The best-known clashes took place over the Blunston Licenses, granted between 1733 and 1736 west of the Susquehanna. These grants on land not yet purchased from the Indians were an explicit attempt to forestall Marylanders, particularly in what was to become York County.[50] Many Germans and Scotch-Irish were guided to this area and came into open conflict with people granted land by Calvert. Although these grants later led to antagonisms between the Penns and settlers, they contributed to occupation of the disputed area and helped to secure more land for Pennsylvania.

The Penns made only a few attempts to control the settling of groups solely by nationality. Welsh of three denominational persuasions—Quaker, Baptist, and Anglican—were located on separate Welsh tracts before 1700.[51] But apparently the Scotch-Irish were involved in the only later attempts of this sort. Besides permitting Scotch-Irish and Germans to settle the area under dispute with Maryland, James Logan, the provincial secretary, encouraged the Scotch-Irish in 1718 to move from what became Manor Township to Donegal in Lancaster County (figure 3) before the Indian title was cleared, ostensibly because of an apparently accepted romantic notion that they would prove good frontiersmen, having so bravely defended Inniskillen against Irish Catholics in 1688. More important, he settled them on his own speculatively held lands.[52] In 1749, reputedly because some Scotch-Irish disputed possession with Germans in Donegal, they were encouraged to move across the Susquehanna to Cumberland. Some went, but many remained.[53] These attempts to encourage or direct some members of national groups seemingly were successful, but in the overall picture they were not a critical aspect of settlement. If people settled in groups they did so more to satisfy their sense of community, not because of external pressures.

Indian title to the land continued as a serious issue of negotiations and controversy. William Penn sought to maintain peaceful relations with the Indians to ensure orderly settlement by purchasing land ahead of settlement (figure 17). In 1700 he prohibited private purchases from Indians without proprietary permission.[54] Later the proprietors' agents made some attempts to restrict settlement; in 1716, for example, they prohibited a survey of London Company land "above" Conestoga Creek and dissuaded Scotch-Irish from settling near the site of Harrisburg.[55] Occasionally, most particularly in 1749, proprietary agents ejected squatters from Indian lands.[56]

Although Penn's sons and agents continued to purchase Indian lands, they permitted some settlements on them. In 1723 German Reformed and Lutheran settlers took up land on Tulpehocken Creek in the Lebanon Valley (figure 1), and by 1729 townships were organized there before title was cleared.[57] In the years before 1736 the sale of Blunston Licenses for settlement in York County and the Cumberland Valley increased tension with the Iroquois as well as with the Marylanders.[58] In 1737 the infamous "Walking Purchase" by which the proprietary gained much of what became Northampton County (figure 17) provoked ill feeling among the Delaware Indians.[59] These failures to deal openly with the Indians contributed to their insecurity and so in part to depredations by them in the French and Indian War between 1755 and 1758 and during Pontiac's uprising in 1763 and 1764. Since the Iroquois, who had held sovereignty over the Delawares and Shawnees, were unable to restrain the latter tribe, settlers were thrown back from areas in the Great Valley adjacent to Blue Mountain and were checked temporarily from entering the "ridge and valley" country beyond.[60]

The overall influence of the proprietors and their agents on occupation patterns was thus small and was primarily indirect. Their practices were as often permissive as coercive when early attempts at regulation gave way to near chaos. Not until 1765 did the Penns fully realize that their well-being depended on full

acceptance of settlers' rights. Policies finally were made to conform with accomplished fact; but within fifteen years the whole
proprietary apparatus was overthrown.

* * *

Quality of the land was undoubtedly a critical influence on
settlement. But this factor did not operate in southeastern Pennsylvania in the way that many analysts have supposed. A comparison of physiographic and soil maps (figures 5 and 6) with the
distribution of people in 1700 and 1730 (figures 7 and 8) gives
little indication that the best lands were sought out. Given the
generally good quality of land in much of the area, this finding is
not surprising. But the scale of these maps is small; the more
subtle data shown by the arrows on the 1700 map and the maps of
population densities, particularly in Chester and Lancaster
counties (figures 7, 18, and 19), suggest that some settlers selected

Figure 18

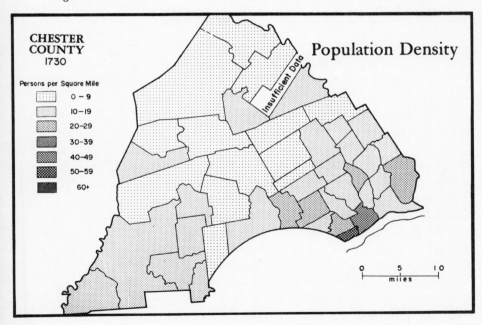

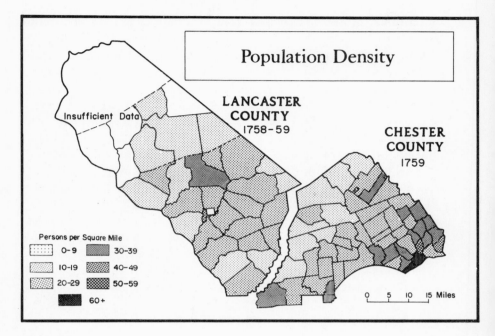

Figure 19

land by this criterion. Townships underlain by limestone and those with gentle slopes generally had greater population densities, while these areas with less desirable soils contained lighter populations.

Other information supports this conclusion. Quakers occupied Chester Valley very early (figure 7); survey drafts dated 1702 show that Caln Township was divided into holdings earlier than the more rolling uplands on either side.[61] The Lancaster Plain, the most extensive area of gently rolling, fertile limestone land, attracted settlers and speculators at an early date. An agent or agents carefully chose the site of the first Mennonite settlement on Conestoga loam between Conestoga and Pequea creeks (figures 1 and 7).[62] Soon after, Huguenots settled Strasburg. Speculators such as Amos Strettle and the London Company early acquired almost 11,000 acres nearby.[63] Several settlements were undertaken by Scotch-Irish and Welsh in what became Donegal, Leacock, Lampeter, Salisbury, and Caernarvon townships (figure

3). Lutheran and Reformed groups also occupied sites in the section. This activity made the Lancaster Plain the most mixed cultural area in rural Pennsylvania. Elsewhere various individuals and groups, such as proprietary agents, Swedes on the Schuylkill, and Germans on Tulpehocken Creek in the Lebanon Valley and in York Valley sought tracts of fertile soils.[64] Hill lands were the least attractive.

Most settlers were probably more concerned with an accessible water supply than with the exact quality of the soil. Drafts of townships in Chester County near the Delaware River show that despite the rectangularity of holdings most of them included stretches along streams.[65] Under "indiscriminate" location, lots were often strung out first along streams, as indicated in the division of Strettle's speculative holding on the Lancaster Plain and by the layout of lots in an early settlement of Scotch-Irish in the Lebanon Valley.[66] Interfluves generally were taken later; most settlers wanted to avoid digging wells, and springs and permanent streams were desirable for domestic and farm use, particularly for irrigating meadows.

The connection between settlers' choices and vegetation is obscure because of the lack of distributional data on flora. In a few instances, selection of Indian old fields was noted in survey drafts,[67] and certain hardwood trees were considered indicators of good soil. How often settlers used species as a guide to soils is not clear.[68]

Nineteenth century writers often asserted that the Germans took to well-wooded lowland limestone areas and the Scotch-Irish to shaly and more sparsely vegetated uplands as a consequence of homeland experience. We therefore must consider the relationship of national groups to various qualities of the land.[69] Because Mennonites and Quakers possessed more wealth than other denominational groups, we might also conclude that their farms were located on better soils. But a comparison of figures 12, 13, and 14 with figures 5 and 6 and other data indicate that land qualities did not coincide closely with particular cultural groups.

Germans did not assiduously seek limestone soils. Even though more Germans than others did settle on limestone lands, this was probably because of their greater numbers and the time of their entry rather than a finer perception of soil qualities, and many occupied other types of land. Many Germans and Swiss, including one of the major groups of Mennonites, occupied soils on somewhat inferior red shales in Bucks and upper Philadelphia (later Montgomery) counties. In Lancaster County some Mennonites actually located on the relatively poor Penn gravelly soils (table 10) in the northern parts of Mt. Joy and Rapho townships (figure 3), while the Scotch-Irish took the limestone soils in these townships.[70] In 1759, of 235 taxpayers in almost exclusively German Cocalico Township, Lancaster County, 49 per cent farmed on "poor" land that constituted 33 per cent of the 25,953 acres assessed. The remaining half were on "middling" and "good" limestone land.[71] Scotch-Irish and English settled on all qualities and types of land—the Scotch-Irish on good crystalline Chester soils and on limestone in Lancaster and Cumberland counties. The Quakers, because they were the first to arrive, took land along the Delaware, then moved onto crystalline soils, the limestone soils in Chester Valley, and those derived from red shale. Frederick Jackson Turner was wrong, at least for southeastern Pennsylvania, when he asserted that a map of limestone soils was also a map of German settlement.[72]

The soils of southeastern Pennsylvania were generally fertile, and some of the poorer soils were good compared, say, with much of New England. Not surprisingly, then, the people were willing to settle in many areas. If Mennonites and Quakers achieved more wealth than other groups,[73] their success should be attributed not to the soils, because they settled on all types and qualities, but to their social philosophy of discipline and mutual aid. As for the national groups, since none were associated exclusively with any type of soil or terrain, recollections of the homeland do not seem to have exercised much influence on decisions about where to settle.

* * *

Most settlers seem to have been concerned with access to markets and courts in county seats and Philadelphia and to their neighbors. The comparative regularity of the frontier zone at various times suggests this conclusion (figures 7, 8, and 9). (Although settlers on the west side of the Susquehanna were rather far from Philadelphia, which was the focal point of activity in the province, they were close to markets on Chesapeake Bay.) Population densities also provide evidence that more people wanted to be close to the market; counties adjacent to the Delaware had greater concentrations of people than those farther away (figure 9).

But most settlers also sought farms of adequate size. Grants were generally from 100 to 500 acres.[74] Therefore new areas were continually being opened up to take care of the influx of settlers. The availability of unoccupied or unsurveyed land undoubtedly was a significant factor in determining where people located. Contemporary reports are somewhat contradictory on the rate and degree of occupation. One Philadelphian asserted as early as 1715 that no unsettled land existed within 50 miles of Philadelphia and that within a radius of from 60 to 100 miles settlers had to buy from speculators or other owners.[75] He exaggerated the situation, probably because speculators had taken up so much land in the back country, particulary in Lancaster County. But James Steel, a proprietary agent, probably understated the scarcity when he said in 1737 that new grants of 3,000 and even of 1,000 acres were impossible to obtain in what is now Lancaster County.[76] By 1740

Table 12

Assessed Acreages Reported, 1760

County	Area (acres)	Reported (acres)	Percentage Reported
Philadelphia	396,160	315,805	80
Bucks	394,800	287,868	73
Chester	604,800	399,674	66
Lancaster[a]	917,120	436,346	48
Northampton[a]	1,189,173	461,440	40
Berks[a]	552,960	208,925	38
York	921,600	256,561	28
Cumberland[a]	837,776	179,185	21

Source: Pa. Arch., 8th ser., 6: 5134, 5141.

[a]Includes some land beyond Blue Mountain. See figures 5 and 9.

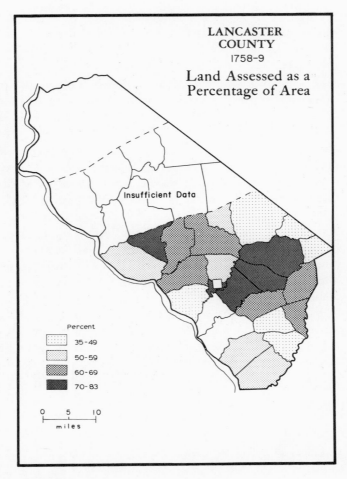

Figure 20

the proprietors had little good land for sale east of the Susquehanna River and south of the Blue Mountain, and people were
anxious for new land purchases from the Indians.[77] The reluctance
of the Indians to sell tracts, their presence in unpurchased areas,
and eventually their violence arising from frustration thwarted
most attempts by settlers to get beyond the mountain, and many
of them passed through Pennsylvania to the Maryland, Virginia,
and Carolina back country.

Possibly these comments on the scarcity of land applied to the better soils, since in 1760 large numbers of unassessed acres were reported in the assembly (table 12).[78] In Chester a third was not assessed. Support for this data comes from township assessments of acreages in Lancaster County; on the more fertile Lancaster Plain a higher percentage of acres was assessed, as much as 83 per cent in Leacock Township, compared with 35 per cent in poorer Colerain Township (figure 20). Many of the reported assessment figures could have been substantial underestimations, possibly because assessors did not fully tax first-generation settlers.[79] But they may indicate that more land, most of it of lower quality, was available than other commentators were suggesting.

Certainly some settlements filled in the area behind the frontier zone. Many Scotch-Irish located in western Chester and eastern Lancaster counties after much of the more easily workable Lancaster Plain had been occupied. Speculators like James Logan sold land to the more affluent immigrants when the value of their holdings had risen considerably.[80] Schwenkfelders who arrived in the 1730s were able to find some open contiguous lands in upper Philadelphia County. As late as 1735 a surveyor was instructed to lay out a 500-acre lot in Caln Township (above the valley).[81] The Penn "reserves" or "manors" were also gradually sold piecemeal, especially in the two decades before 1760, even though squatters occupied some parts of them and other parts were rented.[82] One possible reason for a return in 1760 of only two-thirds of the area of Chester County was that a large part of these tracts remained unsold (table 12, figure 16).[83] Finally, warrant lists show that a considerable amount of land was granted in Chester after 1733 and in Lancaster even after 1752, when York, Cumberland, and a part of Berks had been taken from it (figures 21 and 9). These settlements contributed to a thickening of population and probably retarded areal expansion. Apparently many wanted to be near the market rather than on better but more remote land. As a Quaker in Chester County said in 1725, a settler had to consider "the goodness or else the situation of his land."[84]

The land in older areas, however, was too expensive for most new settlers. In the last analysis, availability of land had to be measured by the affluence of the settlers. By 1740 good occupied

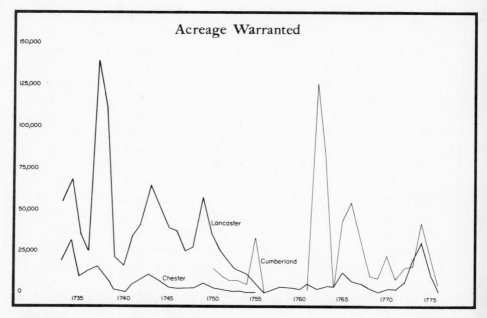

Figure 21

land in Chester County and the Lancaster Plain was worth from £1
to £1 10s. per acre, and by 1760 the value had risen to between
£1 10s. and £3 10s. (table 13). If poor settlers wanted to be near
Philadelphia they had to take poorer hill lands, and this some did,
to their chagrin.[85] More of the "poorer sort" who arrived after
1725 (if indentured after they had served their time of four years,
more or less) went beyond the limits of settlement and speculative
holdings to where land was cheaper. Many went to Maryland and
Virginia, where public lands were less expensive than in Pennsylvania, at least between 1732 and 1765.[86] More immigrants in this
period were poor "church" people than affluent sectarians, as
Muhlenberg and others noted.[87] Together with their later arrival,
their relative poverty helps to explain why more Presbyterians,
Lutherans, and Reformed adherents than Quakers and Mennonites
were in frontier areas in 1760. The "church" people could not buy
land in speculative grants and "manors," but the sectarian "plain
folk," with greater resources and a stronger sense of cooperation

Table 13

Land Values per Acre, Lancaster County
(Mostly from the Lancaster Plain)

Period	Value
1730s	1s. to £1.7, mostly 6 to 15s.
1740s	8s. to £5.5, mostly £1 to £1.5, except mortgaged, 4 to 10s.
ca. 1760	10s. to £10, mostly £1.5 to £3.5
ca. 1789	4s. to £30, mostly £3 to £10.

Source: Deed books, Recorder of Deeds Office, Lancaster.

among members, could buy more readily where they wished.[88] These circumstances led not only Scotch-Irish but many "church" Germans to the edge of settlement (figures 12 and 13). This occupation of the wilderness by Germans denies the conventional belief that the Scotch-Irish were the only true frontiersmen.[89]

* * *

By 1760 settlers had occupied most of southeastern Pennsylvania westward and northward from Philadelphia, the chief point of arrival from Europe. These colonists on land not previously occupied by white men responded to several forces in choosing sites. The distribution of national and denominational groups suggests that many settlers sought holdings next to those with whom they had traveled, to kinsfolk, those of the same regional background in Europe, and persons of the same theological persuasion. But substantial parts of the area contained a variety of groups; thus other factors were also at work, notably actions of the proprietors and their agents, soil quality, availability of land, access to markets, and immigrants' time of arrival.

William Penn attempted to spread the people in a regular fashion backward from the Delaware, but after the first few years his system broke down in several respects. Later attempts by proprietary agents to keep squatters off reserved and Indian lands were not successful. Penn and his agents indirectly contributed to the failure of his orderly program by permitting some settlers on lands not yet purchased from Indians but claimed by Maryland. Penn also initiated a sequence of grants to speculators who controlled the price of land to a considerable extent and so of settlement in areas on both sides of the limits of settlement.

Although more affluent settlers, mostly sectarians, paid attention to soil quality in their selection of sites, the overall high fertility of most of southeastern Pennsylvania meant that soils were not a critical factor to many settlers. No one national or sectarian group was strongly correlated with any particular type of soil or land. Most settlers shunned hill lands, the earliest persons in any area sought streams or springs on their land, and some wanted Indian old fields.

Probably more important than the physical aspects of the land was its availability at various times. Most farmers located adjacent to previously occupied sites, near neighbors and as near as possible to markets, particularly Philadelphia. Only the wealthy could buy behind the line of settlement. Therefore, despite the push and pull of many other forces the factors that most clearly determined a settler's choice of his first farm in the New World were his date of arrival and the location of the nearest available unoccupied land. As a result, members of all national groups located on the edge of settlement, the frontier. The liberal goal of self-determination was therefore partially fulfilled. The people let other forces than the proprietor direct their destinations.

CHAPTER THREE

Movements of Pennsylvanians

Whether early Pennsylvanians were more geographically mobile than Englishmen and other Europeans of the same era is uncertain, although it appears that throughout most of the eighteenth century more Pennsylvanians moved about than New Englanders.[1] No doubt in Pennsylvania many settlers and their descendants moved from their original homes. Some went to the frontier, mostly in groups, in many instances hundreds of miles from their first homes; others traveled to nearby rural communities or to urban places within the region. Only a minority stayed where they had first settled or had been born.

In deciding whether to move or to stay, Pennsylvanians chiefly considered which course would improve their material position or at least prevent a decline in status. But their drive for social improvement was constrained by other pressures. The significance of nationality in this is not easy to determine. A view espoused by many commentators is that the Scotch-Irish may have been more mobile than persons of German or English ancestry. However, many Scotch-Irish settlements persisted where they had begun. Ulstermen may not have had any more of the restlessness often ascribed to them than any other group. Among religious denominations, Quakers, Mennonites, and other sectarians may have staved off decisions to go to the frontier longer than other denominational groups owing to their social philosophy of mutual aid and tight discipline. But late in the century some of these did pioneer in the west. The most prosperous (and proportionately more Quakers and Mennonites were affluent than members of

71

other religious groups) and the very poorest were the least likely
to try new situations. The very large group willing to travel to the
frontier or to try new situations was probably composed of persons resembling their restless fathers and grandfathers who had
come from the middle stratum of western European life. Such
people often possessed barely adequate worldly goods, and so they
often felt dissatisfied with their lot and listened to reports from
other places. Able to travel most easily when economic conditions
were relatively good, particularly after frustrating recessions, they
weighed what they had heard about the quality and price of land
in newly opened areas to the west and southwest against security
of tenure, the price and rent of land near home, and opportunities
in other occupations and in urban places.

Conclusions in this discussion should be considered only as tentative, since measurements of the dimensions of movement—
numbers, rates, directions, and distance—are not precise, nor are
the connections between these and other factors obvious. What
might seem an easy task is, in fact, formidable. Disappearances of
persons can be calculated with difficulty, but establishing how
many of these persons died is virtually impossible. To trace the
whereabouts of most of the others who disappeared is impracti-
cable without a full roster of names of Americans in all areas. A
sample from a few townships in Lancaster and Chester counties
shows that very few persons who disappeared from one township
reappeared in another one nearby. Moreover, uncertainty arises
because two or more persons can have the same name. Such problems are not easily resolved.

More exact measurements on numbers, rates, direction, and
distances of movement have to await a detailed year-by-year study
of names on tax lists for townships where church and probate
records have also survived. These ecclesiastical and legal records
would indicate the proportion of deaths among those who disap-
pear. To provide details of direction and distance, records noting
place of birth (and subsequent moves) are needed. In the latter
case the study would have to focus on destination points, in the
former on places of departure. Therefore it may be impossible to
combine disappearances with direction and distance for any one
area. Unlike New England, where some scholars have attempted to

use the techniques of historical demographers,[2] Pennsylvania handicaps its students with a lack of records at the local level. The township was not an important unit of government, and many records such as estate inventories and wills have been collected at the county level, representing a much larger number of persons. Then too, Pennsylvania townships often held congregations of several different denominations, and church records of baptisms, marriages, and deaths are scarce. Thus the feasibility of dealing with a small community—the only scale at which intensive genealogical work could be undertaken—is severely limited in Pennsylvania. Although these problems are thorny, in the present context some hypotheses can at least be suggested from comparisons among various sets of data.

* * *

During the Revolutionary period, according to Jackson Turner Main, rates of movement were substantial, and in Pennsylvania they may have exceeded the American average. Forty per cent of rural Americans moved "during a few years' time," and the loss rate from an average rural community was about 15 per cent each decade, or roughly 1.5 per cent yearly.[3] The evidence from Pennsylvania indicates that the rates there were higher. Between 1774 and 1785 in Chester County and between 1772 and 1782 in Lancaster, somewhat more than 50 per cent of the adult males disappeared per decade. Allowing for deaths and replacement of some men by their sons, the rate was 30 per cent. In some townships the loss rate was 70 per cent (figures 22 and 23).[4]

Although this unsettled decade possibly should not be considered representative for the century as a whole, scattered information indicates equally rapid turnovers in some other periods. Henry E. Muhlenberg reported in 1747 that half of his congregation of 1742 in upper Philadelphia County was no longer with him, suggesting a rate of attrition approximately the same as that during the Revolution.[5] Even if some of the departed had died (and Muhlenberg may have overstated departures to impress upon the church fathers in Halle, Germany the frustrations of trying to impose discipline on Lutherans), there is little doubt that these

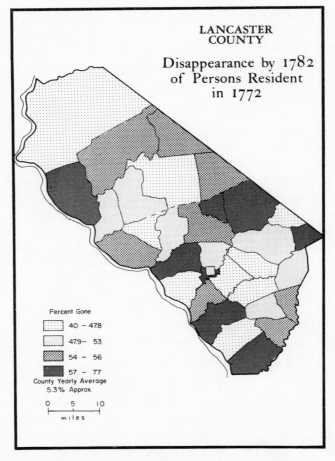

LANCASTER
COUNTY

Disappearance by 1782
of Persons Resident
in 1772

Percent Gone

40 – 478

479– 53

54 – 56

57 – 77
County Yearly Average
5.3% Approx.

0   5   10
        miles

Figure 22

people were mobile. Similarly, on the Penns' manor of Andolhea
in the German Tulpehocken settlement in the Lebanon Valley,
only three of sixteen who originally settled in 1723 remained in
1741 when the land was finally warranted, a depletion rate of over
3 per cent per year. Then only four of twenty-one warrantees or
those appearing to be their sons had lands patented between 1744
and 1776.[6] Even when sons are taken into account, the rate of
loss was very high. The nearby Hanover Presbyterian congregation
was severely depleted twice, in 1760 and 1771.[7]

The rate of movement seems to have been strongest in the 1740s, 1758 to 1763, the middle 1780s, and the early 1790s, but the record is too scant to make firm judgments. If Muhlenberg's assertion can be generalized for the whole area during the 1740s, considerable movement must have occurred, despite a rapid population growth (figure 11). The French and Indian War, especially between 1754 and 1756, slowed movements to the west, if not within the area. After hostilities ended in 1758 Thomas Barton of Lancaster reported to Thomas Penn that "they are daily removing to Carolina."[8] The middle 1780s and early 1790s seem to have been periods of heavy movement. David Shultze of upper Philadelphia County recorded more land sales in his diary in 1786 than in any other year, and in 1793 another diarist commented: "This day being remarkably favourable for Flitting families, it is said 30 waggons loaded on that account passed through West Chester this day."[9] West Chester was on a secondary road, not on the Lancaster Turnpike, the main route westward, where traffic pre-

Figure 23

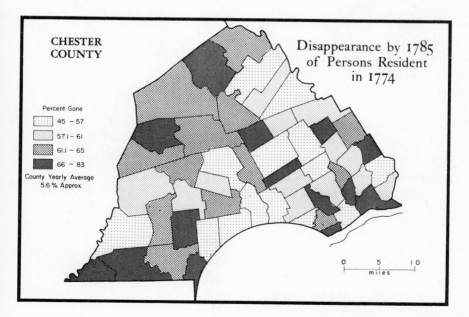

sumably would have been even greater. Movements may have
occurred in generational spurts. Assuming that the original settlers
were roughly of the same age and date of marriage, more sons
would have been available for migration in some years than others.
But, again, evidence is slight.[10]

The directions taken and distances traveled by migrants,
whether local, intraregional, or to the frontier, can be established
only in the most general terms. Population densities continued to
increase in all counties throughout the century, indicating that
more persons stayed home or moved only within Pennsylvania
than moved out of the province. The rate of population growth in
southeastern Pennsylvania declined after 1760, however, possibly
suggesting increased emigration. Unfortunately emigration cannot
now be calculated, and the slower pace of growth probably indicates a decline in immigration, and possibly even a falling birth
rate, as much as emigration. Nevertheless, it is certain that many
people moved to the frontier. Pennsylvania was a distributing
center to the south and west, as is indicated by letters of encouragement to Pennsylvanians from those who had already moved to
the back country of Maryland, Virginia, the Carolinas, and
Kentucky.[11] These movements gave rise to views, certainly exaggerated, such as Thomas Cooper's, who wrote in the 1790s that a
prosperous farmer named McAllister near Harrisburg was "not so
attached to the spot as to be unwilling to remove to the wilderness . . . like almost all the Americans."[12] Similarly in the same
decade, Tench Coxe suggested that the eastern states were contributing their "redundant" population to the frontiers.[13]

The movement out of the region to the frontier has received far
more publicity (if little careful analysis) than have internal shifts
in residence. After 1760 the populations of counties in the back
country, notably Cumberland, grew more rapidly than did those
of the oldest counties on the Delaware, suggesting that many
people went into these areas from the east (figure 11). Direct
analysis of names on tax lists provides one way to find out where
people went, but the results are unsatisfactory. For example, of
forty-nine taxpayers in Bart Township, Lancaster County, who
disappeared from the 1772 tax list by 1782, seven possibly died
and were replaced by sons, but only four others could be traced to

new homes in other townships of Lancaster or Chester counties. If an estimated thirteen others died without being replaced by sons, then one-half of those who disappeared cannot be accounted for, at least without looking at 1782 assessments for every township in North America, and even in Europe.[14] The four presumed to have moved may not have been identified correctly; the James Dunlap who in 1772 owned fifty acres in Bart may not have been either the James Dunlap in 1782 in Salisbury Township, Lancaster, or the one in Sadsbury, Chester. In all aspects of the pattern of movement, then, any description is severely lacking in certainty. To discuss such patterns is necessarily to risk vagueness, but at least some of the factors can be explored.

* * *

Members of all national and denominational groups were mobile. The evidence concerning the extent of their movement is inconclusive; even so, the conventional view that Germans were stable and the Scotch-Irish were the restless frontiersmen has to be rejected or at least severely qualified.[15] Sectarians, notably Quakers and Mennonites, probably stood more firm, or remained closer to home, than did members of other denominations. Yet even some of these eventually traveled long distances to new homes. On such occasions they went together in coherent congregations or as parts of congregations, as "church" groups sometimes did.[16]

Some cases of dramatic change occurred among national groups. Examples include the depletion by one-half in five years of Pastor Muhlenberg's German Lutheran congregation and the departure of groups in 1760 and again in 1771 from Hanover Scotch-Irish Presbyterian Church.[17] Beginning as early as the 1730s, all national groups were represented in the Shenandoah Valley of Virginia.[18] Within southeastern Pennsylvania, Germans and English bought out farms of one another's groups.[19] But these instances are not very satisfactory as the basis for drawing conclusions.

Surnames from assessments (remembering the difficulty of identifying national backgrounds) provide the clearest evidence for measuring change and stability over several years.[20] Consider Lancaster and Chester counties between 1759 and 1782. In Lancaster, the relative strength of the English and Scotch-Irish decreased by 5 and 6 per cent respectively and their actual numbers declined in some townships, while Germans increased relatively and absolutely (table 14). Yet the rate of change varied considerably (table 15 and figures 25, 26, and 3). The proportion of Germans increased by more than 10 per cent between 1759 and 1782 in the ethnically mixed townships of Bart, Donegal, Mt. Joy, and Londonderry, the last three on the western side of the county, and between 1782 and 1800 in Mt. Joy, Caernarvon, Leacock, and Salisbury, the last three in the eastern part of the Lancaster Plain. Thus the decline of the British began earlier on the western side of the county than in the eastern part. In fact, in 1800, three generations after settlement, the Scotch-Irish (or Scots) still composed a third of Salisbury's population. In the southern end of Lancaster County German encroachment was slow. Martic and Bart townships, adjacent to German settlements, still contained substantial numbers of Scotch-Irish. More precisely, the disappearance of individuals between 1772 and 1782 in many German townships, such as Cocalico and Elizabeth, was more marked than that from Scotch-Irish Donegal and Derry.

In sum, comparison of figure 22 with figures 25 and 26 suggests little correlation between total amount of movement and movement within national groups. Most dramatically, the decrease in small, strongly German urban places—Stumpstown, Middletown, Jonestown, and Manheim—was greater over the decade than in any one township (79 to 90 per cent).[21] These figures suggest that individual Germans were as mobile as the Scotch-Irish, at least in Lancaster County, although possibly they did not move out of the county as often as the others or were replaced by Germans from other counties rather than by British. If the British did move beyond Lancaster County, two or more generations of settlement in certain areas by members of many families hardly points to "restlessness" any more innate than that of Germans.

In Chester County the most dramatic changes were the relative decline of the Welsh and the increase of Scotch-Irish between 1730 and 1759. The Germans, though their increases were relatively significant, in 1782 remained important only in the

Table 14

Proportions of National Groups in Two Counties

National Group	Chester Co.			Lancaster Co.		
	1730	1759	1782	1722	1758–59	1782
German-speaking	2%	5%	8%	65%	58%	68%
English	67	59	63		15	10
Scotch-Irish, etc.	12	23	19	35%	19	13
Welsh	17	8	7		1	1
Other and unassigned	2%	5%	4%		7%	9%
Approximate total population	10,800	27,000	34,450	1,400	26,000	47,000

Source: MSS tax assessments and returns, Ches. Co., 1730, 1759, 1782, Lanc. Co., 1758–59; 1722, H. Frank Eshleman, ed., "Assessment Lists and Other Documents of Lancaster Prior to the Year 1729," *Jour. Lanc. Co. Hist. Soc.,* 20 (1916): 174–78; 1782 (Lancaster), *Pa. Arch.,* 3d ser., vol. 17.

Note: Some columns do not add to 100 because of rounding.

Table 15

Changing Population of National Groups, Selected Townships, Lancaster County

Year	Group	Bart	Caernarvon	Donegal	Leacock	Martic	Mt. Joy	Salisbury	Londonderry
1758–59	German	13%	21%	35%	40%	22%	46%	0%	26%
	English	28	25	17	23	27	18	35	28
	Scotch-Irish	48	13	36	26	42	23	63	32
	Welsh[a]	...	32	...	...	...	...	...	...
	Other and uncertain	12%	9%	12%	11%	9%	13%	2%	15%
	Total population	625	337	968	992	1,021	638	992	625
1782	German	33%	28%	62%	39%	36%	60%	9%	50%
	English	19	13	10	16	12	7	33	12
	Scotch-Irish	27	12	17	25	32	10	49	24
	Welsh	...	27	...	...	...	...	...	...
	Other and uncertain	21%	22%	11%	20%	21%	23%	9%	14%
	Total population	765	501	1,221[b]	1,282	1,100	831	957	1,034
1800	German	40%	42%	72%	52%	45%	72%	20%	...
	English	15	10	5	12	10	6	30	...
	Scotch-Irish	23	9	9	10	21	3	35	...
	Welsh	...	19	...	...	...	...	...	...
	Other and uncertain	22%	20%	14%	26%	24%	19%	15%	...
	Total population	682[c]	668	1,416	1,468	1,369	832	1,296	n.a.

Source: Lanc. Co. MSS tax assessments and returns, 1758, 1759, 1800; 1782, Pa. Arch., 3d ser., 17: 713–17, 722–26, 812–18, 818–23, 823–30, 833–37, 843–46, 856–63.

Note: Percentage totals for some years do not equal 100 because of rounding.

[a] If not shown, only a few and included with English.
[b] Excludes Elizabethtown, Maytown, and Falmouth.
[c] List not complete.

northern end of the county, an area adjoining heavily German Berks and upper Philadelphia counties. The Scotch-Irish lost some ground to the English between 1759 and 1782 in the western part of the county while retaining their position, however weak, in townships adjacent to the Delaware River. In terms of *individuals*, more of the Scotch-Irish and English townships in the southwest and west lost more persons between 1774 and 1785 than did townships in the east and south-central part of the county (figure 23). But the pattern is by no means clear. In any case, the overall loss during the Revolution was no greater in very British Chester than in very German Lancaster.[22]

Even though by 1730 Quakers, Mennonites, and other sectarians had established colonies on the frontier, after 1740 they organized very few congregations in new areas in contrast to other denominations (figure 14). Apparently they were concerned with intensifying their community life in areas they had already occupied in order to maintain their cohesion.[23] William Pim's

Figure 24

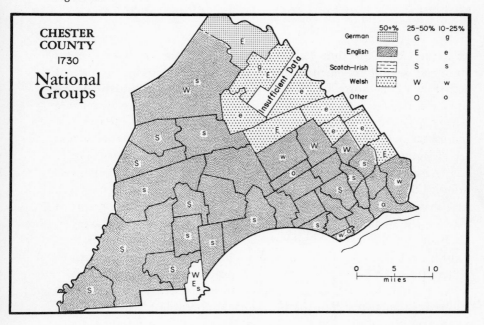

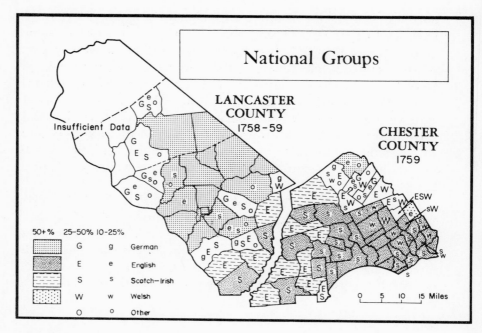

Figure 25

assertion in 1730 that he would sell only to Friends[24] seems
amplified by the lower mobility in strong Quaker areas; the rate of
attrition of persons between 1774 and 1785 in south-central
Chester, though not a clear pattern, was lower than elsewhere
(figure 23). Similarly several of the townships around the town of
Lancaster with heavy Mennonite populations seem to have lost
fewer people than was the case in most parts of the county (figure
22). Although Franklin claimed that English left certain neighborhoods because of offensive German manners, the decline of the
British on the Lancaster Plain was probably as much the result of
Mennonite willingness to pay substantial prices for farms.[25]
Michael Baughman of Manheim Township, who held more than
3,000 acres at one time in many parcels in various townships,
willed these to his family and sold only to other Mennonites.[26]
Even though some Quaker congregations eventually disappeared
from the Lancaster Plain (a situation comparable to the demise of
an Amish community in the Chester Valley early in the nineteenth

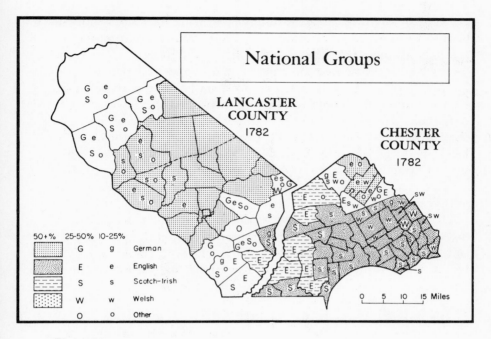

Figure 26

century),[27] and though new groups of Mennonites and Quakers went off to the frontier in the 1780s, in their own stronghold of Chester County they were not and never have been dislodged. In 1790 Quakers probably still totaled more than 30 per cent of Chester County's population and Mennonites nearly 25 per cent of Lancaster's.[28] If many of the Scotch-Irish and Scots had belonged to a strong sectarian group, it is doubtful that we would hear so much of Scotch-Irish restlessness, but of course we can never know. (Incidentally, some of the Quakers were English-Irish from southern Ireland.)[29]

* * *

As in western Europe, the most prosperous Pennsylvanians were the least inclined to move. Many of the poor shifted around, searching for better chances, but fewer may have gone to the frontier than those in lower-middle income levels. Only 15 to 24 per cent of the most affluent disappeared from Bart and Manheim townships between 1772 and 1782, fewer than those in other tax brackets (table 16). The wealthy had good reason to remain; throughout the eighteenth century the upper 40 per cent of Chester County's population, and particularly the top 10 per cent, clearly improved their position in contrast to the lower 60 per cent (table 1). By 1800 the top 40 per cent possessed over 80 per cent of the assessed wealth, 20 per cent more than they had in 1693. The top 10 per cent increased their share from 24 to 38 per cent. Certainly some individuals and families rose into higher levels, but the richest held their position at the top of assessment rolls year after year.

The lower income groups were the most volatile; two-thirds of those in the lowest tax brackets disappeared from the rolls of Bart and Manheim townships between 1772 and 1782 (table 16). Very few of these turned up in nearby townships, suggesting that most

(margin note: Supports Henretta's argument for rising stratification but not necessarily for rising ? poverty)

Table 16

Persons in 1772 Who Remained or Disappeared in 1782,
by Economic Status, Bart and Manheim Townships, Lancaster County

Status (by tax assessed, in shillings)	Remaining	Sons of Deceased (probable)	Gone
Bart			
Low (0–3)	5	0	17
Medium-low (4–7)	10	1	10
Medium (8–12)	9	1	7
Medium-high (13–16)	7	0	5
High (over 16)	11	0	2
Single freemen head tax	1	0	7
Total	43	2	48
Manheim			
Low	8	3	23
Medium-low	4	1	4
Medium	5	0	2
Medium-high	13	4	3
High	23	3	8
Single freemen	4	2 (possible)	7
Total	57	13	47

Source: Tax assessments and returns, *Pa. Arch.*, 3d ser., 17: 194–96, 219–23, 771–74, 833–37.

of them left the county.[30] This evidence seems to contradict
Phineas Bond, who in 1789 observed that indentured servants "for
the most part continue as laborers for years in the neighborhood
where they served, having no immediate means to enable them to
settle lands or to enable them to migrate to a distant country."[31]
A self-image of ineffectiveness undoubtedly hindered the movement of some. When the traveler Johann David Schoepf, after
extolling the Germans in Lancaster County, came in 1783 on the
less prosperous German area of hilly northern Chester County, he
was told by a German-speaking person that "he would rather live
somewhere else, but . . . he had heard that in Kentucky there was
no real winter; and where there is no winter, he argued, people
must work year in, year out, and that was not his fancy; winter,
with a warm stove and sluggish days being indispensable to his
happiness."[32] Obviously this person had little interest in self-
improvement. Partially resolving the apparent contradiction
between those observations and the tax data is the probability that
many of the poor, including the 15 to 20 per cent who were
laborers in town and country, drifted about so much that the
assessors often missed them. To support this contention, the
assessor frequently crossed the names of poor persons off tax lists
and wrote "gone" in their place.[33]

Small farmers and craftsmen in the lower-middle income ranks
were probably the most concerned to make moves to the frontier
that would improve their conditions. They were more likely than
the very poorest people to possess a wagon, horses, farm equipment, and cash to pay for ferriage and food for the trip and a new
start. The lower-middle income people had the greatest reason to
move; over the century their relative share of the wealth in Chester
County fell from over 20 per cent to under 14 per cent (table 1).
Compared with those doing better they had grounds for unhappi-
ness, even though during the last decades of the century fewer
rumblings were heard in Pennsylvania than in New England, where
the "safety valve" of the frontier apparently worked less effectively.[34]

* * *

Besides the characteristics of the people, chiefly religious
denomination and economic status, various external forces encour-

aged or discouraged movements. These included economic conditions, tenure problems, price and availability of farming land, and other opportunities on the frontier and near home.

The level of economic conditions probably contributed to movements at different times. Some comments suggest that movement was greatest during buoyant times, or at least during periods of recovery. The few years after the French and Indian War were prosperous, stimulated in part by the expansion of the money supply from the British army. In 1758 substantial numbers of people apparently moved from Lancaster County to Carolina.[35] In 1760 and again in 1771, both active trading years (figure 4), groups from Hanover Presbyterian congregation left for the frontier.[36] The flourishing early 1790s seem to have encouraged movement, as they did in Long Island.[37] On the other hand, just earlier in 1788, the larvae of the Hessian fly (*Phytophaga destructor*), which sapped moisture from the wheat and lowered yields, was "raging" in Bucks County and so forced some farmers to sell their holdings.[38] Whether this encouraged large movement from the area is unclear. Unfortunately too little is known of the magnitude and duration of the Hessian fly attacks in southeastern Pennsylvania.[39]

The proprietors and their agents in the land office caused some individuals to move through their anachronistic treatment of tenure rights. This problem arose in part from the feudal right of the proprietor to demand escheat, or return of the land, for nonpayment of quitrents, from the law that unnaturalized aliens did not have the right to hold land, and from confusion over surveys and squatting. An example of the escheat problem is offered by the Schwenkfelders. Fifteen years after they and others had settled on what had been Frankfort Company land in upper Philadelphia County, the land office discovered that they had not paid any quitrents. When they refused to pay from the beginning of the Frankfort grant, the land office served them notice to vacate through the county sheriff. The people resisted, and eventually a compromise was reached; but some people moved elsewhere.[40] How widespread these threats of escheat were is not clear. Second, although Penn had encouraged aliens to come to Pennsylvania, no law was passed guaranteeing them rights to land until 1742.[41] One particular case involved the land of Hans Brand of Strasburg Township, who died in 1739, having willed his land to his son. Brand had arrived in 1717, before the loyalty oath was in effect, and had never been naturalized, so the land could legally escheat to the proprietor. Nevertheless the problem was resolved, in part by giving the son the first chance to purchase the land.[42] Solutions such as this suggest that the alien problem was not a serious one in encouraging movement before 1742. Third and probably more important were the many instances of overlapping claims that caused differences among neighbors and with the proprietor. Litigation became quite involved in many cases, and some settlers undoubtedly decided to move to new areas, where they anticipated less confusion.[43] Where the proprietors' agents tried to eject squatters from manors, however, the people resisted rather than moved.[44]

Pressure also arose from the proprietors' raising of prices on common lands. In 1732 Thomas Penn raised the price of land by 50 per cent and quitrents by 150 per cent.[45] Together with the inability to settle western lands because of Indian pressure and the overt conflict with Indians between 1755 and 1758 and again in 1763 and 1764, land prices generated considerable dissatisfaction among persons without warrants or deeds with the proprietor. Many persons left for Maryland, Virginia, and Carolina, where land was cheaper and quitrents lower, even though they had to face tithes for established churches in Maryland and Virginia.[46] In Pennsylvania the problem continued until 1765, when preemption was recognized and the price of land was lowered to £5 per 100 acres, or until the Revolution when quitrents were abolished.[47]

* * *

The Penn family was not directly responsible for the rising prices of land already occupied except where they held their own speculative holdings. But land prices and the size of holdings had a substantial bearing on movements of people. On the Lancaster Plain, where prices were higher than in most other parts of southeastern Pennsylvania, values rose from about 10 shillings per acre in the 1730s, to double that amount in the 1740s. This was re-doubled by 1760, and in 1789 prices were ten times what they had been five or six decades earlier (table 13).[48] A comparison of these increases with the increase in average value of estate inventories, which included debts, grain on hand, and farm and household goods but not land, suggests that the net worth of the average or better-than-average farmer did not keep pace with the land prices (table 17).[49] Inventory values only quadrupled between the

Table 17

Changing Inventory Values[a]

Chester County			Lancaster County		
Period	*Sample*	*Value*	*Period*	*Sample*	*Value*
1713–16	28	£162	. . .	. . .	. . .
1730–31	30	£252	1729–37	80	£105
			1750	61	£153
1761	35	£300	1760	59	£208
1783	34	£464	1783	82	£409
. . .	. . .	. . .	1790	38	£458

Source: Register of Wills Offices, Chester and Lancaster counties.

[a]Land values excluded.

1730s and 1790 compared with the tenfold increase of land values. Unless a young person had considerable capital or a farm to inherit he would have faced the prospect of moving to a place where land was cheaper. Even Mennonites must have felt this pressure in the 1780s when some of them left for what is now Ontario. Needless to say, those who sold out were in a strong position to buy farms on the best soils in remote areas.

The shrinking size of holdings throughout the century limited opportunities at or near home and was partly responsible for increasing land prices. Original holdings could be divided into only so many farms if the success of sons or grandsons was to be ensured. Although properties tended to be relatively small from the beginning of the colony,[50] average acreages in Chester and Lancaster counties dropped until 1760. In 1710 the average size in

Chester was 245 acres and the lowest quartile of townships ranged from 129 to 190 acres; in 1760 and 1782 the average was about 125 acres (figures 27, 28, and 29). In Lancaster the average was only slightly higher than in Chester. By 1782 the averages in some townships was quite low owing to the presence of some very small holdings, especially where some urban subdivisions, unspecified as such in tax returns, had been platted.[51] Nevertheless, in most townships some farms were below the usual sizes of 80 to 200 acres.

The series of maps of holdings actually present a more complex sequence of size changes (figures 27, 28, and 29). In the frontier area of northern Lancaster, the "unimproved" holdings of speculators averaged 366 acres in 1782 and the average of occupied farms was only 95 acres. Sizes apparently decreased for a time in southern Lancaster and western Chester but later increased. In Fallowfield Township, for example, the average was 2,178 acres in 1710, but by 1759 it was only 124 in East Fallowfield and 118 in

Figure 27

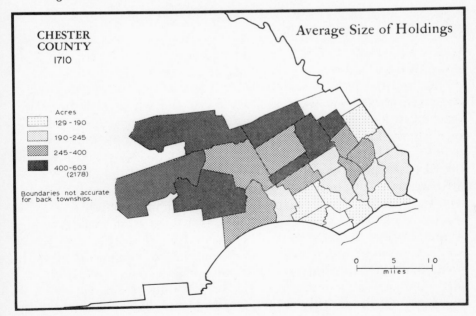

CHESTER COUNTY 1710

Average Size of Holdings

Acres
129 - 190
190 - 245
245 - 400
400 - 603
(2178)

Boundaries not accurate for back townships.

0   5   10
miles

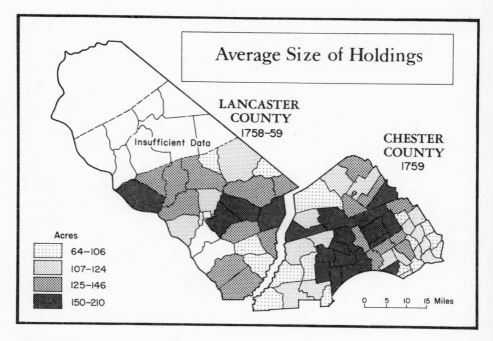

Average Size of Holdings

LANCASTER
COUNTY
1758-59

CHESTER
COUNTY
1759

Insufficient Data

Acres
64–106
107–124
125–146
150–210

0   5   10   15 Miles

Figure 28

West Fallowfield. Yet in 1782 the averages were 153 and 172 respectively. A possible reason for this sequence is that speculators on the frontier at first held large lots but that later the pioneers and even their sons were not taxed for the whole area they planned to have warranted and deeded. A similar situation existed in northern Lancaster; assessors apparently followed instructions to be easy on the poor.[52] Eventually these farms were taxed at their full acreages. This evolution would account for the unlikely drift westward of larger holdings in Chester County between 1759 and 1782, as indicated by the maps. Another interpretation, always possible with these kinds of data, is that assessors' estimates were inaccurate.

Many farmers and public officials recognized minimum economic sizes of farms, though late in the century a few accounts of inadequate holdings were reported. In 1789 five farms on the Lancaster Plain, of 120, 123, 126, 139, and 150 acres, were

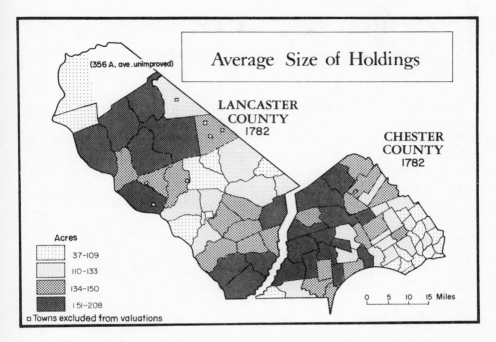

Figure 29

adjudged too small for equal division by neighbors appointed by
the Orphan's Court.[53] Even on the fertile Lancaster Plain, farms of
60 to 75 acres apparently would have been inadequate to sustain
families. The high rate of disappearance by 1782 of persons who
could not find niches, more than 40 per cent of all those listed in
1772 (figure 22), tends to support this view. (At this time, by
comparison, farms in Massachusetts were much smaller and rural
people there probably had a harder time making ends meet.)[54]
How many farms in Pennsylvania had become too small is not
clear. In 1775 and 1800 observers reported this,[55] and in eastern
Chester County many farms were of less than 80 acres. But here
more intensive agricultural practices may have permitted smaller
sizes.[56] Intensively cultivated Amish farms on the Lancaster Plain
today average 40 to 50 acres.

That Lancaster and Chester farms were generally of an economic size reflects rational inheritance practices. Conditions rather

than custom or even law guided decisions on dividing farms in Pennsylvania. In western Europe both partible (division) and impartible (primogeniture or variations of the "stem family") schemes had been used, and many scholars have considered one or the other customary for particular areas. Thus if we were to believe some scholars of European rural history who emphasize tradition, German areas in Pennsylvania should have had tiny holdings because of partible inheritance and English areas large ones owing to primogeniture.[57] But recent work on early modern England itself shows more variation in practice than was originally thought.[58] Pennsylvania farmers who willed their land legally could do as they pleased; even as late as 1782, equal or nearly equal holdings of persons with the same surname implies equal division among sons.[59] Intestate laws, framed in 1700 and 1706, combined division and primogeniture; the eldest son was to receive a double share, excluding cases where the widow was involved. The Privy Council, insensitive to the Pennsylvania situation, attempted in vain to repeal the law in favor of primogeniture.[60] In practice the Orphan's Court of Lancaster followed the intestate law in approximately half the cases and yet showed flexibility in each instance by considering the value of the holding and the circumstances of the family members.[61]

Before 1760, division was probably the practice in much of Chester and Lancaster counties. After that date impartible inheritance more and more became the norm because, given the economic and technological situation, minimum sizes had been reached. As a result one, two, or more sons in the third generation of settlement had to move from the family farm. But through the sale of the farm by the executors to one son, usually the eldest, the other children realized their share. This enabled them to buy farms elsewhere, most obviously on the frontier, if they wanted to farm with a decent standard of living. Crèvecoeur, when he moved from Connecticut to the Susquehanna Valley, pointed to "the desire of contributing to the success of my family, and of assuring its independence after my death."[62]

This reduction in the number of local opportunities and the increased value of land helps to explain why so few landless persons, including single freemen, later possessed land in the same

Table 18

Persons in 1772 Who Remained or Disappeared by 1782,
by Ownership of Land, Bart and Manheim Townships, Lancaster County

Status	Remaining	Sons of Deceased (probable)	Gone
Bart			
Owners	39[a]	2	23
Landless (tenants, inmates)	3	0	18
Landless (single freemen)	1		7
Total	43	2	48
Manheim			
Owners	52[b]	8	20
Landless (tenants, inmates)	1	3	20
Landless (single freemen)	5	1(possible)	7
Total	58	12	47

Source: Tax assessments and returns, *Pa. Arch.*, 3d ser., 17: 194–96, 219–23, 771–74, 833–37.

[a]In Bart, landless achieving ownership, 1782—2 in township; 1 elsewhere in Lancaster or Chester.
[b]In Manheim, landless achieving ownership, 1782—1 in township, plus 5 freemen inheriting land; 1 elsewhere.

townships. In Manheim Township, a strong Mennonite area, for example, of thirty-eight landless persons in 1772 only seven or eight had achieved ownership there or in nearby townships a decade later. This number includes five single freemen who had inherited land within the township (table 18). Two remained landless but most disappeared from the county. Many presumably went to the frontier and others moved here and there in older settled areas.[63]

Given relatively unchanging technologies in farming and manufacturing,[64] the pressure of population growth drove up prices of land and led to division of holdings through two or three generations until minimum economic sizes were reached. As a result, many persons moved to the frontier. More people remained than left, however, as is indicated by the increasing densities of population in all counties (figures 8, 9, and 10). Good opportunities apparently dwindled as each generation passed, as is suggested by the increased relative stratification of wealth (table 1). An increase

Seems to argue against L's thesis

in single freemen in Chester County from 9 per cent of the total number of taxpayers in 1730 to nearly 20 per cent in 1800 possibly indicates that more were forced to marry later than previously.[65] Yet by mortgaging farms, renting farms, or taking up crafts and other activities in the country and in towns, many individuals retained or improved their status or at least postponed a move.

Mortgages on their farms helped some persons. Mortgage deeds appeared in deed books of Lancaster County quite frequently in the 1740s. The Loan Office issued paper money in 1729 and 1773 secured by these mortgages on real property. The records for the latter year indicate that 80 per cent of the mortgages were on farms, notably in the oldest counties of Bucks, Philadelphia, and Chester, where the economic pressure on smallholders was undoubtedly greater than elsewhere because of higher land prices.[66] Yet the Loan Office probably was too cautious and too few mortgages were secured to help a large section of the rural populace.[67]

Tenant farming was much more frequent than we might expect, given the tenacious belief that all farms were freeholds. Even the correspondence of the Penns largely ignored tenancy.[68] But in 1760 and 1782 about 30 per cent of Lancaster's and Chester's married taxpayers were landless (table 19 and figure 30), and about the same number of farmers fell into the tenant category, possibly half of them sharecroppers.[69] Tenancy occurred most frequently in towns and townships where ironworks needed many

Table 19

Nonlandowners as Percentage of Taxables

Area	1758–59	1782
Chester County	27	27
Lancaster County	*	31
(Present day area)	36	32
(Dauphin, Lebanon)	*	29
Lancaster Borough	41	n.a.

Source: Ches. Co.: MSS tax returns; Lanc. Co.: MSS tax returns, 1758, 1759; 1782, *Pa. Arch.*, 3d ser., vol. 17.

*Inadequate data.

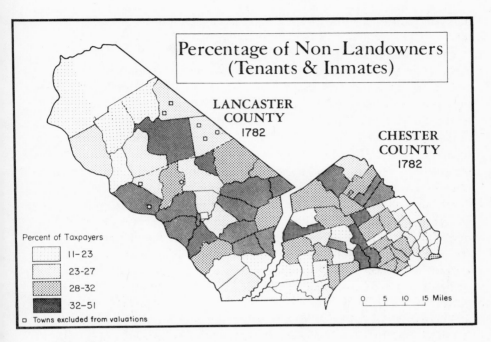

Percentage of Non-Landowners (Tenants & Inmates)

LANCASTER COUNTY 1782

CHESTER COUNTY 1782

Percent of Taxpayers

11–23
23–27
28–32
32–51

□ Towns excluded from valuations

0 5 10 15 Miles

Figure 30

laborers. In the best farming areas, the Lancaster Plain and south-central Chester, however, the number of tenant farmers was higher than on poorer land and in more remote areas, such as northern Lancaster (figure 30). In 1759 John Armstrong informed Thomas Penn, who wanted to lease some of his private lands in inaccessible areas, that "Distance from the Metropolis [Philadelphia] & Want of Water Communication, must make Rents comparatively small," and that renting would be too much trouble for Penn and the settlers.[70] On the good land of the Lancaster Plain some tenants and the owners of their holdings were taxed at comparatively high rates.

To farm good land, even if rented, was better than owning poor land. As a temporary expedient, tenancy may have permitted some to build up capital for a later improvement of status on the frontier or near home. Tenants paying cash rents were probably more likely to improve their position than those on shares, who

paid the landlord more if they increased their inputs to raise production. The evidence, however, is unclear.[71]

Even though we usually think of the people as farmers, many
rural Pennsylvanians and town dwellers were craftsmen. By 1758
and 1759 in rural Lancaster County, about 20 per cent of the
taxpayers were craftsmen, compared with 15 per cent laborers and
60 to 65 per cent farmers.[72] Most of these rural artisans, except
millers, were lower in status than most farmers, including tenant
farmers, largely because most did not own any land. With the
increasing differentiation of wealth throughout the century, the
poorer artisans fell behind, at least in a relative sense.

In large towns, artisans fared better than their counterparts in
the countryside, especially during the first twenty years of Philadelphia's existence and between 1730 and 1765 in the back country during the boom of town building.[73] After this time the
growth of urban populations only paralleled total growth, so presumably opportunities did not improve generally in these larger
places. In fact, many laborers who lived in Lancaster worked only
at harvest time.[74] In 1782 the average tax paid by the residents of
the town of Lancaster, a majority of whom were craftsmen, was
£5 12s. compared with £8 4s. for the county as a whole. Only a
few years earlier in 1774, the average for the town equaled the
county's average.[75] Craftsmen in small towns fared much worse,
probably worse than did rural artisans. In 1782, the smaller the
town in Lancaster County the lower the average tax; most averaged less than a third of that of the town of Lancaster.[76] Apparently only large places provided opportunities, and even then success was less obvious by the end of the century.[77]

* * *

As the eighteenth century passed, Pennsylvanians continued to
move about to improve or at least to maintain their status. Many,
and as yet we do not know the numbers, moved to the frontier. In
the relatively open society there were few restraints on these
movements. Pennsylvanians possibly took advantage of the "safety
valve" of the frontier more than New Englanders when holdings

were reduced to minimum economic sizes or even before. Toward the end of the century the movement to the frontier was as great or greater than earlier as opportunities in both town and country apparently ebbed. However, movements *within* the region may have increased as persons without sufficient capital to buy farms on the frontier sought to hold their status. As indicated in table 1, these people at the bottom were less well off relatively and some perhaps even in an absolute sense by 1800. As always, the most affluent, notably the Quakers and Mennonites in rural areas, were the least inclined to move or only to move nearby. Yet even these had to face the problem once their farms could no longer be divided, if they sired more than one son. In the 1780s Quakers and Mennonites started new communities in distant places. Not until the economic orientation of the state changed toward manufacturing and more intensive systems of agriculture became firmly entrenched, perhaps not clearly before 1840, did the number of opportunities equal those in the early eighteenth century. As long as the frontier was open, however, many people were able to move, and as a result frustrations were dampened and the liberal values of the original inhabitants of the colony were upheld.

CHAPTER FOUR

Territorial Organization of
Farms and Rural Institutions

William Penn believed that settlers should live in agricultural villages set in the midst of small, neatly laid-out townships. He hoped that farmers and others thus would encourage and aid one another and bring up their children in a civilized manner. Ordered space would mean orderly and happy lives.

But the Quakers and most of those who followed, though many had lived in agricultural villages in Europe, wanted to avoid the constraints of living in close proximity and so sought a different territorial structure. Farmers were inclined to settle at some distance from one another in farmsteads set in the midst of contiguous fields. Other community institutions such as meetinghouses, schools, and business and manufacturing operations were also dispersed in an apparently haphazard fashion. As a result, the areal pattern of rural communities was not sharply defined and did not correspond with townships, congregational or school districts, or local economic regions. Rural communities were complex, open-country neighborhoods without certain edges or centers. To Penn this pattern seemed chaotic, contrary to reason and to what he regarded as Quaker ideals.

Contemporary and later commentators on the scene have considered this style of rural life to be the consequence of cultural traditions of the settlers, cheap land on the frontier, or lack of conflict with Indians. But neither Penn nor subsequent interpreters appreciated the changes taking place in the seventeenth

98

century in rural western Europe and elaborated in early Pennsylvania. They failed to recognize adequately the strong trend in Europe toward operation of farms by the heads of nuclear families and the individualization of decision-making. In England, especially, the tendency was apparent with the movement toward enclosure begun under Elizabeth I. The division of Christendom into denominations and their spatial mixing in the new environment meant that old territorial forms of parishes had less relevance. But despite the considerable movement of people to and from the region and the apparent confusion of social connections that arose, local communities did exist. Partly because they were established, the area became by European standards a stable and affluent rural countryside.

* * *

Penn at the outset laid down plans for rural communities. "For the more convenient bringing up of youth . . . so that neighbors may help one another . . . and that they may accustom their children also to do the same," Penn proposed a township system in which farmers, craftsmen, and others would reside in villages.[1] Meetinghouses were to be placed at the center of the villages, and presumably the townships were to have considerable administrative significance. Individual holdings would extend outward from the village centers and were to be divided in a regular fashion. But except for home lots, farms would be of one piece, with contiguous fields, unlike the open-field system of scattered strips, with which agricultural villages in Europe were often associated.[2] The road pattern would be rectangular. By his charter Penn had full power to determine tenure rights: "in fee simple, fee tail, or for a life or lives, or a term of years, and by such services, customs, and rents as might appear . . . expedient." He could create manors for others, demand escheat of unsettled land, and require quitrents. Settlers did not have full rights of alienation. He was to control ferries and mills. Thus the plan and charter had strong manorial and centralizing overtones.[3]

Penn publicized various schemes to flesh out his general plan. He said townships should normally be of 5,000 acres, with farm

sizes dependent on the financial ability of settlers or purchasers.[4]
He advocated ten, fifteen, or twenty families for each township
with holdings of 100 to 500 acres.[5] Two specific proposals related
to the disposition of farm shapes and sizes. One called for farms of
100 acres to be laid out along a "street" road dividing the township in halves, with the remainder of the township land held in
reserve for children (figure 31).[6] The other was based on the
assumption that groups would consist of ten families. Each of
their 500 acres would be divided into farms of 450 acres and home
lots of 50 acres. The ten home lots would lie in a 500-acre rec-
tangle (not a green) with the residences presumably placed around
its outside facing the farms, which were to be wedge-shaped (figure 32).[7] For servants who would be unable to purchase land at
the end of their service Penn suggested 50 acres per head and even
a separate township of 6.000 acres.[8]

To implement these orderly concepts, Penn sold blocks of
township size to some of the Quaker "First Purchasers" (5,000

Figure 31

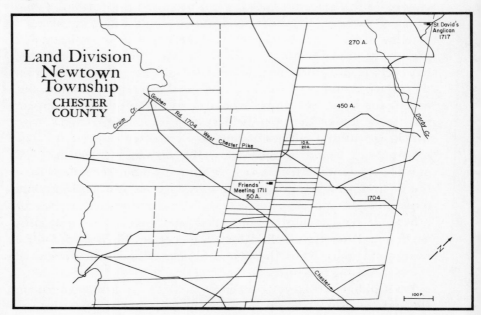

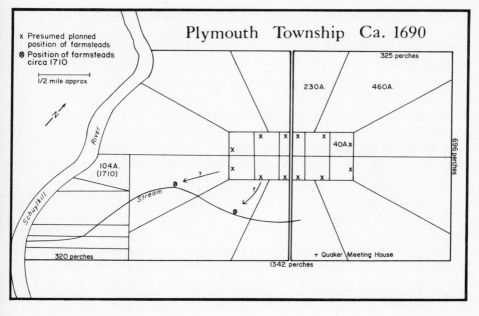

Figure 32

acres for £100). But to many who lacked funds he had to sell
relatively small holdings of 500 acres and less.[9] He hoped that the
possessors of townships, supposedly the "natural" leaders, would
sell to settlers and organize them into communities. To hasten the
process, in 1684 he required that the sites be occupied within
three years or the land would escheat to him.[10] Penn or his agents
would place poorer "First Purchasers" in townships by a method
that unfortunately was never made clear. To encourage sales he
offered lots of 10 acres in Philadelphia for each 500 acres purchased, a 50-acre bounty for each servant settled, and a three-year
period free from quitrents.[11]

During the first twenty years of the province the proprietor
maintained certain aspects of the ordered plan. In 1682 Penn instructed Thomas Holme to survey townships, and until 1696,
when he died, the surveyor-general had control over the disposition of land. His map, republished with additions several times,
indicates through its regular pattern that surveys preceded occupa-

tion by settlers (figure 15).[12] Even after 1700 speculative holdings
continued to be laid out in a regular rectangular fashion (figure
16).[13] Penn remained optimistic in this period. "I settle them in
villages," he wrote in 1684, and the next year he repeated his plan
in greater detail, enthusiastically asserting that fifty townships had
been laid out.[14]

In 1690 he published his plans for a second great orderly settlement on the Susquehanna, which was to be focused on a large city
and would progress eastward. But this plan failed, and even in the
earliest settlements on the Delaware there were indications that
Penn's ideas for community life were being frustrated.[15] Agricultural villages did not materialize and farmsteads were dispersed.
Indiscriminate settlement after 1700 led to irregular holdings, and
farms definitely became the decision-making units as the few
feudal ties were loosened. Townships were not maintained either
in form or function, and social and economic institutions, apparently lacking spatial regularity, appear to have done little to foster
order and participation in community life.

* * *

Although Holme's map (figure 15) shows many regularly laid-
out townships, it also reveals a dearth of agricultural villages.
Despite Penn's optimism in 1684, his plan for village living was a
failure from the outset. The only villages on Holme's map are
Newtown in Chester County (figure 31) and Newtown and
Wrightstown in Bucks. The latter two had large squares, as proposed by Penn. Germantown does not appear on Holme's map,
but it was platted as a street village, with home lots of three
acres.[16] A later survey of Plymouth Township nearby, after 1700,
shows a tentative attempt to follow Penn's village ideas (figure
32). But this draft shows two farmsteads on streams some distance
from where Penn would have wanted them.[17] Only Germantown
and Newtown, Bucks, survived as villages, although chiefly as
urban centers and not as clusters of farmhouses. Somewhat later
the Moravians lived for a generation in the communal villages of
Bethlehem, Nazareth, and Lititz, and there was another communal
group at Ephrata (figures 34 and 35). These places did not follow

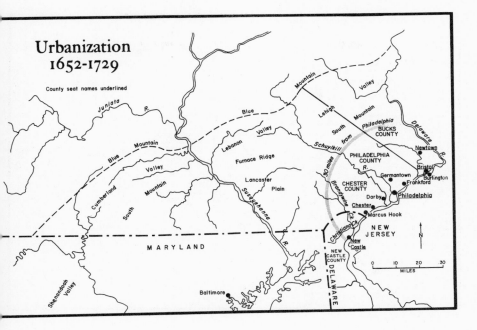

Urbanization 1652-1729

County seat names underlined

Figure 33

Penn's scheme and were eventually transformed into urban centers. Farmsteads were widely dispersed; in the 1790s Weld observed that between Philadelphia and Lancaster he found "not any two dwellings standing together" except at Downingtown (figure 35).[18]

Individual lots grew less regular as the dispersed pattern of farmsteads spread. Because of the weakness of the land office after 1700, settlers were able to mark off the land they wanted, even within some of the jealously held "manors" of the Penns.[19] As late as 1752, Richard Peters thought indiscriminate location by settlers was a "promiscuous" practice.[20] Although the laws officially conceded 6 per cent more than the amount specified by survey warrants to cover "barrens" and roads, and although surveyors were explicitly instructed to allow only four corners to a survey, the settlers had their way and a haphazard metes-and-bounds pattern emerged in most areas.[21] Some holdings had a

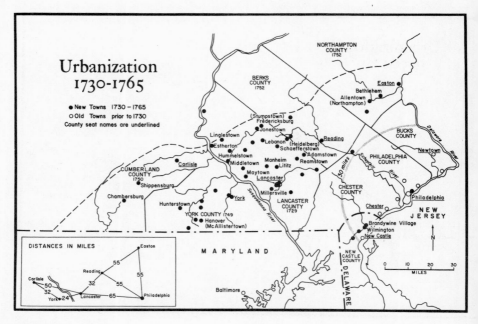

Figure 34

score or more points; a very small number had as few as four.[22]
Surveyors and even high officials contributed to the apparent
chaos by taking only land with good soils, tall timber, gentle
slopes, and the like and excluding poorer pockets.[23] The only
clear signs of remaining regularity were the straight survey lines, at
least on the drafts, and river lots that were often three times as
long as wide.[24] The locations of farmsteads contributed to the
irregular appearance; Schoepf reported in 1783 that they were
frequently set far back from roads, most often adjacent to springs
or above streams.[25] This tendency had actually been apparent very
early in eastern Chester County, where lots were laid out fairly
regularly yet also conformed to the deeply incised streams in the
area (figures 2 and 31).[26] Particularly after 1700, the settlers'
perception of natural conditions rather than an abstract survey
system dictated form. Not until the end of the century and at the
far western end of Pennsylvania did the government reintroduce
the rectangular system.[27]

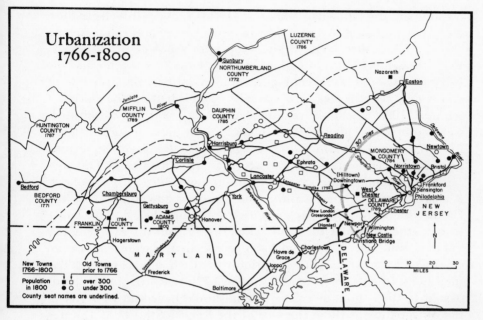

Figure 35

Changes in the legal status of individual holdings also indicated a shift in power toward farmers. As shown by the plans outlined above, Penn himself recognized that settlers wanted individual holdings with contiguous fields rather than strips in open fields. His compromise schemes were offered "so that the Conveniency of neighborhood is made agreeable with that of the Land."[28] He also sold rather than granted most land, an indication that he fully accepted the modern view of land as a marketable commodity. In these two respects Penn's practices differed from those of the earliest Massachusetts settlements[29] and from the communitarian idea of land held and worked in common, as in the Moravian "General Economy." Nevertheless his views remained too manorial and centralized for the Quaker farmers.

Although Penn did not spell out all aspects of tenure, many Quakers felt that they were hedged in by his charter rights. These restrictions, and thus the uncertainty of tenure, led the assembly in 1701 to pass a "Charter of Property." Largely through the efforts of the speculator-farmer David Lloyd, this legislation guaranteed to landowners confirmation of titles and full power to alienate lands and revoked the proprietor's power of escheat.[30] Even though Penn retracted his signature from this charter and the Privy Council did not accept its recommendations, the principle of grants in "fee simple" was virtually established as the norm of tenure.[31] The assembly remained powerful, and the proprietors were completely unable to influence it on most tenure matters. Eventually, in 1765, the Penns recognized the legality of squatters' preemption rights after years of acceptance in practice.[32] The only remains of feudal practice, the quitrents, were difficult to collect. Richard Peters at midcentury said "such is the humour of the People that they woud [sic] give twice the sum they do [for land] to have the present Quit Rent taken off."[33] But it was essentially a minor issue. Once the land had been deeded, warranted, or even possessed by squatters, the proprietors really had little power. The final blow to the Penn family came in 1779 when the public lands passed to the commonwealth.[34] Penn should have known better at the outset than to fly in the face of the English Statute of Tenures of 1660 guaranteeing individual rights.[35] Private ownership of property and individual operation of farms were becoming the norm.

Why did the people, many of whom had lived in villages in open-field areas, wish to assert their independence from Penn's ideas? The inability of the Penns and the land office to control the disposition of land cannot alone explain the dispersion of farmsteads, the irregularity of holdings, and the definite establishment of individual ownership. At least five explanations have been offered for the dispersed rural settlement and individual farms in Europe and America: ethnic traditions, European practices of agricultural land use, the form of the land, the cheap land in America, and less need for defense. Ethnic traditions have been called forth frequently in the past, although Meitzen's classic work attributing dispersed patterns to Celts and nucleated agricultural villages to Teutonic peoples has been discredited by many scholars in Europe.[36] Yet a well-known anthropologist affirmed relatively recently that the dispersed pattern in Pennsylvania resulted from traditions on the Atlantic Celtic fringe of Europe.[37] In the 1930s, on the other hand, a geographer traced origins of the *"einzelhofe"* to the "remote hills bordering the Rhine."[38] But Pennsylvania patterns cannot be attributed to either the Scotch-Irish or the Germans because the English Quakers were already living in isolated farmsteads when the others arrived; many Germans, per- haps most, came from areas with agricultural villages, such as Württemberg and Baden; and recent studies have concluded that dispersed settlement in Ulster developed only in the nineteenth century.[39] Besides, and more important, the dead weight of ethnic or national antecedence cannot explain the decisions and actions of such achievement-oriented people as Pennsylvanians regarding settlement patterns. We have already seen that inheritance prac- tices varied with conditions and could not be identified with tradition.[40]

The traditional explanations relating to land uses and landforms are not relevant to the situation in Pennsylvania, even though they had partial validity in Europe. Some have identified dispersed settlement in Europe with livestock raising and the village open- field system with grain production. In Pennsylvania farmers prac- ticed mixed agriculture with some emphasis on grain, especially wheat, yet no open fields resulted. Dispersed settlement was found both on plains and in hilly areas in Pennsylvania, whereas scholars often have identified the dispersed pattern in preindustrial Europe with hill lands, and villages and open fields with plains. They have argued that in hilly areas arable pockets are so scattered that vil- lagers would have spent too much time in travel to them. On plains this restraint did not operate, so that water supply was the critical factor encouraging people to cluster at springs and well sites. But even in Europe the patterns did not always fit this theory.[41]

Neither is the relatively cheap land in Pennsylvania, permitting large farms, an adequate explanation for dispersion.[42] Because the mystique of free land has obscured our understanding of farmers' decision-making processes, we need to assess the size of farms and travel distance to fields. Although many holdings were large by European and nineteenth-century standards at the outset, they were not huge. The modal size of the first purchases was 500 acres, and in 1710 Chester County holdings averaged 245 acres and between 100 and 200 acres near the Delaware River. From about 1760 to at least the 1780s the average size of holdings in Chester and Lancaster counties was about 130 acres (figures 28 and 29). In the hypothetical plan of Plymouth Township (figure 32), with its 500-acre farms, the greatest distance from farmstead to the edge of the farm would have been about 1¾ miles, well within the average distance of 2½ miles to fields that Michael Chisholm has suggested would be the maximum distance that the average preindustrial farmer in various parts of the world would travel.[43] Therefore in Plymouth and certainly on the smaller farms of later years farmers could have lived in villages without limiting their activities. This point can be strengthened by comparing the limit of intensive agriculture argued by Chisholm. He has found that farmers will put less labor and capital into fields beyond 5/8 mile from the farmstead. In early Pennsylvania farmers emphasized grain production, and so capital and labor were used rather sparingly. Demands on labor were great only at harvest time.[44] As a result not only farther fields but most nearer ones were not intensively cultivated. Certainly then, Penn's plan for wedge-shaped farms could have been combined with village living. But Pennsylvanians dispersed their farmsteads regardless of cheap land or the size of their holdings. Even in the first and second generations of settlement in Massachusetts, where holdings were smaller than in Pennsylvania, many farmers moved away from villages onto their farms.[45]

Peaceful relations with the Indians may have permitted farmers to disperse, but like the weak administration this was essentially a negative factor.[46]

The people could have lived in villages, but something led them to prefer living on their own farms. If it was not chiefly the factors examined above, what was it? Apparently the fundamental force leading to dispersion was the rise of individualism over peasant values in western Europe.

By the turn of the eighteenth century the agricultural village had become, in social terms, an anachronism. Its meaning lay partly in the feudal open-field system, which had been sustained by a medieval attitude encouraging equitable distribution of all qualities of land, and partly in its usefulness to lords in controlling the peasants.[47] By 1700, except for corporate farms in eastern Europe, the medieval structures were clearly on the wane. Farmers were becoming individual operators, even where their land was fragmented and where a majority were tenants.[48] Their freedom from personal dues and participation in the market economy signified this, as did the willingness of many English tenants to cooperate with landlords in the enclosure movement.[49] It is not surprising that in Pennsylvania these Europeans subscribed to what seemed then to be the most rational and efficient way of organizing farms. As individual operators, two-thirds of them owners,[50] they wanted the power to decide as many of their own actions as possible and not to be obligated to cooperate with others. By living on their own land they did not have to compromise at all on travel time to the fields, as they felt they might had they lived in villages. Given the size of their holdings, Quakers could have resided in villages, but notwithstanding their enthusiasm for the "holy experiment" they initiated the dispersed pattern. As the Anglican Andrew Burnaby stated (partly in another connection and with some antagonism): "Quakers struggle for preeminence and evince in a very striking manner that the passions of mankind are much stronger than any principles of religion."[51] Most of the others, including sectarians except for the utopian Moravians, followed the Quakers. As in New England, the influences of the times were irreversible; by 1680 Puritans probably were not laying out open fields or agricultural villages. By then land was sold rather than granted as the free enterprise system developed on and off the farm.[52] In Virginia, too, most farms were relatively small during the Revolutionary period.[53] Only with the rise of corporate farming today does it seem possible to view the family farm as a phase in European and American history and not as something established for all time largely by the settlers of Pennsylvania.

[handwritten margin note: But the sect-type Germans in Lanc Co were notorious for communal presence!]

* * *

Despite the early tendency toward dispersed farms, in the first years of the colony and even to 1740 the community idea based on townships and parishes was not entirely rejected. Small, regular townships of around 5,000 acres were laid out where possible in Quaker areas, with some attempt to establish centers, as in New-town, Chester (figure 31). The Quakers in the Nottingham Lots, the Mennonites in Bebber's Township, the Conestoga Mennonites, the Huguenots of Strasburg, and even the Scotch-Irish Presby-terians in Donegal, Marsh Creek (Gettysburg area), Conocoheague (near Chambersburg), and elsewhere all thought of their "settle-ments" as discrete communities and named them accordingly (figures 3, 7, 34, and 35). Presbyterians seemed to have had a policy of dividing areas into congregational units, and so Presbyte-rian churches at first were fairly evenly placed six to nine miles apart in strong Scotch-Irish areas of Chester County and in the Cumberland Valley.[54]

The most interesting early cases of community exclusiveness involved the sectarians of Germantown and the Welsh, who wanted separate political and judicial powers. In 1684 Francis Daniel Pastorius at Germantown asserted, "I for my small part could indeed wish that we might have a separate province, and so might the better protect ourselves against all oppression."[55] For a short time Germantown had borough status and a separate court.[56] The Welsh sought to have a separate colony; the pro-prietor had a tract laid out for them in Chester County and per-mitted separate courts for a while (figure 16).[57] These various developments of early townships, the Presbyterian districts, Ger-mantown, and the Welsh Tract came the closest to Penn's notion of communities corresponding to townships.

These attempts to create strong "townships" and spatially de-fined "parishes" largely failed for several reasons. Among them were the structure and actions of branches of the government, but more basic were the lack of communitarian discipline within most groups, the pluralistic society, and the individualistic values of the people. Structurally speaking the government and even the pro-prietor undercut the political powers of separate communities. Germantown lost its borough status and its separate courts in 1707. Queen Anne or her ministers regarded the courts as a threat to the royal legal structure and insisted on integrating them.[58] Lack of interest in local offices was one reason for the loss of borough status, but the action of the assembly was certainly another.[59] Even as early as 1690 the Welsh Tract was doomed as a separate entity. In that year the Provincial Council divided the tract between Chester and Philadelphia counties (figures 2 and 16) to dissuade the Welsh from pretensions of autonomy.[60] Thus it seemed that no one would tolerate separate townships.

Fundamentally, wide township powers were impossible because counties were made very strong.[61] If Penn really had been interested in political townships as the basic communities, he would have provided in the constitution for strong officials with sufficient powers to govern them.[62] But for reasons yet unclear he did not. The Quakers were not interested in politically strong townships and possibly felt that they could control the province and its style of life best through counties. Until midcentury they did.[63] By 1725 the county commissioners had become elective, and the assembly assigned them substantial powers.[64] An ironical aspect of the township scheme was the vestigial phrase "according to a system of townships appointed by me" that continued to appear on survey warrants until 1809.[65] Samuel Blunston, a Quaker surveyor in Lancaster, questioned the phrase in 1734: "I also observe the Lands are to be laid out according to the method of townships, to which method I am . . . [a] Stranger."[66]

Political townships continued to exist but merely as convenient units of assessment for the counties, with weak justices of the peace.[67] Although the people sometimes petitioned for new townships and suggested names for them, indicating a feeling of identification with them, townships were not powerful political or social units as in seventeenth century Massachusetts or in the Delaware Valley before 1680.[68] The weakness of townships seems to be signaled in the shift after 1700 toward larger and more irregular areas with streams and hills as boundaries rather than straight survey lines (figure 2). Similarly, when the original Mennonite tract of 1710 in Lancaster County was divided in 1729 between Conestoga and Lampeter townships the inhabitants voiced no obvious protest. The allegiance of the people and the political power lay elsewhere. Unless one recognized the assessment sheets lying on the tables of assessors for several days in winter, the documents of justices of the peace stuffed into desks, or the names of townships on maps, in many cases inaccurately placed, then the townships' visibility was singularly low.[69]

Most parishes as well as political townships did not materialize as communities, at least in the strict sense of areally defined units. This failure was, first of all, a consequence of the lack of leadership; ministers were often in short supply among church groups. But the people also tended to resist the exercise of religious authority. Henry M. Muhlenberg and Michael Schlatter, sent over in the 1740s to bring order to the Lutherans and the Reformed, found that decisions were made by majority vote rather than by ministers or even elders on the basis of church discipline. Pennsylvania may have been a "heaven for farmers" and a "paradise for artisans," but in this voluntaristic situation it was a "hell" for preachers.[70] The Great Awakening loosened what had been the reasonably secure Presbyterian discipline and fostered splinter groups. The decentralized ecclesiastical situation paralleled the people's desire for individual success.[71]

Parishes also failed partly because of the pluralistic denominational patterns. Although Quakers and Presbyterians occupied some areas exclusively for a time, few groups, especially German congregations, found themselves alone for long.[72] Lutherans and Reformed generally were distributed together and, in 60 per cent of the congregations, used the same buildings.[73] On the Lancaster Plain and elsewhere many groups were mixed (figures 13 and 14). Churches in towns often were excluded from central squares and placed on back streets, even though many were impressive structures, such as the Lutheran Church in Lancaster built in the early 1760s.[74] In this chaotic and diverse social environment many clergymen were appalled that they could not organize parishes or establish their church, and as a result many left for more traditional Virginia and Maryland.[75]

One might argue that the throwing together of disparate groups in the new environment was the sole explanation for lack of parishes.[76] But the denominational attitude, that is, mutual toleration among groups, which was so clear in Pennsylvania, had already developed in Europe by the late seventeenth century. Quakers could appear openly in England without persecution.

Although sectarianism was obvious in Pennsylvania's early years, the Great Awakening had the effect of pushing denominationalism one step further and weakened distinctions. Increased tolerance diluted divisive dogma (though certain tenets were strongly held), and denominations and local churches more clearly became voluntary societies for personal identification and salvation than institutions that embraced the totality of social and economic life.[77] In Pennsylvania, then, the American pattern of religious life without discrete areal parishes appeared early, and tendencies toward individualism ripened where power was not sharply focused.

The Quaker position toward parishes was ambivalent. Without doubt their distinction between the visible and invisible church fostered this attitude. They seem to have had little interest in Penn's townships as parishes; not all townships had meetinghouses, nor were those that were constructed centrally located (figure 32). Although Penn at first promoted his "holy experiment" among sectarians, eventually the Quakers allowed all sorts of people into Pennsylvania, apparently including many without denominational affiliations (table 6). But when the Quakers' political power was weakened in the 1760s, and while other groups were accepting denominationalism, rural Quakers, such as those in Chester County, turned inward and became more exclusive—more sectarian. In their little holy commonwealth righteousness turned to self-righteousness, and critics were able to attack the hypocrisy of "birth rights" and attachment to wealth among these pious folk.[78] Many Mennonites at this time seem to have been less prone to retreat from the world, partly because they had little to lose owing to lesser involvement in public affairs.[79]

As churches moved from being sharply defined means of child socialization and social control, as conceived by Penn, to voluntary means of social participation, secular schools gradually appeared.[80] The earliest schools were explicitly denominational, organized by Quakers, Presbyterians, and others. Among Lutherans and Reformed Germans the first buildings often were schoolhouses, and teachers became ministers through consent of the people.[81] Some Presbyterian ministers ran academies for teaching the classics. Later, although Germans protested the "charity

school" movement in the early 1750s, which would have forced
integration into English culture, some of them organized their own
schools for teaching English, ciphering, and, of course, morality.
These were organized by neighbors of various denominational persuasions—in Strasburg Township, for example, by Mennonite,
Lutheran, and Reformed folk. In the following advertisement their
interest in English, the classics, and moral training, as distinct from
sectarian catechetic teaching, is obvious:

A certain George Hadams, an Englishman, by profession a schoolmaster [is] a
perpetual talker, great bragger, pretends great knowledge in having both English and Latin. [He is] a notorious cheat, a wilful liar, and a wicked de-
bauched person unworthy to live among civilized people, [and so] we think it
is incumbent on us to caution the public against such an atrocious villain.[82]

The writer was sufficiently secularized to say "civilized" rather
than "Christian" people. Despite the group's forthright dislike of
Hadams, it requested another English teacher.

Whether this kind of school was established in every neighborhood is uncertain. The scant evidence suggests that the people at
this point felt no need for an elaborate educational system. Technology was simple, and except for some enthusiasm among some
Presbyterians and others for classical studies education's purpose
was simply to provide assistance in carrying out the business of
everyday life. As a result schools were scattered, often on a corner
of a generous farmer's holding or near or in a church.[83] School
districts were *ad hoc* affairs, and probably relatively few children
were educated by professional or semiprofessional teachers. In
contrast to today's suburban neighborhoods, schools did not provide a clear focus for rural communities.

The haphazard open-country pattern was also apparent in the
scattering of economic institutions. Many hamlets sprang up at
crossroads and around taverns, mills, and ferries, and speculators
laid out urban villages and towns. But hamlets and villages ex-
hibited no definite pattern of association with local communities.
The relatively unspecialized economic system and technology (by
modern standards) contributed to this. Processing of goods was
undertaken for the most part by individual proprietors rather than
by corporations. In 1783 Johann Schoepf noted the sorry-looking

artisans' cabins along roads.[84] Butchers, shoemakers, tailors, and tinkers were often itinerant, using the raw materials provided by consumers to finish goods.[85] Prominent farmers distilled liquor for sale.[86] Weaving was mostly a cottage industry, even in the production of commercial textiles.[87] Blacksmiths were distributed near the purchasers of their goods because it was cheaper to ship their raw material, iron, than completed goods such as horseshoes and wagon tires. Moreover, since the finished product was custom made, specifications had to be given firsthand. Despite the importance of blacksmiths, they could not be the sole focal point of communities with their wide range of needs. Millers were tied to streams, their source of power. Howell's map of 1792 shows mills on permanent streams every two miles or so.[88]

Many commercial activities were uncentralized and transportation was undeveloped. Keepers of shops and taverns operated on the local scene. Because of the relatively low key of trading, however, only a handful of transactions a day, most shopkeepers had little need for frequent market information. As a result, they had little need to cluster in urban places, at least before 1730. Few shopkeepers assessed the optimal location among various alternatives. Shopkeepers carried on banking operations, as did affluent farmers. As estate inventories show, some farmers and shopkeepers made numerous loans.[89] Roads were usually poor, even by post-1800 standards. County officials ordered roads built in response to the petitions of inhabitants who had particular needs. When a new church or mill was erected those who stood to benefit most, not whole communities, would request a road to serve it. These often conformed to natural features of the landscape rather than to the principle of shortest distance.[90] Few of Penn's planned straight roads were laid out (figures 31 and 35).

* * *

Thus we see that Pennsylvania's dispersed and apparently haphazard patterns of spatial organization of various institutions, while appearing chaotic to Penn and others, involved a complex network of interconnections among residents.[91] In spite of their individualism, the people could not live entirely without commu-

nity. Security was found in various ways. Relatives, notwithstanding the preeminence of the nuclear family and the high
degree of mobility, provided a major focus of interdependency.[92]
Local congregations, despite their lack of social control over most
persons (except among sectarians), their divisiveness, and their
weakened powers of education, were still crucial means of social
participation. The ideology of these churches supported middle-
class needs for order and individual success. As in Europe, the
numerous taverns provided social participation for many, particularly the less pious and the unsuccessful.[93] Millers, shopkeepers,
and affluent farmers who loaned money and distilled whisky were
important points of contact. But these institutions and establishments were not enough in themselves to hold communities together.

One obvious direct means of encouraging order was through
voluntary neighborhood cooperation. As we saw earlier, considerable interaction occurred at the grass-roots level among members
of religious and national groups, and this extended to such institutions as schools. Barn-raisings were also occasions of mutual help
and temporary recognition of community, besides being times of
revelry, not only within cultural groups but between members of
different groups. In 1769 James Burd of Paxton Township, of
English ancestry, commented that a hundred neighbors, German
and Scotch-Irish, turned out to his raising. (About the same time
he and his wife were invited to the German church in Middletown.)[94] Around 1760 the numerous lotteries for church buildings
usually involved sellers and even organizers from various denominations and nationalities.[95] Voluntary cooperation within communities and their social viability resulted from the recognition by
individuals that they had to discipline themselves to a degree of
cooperative aid to ensure their own individual success and the
building of a good if not holy society.[96] If Benjamin Franklin
expounded his aphorisms of achievement through "Poor Richard"
to encourage the weak, he was probably also representing a large
bloc of opinion. Pennsylvanians were fortunate, however, that the
land was so productive that the aspirations of most could be fulfilled at the same time that local institutions could be so poorly

defined socially and spatially. Likewise, partly because of their skill, Pennsylvanians in local communities were able to participate effectively in the larger units of the county and the region, to which we now turn.

CHAPTER FIVE

Territorial Organization of Towns, Counties, and the Region

If William Penn and the Quakers disagreed on the form of rural settlement, they concurred on the need for towns to foster the expansion of the economy, to maintain order and to sustain social values. Penn, his sons, and other Pennsylvanians founded more than a hundred urban places during the course of the century, and many unplanned hamlets appeared. These towns, by acting as channels for information, ideas, and goods, gave a definable shape to many activities throughout the region. Urban and country life were closely tied and not in basic conflict.[1]

* * *

Towns ranged in size and importance from Philadelphia, the metropolis, to minuscule hamlets. The different types, indicated on table 20, are defined by the dominant kinds of activities of residents and by their populations.[2] Commerce, transportation, public administration, and processing were the chief economic sectors, but the importance of social identification and interaction cannot be discounted. In that preindustrial time commerce was the most universal and obvious characteristic of all urban places; Isaac Weld was nearly correct in 1795 when he asserted that "the size of all towns in America has hitherto been proportionate to their trade."[3] Hence most towns can be classified as service centers, or "central places" within their tributary trade areas.

Successful central places were points of nearly optimum accessibility for buyers and sellers. These places varied in size and complexity; places of lower order or rank had fewer people and kinds of activities than those of a higher order because the latter served larger areas and populations. Higher-order activities thus had higher thresholds for entry than lower, less specialized ones. For example, lower-order places did not have clockmakers or merchants who emphasized buying and wholesaling. Higher-order places also included the unspecialized shopkeepers and blacksmiths usually found in small places. There were fewer high-order than low-order centers; many hamlets existed, but only one Philadelphia. The hinterlands of the hamlets were local, but the operations of some Philadelphians ranged over the whole region. Yet all towns were foci within the mercantile network that developed in the area.[4]

Other activities contributed to the development of the urban hierarchy. Although financial dealings were much less concentrated than after the rise of banks in the 1780's, many merchants who lived in higher-order central places were the most important bankers and lenders. Transportation was closely but not entirely connected with commerce. The larger central places were on major roads or navigable streams, but the chief purpose of some smaller places was storage and transshipment.[5] Many hamlets owed their existence to taverns that were resting points. The political functions of Philadelphia and several county seats accentuated their importance (table 20).

Larger places thus enhanced their position through "agglomeration" or "external" economies.[6] Less effort was expended when trips could combine public and commercial transactions. The presence of one activity helped to support others. In the colonial northeast it was no accident that Philadelphia, New York, and Boston were capitals and the largest places. The public administration and commercial functions of these higher-order places thus contributed to their value as points of social interaction and identification. Rural dwellers could meet friends who lived beyond their immediate neighborhoods. Many persons settled in these places because they wanted the stimulation of daily contacts among many people, even though they might have become more

Table 20

Classification of Towns by Dominant Function, Population in 1800,
Rank in Central Place Hierarchy, Period of Founding, and Location

Dominant Function	Population Range, 1800	Rank or Order	Places, Period of Founding, and Location
Service			
Metropolis	Over 10,000	5	Philadelphia (and Baltimore)
County seat			
Strong, growing	1,000–5,000	4	Midcentury (1730–65): Lancaster, York, Reading, Carlisle, Easton (back country)[a]
	1,000–2,000 500+		Late century (1766–1800): Harrisburg, Chambersburg Gettysburg (back country)[a]
Weak, stagnant	300–500	3	Early (1652–1700): New Castle, Chester, Bristol (near Philadelphia)[b]
	300	2	Newtown (near Philadelphia)[b]
	300–500	3	Late: Norristown, West Chester (near Philadelphia)[b]
Other	500–3,500	4	Midcentury: Lebanon, Allentown, Shippensburg, Hanover (all back country)
			Wilmington (near Philadelphia)[b]
	300–500	3	Midcentury: (mostly 1750–65): 9 planned towns
	100–300	2	Mostly midcentury and late: ca. 70 planned villages
	100	1	Hamlets

Transport points	. . . . . .	1,000–5,000 300–1,000 <300	. . .	Early: (New Castle, Chester)[c] Midcentury: (Other county seats, esp. Easton) Middletown, (Shippensburg), (Hanover) (back country) Late century: (Harrisburg), Columbia Christiana Bridge, Newport (near Philadelphia) Also hamlets around taverns, at crossroads and ferries
Processing towns	. . .	300–2,500		Early: Germantown, Frankford (near Philadelphia) Midcentury: (Wilmington), Brandywine Village, (county towns in back country) Also hamlets around mills, mines, iron works
Religiously oriented towns[d]	. . .			Early: (Germantown) Midcentury: Bethlehem, Nazareth, Lititz—Moravian; Ephrata

Source: Various. See n. 2, chap. 5.

[a] More than 30 miles from Philadelphia.
[b] Within 30 miles.
[c] Towns in parentheses have already been noted above in table.
[d] Initially self-sustaining agricultural villages; later central places and manufacturing towns.

affluent by farming.[7] Because of the attraction of the larger places they became the centers of culture and ideas.

As for manufacturing, although a majority of town dwellers were craftsmen engaged in processing materials, most of them were also retailers. Besides, in the prefactory era most of the larger operations, such as milling and ironmaking, were located in the countryside.[8] Thus few towns had processing as their chief concern. Merchants, shopkeepers, tavernkeepers, and public officials, not industrialists, were the key figures. Although this study focuses on southeastern Pennsylvania and northern New Castle County (figures 33, 34, and 35), we shall note here some places in Maryland and north and west of Blue Mountain in Pennsylvania that had functional relationships with this area.

* * *

Five periods and two zones can be defined fairly clearly in considering the founding and growth of the various types of towns. The periods were: the pre-Pennsylvania, 1652-1680; the establishment, 1681-1700; the quiescent, 1701-1729; the boom, 1730-1765; and the period of stabilization, 1766-1800. The two zones were separated by a line roughly thirty miles or a day's journey from Philadelphia (figures 33, 34, and 35). Within the first zone urbanization was much more inhibited by the overwhelming importance of Philadelphia than in the "back country" beyond.

During the period before the establishment of Pennsylvania, New Castle was founded by the Dutch in 1652 and Upland, later Chester, by the Swedes, both on the Delaware.[9] Between 1681 and 1700 Penn and others laid out Philadelphia and other towns on or near the Delaware (tables 21 and 22).[10] Philadelphia grew so rapidly that it soon contained a quarter of Pennsylvania's population. In the period of quiescence no towns were laid out even though settlers were occupying the back country. Philadelphia so dominated the scene that other towns stagnated. When Lancaster, in the back country, and Wilmington, in adjacent Delaware, were established in 1730, the process of urbanization was revitalized, and it accelerated between 1740 and 1765. In this boom period William Penn's sons and other developers laid out a larger number of towns, mostly in the back country, and several places, notably Philadephia and county seats in the back country, grew rapidly. In general, these events paralleled the formation of new counties and substantial economic expansion.

During the last third of the century, the period of stabilization, the rate of urbanization was less spectacular. Philadelphia grew somewhat more rapidly than it had in the previous period, in spite of severe competition from Baltimore, and in 1800, with its suburbs, contained 20 per cent of southeastern Pennsylvania's population (figure 11).[11] But county seats grew more slowly, and the number of new towns laid out during the last two decades of the century did not equal the number platted from 1755 to 1765.

* * *

In 1800 the functions of towns were much the same as in 1700, as was the orientation of the economy. During the preindustrial era in this rural society, most towns acted as central places for exchanging farm commodities for those of other counties. Yet urbanites contributed their skills to the economic, political, and social organization of the region.

William Penn's charter gave him the authority to erect cities and boroughs as well as counties, townships, and "hundreds" (county subdivisions with their own courts).[12] Recognizing that cities were needed to encourage commerce, he ordered his surveyors to lay out Philadelphia in 1682 on the neck between the Delaware and Schuylkill rivers. The city was to be both a "greene countrie

Table 21

Number of Towns Founded
(Five Year Intervals after 1740)

Before 1680	1	1746–50	4	1771–75	3	1796–1800	2
1681–1700	7	1751–55	6	1776–80	5	Uncertain:	
1700–1729	0	1756–60	10	1781–85	4	1681–1729	1
1730–40	3	1761–65	19	1786–90	7	1730–1765	4
1741–45	7	1766–70	3	1791–95	1	1766–1800	17
						Total	104

Source: Local histories, maps. See n. 2, chap. 5.

Table 22

Counties, County Seats, Founding Dates, Founders, and Boroughs

County	Founding Date	Seat	Founding Date	Founder	Borough Status
Philadelphia	1682/83	Philadelphia	1682/83	W. Penn	1701 (city)
Chester	1682/83	Chester (Upland)	1701 (part)	J. Sandelands	1701
		West Chester	1786, seat 1789	several persons	1799
Bucks	1682/83	Crewecorne?	1683, hamlet		
		Bristol	1679, seat 1705	Prov. Council	1720
		Newtown	1680s, seat 1724	W. Penn	. . .
New Castle, Del.	1682/83	New Castle[a]	1652	Dutch	. . .
Lancaster	1729	Lancaster	1730	J. Hamilton	1742
York	1749	York	1741	Penns	1787
Cumberland	1750	Carlisle	1752	Penns	1782
Berks	1752	Reading	1748	Penns	1783
Northampton	1752	Easton	1752	Penns	1789
Bedford	1771	Bedford[a]	1766	Penns	. . .
Northumberland	1772	Sunbury[a]	1772	Penns	. . .
Montgomery	1784	Norristown	1784	W. Smith	. . .
Franklin	1784	Chambersburg	1764	B. Chambers	. . .
Dauphin	1785	Harrisburg	1786	T. Harris	1791
Delaware	1789	Chester[b]			
Adams	1800	Gettysburg	1780	S. Gettys	. . .
		Other Boroughs			
		Germantown	. . .	. . .	1691–1707
		Wilmington, Del.[a]	. . .	. . .	1740
		Lebanon	. . .	. . .	1799

Source: Various. See n. 2, chap. 5.

[a]Not in southeastern Pennsylvania but relevant to discussion.
[b]Already cited under Chester Co.

towne" and a metropolis. Although in 1690 Penn opened a sub-
scription drive to found another city on the Susquehanna, the
plans never materialized.[13] One metropolis sufficed in the area, at
least until Baltimore emerged after 1750 to serve part of the
region. Philadelphia was Penn's most notable success in his "holy
experiment."

Our discussion must begin, therefore, with the recognition of
Philadelphia as the nodal point of the province. Its growth to
about 6,000 within its first decade and its overwhelming size
between 1730 and 1800 compared with the next largest town,
Lancaster, are apparent from figure 36. It was clearly the "primate" city;[14] in 1800 its population was about 62,000 (including
suburbs) compared with 4,300 in Lancaster. Eight per cent of the
region's total urban population lived there. (If Delaware and West
Jersey are included, Philadelphia's share is still at least 60 per
cent.) As Penn intended, Philadelphia immediately became the
focus of many regional and county activities: commerce, shipping,
the Quaker Yearly Meeting, the creative arts, technology, science,
and county, provincial, and later state and federal administration.
Within ten years of its founding its Quaker merchants created their
own patterns of trade within the British mercantile system and
their city emerged as a rival of Boston and New York.[15] Grain and
especially flour from Pennsylvania, West Jersey, and Delaware was
sold to the West Indies and later to southern Europe, New England, and even England. Flaxseed was shipped to Ireland, especially after 1740, when a period of rapid growth in trade occurred.
Corn, pork, and beef were also exported. After 1750, iron, the
production of which was financed by Philadelphia merchants, was
shipped abroad. Exporters became more effective in collecting
commodities for shipment, in large measure through agents in
other towns. These activities resulted in exports totaling more
than £800,000 by 1775. In flour, wheat, and flaxseed alone this
meant an increase in per capita exports to about 41 shillings compared with 17 shillings in 1730 (figure 4).[16] Following the Revolution old markets were regained and new ones established so that
by the early 1790s exports reached prewar levels.[17]

Goods were imported from England and elsewhere and distributed in Philadelphia's hinterland. Some merchants who origi-

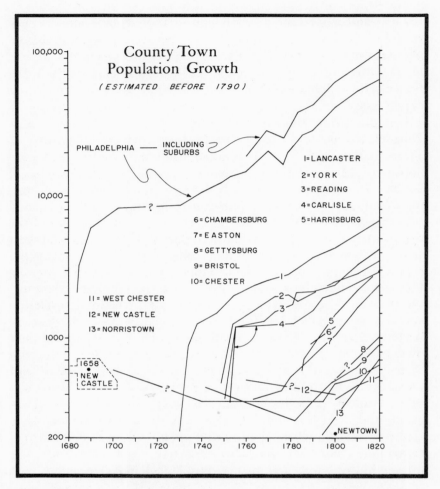

Figure 36

nally handled both exports and imports developed sufficient
volume by 1750 to allow them to specialize in imports. Back-
country merchants who sent goods to the city had their wagoners
bring back goods from these wholesalers.[18] Although Philadelphians were constantly in debt to London merchants and the value
of imports fluctuated greatly, the long-range trend of imports was
upward. According to Benjamin Franklin, the value of imports

rose seventeen times between 1723 and 1757 while the population quadrupled; although the volume of imports actually increased only ten-fold during that period, the gains were impressive on a per capita basis.[19] After 1760 per capita imports were at modest levels except in 1772.[20]

In contrast to Pennsylvania, the tobacco colonies to the south had a lower average living standard, a slower rate of white population growth, and few substantial towns, at least until they turned to wheat production. Unlike Pennsylvania's farmers and merchants, Virginia planters were tied to London and Glasgow merchants in a commercial structure that permitted less autonomy and flexibility. Much of their retail trade was handled by agents of British merchants.[21] After 1750, when some parts of Maryland and Virginia turned to wheat production, Baltimore rose quickly to handle the trade. Its merchants, some of whom moved from Pennsylvania, also tapped part of Philadelphia's hinterland west of the Susquehanna.[22] Although this intrusion from the south resulted in severe competition for Philadelphia's merchants, Baltimore's activities actually contributed to a tightening of commercial organization in Pennsylvania. Philadelphia's development was not hampered, and its rise to the rank of chief city in America coincided with the blossoming of Baltimore. Commercial interconnections between these and other large cities contributed to their success.[23] The ability to organize commerce within the British commercial structure but to remain partly autonomous of it nourished urban and economic development.

Philadelphia's position as a major organizing center for the export trade of Pennsylvania and adjacent areas contributed greatly to its growth and specialization. Many clerks were needed, and many other persons were employed in transport (table 23).[24] Some merchants became specialized insurance underwriters. However, the port function was secondary to the commercial role in fostering growth. Had the trade of Pennsylvania been organized directly from London and Glasgow, as was much of Virginia's, where no large city emerged, many shipping points such as Bristol, Chester, New Castle, Wilmington, Charlestown, and Havre de Grace might have developed more and the result might have been a much smaller Philadelphia.[25]

Table 23

Occupational Percentages of Taxables

Occupation	Phila. 1790	Lancaster 1759	Lancaster 1773	Lancaster 1789	Lancaster 1800	Reading 1773	Reading 1785	Reading 1805	York 1783	York 1800	Carlisle 1781
Primary production	0.5%	0.3%	0.0%	2.2%	2.9%	4.9%	0.6%	4.9%	0.0%	0.2%	0.0%
Crafts	41.5	59.9	65.8	61.2	57.1	60.7	58.0	64.5	62.4	62.2	43.4[c]
Trade and finance	30.0	15.5	15.1	10.6	10.2	14.8	13.3	11.1	15.8	12.0	15.9
Transport	3.8	3.5	1.3	0.4	0.9	1.2	3.3	0.7	1.5	0.9	2.1
Public service	8.0	0.8	1.8	2.4	5.1	4.9	2.1	3.1	1.8	4.0	4.2
Personal and social service	7.4	3.8	3.3	4.8	4.9	3.3	2.7	3.8	3.0	5.4	4.2
Laborers	8.7[c]	16.5	13.1	16.0	16.0	9.4[c]	15.8[b]	11.1[b]	14.8[b]	14.8[b]	30.2[b,d]
Others	0.0%	0.0%	0.0%	3.6%	3.2%	0.8%	4.2%	0.9%	0.6%	0.7%	0.0%
Taxables listed[a]	3,434	438	436	564	857	280	388	588	360	517	222
Taxables with occupations	2,758	404	398	501	724	244	331	451	330	426	189

Source: Philadelphia: Rossiter, A Century of Population Growth . . . (Washington, 1909), pp. 142–43; Lancaster: 1773, Pa. Arch., 3d ser., 17: 454–65, Lanc. Co. MSS tax returns, 1759, 1789, 1800; Reading: MSS tax returns, Berks Co. Hist. Soc.; York: MSS tax returns, York Co. Hist. Soc.; Carlisle: MSS tax returns, Cumberland County Courthouse, Carlisle.

Note: Some percentage totals do not equal 100 because of rounding.

[a] Excludes single freemen.
[b] Adjusted; see n. 24, chap. 5.
[c] Probably too low.
[d] Probably too high.

Penn and the Quakers did not doubt that the commercial center should also be the focus of government and social life in the province. Although the number of public servants in Philadelphia was small compared with commercial sectors (table 23), all settlers were required to visit the land office, and the provincial courts met there. The Yearly Meeting of Quakers attracted many prominent farmers from the adjacent counties, not only to seek silence and inspiration but also to purchase imported goods and to negotiate loans with merchants, the chief lenders.[26] The work of county courts, the recording of deeds, the registration of wills, and the activities of lawyers all assisted Philadelphia's "pulling" power. Eventually, as the urban population grew, the local marketplace drew farmers' garden produce within a radius of about fifteen miles; in 1765 300 wagons were observed at the market.[27] Craft manufacturing developed, and by 1800 a few cotton mills appeared not far outside the city.[28] These in turn attracted larger imports of cotton and then machine-makers. Thus the advantage of being the area's first capital and the ability of its merchants to organize the Atlantic trade of the area spurred the development of a large city with a wide range of activities. Philadelphians helped to build an increasingly complex network of interconnections within the area that promoted economic growth. As a result, travelers from overseas were impressed by the city. Its population and the quality of its buildings surpassed most other cities in the western world in 1776.

After the Revolution, Philadelphia's position in the state weakened somewhat and it lost its preeminence in America. Baltimore's merchants markedly increased their activity, and by 1800 its millers were drawing additional trade away from the Delaware.[29] Back-country pressure for an inland site for the capital also led to the removal of the state governments to Lancaster in 1799. People to the west had balked at Quaker control of the assembly in the 1760s and up to 1766 had complained about underrepresentation, but not until the end of the century were they able to negotiate a change of the capital to a more central position.[30] Yet because the economy by then operated more independently of the political system, the shift was of little direct significance to the economic strength of Philadelphia. Nevertheless, the loss may have damaged Philadelphia's image and weakened its merchants' commercial vigor. Whatever the reasons, by 1800 New York's population had surpassed Philadelphia's and Baltimore had made a dramatic gain.[31]

* * *

Penn, we have seen, had plans for politically strong townships with agricultural villages; instead, counties became the chief units of local government and rural settlement was dispersed over the countryside. As counties were formed, towns were laid out as seats for courts and administration. County seats besides Philadelphia divide into two groups: those founded within thirty miles of Philadelphia, which failed to grow, and those farther away, which grew and became the most important centers outside Philadelphia. The first group can be divided into those established early and those founded in the 1780s, and the latter group into those created by the Penn family and those laid out by others that became seats after the Revolution (table 22).

Some in the first group were founded quite early: Bristol, Newtown (replacing Bristol in Bucks County in 1724), Chester, and New Castle (figure 33). The circumstances of the founding of most of these places are not entirely clear. Bristol was platted in 1697 by order of the Provincial Council in response to a petition of inhabitants, and in the 1680s Newtown was laid out, intended as one of the few agricultural villages in the province (figure 15).[32] Chester was an outgrowth of Upland, the site of a court under the Duke of York, who held jurisdiction over the Swedes in the Delaware Valley after 1674. Apparently little subdividing was undertaken there until 1700, when James Sandelands platted part of his land.[33] New Castle, established by the Dutch in 1652 and the earliest town in the Delaware Valley, remained the seat of New Castle County after 1682.[34]

These county towns stagnated throughout most of the century (figure 36), although they held courts, supported recorders of deeds and registers of wills, and, in the cases of Bristol and Chester, received borough charters that permitted market days and fairs. New Castle probably lost population after 1682, when Philadelphia was founded. In 1753 Lewis Evans observed that Bristol,

Chester, and Newtown had "been long at a stand."[35] Chester and New Castle were reported in a state of physical decay.[36] The two county seats established in the 1780s, West Chester and Norristown, also failed to grow rapidly at first (figures 35 and 36).

The stagnation of these county towns was paralleled by an almost complete lack of development of other towns in the three original counties near Philadelphia. At least until after the Revolution, hamlets rather than planned towns were the only signs of urbanization. Compared with the back country, little drive toward the organization of towns was evident (figures 33, 34, and 35).

Philadelphia's preeminence inhibited the establishment and growth of other urban centers, at least in the longest-settled counties. It preempted central place, transport, and craft activities and so overrode the external economies provided to other county seats by their administrative functions. Quaker farmers were quite willing to divide their travel. Although they could not avoid courts in their own counties, most of the lawyers and merchants with whom they dealt apparently lived in Philadelphia.[37] As early as 1703, farmers in the Welsh Tract and Goshen Township in Chester County petitioned for a road to Philadelphia, "their chief present market."[38] Philadelphia's status gave it what would seem to be more than its fair share of lower-order activities. As a consequence, nearby county seats did not rise above third-order status in the mercantile hierarchy and speculators were discouraged from laying out additional towns. Bristol's continued existence kept Newtown at even a lower order of importance than the others (table 20).

* * *

In contrast, the county towns in the back country south and east of Blue Mountain grew substantially and remained "strong" in the central-place hierarchy. The first of these were laid out between 1730 and 1752: Lancaster, York, Reading, Carlisle, and Easton. Others became seats after the Revolution (tables 21 and 22).

The laying out of Lancaster in 1730 ended a long drought in town founding, leaving aside the spontaneous rise of hamlets around taverns and mills. Twenty years elapsed between the first settlement in what became Lancaster County and the establishment of the town. The formation of new counties was impeded by the recalcitrance of the Quaker assembly, which wanted to keep power in the older counties.[39] Urbanization was retarded by the relatively slow influx of immigrants before 1720 and by slow growth in the economy, most clearly between 1700 and 1725 (figure 4). With the founding of Lancaster more rapid growth began.

The process of the founding of these places as a consequence of speculative initiative, population growth, legislative action, and economic conditions indicates their importance as central places or, as they were called then, "market towns." The site of Lancaster was land owned by a Philadelphian, Andrew Hamilton, then prothonotary of the supreme court in the province. He had only lately acquired the land, which had no site qualities to commend it, as its center was a mile from the Conestoga Creek. Apparently Lancaster's site was determined only by the location of Hamilton's holdings, and Hamilton's political influence in Philadelphia determined that the seat was to be his possession. He and his descendants collected quitrents and sold lots in the town until 1815.[40] In spite of deficiencies, Lancaster was well situated in a rich agricultural area more than sixty miles from Philadelphia.

All other new county towns established before 1775 were created by the Penn family. Thomas Penn's arrival from England in 1732 marked the beginning of a new era. Proprietary administration, in a confused condition during the previous decades, was reorganized. Land policies were reformulated, and the proprietary charter right of laying out towns was affirmed. In some instances the Penns anticipated the formation of counties by founding towns, as with York and Reading; in others they waited for the assembly to act, as was the case with Carlisle and Easton.

The decisions involved in locating York, Reading, Carlisle, and Easton were serious matters. Situations and sites were carefully considered in the correspondence between the Penns and their surveyors and agents.[41] They clearly stressed situations; centrality within counties, accessibility to Philadelphia, and distance from

other county seats and from Philadelphia were guiding principles.[42]

As for centrality, a principle applied many times in locating
state capitals in the United States, the Penns relied upon their own
sense and inhabitants' petitions.[43] Choosing the point of optimum
accessibility within counties (involving the least aggregate travel
time) would facilitate the movements of people to courts and,
they surmised, would help trade and commerce. Apparently both
the Penns and the inhabitants expected these places to be the
focuses of commerce within counties, which correspond roughly
to trading areas. The Penns also anticipated high profits from the
sale of lots. In most instances in southeastern Pennsylvania the
principle of centrality was observed to a degree (figure 34), but it
had to be reconciled with the second requirement, accessibility to
Philadelphia.

Compromises between these principles were openly discussed in
the correspondence. Thomas Cookson, reporting to Thomas Penn
in 1749 on the site of Carlisle, wrote that "the People will expect
it to be as near Central as may be, but that ye advantage should be
allowed on the Side nearest Market," that is, Philadelphia.[44]
Reading was the only case in which the two factors were easily
reconciled; it was centrally located in Berks County, in the area of
population concentration south of Blue Mountain, and was on the
Schuylkill River and a main road to Philadelphia. Easton was least
centrally located because the Penns emphasized a site with accessibility, at the forks of the Delaware. In 1736, sixteen years before
its founding, they spoke of the transportation advantages of this
place.[45] The sites of Carlisle, as noted above, and York were established toward the eastern sides of Cumberland and York counties
to compensate for greater distances to Philadelphia than in other
counties, the costly and time-consuming crossing of the wide Susquehanna River, and competition from Maryland merchants.
Despite this attempt to point York toward Philadelphia, immediately after York was laid out in 1741 its citizens participated
in the construction of a road to the Chesapeake Bay at Joppa
(figure 35), and Baltimore's rapid rise after 1750 was partly a
consequence of the development of trans-Susquehanna Pennsyl-

vania.[46] This emphasis on accessibility in locating Easton, York, and Carlisle resulted in the establishment or development of Allentown, Bethlehem, Hanover (then called McAllisterstown), Chambersburg, and Shippensburg as important central places and transport centers at major crossroads.

On the distance of new county towns from the metropolis and from one another, all these towns were at least fifty-five miles from Philadelphia, as indicated on the inset of figure 34. Their county's boundaries were at least about forty miles from the city, well beyond a day-long round trip of thirty miles. Wagoners and farmers doubling as haulers were not likely to drive their wagons to Philadelphia frequently. Thus these county towns were not overshadowed as were those nearer the metropolis. The towns were closer to one another than to Philadelphia, but at least twenty-four miles separated them. The shortest trip, from York to Lancaster, was at least as great in cost and time as one from Carlisle to York or from Reading to Lancaster (thirty-two miles) because of the mile-long Susquehanna ferry ride. The county boundaries running between these places marked approximately the limit of a daily thirty-mile return trip and thus also indicated trading areas. Although the Penns were responsible for setting these locations at reasonable distances, the assembly assisted by determining what seem to have been realistic county areas for the population densities at the time.

Although York, Reading, Carlisle, and Easton became the most elegant examples of Thomas Penn's planning, he and his brothers were also responsible for Bedford (1766) and Sunbury (1772). Both had splendid sites, the latter at the forks of the Susquehanna and the former on the Juniata River. Their growth was slow because of sparse hinterland populations. Although their locations were not strictly in the area under study south and east of Blue Mountain, their establishment clearly indicates that the Penns controlled the founding of county towns between 1741 and 1776 and supports the contention that many people expected that such towns would be functionally important.

Between the Revolution and 1813, in response to demands for smaller counties and because the original seats were off-center, the legislature divided all counties except Bucks.[47] None of the new county towns in the back country were laid out by the Penns, who lost the "public" land in 1779, but were chosen from among those already established by others. Chambersburg (1764) and Gettysburg (1780) were selected from among several existing places. Political favoritism may have been involved in these choices, but Thomas Harris was assured of Dauphin County's seat only when he promised land for the courthouse and for state buildings.[48] (The capital of Pennsylvania was moved to Harrisburg in 1812 after resting for thirteen years in Lancaster.) Flourishing Middletown might have become the seat of Dauphin County had the owner of much of the land there shown greater enthusiasm for the project. Middletowners probably regretted his indifference a few years later when they compared the bustle and growth of Harrisburg with their town's slackness (figures 36 and 37).[49] Lancastrians who feared Harrisburg's commercial significance and opposed the new county were wrong in thinking that Lancaster would suffer seriously, since it continued to grow and remained the largest place in the area until after 1820. Nevertheless they were correct in assuming that Harrisburg would flourish as a county seat, particularly because it was located on the Susquehanna.[50] Town founders and others with foresight anticipated growth and prosperity for these later county towns, as the Penns had when they laid out the earlier seats.[51] But Harrisburg excepted, these new towns were probably less significant as generators of economic growth than their counterparts had been earlier.

The expectations of the Penns and others in locating county towns were borne out by population growth. Lancaster and the Penns' towns south and east of Blue Mountain, except Easton, quickly grew to 1,200 or 1,300 persons. Even Easton eventually outstripped other towns in Northampton County (figures 36 and 37). Because of continuing similarities in the proportion of taxpayers in each occupational sector of these county towns (table 23),[52] Lancaster's earlier start apparently gave it the momentum to keep its population ahead of other towns. Less spectacular but sustained growth continued in these places after the first decade.

The growth of these towns delighted the Penns' agents; their letters were optimistic in the early years.[53] Travelers were impressed by the quality of buildings, at least after brick and stone

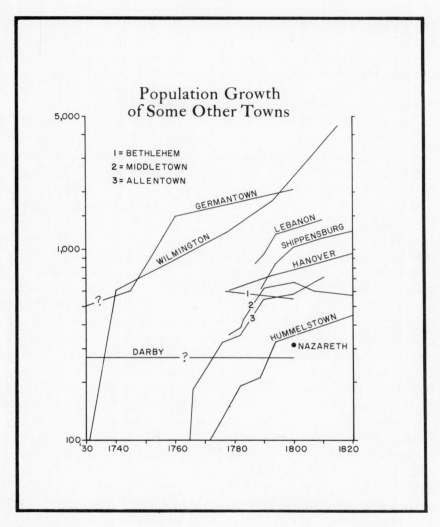

Figure 37

houses began to replace those built of logs. In the early 1760s especially, both private and public buildings were improved.[54] In 1783 Johann Schoepf commented that these market towns were the "object of diligent care," and others compared them favorably with English county seats.[55] Lancaster in particular was praised;

almost invariably it was referred to as the largest inland town in America, and its population was exaggerated.[56]

Postrevolutionary county towns in the developed back country also grew. Harrisburg's rapid growth astonished European travelers and others;[57] the populations of Chambersburg and Gettysburg also increased, but less dramatically (figure 36). County-seat status in the area beyond Philadelphia's dominance appears to have provided towns with the means of acquiring central-place functions of the fourth order.

Political, commercial, craft, and social functions brought rapid early growth and sustained growth later to these county towns south and east of Blue Mountain. The courthouse, situated in most cases in the middle of the central square, was their focal point. The courts met in the spring and fall. Lawyers and recorders of deeds handled changes in land holdings, and litigation was epidemic because of the metes-and-bounds survey system. Tax appeals had to be filed at the courthouse. Rural people who petitioned for new counties were serious when they argued that convenience to courts was important to them.[58]

Unlike the county towns near Philadelphia, in the back country the administrative function stimulated the development of commercial central-place functions. Farmers and shopkeepers from smaller towns dealt conveniently in these places with buyers, retailers, and craftsmen, with stall-holders in the marketplace, and with other farmers at fairs. Although there were proportionately fewer persons engaged in commerce and transport here than in Philadelphia (table 23), many merchants and agents of Philadelphians quickly settled in these towns. In Lancaster, Simon and Levy helped to organize the fur trade and purchased agricultural products. After 1750 Edward Shippen, a prominent Philadelphia merchant, moved to Lancaster.[59] As the chief buyers, retailers, wholesalers, money lenders, and creditors within the county trading areas, these merchants organized a large share of the sale of imports and locally manufactured goods to settlers and farmers and the shipment of grain and flour (the chief products of the area), flaxseed, hemp, livestock, and other commodities to Philadelphia and Baltimore. Some owned mills in the countryside.[60] Although flour was not milled in the towns and did not have to be shipped through the towns (except for Easton and Harrisburg, which became storage and shipping points), traders had to handle the paperwork. As creditors, merchants made advances to farmers and rural and village shopkeepers. The high level of good debts listed in inventories attests to the importance of many merchants.[61]

County towns held markets and fairs, although technically they were prohibited from doing so without borough status.[62] After Wilmington (1740) and Lancaster (1742) received charters, leaders apparently felt for a few decades that towns did not need borough status to function adequately. County commissioners instead of burgesses looked after streets and regulated the markets and fairs.[63] Marketplaces were busy twice a week. Butchers serving the townspeople seem to have been more prominent in them than farmers. In Lancaster, at least, the burgesses were preoccupied with their operations, regulating their handling of meat, protecting their trade and that of shopkeepers from farmers who peddled produce when the market house was closed, and maintaining fair prices by preventing forestalling.[64] As the towns grew, the importance of their markets as a source of income increased for many farmers in Lancaster County and elsewhere, but this was more a consequence than a cause of urban growth.

Semiannual fairs were important before the Revolution, indicating the lack of fully developed trade organizations. At York the spring fair was the time for trading plough horses and milch cows, and at the fall fair the attractions were beef, cattle, butter, cheese, winter milch cows, bacon, hogs, and pork.[65] After 1775 fairs declined in importance, judging by the marked decrease in the number of stalls rented at Lancaster.[66] Although drinking and other misdeeds were the explicit reasons for discontinuing fairs (e.g., Bristol in 1796), the rise of middlemen and, in Lancaster's case, of stockyards was probably the chief reason.[67] Greater demand helped increase the frequency and regularity of farmer-merchant contacts.

Employment in transportation also developed. The county towns were originally located on major roads (figure 35), and growth accentuated their role as transport centers. Although the Lancaster-Philadelphia Turnpike of 1792 was the first major road improvement in the state, the poorer earlier roads were used heavily, and most goods were moved by wagon.[68] Easton's slow early growth was partly the result of limited trade on the Delaware, which eventually increased. Harrisburg became an important unloading point for wheat, flour, whisky, and lumber shipped down the two branches of the Susquehanna.[69] Certainly the taverns, numerous by European standards (at least thirty-eight in Harrisburg by 1795), catered as much to those who moved goods as to visitors on business.[70]

Craft manufacturing emerged in county seats to supply local, county, and even regional markets. In 1754 Thomas Pownall observed that Lancaster was noted for its gunsmiths and saddlers, who were involved in the business of outfitting settlers, soldiers, and transporters.[71] Eventually weaving increased in importance. Production of cloth in twelve months during 1769 and 1770, encouraged by nonimportation agreements, was 27,739 yards in Lancaster. By 1810 output was nine times greater.[72] Reading became renowned for its hats by 1794, and Harrisburg shipped its hats up the Susquehanna.[73] As the towns grew the number of craftsmen increased. But although there were more craftsmen than service people in these towns, industry trailed commerce as a source of income. Much spinning and weaving were done in the countryside, as was most of the flour milling. Dispersed energy sources, small enterprises, a lack of specialization, and severe competition from cheap English goods retarded the development of factories.[74]

Although less obvious than administrative and commercial functions, the social functions of county seats were important. Many inhabitants of counties probably fixed their loyalty on the centers where they thought important decisions were made and big events happened. When Penn's plans for tightly knit townships failed to materialize, local communities were not clearly defined by institutions. In much of the area a diversity of denominational loyalties hindered the development of strong neighborhood communities. With well-defined local communities lacking, the importance of county seats was heightened.[75]

Social institutions, the arts, and architecture reflect this sense of participation in the life of county seats. When Witham Marshe visited Lancaster in 1744 he complained that the people were "wretched sluts and slovens" and that the town was in miserable condition.[76] If he had returned only a few years later he would

have found fire engines, a newspaper, a library, and elegant
churches with regular ministers, unlike many rural congregations.[77] Since their ministers were the most prominent, these
urban churches eventually helped to integrate denominational
bureaucracies throughout the area. Lancaster attracted inventors
like William Henry. By 1760 this town was in many respects a
Philadelphia in microcosm, proud that it could emulate the metropolis. After the Revolution all the county towns had weekly
newspapers that circulated throughout their hinterlands.[78] Town
dwellers were about as affluent as rural folk, another mark of
urban maturity, despite the disparity between incomes of merchants on the one hand and laborers and weavers on the other.[79]

In sum, then, the back-country county towns emerged and grew
because they served their counties as nodal central places next in
rank to Philadelphia. Political, economic, and social functions
were wedded; although commerce was the compelling interest of
many persons, concentration resulted primarily from the location
of courthouses. Manufacturing developed as populations grew and
the area became increasingly complex economically and socially.

Despite the significance of these county seats as central places
and their heightened sophistication, signs of limitation on their
rate of growth and on their functions were apparent. Before 1800
they remained open and loosely built-up in form—large lots with
dairies, gardens, and orchards.[80] The row housing now so characteristic of these places was built later. Land values in Lancaster
were no higher in 1790 than in 1760.[81] Many laborers, from 10 to
20 per cent of taxable town dwellers (table 23), earned a large part
of their income from harvesting hay and grain in the countryside.[82] The rate of specialization in occupations was perhaps
slower than the rate of population growth of towns (table 24).[83]
The populations of county seats continued to grow but declined as
a proportion of the county totals (except for Philadelphia),
staying below 8 per cent (table 25).[84] These indications of circum-
scription were the results of limitations in the economic system
and the continued location of much manufacturing outside towns.

* * *

Only a few towns that were not county seats grew to be fourth-
order central places. Chambersburg, Gettysburg, Allentown, and

Table 24

Degree of Occupational Specialization[a]

Town	Year	Number of Occupations	Persons with Occupations Listed	Average Number of Persons per Occupation
Lancaster	1759	70	404	5.8
	1773	66	398	6.0
	1789	77	501	6.5
	1800	104	724[b]	7.0
Reading	1773	62	244	3.9
	1785	67	331	4.9
	1805	72	451	6.3
York	1783	58	330	5.7
	1800	69	426	6.7
Carlisle	1781	39	189	4.8

Source: Based on data in table 23. See n. 83, chap. 5.

[a]Includes single freemen only with occupations listed.
[b]Includes state government employees.

Table 25

County Seat Populations as Percentage of Total County Populations

	1760	1770	1780	1790	1800
Lancaster	7.1	7.8	6.0	a	a
Reading	7.5	7.7	6.6	7.1	7.4
York	8.0	7.6	5.9	5.4	a
Carlisle	14.5	6.7	5.4	a	a
Chester[b]	1.3	1.2	1.0	a	a

Source: Various, including tax lists, censuses of 1790 and 1800 (see n. 2, chap. 5), and directly from figs. 36 and 11.

[a]Boundary changes preclude accurate assessment.
[b]Estimates; Chester not separated from township data.

Lebanon reached a population of 500 or more (figures 36 and 37) before becoming county seats, the latter two after 1800. All of these places were sufficiently distant from earlier county seats so that when the population increased they could perform as centers of the fourth order. Despite competition from nearby towns they were able to prevail, apparently because of stronger central situations and possibly because of the skill of their merchants. Lebanon, for example, grew more rapidly than neighboring towns even though it had to compete with several of them for trade in the Lebanon Valley. Chambersburg, aside from its central-place functions, became an outfitting point for the trans-Allegheny trade because of its proximity to gaps in the mountains.

Chambersburg, Lebanon, and Gettyburg were among a host of towns (or perhaps most should be called villages) purposely laid out by private persons, most of whom were not well known otherwise (table 22 and figures 34 and 35). To encourage systematic settlement and efficient disposal of land, these places, like the Penns' towns, had a regular form. Some were square, others long street villages that reminded travelers of German and English villages.[85] Most had a market area, either a square, as in Schaefferstown, or a widening of the main street, as in Linglestown. A few, such as Maytown, had central greens. As in county towns, outlots for horses were laid out beyond the limits of house lots, or sometimes a common pasture was provided.

To understand why these places were established some locational and temporal aspects need to be considered. Three were laid out adjacent to Lancaster and one to York as suburbs; eventually they were absorbed into these towns.[86] A few were on navigable streams, notably Middletown and Wilmington. Many were located on main roads along which taverns and hamlets had sprung up. An example was Downingtown; the Downings may have felt that they could gather more transport business by attracting taverns and consequently craftsmen catering to wagoners. Some places, however, were distant from main roads—Maytown and Millersville in Lancaster County, for example.[87] Apparently the founders primarily expected to attract shopkeepers and craftsmen to supply and buy from nearby farmers.

One wonders if central-place functions—that is, the need to control various activities in a trading area—were understood by many developers, since many places were uncomfortably close to one another—for example, McSherrystown and Hanover, Millersville and Lancaster, Stumpstown and Jonestown. Although distances between places varied greatly,[88] the overall pattern was not random; in the Lebanon Valley, in the northern part of present-day Lancaster County, and in western York and Adams counties villages had a definite tendency to cluster. As noted earlier, towns were conspicuously absent in the counties bordering the Delaware River, at least before the Revolution.

This clustering in three back-country areas and the large number of new towns platted between 1755 and 1765 (table 21) point to town-making fever. The Lutheran patriarch Henry Muhlenberg thought that defense against Indian uprisings was the motivation for town building, for the settlers suffered materially from Indian attacks between 1755 and 1758 and again in 1763. More likely, since the French and Indian War brought British military funds into Pennsylvania and its conclusion released optimistic feelings about the future, speculators wanted to take advantage of the freer money and to emulate the Penns' success with county towns. Some promoted their towns by advertisements in newspapers and by the sale of lottery tickets.[89] Even poorer economic conditions after 1760 did not head off the town-building rush until 1765.

Although population growth and improved economic conditions underlay the burst of urban subdividing, why the urge to build was concentrated in only a few areas is not clear. Population densities, agricultural practices, and the quality of land were not significantly different in other parts of the back country.[90] In Lancaster and the Lebanon Valley Mennonite, Lutheran, and Reformed Germans were prominent, but in western York there were many Scotch-Irish. Not only Germans were inhabitants of towns; German neighbors were said to have scoffed at McAllister when he laid out what was later named Hanover, and a majority of founders in all three areas were British.[91] In the older counties the great economic power of Philadelphia seems to have prevented the emergence of some proposed places.[92]

Although the motives for laying out towns are not readily apparent, many that were established did not succeed because their founders failed to recognize their poor situations or because they lacked capital. By 1800 some fourteen towns had achieved populations of between 300 to 500, but about seventy planned towns fell short of 300. Indeed, many probably failed to reach 100 (tables 20 and 26).[93] Third-order status can be assigned to

Table 26

Number of Towns, with Approximate Population, 1800

0–100	6+	400–500	5	800–1,000	0	3,000–4,000	0
100–200[a]	14+	500–600	4	1,000–1,500	5	4,000–5,000	1
200–300	19	600–700	1	1,500–2,000	0	Over 60,000	1
300–400	9	700–800	1	2,000–3,000	5		

Source: Various. See n. 2, chap. 5.

Note: Hamlets and towns in New Castle County excluded.

[a]Inadequate data for 33 other towns (probably less than 200 persons each).

those over 300 but only second-order and even first-order status to places under that. These places (which were sometimes called villages) lacked the specialized craftsmen and merchants who emphasized the collection and wholesaling of goods that fourth-order places and Philadelphia had. They had one or two shopkeepers, a tavern or two, a blacksmith, and some other craftsmen, as well as laborers, some of whom worked on farms part of the time.[94] The stagnation of many of these places can be inferred from the few extant records; in McSherrystown subscriptions for lots were unfilled and many lots taken by others were not sold but passed on to heirs, and in 1782 taxes in most small towns in Lancaster County averaged less than £2 compared with £5 in Lancaster town.[95] Some speculators went into receivership, especially during the late 1760s, a period of foreclosure, because of a shortage of credit. Baron Stiegel, the founder of Manheim and its glassworks and of ironworks nearby, was the most notable failure.[96] Town building was not very profitable for many because they speculated beyond their means and beyond the ability of the mercantile structure to carry so many central places. Despite a revival of townsteading in the 1780s here and there, but particularly near Philadelphia, many of the villages now thickly dotting the Pennsylvania landscape appeared at various times in the next century.

Numerous unplanned hamlets can be considered as central places of the first order, even though many could scarcely be distinguished from the rural countryside. At this level, despite scant evidence, we can identify the hamlet as a settlement where more than one operation existed. A mill, tavern, or shop standing alone or on a farm is thus placed in the open countryside. Moreover, many hamlets were involved chiefly in servicing travelers or were clustered around manufacturing establishments. Taverners and millers, frequently acted as shopkeepers, and mine, forge, or furnace operators often serviced their laborers from company stores.[97] According to Reading Howell's map of 1792, taverns and mills were located every two or three miles along main roads and on permanent streams.[98] On the Lancaster Turnpike there was a tavern approximately every mile.[99] In 1772 there were 139 tavern applications in Lancaster County, one for every 250 persons.[100] Shopkeepers expedited commerce and trade as collecting points in the mercantile network. Hamlets were especially important in Chester, Philadelphia, and Bucks counties and stand out on maps such as Howell's because of a dearth of planned villages in that area. Many, such as New London Crossroads in Chester County around 1800, were assigned post offices,[101] and many of them probably became larger than unsuccessful planned places (figure 35). Downingtown, a milling center and important stopping point for travelers where the Lancaster road crossed the east branch of Brandywine Creek, grew sufficiently to encourage the platting of land about the end of the century.

* * *

Aside from many hamlets, a few towns, some on water and others on roads, became strong links in the transport network. At New Castle pilots boarded ships bound up to Philadelphia. According to tax returns, several men in Chester ran boats to the metropolis.[102] Easton eventually capitalized on its location at the

forks of the Delaware to become a transshipment point. Shippensburg was an early depot for trans-Allegheny trade before it took
on central-place significance, and Hanover was located at a major
intersection, where the Shenandoah-Philadelphia Road (sometimes
called the "Great Philadelphia Road") from York to Frederick and
the Carlisle-Baltimore Road crossed (figure 35). Middletown's
population grew to nearly a thousand as a transfer point for
lumber and wheat sent down the Susquehanna. A large mill was
built there to reduce the bulky wheat to flour and so reduce
shipping costs. After 1785 Middletown failed to grow partly because Harrisburg captured its trade and partly because of the invention of flat boats capable of carrying goods on the Susquehanna during the spring freshets upstream beyond Middletown to
Columbia and down to Havre de Grace on Chesapeake Bay, thus
diffusing trade.[103] In northern Delaware State, Wilmington, Newport, and Christiana Bridge became shipping points. Many Conestoga wagons from southern Lancaster and western Chester
counties traveled the Newport Road to these towns. From them
shallops transferred wheat and flour to Philadelphia. Apparently
this route was cheaper for many than the direct wagon trip to
Philadelphia.[104] Another reason for this direction of the flow of
goods was the concentration of flour mills near Wilmington on
Brandywine Creek.

* * *

Apart from many hamlets that grew up around mills and ironworks, few towns can be classed primarily as manufacturing
centers in this prefactory era. Perhaps Wilmington can be considered as such because of its shipbuilding and milling. The first
Brandywine mills appeared in the 1730s and increased in number
to eight by 1772 and to thirteen by 1795. They probably contributed greatly to Wilmington's growth, helped to secure it borough
status in 1740, and kept it from the atrophy that other towns
suffered under the commercial shadow of Philadelphia.[105] The
mills concentrated here to take advantage of the combination of a
steep stream gradient for power and the tidewater, which elimi-
nated transshipment of loaded barrels. A cotton mill and, after

1800, powder mills were attracted to the site.[106] But initially Wilmington was not so much a manufacturing town as a central place. This seems clear from its site; it was laid out beside Christiana Creek rather than on the Brandywine a mile or so to the north at Brandywine Village, where the mills were located.

Frankford, near Philadelphia, was also a milling center, and dwellers of Kensington worked in shipyards and ropewalks.[107] Nearby Germantown, originally a community of sectarians who sought to be virtually independent politically, capitalized on the weaving skills brought by settlers from Crefeld on the lower Rhine. Germantown cloth came to be well known throughout America, and as the demand increased additional weavers were attracted there. Several mills were located on nearby Wissahickon Creek, including quite early a paper mill.[108] Manufacturing seems to have been Germantown's chief stimulus to growth. Part of the development of the Moravian communities, Bethlehem, Nazareth, and Lititz, resulted from manufacturing. Even more disciplined than the sectarians at Germantown, the Moravians had fostered agricultural self-sufficiency in their communistic "General Economy," but eventually their shops began manufacturing for regional rather than strictly local purposes.[109] County towns, too, gradually developed more and more manufacturing. In Lancaster and Reading, for example, weavers became known for producing cloth and hats.

Nevertheless, processing by and large remained scattered. In 1760 and even toward the end of the century, from 30 to 40 per cent of the rural taxable persons in Lancaster County were non-farmers, although most produced some food for themselves.[110] Besides laborers and a few peddlers of manufactured goods, coopers, blacksmiths, weavers, itinerant tailors, and shoemakers provided services. Distilling was restricted to some affluent farms. Spinning was done by farmers' wives. Flour milling, the most important industry, was scattered because of its dependence on water power, the predominance of small proprietary firms, and the relatively simple labor demands. Although in the latter half of the eighteenth century this region led the seaboard in manufacturing, true industrial towns had to await the use of steam power and the integration of stages of processing under the factory system, with its sharper divisions of labor. Only after 1820 did such factories appear in significant numbers.[111]

* * *

Weld's assertion in 1795 that the population of towns was proportionate to their trade[112] pointed to commerce as the key to understanding the organization of regions. But towns were viable only if they actually could perform as service centers without crowding either one another or their trading areas and if they fitted to some extent into a hierarchical network of centers. The formulation of this theory by Walter Christaller states that there should be a relatively even distribution of towns in the hierarchy with one of the top order, two at the next level, six at the next, and so on. Towns should also be evenly spaced and centered in hexagonal trading areas.[113]

Early Pennsylvania conforms to this model to a degree. We have distinguished a hierarchy of towns based on size and function from the first through the fifth order, though distinctions at lower levels are unclear. Distance and transport costs helped to determine the grid. Fourth-order towns, the back-country county seats, were reasonably equidistant from one another and from Philadelphia.

But several deviations from the model are obvious, especially in the hierarchy of places by size (table 26). Philadelphia far outranked other towns, partly because of its external commercial connections.[114] The metropolis's primacy suppressed urbanization in the region generally and particularly in adjacent counties. Within each county there were few if any middle-sized towns; in counties with a population of, say, 24,000 and a seat of 3,000, the theory calls for two places of 1,500 and six of 750 to ensure an optimum distribution of goods and services. Second- and third-order places also were not evenly spaced; they were absent in some areas and clustered, even crowded, in others (figure 35). In the nineteenth century the pattern would be filled out somewhat with the founding of more towns, but this was not the situation by 1800. Functions other than commerce contributed to the urban pattern. Transport routes, chiefly roads, resulted in a linear pattern of taverns and also of hamlets. Public administration and cultural activities accentuated the primacy of Philadelphia over other

towns and of county seats within their counties. With industrialization in the nineteenth century, city sizes may have become
more evenly distributed along a hierarchical continuum, but the
areal distribution of cities became even less regular.[115]

In spite of an incomplete urban hierarchy, towns contributed
greatly to the economic growth of the region and stability in its
society so that the standard of living rose by 1770 to a point not
finally surpassed until 1830.[116] The metropolis and fourth-order
county seats in the back country were particularly responsible.
Philadelphians tied the region with the Atlantic world, especially
Britain. Back-country merchants kept in touch with Philadelphia
and Baltimore through newspapers, their wagoners, and mail car-
riers. Merchants and some middle-class farmers possessed a strong
sense of involvement in county life, even though these counties
were larger in area than those in the south. The elections of commissioners and sheriffs at large generated considerable interest.[117]
County inhabitants identified with the seats where they did much
business, both legal and commercial. Fairs before the Revolution
contributed to a strengthening of this focus. The counties and
their seats thus compensated for a lack of sharpness in contacts at
the lower scale of everyday community life. Possibly this regional
framework broadened the horizon of rural people. Had they identified more strongly with local communities or townships, as occurred awhile in New England,[118] many might have been less successful farmers.

After the Revolution, Pennsylvania's development was not as
rapid as it had been. Although towns continued to grow, their
increase was not rapid enough to absorb the surplus rural population. On the other hand, some towns may have grown too quickly
at first to provide an adequate standard of living to their lower
class. Philadelphia's merchants seem to have become less capable
of encouraging growth, as is shown by their tardiness in financing
internal transport improvement schemes.[119] The rise of German
newspapers in county towns noted in chapter 1 may indicate that
people felt divided along national lines more than they had previously, a change exploited by politicians such as Benjamin Rush.
Businessmen, however, were not solely responsible for slower development; farmers continued to work much as they had earlier
and had not significantly raised production per acre by 1790.

CHAPTER SIX

General Mixed Farming and Extensive Use of the Land

A majority of early Pennsylvanians were farmers, and many became well off. By contemporary English and modern American standards, however, farmers generally did not exploit the soil extensively or efficiently. As late as 1801, echoing the lament of others, William Strickland claimed that "agricultural knowledge is at the lowest ebb." A quarter of a century earlier the anonymous author of *American Husbandry* asserted that "their system is the first thing that demands attention, because a thousand evils flow from this alone."[1] Although southeastern Pennsylvania was "better cultivated than any other part of America," farm production was lower per acre than it might have been, considering the high quality of much of the soil and the relatively small size of farms.[2] Farmers did not take good care of the soils, crops, and livestock. English and domestic reformers particularly attacked ill-defined rotation schemes and the inadequate use of fertilizer. They also found the techniques of tillage, land clearance, and livestock feeding wanting. To the critics, Pennsylvanians above all lacked the spirit of innovation.[3]

These criticisms failed to recognize that average or above-average farmers found their returns from general mixed farming satisfactory and so felt little incentive to adopt more specialized and intensive kinds of agriculture such as dairying. Economic conditions throughout the century prohibited major changes and encouraged a remarkably stable and uniform type of mixed

[handwritten margin note: Suggests another limitation to L's modernization thesis]

150

farming that involved fairly extensive use or superficial working of the land. In this chapter, then, we will consider the average system of general mixed farming (especially during the latter part of the century): the divers land uses and yields, the techniques that farmers used, and the conditions—notably the labor supply, availability and price of land, patterns of household consumption, local and external markets, and social attitudes—that influenced the farmers' activities. Central to the argument is a comparison of total yields from crops and livestock with household use and sales, which attempts to indicate why farmers were content with their lot and their techniques. In the next chapter we will consider regional variations within this general pattern.

* * *

Farmers used their land to produce a wide range of crops and livestock for home use and for sale. Plowland, meadows, gardens, and orchards yielded crops, and pastures and fallow land provided forage for animals. Wood lots supplied wood for fuel and construction and also were used for grazing. Rock outcrops were sources of construction stone and lime fertilizer. Unfortunately tax lists do not distinguish all of these categories, and other sources, notably newspaper advertisements and travelers, make use of terms that are not always clear.[4] Plowland probably included only fields in crops or being prepared for them. "Pasture" and "fallow" were rarely defined. The former sometimes included meadow and upland pastures that were occasionally worked into rotations but usually were not. Fallow seems to have referred to areas out of cultivation for both short and long terms; the latter apparently reverted to bush. The appearance of bush fallow, together with the girdling of trees as the chief (but slow) means of clearing land and the use of woodland for forage, helped to confound the judgments of foreign visitors who were familiar with a cleaner landscape found in parts of Europe where fields were enclosed by hedges or lines of trees. Because they could not see the system and the proportions of land devoted to various uses clearly, visitors' comments have to be assessed cautiously. Nevertheless, by comparing their impressions with other data we can put forward some esti-

Table 27

Hypothetical Annual Production from an Average Farm of 125 Acres after 1760
in Lancaster and Chester Counties

Crops	Yields per Acre	Acres	Yield
Wheat	10 bu. (1 bu. sown)	8	80 bu.
Rye	12½	2	25
Oats	15	4	60
Barley	15	2	30
Buckwheat	15	2	30 (or green manure)
Indian corn	15	8	120
	Total	26	345 bu.[a]
Flax and/or hemp	150 lb. hackled, 5 bu. seed	2	300 lb., 10 bu.
Potatoes, turnips	100 bu.	3	300 bu.
Fruit	6 bu. per apple tree at 70 trees per acre		
Hay	1½ tons	2	800 bu.
Other vegetables, tobacco	Amounts uncertain	20	30 tons

Livestock	Size (live)	Number	Food Requirements for All Livestock			Yield
			Grain	Hay	Pasture	
Cattle	700 lb.	7:3 cows, 1 steer, 3 calves	100 bu. (13 acres)	20 tons (13 acres)	10–15 acres plus browse in forest and stubble	Meat: 450 lb. (1 carcass dressed) Dairy: milk, 300 gal.; cheese, butter
Horses	1,000 lb.	3–4:1 young	80 bu. (5 acres)	9 tons (6 acres)	3 acres, etc.	Plowing, road transport
Swine	175 lb.	8	30 bu. (2 acres)		Yes plus mast	Meat: 500–600 lb. dressed (4–5 carcasses)
Sheep	50 lb.	10:2 young (fall)	5 bu. (1/3 acre)	1 ton	1 acre	30 lb. wool
Poultry	. . .	. . .	. . .	. . .	. . .	Meat, eggs
Bees	. . .	1 or 2 hives	. . .	. . .	. . .	Honey, pollinated clover, etc.
			Total 215 bu.	30 tons		

Source: Various. See n. 86, chap. 6.

[a]Of which 30 bu. for seed and 215 for animals.

mates on the types and production of crops and livestock, their uses, and the kinds of land uses (table 27).

"Wheat is the grand article of the province. They sow immense quantities . . . ," exclaimed the anonymous author of *American Husbandry* in 1775.[5] He had little need to stress the point; as early as 1700 James Logan asserted that "wheat [was] the farmer's dependence," and in 1728 a German diarist wrote that "wheatbread is eaten in almost all places."[6] In the early 1780s in twenty townships, most of them near the Delaware River, the average farmer sowed only slightly less wheat than he had in the fall of 1759.[7] Other evidence indicates that wheat continued to be Pennsylvania's key crop. Wheat products clearly furnished the citizens' tables more than other grains (table 28), and flour, bread, and wheat composed the largest element in the region's foreign trade.[8]

Despite the great importance of wheat, yields per acre were low. From newer land twenty, thirty, or even forty bushels per acre were reported; but abundant comments suggest that five to twelve bushels was all that could be expected on old land.[9] Around 1750 Aaron Leaming, an affluent resident of Cape May County, New Jersey, thought eight bushels per acre was a good harvest. David Shultze of Montgomery County threshed out five to eight bushels from one bushel sown per acre, and in Chester County arithmetic workbook calculations were based on six bushels.[10] Three Chester County farmers estimated their losses to British troops, who foraged through their area in 1777, on the basis of ten, twelve, and fifteen bushels per acre.[11] In such circumstances we would hardly expect them to underestimate these figures. In 1790 six to eight bushels were though common near Philadelphia. According to a correspondent of George Washington, fifteen bushels were general on limestone soils in York and Cumberland valleys (York and Franklin counties), twelve to seventeen on red shales north of York, and ten to twelve in the poorer "barrens" in southern York. (This reporter asserted that forty to fifty bushels were known in Lancaster County. Did he hold a romantic view of the land across the Susquehanna and the Mennonites?)[12] Travelers late in the century usually recorded yields of ten to twenty bushels.[13] John

Table 28

Needs of an Average Family (Based Primarily on
Goods and Money Specified for Widows in
a Sample of Wills of Farmers, 1740-90)

Item	Frequency in Wills	Average Allotment in Wills	Family (×5)
Pork	84	101.8 lb.	500 lb.
Beef	58	51.3 lb.	250 lb.
Mutton	0		
Eggs	2[a]		
Butter	1[b]		
Wheat	116	13.2 bu.	60 bu.
Rye	58	5.4	25
Barley and malt	17	3.8	20
Oats	11	9.0	45
Buckwheat	6	4.8	20
Indian corn	13	6.3	30
			200
			+90[c]
			290 bu.
Potatoes	3[d]		
Turnips	3[d]		
Cabbage	5[d]		
Apples	68		
Cider	49	2.4 bbl.	10 bbl.
Liquor, various	23		
Beehives	2		
Flax	42 ⎫	¼-½ acre, or	
Hemp	17 ⎬	10-20 lb. hackled	50-100 lb.
Flax/hemp/tow	35 ⎭		
Wool/sheep	74	6 lb. or 2 fleeces	30 lb.
Hay	9		
Meadow, use	6	¼-3 acres	
Horses, use	1	Often	
Money, annual	59	£7.7	£40
Money, lump sum	24	£114	

Source: Register of Wills Offices, Lancaster and Chester counties.

[a] Use of chickens cited frequently.

[b] Use of one or two cows usually.

[c] Addition to compensate for underendowment of grain. Widows' sons presumably fed some livestock and provided some seed from their granaries. See text and table 27.

[d] Use of garden often.

Beale Bordley, the dean of agricultural reformers, stated in 1792 that six to twelve bushels was most common, but where wheat rust and the larvae of the Hessian fly had attacked the yield was frequently less than five.[14] In 1759 and in the early 1780s an average farm of 125 acres, at least in Chester and Lancaster counties, produced sixty to eighty bushels of wheat on eight to ten acres (table 27).[15] Farmers sowed lightly usually one bushel per acre, and reaped lightly. Pleas were voiced to buy improved seed from other areas (and thus enrich what today would be called the gene pool), to rotate crops, and to fertilize grain fields, but before 1800 few farmers sought to improve wheat yields.[16]

Rye was an important fall-sown crop, but "far more wheat is grown than rye," observed the German diarist in 1728.[17] In a sample of estate inventories, rye in storage usually amounted to between 15 and 50 per cent of the total for wheat. In the 1777 inventories of military losses by Chester farmers, rye was listed at 2,324 bushels, or about a quarter of the wheat inventory of 9,062 bushels.[18] Although when wheat prices were high farmers sometimes ate rye bread to increase their incomes, the amount of wheat flour consumed among Mennonites, at least, was apparently significantly higher than that of rye flour (table 28).[19] Had the Germans as well as the Scotch-Irish not distilled it into whisky, less rye might have been grown.[20] On the average farm of 125 acres perhaps ten acres was devoted to winter grain and two of this to rye.

Spring grains, oats, barley, buckwheat, and Indian corn were grown on most farms. Oats was the most significant of the spring grains introduced from Europe. In Chester the farmers' claims against the British troops for oats were twice those for rye and nearly half as much as for wheat. This amount represented the production of four or five acres on an average farm at yields of ten to fifteen bushels per acre.[21] The great number of horses in Pennsylvania, generally three or four per farm, was the major reason for the substantial production of oats. Just as no evidence is available on whether Germans preferred rye for bread, nothing shows that the Scotch-Irish preferred oats for either bread or porridge. Barley was not widely grown because "sufficient encouragement has not been given to raise it."[22] Even though many Germans lived in the area, not much beer was brewed. Rye whisky, cider, and rum seem to have been drunk more frequently.[23] Buckwheat was fairly common yet was grown in small amounts. Often plowed under as green manure and a catch crop, it was generally consumed by the least affluent. Henry Muhlenberg sympathetically noted that when buckwheat failed "it is hard for the poor."[24]

Despite Peter Kalm's fine report on maize, we need to know more about its production and uses. In the nineteenth century the amount of corn grown far exceeded that of wheat.[25] Kalm observed in 1750 that it was grown in little fields on nearly every farm, but the author of *American Husbandry* thought it was neglected in Pennsylvania compared with New England and the South because of a commercial bias in favor of wheat. The war claims of Chester farmers list only 650 more bushels of corn than of rye, yet in nine cases an average of the production from six acres was reported. Other evidence would suggest that up to ten acres was common, but we really do not know.[26]

Maize tended to be more productive than other grains, particularly when sown on new land. In 1714 a letter to Wales emphasized the copious corn yields, saying, "which graine produced more increase than any other Graine whatsoever." Others thought that returns of twenty to thirty bushels were common, but in the 1790s Morse estimated fifteen as the average.[27] The practice, adopted from the Indians, of planting in hills rather than in rows may have restricted yields.[28] Squirrels fancied corn and reduced harvests. Around 1750 in Lancaster County a concerted attempt to protect corn by placing bounties on squirrels' heads was a boon to the poor. But it was too costly for the county treasury to maintain, so both the poor and the squirrels remained.[29]

Humans, except the poor, directly consumed corn sparingly (table 28).[30] Most farms, however, possessed from five to ten hogs. Undoubtedly the "corn belt" practice of feeding corn to them, and also to cattle and sheep, was initiated before the mid-eighteenth century here and probably in other areas on the eastern seaboard.[31]

Small acreages of a number of other crops were planted. Flax (*Linum usilatissimum*) and, to a lesser extent, hemp (*Cannabis sativa*) were prominent sources of fiber and oil. In 1747 Franklin claimed that Pennsylvania was "a great country for flax" and possessed many oil mills. Tax returns apparently do not show all of them; in 1759 only five were reported in Lancaster and, in 1782, six in Chester (table 34). During the middle 1730s seed became an important export to northern Ireland. For domestic use a half century later flax was considered as essential as wheat.[32] Most plots of flax seem to have amounted to one-half to two acres.[33] The planting of hemp was officially encouraged from time to time, but in general it never became as important a crop as flax.[34]

Horticultural crops were ubiquitous. "Scarce an house but has an apple, peach, and cherry orchard," one letter reported.[35] A German servant commented that Pennsylvania was altogether unlike his homeland, where few orchards were planted, and a Scotsman who settled in Franklin County in 1770 was likewise impressed: "We who are Country people used always to think it a great matter that the gentlemen in Scotland had orchards."[36] Newspaper advertisements in the 1720s recorded orchards of from 200 to 400 trees, and one writer said that an orchard of 50 trees was small.[37] Probably 100 to 150 trees per farm were common. Assuming 60 to 70 trees per acre, the average farm had approximately two acres devoted to fruit crops. Yields of apples averaged from four to ten bushels per tree, and two or three trees provided apples for one barrel of cider. Dried fruit and brandy as well as cider were produced for home use, and hogs ate large numbers of waste peaches and apples in August and September.[38]

Vegetables were grown on most farms. Potatoes and turnips were fed to animals, but in far smaller quantities than in eighteenth-century Europe.[39] The earliest known reference to potatoes was made in 1683 and to turnips in 1724.[40] Potatoes were produced with maize in newly occupied areas by 1733, in one instance at least, and the frequency of their production probably increased, for by 1800 they were grown "in great plenty on every farm."[41] Fewer turnips were raised because the hot summers did not favor their growth and they required more labor than did grain. Acreages were small for both: claims in 1777 against the British in Chester County averaged one-half to two acres of potatoes.[42]

For forage and hay, farmers produced a great variety of grasses and legumes as well as using forest browse, mast (nuts), fruit, pumpkins, and flaxseed cakes. Bluegrass, white and red clover, timothy, presumed by some as native to New England, and other grasses were introduced from Europe. These crops were quite important, since for cattle "ye country grass is very rough and course [sic] in hand as most things by nature" while "English hay does very kindly, especially white honey suckle [white clover]."[43] Before 1700 bluegrass (especially *Poa pratensis*) and white "Dutch" clover (*Trifolium repens*) appeared both spontaneously and under cultivation.[44] The general phrase "English grass" occurred in farm advertisements in the 1720s but not later, apparently because growth of these grasses and legumes had become so widespread. In the 1730s the sowing of clover was reported in some backward parts of Chester County. Nevertheless white clover did best on limestone soils and would not grow spontaneously on depleted soils.[45]

Red clover (*T. pratense*) was even more difficult to handle and may have been a later arrival from Europe. In 1723 red clover seed was advertised in Philadelphia, and in 1754 a Chester County farmer requested some from Lancaster County, since it was not grown nearby. The next year William Logan, an experimenting gentlemen farmer, wrote to Jared Eliot in Connecticut that "we are getting into it fast." Five years later Logan, too, received seed from Lancaster County. In 1790 red clover was reported from New Castle County, near Carlisle and the Chester Valley.[46] Nevertheless, one traveler at the time said it was grown only around Philadelphia, whereas in Northampton the Germans were "only beginning" to sow it and in York it was referred to as a "valuable new article, CLOVER."[47] These references would seem to suggest that red clover was only spottily grown before 1790, even though bees were available for pollination. Toward the end of the century the incorporation of clover into rotation schemes and the extensive use of gypsum may have encouraged its wider use.[48]

Timothy (*Phleum pratense*) was apparently well known as a crop by 1750, since Franklin, who knew little about agriculture, rebuked Eliot for sending the seed of "mere" timothy, or "Herd's

Grass," to him. But the earliest explicit reference to timothy in 1740 may indicate that it had not been around long.[49] Although this grass was able to grow without man's help, it apparently was not spontaneous everywhere; in 1770 a grazier of horses beyond Blue Mountain was told by his landlord "not to neglect getting the timothy seed if you Ride a Hundred Miles for it." This order also points to its value, and in 1790 it was asserted that "the oecumenical use of the grass is universally known."[50]

The production of hay varied greatly. One observer reported 400 pounds per acre from one poor area but another 8 tons, undoubtedly an exaggeration. In 1790 in York County a correspondent of Washington's stated that 2 tons of timothy and 1½ tons of clover per acre could be made on the first cutting, 1 ton of clover on the second.[51] These averages referred to limestone land on which clover probably did particularly well, if today's yields are an indication (table 10). Production then was probably generally lower, perhaps 1½ tons per acre or 30 tons from twenty acres of meadow on the average farm.[52]

Almost all farmers raised livestock. More families owned cattle than owned other animals. Even many town dwellers, widows, and laborers kept one or two cows. Farmers kept more horses here than elsewhere in the colonies, but fewer oxen. Sheep were found on fewer farms than were cattle and horses. Swine apparently were everywhere, as were fowl and bees. Enough information is available to consider breeds, numbers, and feed requirements of cattle, horses, sheep, and hogs, as well as yield and consumption from these four animals.

In 1750 Peter Kalm claimed that most cattle were of Swedish ancestry. Actually little is known of their pedigrees. Undoubtedly the Swedes sold cattle to the early Quakers, but similar types were probably imported. The motley variety of colors of animals advertised around midcentury in newspapers suggests different breeds.[53] Increased concern for breeding became apparent toward the end of the century; in 1770 "a likely young bull of the English breed" was advertised, and after the Revolution the names Sussex old red, Suffolk polled, shorthorn or "Teeswater," and Devon appeared frequently.[54] Although reformers became more interested in better breeds, emulating Coke of Derby and others in England, the average farmer apparently was little affected by such developments before the end of the century.

Functional distinctions among cattle apparently came slowly. Early in the century the record refers to all-purpose "neat" cattle. By 1750 however, "milch," "beef store," "fat steer," "oxen," and "bullocks" were specified in various sources. Dairy cattle undoubtedly continued to be slaughtered for meat, and oxen may have been much more important in early years than later. In 1782 the return for Upper Darby reported only 20 oxen compared with 247 cattle and 149 horses.[55] This tax list contains one of the few explicit references to oxen.

Except for the first two decades, when the rapid growth of Philadelphia placed excessive demands on the supply,[56] farmers usually kept sufficient cattle for their own needs and produced a small surplus for markets. Few complained of shortages in later years. Indeed, in 1747 farmers in Chester and Lancaster counties protested to the legislature on the great number of cattle being driven from Virginia.[57] Again in 1783, Schoepf, discussing imports of "black" cattle from Carolina, said that "the Pennsylvania farmer squints at this business because he himself raises enough cattle to overstock the market."[58]

The number of cattle at various times can be estimated roughly. Estate inventories from Chester and Lancaster counties for various years between 1713 and 1790 (table 29) suggest that farms generally held from 7 to 10 cows, nearly 50 per cent of which were young. Tax lists cite only those over three years of age, so averages from these lists are lower—in 1773 for the whole of southeastern Pennsylvania about 29 per hundred persons and in 1760 and 1782 in Lancaster and Chester counties about 3½ per farm.[59] Adding 50 per cent for the young, the average farm in these two counties kept 6 or 7 cows, about the same as in eastern Massachusetts and Virginia but possibly fewer than in North Carolina.[60] Large herds were not common.

Even toward the end of the century Europeans complained about the small size and low yields of meat and dairy products from American cattle, notwithstanding the "fat animal craze" that

Table 29

Average Number of Livestock in a Sample of 207 Inventories,
Chester and Lancaster Counties

Period	Inv.	No. of Cattle	% of Young	Inv.	No. of Horses	% of Young	Inv.	No. of Swine	Inv.	No. of Sheep	% of Young
1713–16	22	8.6	58	26	6.0	21	9	9.7	11	15.6	9
1728–37[a]	72	9.6	56	80	6.7	33	32	8.9	42	12.0	5
1750	27	8.3	57	35	3.8	22	14	6.7	22	12.3	8
1761	74	9.3	39	71	4.2	22	59	5.8	53	12.3	4
1772	38	9.4	47	41	3.9	19	33	7.3	33	14.9	6
1783	60	7.2	46	58	4.2	20	39	8.6	40	10.5	9
1790	28	8.9	38	23	3.3	13	21	7.4	17	12.4	6

Source: Register of Wills Offices, Lancaster and Chester counties.

[a]Chester, 1730–31.

captivated some affluent farmers.[61] Data are not plentiful for sizes
or quality. In the early 1730s William Pim of Chester County
slaughtered nine cattle, cows, steers, and oxen, all probably about
six or seven years of age. Their dressed weight ranged from 337 to
507 pounds, so their live weight would have been from 600 to
1,000 pounds.[62] Assuming the average dressed carcass to have
weighed 450 pounds, 250 pounds would have been consumed at
home (table 27) and the remainder would have been available for
sale. In several of these cattle the forequarters were larger than the
hindquarters, a condition deplored by the reformer Bordley sixty
years later. During the "craze" in 1774 a fat steer named Roger
dressed at 1,678 pounds, and Jefferson, in response to
European critics of American beasts, mentioned steers of 1,800
and 2,500 pounds and some calves' quarters that dressed at 64 to
72 pounds. Because Bordley wanted to improve breeds for ordinary farmers, he lamented this penchant for size among affluent
breeders and so bred smaller cattle.[63]

Dairy production was low by modern standards. A cow that
gave 4 quarts of milk a day was considered very good, but perhaps
1 quart was more common. On an average farm, if each cow
yielded a quart or so and two were producing at a time, the supply
would have been 2 or 3 quarts per day, or no more than 300
gallons per year. No estimates were available for the length of dry
periods. Apparently 2 gallons, or a third of a week's production,
was needed to produce enough fat for a pound of butter, and 1
gallon yielded a pound of cheese.[64] Most of the dairy produce
probably was used at home.

The generally small size and poor quality of cattle resulted not
from lack of feed but from lack of concern about feed quality and
care. Travelers and new settlers were displeased with the handling
of cattle by Americans. In 1794 Parkinson saw half-starved cattle,
many with "hollow-horn," an infection of the sinuses induced by
cutting horns too short. Random breeding among cattle fending
for themselves in the open did not produce improved offspring. In
the 1680s the Swedes were said to let thin cattle run in the woods
in all seasons "so that they derive little profit from them," and in
1724 Christopher Sauer remarked that few stables had been constructed.[65] Although stables appeared without doubt by 1790 and

stall-fed cattle even by 1760, as late as 1769 Edward Shippen, speaking of the area immediately adjacent to Lancaster, complained that trees would

decay and be blown down and the Ground left bare at Last; unless young wood grow up in their places; but the Succession is never to be expected on Land adjoining Towns and Citys, where there are great quantities of Cattle browsing all the season of the Twelve Months.[66]

Thus even near Lancaster, which was set in the midst of the rich Lancaster Plain, German farmers apparently were little concerned either with the forest or with their cattle. This helped to keep cattle in a low state of productivity.

Given six or seven cattle (half of which were under three years of age) averaging 700 or 800 pounds, acreages on the average farm to support them can be estimated (table 27): ten acres of meadow to supply 15 tons of hay, seven acres of grain to provide 100 bushels of grain, ten to fifteen acres of pasture, fifteen to twenty acres to fallow land, and twenty to twenty-five acres of woodland for browse.[67]

In eighteenth century Pennsylvania, horses were overwhelmingly more important than oxen for hauling wagons and plowing, even though in 1790 a working horse was worth more than a yoke of oxen or two good cows.[68] In 1773 there were twice as many horses per person in Pennsylvania as in eastern Massachusetts and probably proportionately more than in most other areas in America and even in Europe. In the Shenandoah Valley, as much an extension of Pennsylvania as a part of Virginia because it was settled from the north, the average farm had as many. From the early years, careful horse breeding was encouraged. Laws were passed to reduce uncontrolled breeding. In 1724, for example, stallions over eighteen months were not to run at large unless they were at least thirteen hands tall and of "comely proportions."[69] Stud horses were imported during the first years of the colony and from time to time afterwards. Later, affluent farmers kept records of their studs' services and advertised them in newspapers. In 1774, between April and July, according to the diary of Richard Barnard, his horse served forty-two mares. Shortly thereafter a horse named "Pennsylvania Farmer" was advertised as ready at Clark's in Lampeter Township, Lancaster County.[70]

Presumably the ill-defined "Conestoga" and other types emerged from these breeding activities. The famous Conestoga supposedly dominated the local scene until replaced by Percherons in the 1840s.[71] European travelers, told that they were "fine horses" by Americans, thought they were strong but "ill-shaped large clumsy horses" that stood fourteen to seventeen hands high.[72] Germans of Lancaster County on Conestoga Creek have been credited with the Conestoga's development, but there are no references to "Conestoga" horses in the literature of the time. The term may have been derived from the wagon dubbed "Conestoga" by Philadelphians, who early identified that particular area with the back country. To further cast the matter in doubt, "Conestoga" wagons were referred to as "Dutch," "Irish," "road," and, in Lancaster County, "Philadelphia."[73]

Because of the greater capital expense, fewer horses than cattle were raised in the area, and not as many persons owned horses.[74] In 1760, according to tax lists, there were 2.44 horses per farm in Lancaster and Chester counties (figures 46 and 47). An inventory sample averages 4½, with 15 to 25 per cent of the sample colts under three years of age (table 29). Although the data for early years are exaggerated by the inclusion of inventories of horse traders who lived on the frontier,[75] the wealthier farmers, perhaps a third of the total, probably owned 4 adult horses. This was the minimum number needed to haul a wagon with a capacity of a ton or more over the long trips to Philadelphia, Baltimore, or Newport and Brandywine Creek in northern Delaware. Burnaby's frequently quoted 1759 figure of 9,000 wagons, one for every twenty persons or every four families, conveys the importance of horses in early Pennsylvania. If an average farmer owned 3 horses, he needed eighty bushels of grain, especially oats, from six acres; hay, especially timothy, from three acres; and three acres of pasture, as well as fallow land and woodland, to feed them generously (table 27).[76]

Swine were almost certainly common, and twice as much pork as beef was consumed in the home (table 28), but the extant record supplies surprisingly little information on them. Although "Chiney," Guinea, Berkshire, and Wiltshire breeds were mentioned after the Revolution and reformers experimentally crossed them, Parkinson at the end of the eighteenth century described American razorbacks with long snouts as the most common type and inferior to the English varieties.[77] Because of a desire for fat meat, hogs were not as small by today's standard as were cattle and sheep. Between 1750 and 1790 Shultze in his farm diary recorded the slaughter of twenty-five hogs yielding 134 pounds average dressed weight, ranging between 82 and 250 pounds. Just after the Revolution a Chester County farmer described a "big white" at 304 pounds and others at 286, 225, 224, 204, and 60 pounds. Bordley complained that farmers catered too much to laborers who wanted fat pork and so raised hogs of several hundred pounds. He grew smaller animals by crossing Chinese and American whites and killing them at eighteen months, when they weighed only 160 to 200 pounds.[78]

Inventories provide the only systematic data on the number of hogs. Apparently most farms kept between five and ten (table 29), and the maximum is thirty. A decline in average numbers throughout the century is suggested by table 29, yet this seems unlikely. The inadequacy of the sample precludes a final judgment.

An average farmer owning eight hogs averaging 175 pounds live weight would have required about thirty-two bushels of grain, especially maize, besides mast from oak and beech woods and pasture (table 27). By 1740 maize was fed to swine and the "corn belt" system was foreshadowed. When prices were low for wheat, however, this grain was given to pigs in some areas despite protests by the frugal-minded.[79]

Compared with parts of England and eastern Massachusetts, Pennsylvania's stock of sheep per farm was small.[80] According to tax returns in 1759, fewer than half the taxpayers in Chester and Lancaster counties kept sheep, and the number of sheep per farm averaged about seven with a range of from five to eleven. In 1782 averages were slightly higher.[81] Inventories of better farms report an average of thirteen (table 29). There were few large flocks; in 1759 only eleven farmers in Lancaster and four in Chester owned more than twenty-five sheep.

Gentlemen farmers sought to improve breeds for wool, which was in greater demand than was mutton (table 28). Even though by 1770 Merinos were found in Chester County, major improvements came only after 1800. Some commentators blamed the Pennsylvania weather for the poor quality and small size of sheep; hot, humid summers and cold winters were inimical to their health. Others asserted, however, that farmers sold their best animals to the butcher and thus kept poorer breeders.[82]

Sheep were generally small and little food was allowed for them. If the average farm had ten sheep averaging fifty pounds and about 10 per cent of these were young, only about four bushels of grain, including maize from one-quarter of an acre, a half-ton of hay from one-third of an acre, and an acre of pasture, besides fallow, woodland, and fence rows, would be a sufficient food supply (table 27).[83]

Poultry and bees should be mentioned. Chickens, geese, turkeys, "dunghill" fowl, and even Muscovy ducks were found on farms. Widows' dowers cited in wills frequently mentioned chickens (table 28). Undoubtedly Pennsylvanians used these for food in substantial but unknown quantities. For Christmas, turkeys may have been preferred.[84] Bees, the "Englishman's flies" to natives, were common. Some farms had as many as six or eight hives, and four, nine, and ten swarms were mentioned in Shultze's farm diary.[85] Sufficient bees were probably available to pollinate clover, but like so many other details of agriculture the record does not inform us. Nevertheless, in sum, this survey shows that the average farm yielded a substantial and wide variety of produce.

* * *

The acreages needed to produce the various requirements we have traced for the average farm of 125 acres would have been perhaps 26 acres in grain; 8 or 9 in flax and/or hemp, roots, other vegetables, fruit, and tobacco; 13 of meadow for hay; 20 for pasture; 3 for the farmstead; and the remaining 55 to 60 acres in fallow and woodland (table 27). We cannot easily confirm the figures for this tentative construct. The land in crops, 35 acres, does come very close to the average of twelve cases specified in farm advertisements, which nevertheless reveal wide variations. In advertisements meadowland averaged 13 acres, but this also varied considerably from case to case.[86]

Woodland acreages are also indefinite. According to tax returns in 1759, the amount of cleared land per taxpayer averaged about 52 acres in Chester County and about 40 acres in Lancaster.[87] This would suggest 75 and 95 acres respectively in woodland on farms averaging 125 to 135 acres. The amount of uncleared land before and after 1760 can be calculated only approximately. In 1715 in Thornbury Township, Chester County, only 18 per cent of assessed land was cleared; by 1760 in a nearby area the figure was 40 per cent.[88] This represents an increase of about 0.5 per cent of cleared land each year. If this rate is applied in the period after 1760, by 1790 about 60 per cent, or 75 acres, would have been cleared, leaving 50 acres uncleared on the average farm in that area of Chester County.

Comments of residents and other data suggest that these calculations exaggerate the amount of uncleared land or of woodland. In 1771 Muhlenberg, who lived twenty-five miles northwest of Philadelphia, regretted that he had sold his woodlot of forty acres because "wood is becoming scarce in these parts." Rental agreements specified that only a certain amount of land was to be cleared.[89] As early as 1740, some complained that squatters and others were selling or destroying timber. In the 1790s only 15 per cent of what was termed a typical farm in Bucks County was woodland.[90] Near Philadelphia some travelers commented on the barrenness of the land. By 1775 firewood was brought down the Delaware to the city, and Shippen's complaint about heavy sylvan grazing near Lancaster implies an impending shortage of wood near larger urban centers.[91] Finally, in sixteen Chester County townships only 21 per cent of the area was assessed as "woodland" as distinct from "uncleared" in 1764.[92] Perhaps, then, a more realistic estimate for uncleared land or woodland in 1790 would be twenty-five acres, or 20 per cent, in long-settled areas beyond the immediate environs of the metropolis and other towns.

Acreages of fallow and upland pasture are particularly difficult to assess. Some cleared land apparently reverted to woodland from time to time. In 1801 Pearson observed tracts of saplings on fertile limestone soils between Lancaster and the Susquehanna, and nineteenth century historians spoke of "grubenland."[93] The presence of these sapling lands may indicate that farmers practiced some kind of shifting cultivation with long fallows. If so, this would account for the large proportion of uncleared land in tax lists and also for the large acreages left over after taking into account plowland, meadow, and pasture. The figure for upland pasture, twenty acres, is likewise conjectural since there is no clear data. All that can be said with certainty is that of land not in crops or meadow, some was in grass, stubble, rubbish fallow, long fallow that was reverting to woodland, and woodland.

The very lack of data suggests a lack of concern over systematic and careful use of land and supports a contention that land was extensively rather than intensively used. This extensive agriculture can be seen more clearly by considering farmers' land practices directly.

* * *

Careless and poorly developed rotation patterns, failure to apply fertilizer properly, if at all, and superficial tillage are the clearest direct signs of extensive use of the land. Reformers were undoubtedly incorrect in many of their prescriptions because they often followed English farming models uncritically and failed to recognize the unique environmental and economic conditions in Pennsylvania. They did recognize, however, that too few farmers tried to achieve optimum relationships between livestock and the land.[94]

Under the "old American system" of rotation, as it was called in 1797 by a Chester County farmer,[95] two phases were distinguished: (1) an initial pattern and (2) a three-field or four-field pattern with fallow representing a cycle of three or four years, after farmers no longer cleared "fresh" land on their farms.

In the first phase the procedure seems to have been to sow corn, hemp, flax, or even hops and to plant potatoes to "reduce the first fatness" of the soil for subsequent sowing of wheat, which would run to straw if the land was too rich.[96] Later, spontaneous crops of white clover were often followed by several years of wheat, but if grain was sown year after year the soil began to "run out." Then noxious European plants like garlic (*Allium vincale*) and St. John's wort (*Hypericum* sp.) replaced clover. Eventually old fields were left in rubbish fallow for from five to seven years or even ten years.[97]

Within this long rotation cycle a shorter sequence of three or four years developed; in areas where less land was available it superseded the long pattern, inaugurating the second phase.[98] Even by midcentury some tenant agreements insisted that winter grain could not be sown more than once every three or four years and that one field had to be left fallow and the other one or two fields in spring grain.[99] Yet such a sequence inevitably failed to maintain soil quality and, with deterioration of seed, resulted in low grain yields.

Newspaper advertisements indicate that more fields were gradually entering rotation schemes.[100] Although Bordley remarked that most farms had between two and five fields, in 1789 Tilton reported from New Castle County that, despite "no established mode of farming," six-field rotations were the most approved: a year each for wheat, barley, and Indian corn, followed by three fallow years; or two years of wheat, one of fallow, one of corn, and two more of fallow.[101] Yet with grains the dominant crops, an increase in the number of fields was not itself enough to increase yields per acre.

Grass and clover were needed in rotations to improve productivity. By 1650 or soon after, fallows sown with grass and clover had become common in England. Many Pennsylvanians must have been aware of the development, but they were slow to follow England's example. Even where bluegrass, white clover, and timothy were sown, the purposes seem to have been to create "permanent" upland pasture and to seek better yields for marsh meadows, not to improve the land for other crops. Farmers who did sow clover on depleted grain lands were disappointed with the results, and so rubbish fallow too easily persisted.[102]

Not until after 1750 did farmers employ new rotation schemes involving clover or grasses, and apparently they were not common even among better farmers until the 1780s. In 1761 a Chester

County farmer in his diary noted the plowing of his upland meadow, which implies rotation with grass. Schoepf described in 1783 a very simple six-field pattern used near Philadelphia that apparently emphasized the fattening of livestock: corn, wheat, and four years of "English grass." In Darby Township fifteen years later this was the general pattern on seven fields (table 30).[103] Other rotation schemes placed more stress on grain production, as in Cazenove's record for the Great Valley (items 5, 6, and 7 in table 30).[104] Notable in these schemes, besides the obvious lack of roots, is that barley appears more frequently than seems indicated by other data and that buckwheat was frequently used as a catch crop or as a cover crop for clover or was plowed under as manure. In any case, "quick renewals of clover in entire fields [were] coming into practice" in rotation on a greater number of fields than previously; indeed, near Philadelphia clover had given "many old farms . . . a new appearance."[105]

Gentlemen farmers and travelers generally were dissatisfied with the emphasis on grain, even though improvements were finally appearing. Impressed by the virtues of the Norfolk system of "Turnip" Charles Townshend, in 1784 Bordley advocated the general use of root crops, especially turnips and potatoes, and also the inclusion of peas and beans in rotation. The Philadelphia Society for Promoting Agriculture offered prizes for courses including roots and pulses.[106] These advocates of reform failed to recognize that American conditions differed from those in England. Pulses and roots would not grow well during the hot summers, and they required greater inputs of labor than were usually available in Pennsylvania. Reformers similarly argued against sowing wheat, which remained Pennsylvania's chief export. Farmers responded more to market conditions than their would-be saviors, even though they were content with low yields and a sloppy landscape. Tightly regulated rotation schemes were feasible only where fattening and dairying were greater sources of income than wheat. By 1790 farmers were beginning to stress livestock in some areas, but even in these places corn instead of roots was grown for feed, and Bordley himself had to concede that it was undoubtedly a better crop considering American conditions (item 8, table 30).[107]

Table 30

Rotation Schemes Reported in the 1790s

Area		Years/Fields					
	1	2	3	4	5	6	7
Chester Co.							
Darby Tp.	Corn	Wheat	Wheat	Clover	⟵———— "English Grass"		...
Birmingham Tp.	Cn	Barley, Oats, Flax	W, Rye		Cl	...	...
E. Bradford Tp.	Cn, Pot, Pumpkins	By	Cl	W	W, BW		...
Lancaster Plain	Cn, O	W, R / By (winter)	Cl or BW	Cl	Cn		...
Allentown	W	O, Cn, By	Cl	Cl or plowing (recent innovation)			
Lebanon (new land)	W	W	O	Fallow	W	F	...
(old land)	W	By	Cn, O	F or BW	F, then W	...	...
Carlisle	W	O, Cn	Cl	F, then W	...	...	...
	W	By	Cn	O	F	F, then W	
(new land)	Turnips, Sw. Pot.	Flax					
Bordley's "new scheme"	Cn	W or By	Cl	R, By (winter)	Cl	Cl	...

Source: Various. See nn. 103, 104, chap. 6.

Bordley correctly observed that "the two principal links in good farming, are proper Rotation of Crops and Manures." Most commentators were not reluctant to point out that Pennsylvanians failed to appreciate not only proper rotations but also the value of fertilizer, whether cow manure, lime, or gypsum. In 1684 Pastorius noted that the soil was rewarding "if one will duly work and manure it, both of which things are for the most part lacking" among the Swedes. In 1733 Hassert reported that farmers "know of no manuring." Although rental agreements stipulated the dunging of grain fields, in 1773 Francis Alison thought "as new lands are easily purchased, few were at pain to manure their old farms."[108] A comment by Hummel, who founded a town in what became Dauphin County, that manure was unnecessary made Schoepf the traveler indignant. He complained to his readers that

such over-confident opinions regarding the inexhaustible goodness of his soil puts the farmer's industry to sleep, and when, finally betterment is necessary, many of them had rather move on to take up fresh land than be at the trouble of improving the old.[109]

Not only did farmers neglect fertilizers, some very positively rejected them. Schoepf observed this attitude, as did a correspondent to a German newspaper in 1787, although he excepted Mennonites and Schwenkfelders from his indictment.[110] John Adams found that Germans in New Jersey believed, "Lime makes the father rich, but the grandson poor,—i.e., exhausts the land." Other observers noted that because lime had been improperly handled—for example, excessive applications had burned crops—many farmers declined to use it.[111]

Although laziness, self-satisfaction, prejudice, and inefficiency contributed to the widespread failure to use fertilizers, manure was probably in short supply. In 1796 a rural Quaker complained that under the "old system," which did not include clover on fallow, farmers never had enough manure for grain lands after treating the small plots, gardens, and meadows.[112] Although cattle and horses in Philadelphia supplied manure for nearby farms,[113] most farms had too few cattle, an average of six or seven, to produce enough manure. If one cow produced five tons a year (much for the time) and if three to four tons per acre were required to increase yields, then cattle could supply substantially less than half of the thirty-five acres in crops on the average farm (excluding hay and fallow land), even if proper care was taken to save manure.[114] In short, the ratio of cattle to land was low. In western Europe at the time farms raising crops were generally much smaller than in Pennsylvania, and larger stock farms kept about twenty cattle.[115] Even in the 1780s, when cattle feeding became more prevalent nearer Philadelphia, complaints that farmers owned far too many horses and too few oxen and sheep arose, in large measure, from a concern for dunging.[116]

After 1750 lime and eventually gypsum were applied in some areas. In the early 1750s Lewis Evans reported that in the Chester Valley "every farmer has a lime-kiln for manure" but that few farmers knew how to use lime. In the 1760s and 1770s advertisements for that area and for Strasburg on the Lancaster Plain specified its use.[117] Yet as late as 1789 in the Chester Valley a writer could complain that "prejudices unhappily prevail, with many against its use," possibly because some had used it excessively.[118] If this was the situation where limestone was readily available, farmers elsewhere had less opportunity even to try it.

From about 1772 gypsum was imported. By 1783 its use "for grass and plowlands has recently become a favorite practice" from Philadelphia to York. In 1789 and later its application was said to be "very general in this state."[119] Correspondents from various areas reported to Judge Peters, the commodity's chief publicist, that it had been successfully introduced, especially for stimulating the growth of clover on upland pastures.[120] The rate of its adoption in Birmingham Township, Chester County, testifies to its apparent success. In 1790 and 1792 at Amos Brinton's mill a few farmers bought some. Then in 1793 twenty farmers, mostly Quaker, ordered large quantities ground, in some cases as much as 4½ tons. In 1796 substantial amounts again were crushed.[121] Despite this flurry among Quakers, German farmers around Kutztown in Berks County resisted it, claiming "that it uses up the land." Whether the latter had applied overdoses is not certain. In any case, by 1815 even Judge Peters admitted that gypsum was not the catholicon for the ills of Pennsylvania farming.[122] Other techniques were also needed.

Jethro Tull's *Horse-Hoeing Husbandry* inspired some reformers to stress deep plowing rather than manure, but others recognized that both were necessary.[123] Toward the end of the century plows with a cast-iron moldboard, like the "Bucks County," and drill plows appeared and gradually replaced the lighter wooden plows with strips of iron on the moldboards. Fields worked with these light plows had to be plowed "thrice over."[124] This amount of labor must have meant that clean and careful tillage was not common. Although Peter Kalm and John Adams reported ridges and furrows "in the English manner" that were "straight as an arrow" near Philadelphia, throughout much of the area lightly scratched fields full of weeds and even stumps were probably more frequent.[125] Superficial plowing and light sowing of seed did not exhaust the soil as long as farmers were content with low yields that did not place excessive demand on nutrients.[126] By the end of the century, however, farmers on small holdings probably were finding it difficult to make ends meet, as is implied by the gradual relative deterioration of the lower economic ranks.[127]

Because yields from upland meadows were hard to maintain, low-lying areas along streams were favored for hay and grazing. To control the flow of water many farmers built drainage channels, dikes, and irrigation ditches. Dikes and channels appeared very early on the flats along the Delaware from New Castle northward.[128] These areas became choice lands for grazing cattle and for hay. As urban markets and shipping developed, producing an increase in the demand for meat, choice flats became so scarce and expensive that some were held cooperatively.[129]

Irrigation works were installed along many small streams. By 1790 irrigation was so general that an English traveler remarked that "the Americans seem more alive to the benefit of irrigation than any other kind of agricultural improvement."[130] When and where dams and sluices became common is not definitely known. In 1754 Pownall said that the first irrigation works he had seen in America was on a "Switzer" farm in Lancaster County, and later Strickland attributed them to the Germans. Yet wills written in the 1750s indicate that the Scotch-Irish in Lancaster County used sluices. Strickland himself suggested that English settlers from England had brought the idea of irrigation to Connecticut, and

recent research in the west of England, from where many Pennsylvanians came, shows that irrigation was practiced there early in the
seventeenth century. Whatever its origin, irrigation was one of the
few marks of intensive working of the land. Ironically, by 1795
the marsh meadows were considered redundant around Bethlehem, where gypsum had made upland meadows more productive,
and about then Bordley asserted that meadows were now "lightly
thought of."[131]

* * *

Methods used to care for crops and livestock were also part of
the agricultural system. They included fencing and other
means of guarding against depredations in the fields, and barns and
other structures for storing crops and for keeping livestock.

Fencing fields was costly, but because it was thought necessary
it was not neglected as much as other practices. Before 1700
Pastorius recognized that "it is especially difficult and expensive
to fence all the land, yet on account of horses, cattle and swine
running at large we cannot dispense with doing it." Laws were
passed to keep livestock out of cultivated fields, and rental agreements often specified keeping fences in order around grain fields,
meadows, and gardens. Various kinds of wooden fences such as
post and rail, worm, and the Swede's (with an X perpendicular to
the rails) were built. Ditches and privet and thorn hedges were
eventually used as an alternative to save wood in older settled
areas, especially, it seems, in New Castle County.[132]

While some control over the movements of domestic animals
was possible, farmers could not deal so easily with native animals,
disease, insects, genetic deterioration, or the weather. Neither
bounties nor chemicals were very successful in protecting maize
from squirrels.[133] Rust, mildew, "black blast," "scab," "field
lice," locusts or grasshoppers, "fly weavil," and possibly by 1787
the "Hessian fly" attacked wheat and other crops in Bucks, the
most easterly county.[134] To overcome some of these problems and
also genetic deterioriation, seed was traded from place to place,
though not as often as reformers wished. In 1787 Long Island seed
supposedly resistant to the Hessian fly was imported, and in 1793

a farmer in East Bradford Township bought some seed wheat from the Susquehanna area "of the old yellow sort that used to be in these parts 25 years ago."[135] Seeds of various plants were imported from England.[136] Farmers who dunged their land and sowed on better land apparently suffered less than those who did not. Low wheat yields would seem to indicate not only soil depletion but failure or inattention regarding seed problems. Weather conditions affected harvests to the degree of influencing the amount of grain available for export. Drought, heat, and severe cold sometimes lowered yields from orchards or threatened the lives of animals.[137] But Pennsylvanians operated in a climate that did not present difficulties over the long run.

Barns and other buildings were used to store crops and to stable animals, but proper care of animals and crops was not universal. Throughout the period haystacks and barracks were commonly exposed to the elements. At first even grain was left outside, but later granaries were built in the lofts of houses.[138] By 1750 barns and other buildings had become more frequent, as indicated by inventories and advertisements; Kalm noted corncribs, and farmers built barns 50 feet long. Barns of this length were apparently common at the time; in 1739 John Ross, the manager of the Penns' Blue Rock farm in Conestoga Manor adjacent to Mennonite settlements, reported that he had built one 50 by 25 feet "as good work as any I believe in ye Country."[139] By 1770 advertisements showed that some affluent farmers were building barns as long as 70 or even more than 100 feet. Yet not many barns could store all the farmers' hay and grain in sheaves, and in 1782, in strongly Mennonite Conestoga Township in Lancaster, log barns were still much more common than the presumably larger stone and frame barns. Indeed, more stone houses existed here than stone barns, which hardly supports Benjamin Rush's view that Germans looked after the comfort of their animals before their own. Only in the 1790s did discussions of bank barns appear in the literature.[140] Mennonites in Lancaster County apparently built the great "Swisser" barns only after they had prospered during the Revolution.[141]

The low level of technology and invention point indirectly to extensive rather than intensive agriculture. During the yearly

round of work on farms, the most demanding periods were June
and July, when hay was cut and small grains harvested. Moreover,
although threshing was usually a protracted process, many farmers
were anxious to have it done when market prices were high, sometimes early in July.[142] Maize harvesting, second cuttings of hay,
two or three plowings, manure spreading, and wood cutting were
less associated with specific periods and so did not require as
intensive labor.

We might expect that Pennsylvanians would have shown much
interest in labor-saving devices to expedite harvesting and
threshing of small grains. Yet they seem to have been little concerned with harvesting tools and only slightly more with threshing
equipment. Cradles fitted to scythes, used to cut tight-headed barley and oats, appeared in inventories as early as 1717 and may
have come into wide service.[143] Sickles, however, remained the
chief means of cutting wheat and rye to prevent loss of grain. As a
result, many people—farm wives and children, transient laborers,
and even laborers from towns—worked long hours during the
harvest period.[144] Somewhat more concern was expressed for
threshing, recognized as "a laborious task . . . abhorred by
jobbers . . . and costly and hard to get done at the right time."[145]
"Dutch fans" and threshing devices were employed. The fans, designed to blow the chaff, were mentioned as early as 1736 and
were frequently referred to in newspapers and inventories.[146] In
1757, a threshing mill was listed in an inventory of a York County
German, and in 1764 John Clayton of Chester County received
assembly approval to construct a threshing machine he had invented.[147] In 1782 another threshing device was designed.[148] But
flailing and treading remained the chief means of threshing because "both modes are fixed habits."[149]

With the exception of threshers and fans, very few labor-saving
devices were invented. Land clearance continued to be an arduous
task, even though girdling was practiced.[150] A seed drill to improve crop production probably was more laborious than was
broadcasting.[151] Water wheels were used to lift water. That so few
mechanical improvements came into farming seems remarkable,
especially considering the adoption of such inventions as the
Conestoga wagon, rifles, steam engines, and the labor-saving con-

veyors and elevators designed for the Brandywine mills by Oliver
Evans.[152] It is also surprising that gentlemen farmer reformers
were more concerned with increasing production through soil-
preserving techniques and the improved care of crops and livestock
than by saving on labor in a world supposedly long on land but
short on labor.

* * *

To explain why an extensive rather than an intensive agricultural system developed in Pennsylvania we need to consider some
basic economic and social conditions: the labor supply, the availability of land, household consumption, the market, and attitudes
of the people.

Together with a general lack of interest in labor-saving improvements, the short supply of labor contributed directly to poor
farming practices. Wages were supposedly from 30 to 100 per cent
higher than in England, and complaints were expressed from
earliest times concerning the cost of labor. Few farm hands could
be hired, laborers received "victuals in the bargain," and good
tenants were scarce. Toward the end of the period one traveler
explicitly blamed the labor shortage for poor farming.[153]

Yet labor was not always scarce. In 1737 Durs Thommen in the
Lebanon Valley wrote to German relatives that landless people
nearby "work where they can." As noted in chapter 1, unemploy-
ment occurred in other times and places. More accurately, the
labor supply fluctuated, and the role of the supply and cost of
labor in the lack of innovations in agricultural practices is not easy
to measure. During recessions when money was scarce, as in 1764,
laborers were plentiful. Such periods were marked by foreclosures
on poor farmers and by little migration.[154] But during times of
prosperity, especially when high demand for wheat outside Pennsylvania raised farm values, many poor farmers moved to the
frontier and laborers were able to build up capital and so move on
to new areas or to rent land. At these times immigrant laborers
were in great demand, and farmers could pay high wages without
feeling any pressure to make technological changes. Bordley
claimed that even in good times "tillage by hired laborers is cheap,

the *net gain* greater," despite higher wages.[155] The labor supply probably had relatively little influence on the extensive agriculture of the time.

Moreover, land was not free or plentiful in older settled areas. As early as 1700 letters to England and Germany complained of high land prices.[156] Values increased throughout the century, as is implied by the increased density of population (figures 7-10)[157] and by the reduction in farm sizes by 1760 to economic levels of 80 to 200 acres (figure 28). In Lancaster County, deed books show that prices rose throughout the century (table 13). Increases in land value, however, do not seem to have evoked a concerted effort to improve yields by better practices. Other factors were at work.

At bottom, extensive farming was the result of the satisfaction of the average farmer and his response to economic conditions. He produced enough for his family and was able to sell a surplus in the market to buy what he deemed necessities. Since he was not in a strong position to change external market demands, he responded to them in a sensible way, more sensibly than the plans of gentlemen would suggest. To support these contentions it is necessary to assess the relative importance of home consumption and sales.

The total domestic consumption of the average farm family can be estimated roughly from endowments of goods or money specified in wills of farmers, mostly Mennonites and Quakers from the Lancaster Plain. The calculations based on the sample of wills (table 28) assumes that a widow's annual consumption would be average for a family of five and takes into account livestock feed (table 27) and seed grain.[158] Annual consumption amounted to approximately 750 pounds of meat, 295 bushels of grain (50 for direct use, 215 for animals, 30 for seed), linen, wool, and other commodities. The total value of these goods for home use at 1790 prices was between £50 and £60. Since the average farm then earned a yearly income of £100, at least £40 was available through the sale of various commodities to purchase imported textiles, tea, coffee, rum, and iron goods and the services of lawyers, ministers, millers, blacksmiths, shoemakers, other craftsmen, and laborers.[159] This annual surplus of £40 (or 40 per cent) per family corresponds closely with the £7 7s. granted to the average widow who received money instead of goods (table 28), especially among Quakers.[160] A comparison of yields (table 27) with home consumption (table 28) suggests that about 50 bushels of grain (especially wheat), 100 pounds each of beef and pork, flaxseed, hay, and probably other goods were available for the market.

One market for the surplus production was local. Grain, meat, hay, and other products were sold to craftsmen and laborers who, in the latter half of the century, composed approximately a third of the population. Farmers traded hay and grain with one another and bought and sold livestock at fairs, especially before 1775 (chapter 5). In 1790 Pennsylvania's population was nearly 25 per cent urban and therefore provided an outlet for increasing quantities of goods from the region's farmers.[161]

Ship provisions and foreign markets also absorbed the surplus. Flour, wheat, corn, flaxseed, meat, lumber, iron, and small amounts of other commodities were involved in the trade. In the best year of the early 1770s, 1772, exports through Philadelphia were valued at £800,000 sterling, or £1.2 million in Pennsylvania currency (figure 4). The large flour and wheat exports contributed to Pennsylvania's reputation as an agricultural cornucopia. At this time about one-third of the wheat produced in the area was exported, chiefly as flour and bread. In 1770 the value of this commodity was £554,044 (Pa.), about £15 per family or £27 per farm.[162] Nearly half of Pennsylvania's export income and probably half of the average farm's earnings from sales came from this source. Exports of corn and flaxseed added £12,000 and £30,000 respectively in 1770.[163] In this period meat for ships' larders and other colonies per annum totaled about 7,000 barrels a year, or 1,400,000 pounds, valued at £25,000. This amounted to about £1.25 per farm, or a quarter of the 200 pounds of meat sold by the average farm each year (table 27). Unlike wheat, most of the meat was apparently sold within the province. In 1770 iron exports amounted to £39,000 and lumber, some from farmers, to at least £33,000.[164]

Pennsylvanians thus sold a wide variety of products internally and abroad, but wheat was clearly of greatest significance. Although farmers maintained mixed farming, the emphasis on wheat

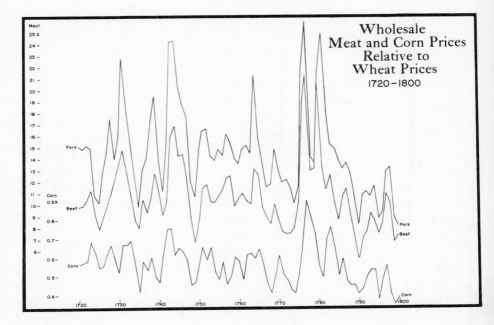

Figure 38

and flour exports undoubtedly hindered a shift to livestock that would have promoted the use of clover and manure and thus a more intensive and productive use of land. The "Agricultural Revolution" that developed in Britain by about 1650 was the result of this emphasis. But Pennsylvanians who were sensitive to market conditions could not convert aggressively to livestock. Only in the early 1740s and the early 1780s did rises in pork and beef prices in relation to wheat encourage a shift (figure 38). It was after these short-lived periods that farmers complained, supposedly because of a glut, of too many cattle driven from Virginia and Carolina.[165] Acreages of wheat increased even more when grain prices rose in relation to those of meat, as in 1772.[166] Extensive use of the land therefore was largely a consequence of the emphasis on wheat exports. Most Pennsylvania farmers were so satisfied with their incomes from wheat and other products that they felt no urge to risk these certain returns by pressing for new

kinds of markets, and so in the course of a century they did not
much alter their mode of agriculture.

* * *

European travelers and native reformers who complained that
farmers were "not . . . inclined to make many innovations upon
the ancient practice of agriculture" missed the mark. Their goal of
"promoting a greater increase of the products of the land," as the
1786 constitution of the Philadelphia Society for Promoting Agriculture stated it, was commendable.[167] Yet this goal carried little
weight with a satisfied group of farmers, two-thirds of them operators of their own farms, who, as one said, had always been able to
get along without the advice of reformers.[168] With one exception,
reformers did not cite the practices of Pennsylvania Germans or
other Pennsylvanians as models of improvement.[169] Nor did they
look to Germany, since few innovations appeared there before
Thaer publicized English schemes just before 1800.[170] Like Thaer,
all American promoters—from Eliot, Bartram, and Read at midcentury to Alison and Jacobs around 1770 and to William and
George Logan, George Morgan of New Jersey, and others of the
Philadelphia Society in the late 1780s—were enamored of English
farming practices. Bordley's advocacy of root crops failed to
recognize that maize was a better feed in America, and others who
praised oxen did not see that horses were much more useful for
road transport.[171] The uncritical adherence to English ideas did
not lead anywhere and possibly even diverted these creative minds
from more realistic goals such as improved harvesting equipment.
In the long run the reformers probably were correct on the need
for more intensive use of the land and for building up the soil. But
most farmers were not convinced before 1800. By that time however, some few signs of improvement and of regional specialization
were appearing as harbingers of nineteenth century change.

CHAPTER SEVEN

Regional Variations in the Use of the Land

In 1826 Johann von Thünen, the owner of a large farm near Rostock on the North German Plain, published his model of regional agricultural patterns. In what he called the "isolated state" the key variable determining agricultural zones was distance from one market center. To demonstrate the working of this factor other conditions were assumed to be constant: a homogeneous physical environment, the same means of transportation, a static population and, not least, optimizing farmers with full knowledge of current technology and of the market.

Since transport costs would increase radially from the market center of this closed economy, more distant farmers would tend either to change the methods used in producing the same crops or animals or to change the crops and animals raised. In the former case, distant farmers would generally compensate for higher transport costs by using less labor and less capital per unit of land than those near the market. Therefore yields per acre of more distant farmers would generally be lower then those near the center. To derive incomes equal to those of farmers near the town, the distant farmers would tend toward more extensive methods and larger farms. Where farmers changed the kinds of crops and livestock, the degree of intensity would vary between cropping systems. For example, firewood production would be extensive by land and labor standards, yet it would occur near the market because of high transport costs. Perishability and value added in later processing would similarly influence the type of production: milk for sale had to be produced near the market for reasons of perishability, hence transport costs; grain for whisky could be grown at a greater distance than grain for milling.

The regional pattern as developed by von Thünen in his scheme was roughly as follows: in the zone nearest the market, market gardening and fluid milk; then moving outward, finishing of livestock for butchers, forestry, grain without fallow, grain with fallow in an open-field pattern, butter and cheese production, and finally livestock raising.[1] He also relaxed his constants to observe the consequences of introducing, for example, a river and other market centers.

Von Thünen himself recognized that his conclusions on land use grossly simplified physical and economic conditions and saw his model as a starting point for understanding and programming farm operations. But subsequent studies have used his ideas, and even today, after major technological changes, variations on his model can be used effectively. It is a useful basis for a discussion of changing regional patterns in early Pennsylvania, where distance was a variable of some importance.

A search for von Thünen rings here fails to disclose obvious regional patterns, however. The land was not homogeneous in quality, although marked variations were not as apparent as they were in other parts of America. Wagons, the chief means of transport, were supplemented by river boats. Rather than one major market center, after 1750 there were two, Philadelphia and Baltimore, and several large county towns. All goods were not sold in these places. Much of the produce was shipped outside of the area, so the market system was not closed. Almost all of the area fell within 132 miles of the two centers, the limit of the fourth of the von Thünen rings (figure 44). Most farmers were not optimizers. Even taking into account these deviations from the model, however, one would think that more regional specialization would have appeared than did. Imprecise tax collectors' records and the paucity of other data may account for some of this lack of regional clarity. It is clear, however, that most farmers continued to produce a wide range of crops and livestock, much for domestic comsumption, and emphasized wheat, "the standing staple of the province," for export.[2] These were key factors obscuring potential patterns of specialization. Had farmers not been so dependent on wheat for their incomes, von Thünen rings of specialization might have appeared more distinctly than they did.

Yet, imprecise as the regions were, they need to be discussed to clarify some of the issues influencing farmers' decisions and the processes affecting land use. We can assess, first of all, regional variations of economic status as an indicator of productivity, and then various crops and livestock that showed some regional variations. Religious affiliation, quality of the land, and distance from markets affected the regional pattern of economic status and the kinds and degree of various types of production. Identification of farmers with national groups will be considered.

* * *

Economic status, as indicated by the amount of taxes assessed, provides the clearest sign of the productivity of farmers. In southeastern Pennsylvania the provincial (later state) taxes per capita or family varied from county to county (table 31 and figure 1). By 1760, the first year that full tax details by county are available, virtually the whole area had been occupied, and the occupants of at least the best lands were of the second and third generations. In 1760, 1778, and 1785 Philadelphia, Montgomery (not created in the first two periods), Chester, and Lancaster counties were rated the highest, with Bucks not far behind. Berks, Northampton, and the trans-Susquehanna counties of York and Cumberland generally were assessed at lower rates than were Lancaster and the counties nearer Philadelphia, but the differences do not necessarily indicate that farmers in more distant counties were less commercial in orientation.[3] The average rates of assessment for Chester and Lancaster counties, which were set by the legislature, were corroborated by county assessors (table 32). In the latter half of the century the average taxes for Chester, which was 60 per cent English, and Lancaster, with as many or more Germans, were about the same.

Within Chester and Lancaster counties, however, the assessors distinguished among townships. The chief distinction was the eval-

Table 31

Average Taxes Levied on Counties by the Legislature

County	1760 (per taxpayer)	1778[a] (per person)	1785 (per person)
Chester	£1.1	£0.69	£0.23
Lancaster	1.1	0.71	0.23[b]
Philadelphia	1.15	1.30	0.27
City	2.25	. . .	. . .
Montgomery	. . .	. . .	0.29
Bucks	1.05	0.67	0.20
Northampton	0.7	0.48	0.15
Berks	0.8	0.65	0.21
Cumberland	0.8	0.62	0.17[c]
York	0.8	0.53	0.18

Source: Pa. Arch., 8th ser., 6: 5141 (Votes and Proceedings of the House of Representatives, 1760); Mitchell and Flanders, *Statutes at Large, Pa.*, 6: 231; 5: 465–67.

Note: The ratio for 1778 was calculated from 1779 population figures and for 1785 from 1786 figures. The taxes levied were £232,607 and £76,945 for 1778 and 1785 respectively. Only relative amounts are important.

[a]Pennsylvania currency, which in 1778 was inflated.
[b]Includes Dauphin Co.
[c]Includes Franklin Co.

Table 32

Average Taxes Levied by County Assessors in Chester and Lancaster Counties

	1758–59	1782
Chester	16.6s.	£7.9
Lancaster	14.9s.	£8.2

Source: Ches. and Lanc. Co. MSS tax assessments, 1758, 1759, 1782 (Chester); 1782 (Lancaster), *Pa. Arch.*, 3d ser., 17: 689–898.

uation of land, but the value of livestock, winter grain sown, occupations, and other property were also used (figures 39–43).[4] Between 1730 and 1759 higher valuations shifted westward in Chester County. In 1759 and 1782 the most productive areas seem

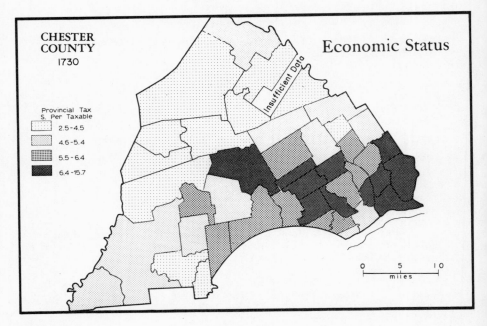

Figure 39

to have been the central and south-central parts of Chester and
especially the southern part of the Lancaster Plain. The lowest
areas of taxation and land value remained southwestern Chester
and adjacent Lancaster, northern Chester, and most of the
Lebanon Valley. These patterns correlate positively with the distributions of relatively costly horses; in 1758–59 particularly,
fewer horses were found on the average farm in southwestern and
northern Chester than on the more affluent Lancaster Plain and in
the remainder of Chester (figures 46 and 47).

Denominational affiliations notably influenced these patterns
throughout Chester and Lancaster counties and throughout southeastern Pennsylvania as well as land quality and distance from
markets. Quakers and Mennonites dominated the top tax brackets
in the most productive areas of the two counties, and large numbers of them lived in highly taxed Montgomery County. In 1782,
only 24 per cent of the population and 37 per cent of the Germans in the area of present-day Lancaster County were Men-

nonites, but 39 per cent of the population and 58 per cent of the Germans who paid more than £40 tax adhered to that group.[5] Even in the poorer parts of Chester and Lancaster, Quakers were the leading taxpayers. Because many Scotch-Irish resided in these areas we might be led to conclude that as a group they were generally poorer. But in 1782 their representation among the top taxpayers in Chester and Lancaster counties was the same as their share of the whole population, and certainly proportionately more of them were affluent than Germans who were Lutheran and Reformed. Germans were the largest national group in relatively poor northern Chester and in the eastern part of the Lebanon Valley. If many of the Scotch-Irish had belonged to some distinctive sect with social characteristics similar to those of Quakers and Mennonites, our task of judging the relative worth and success in farming of national groups might be easier.

Figure 40

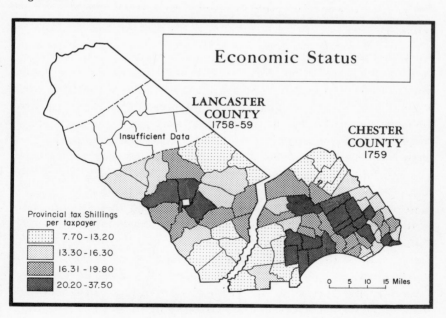

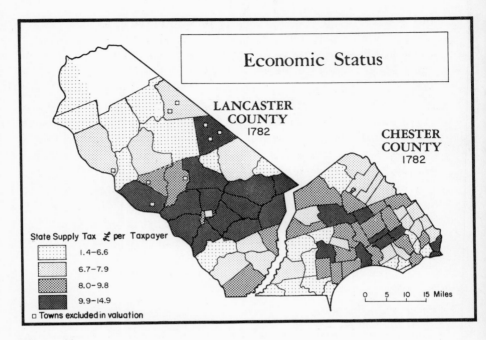

Figure 41

Contemporary comments stressed the wealth of the "plain folk." In 1760 the Reverend Thomas Barton reported that "the country round about Lancaster for several miles is posses'd by Mennonists, who by their industry and great economy have acquired riches and plenty." In 1786 a correspondent to the Germantown paper excluded Mennonites and Schwenkfelders from the opprobrium of poor agricultural practices, a view upheld by Cooper and others who were impressed by the productivity of the Lancaster Plain. Henry Muhlenberg complained that all sectarians could support schoolmasters but that his Lutherans could not. Although Mrs. Thomas Barton could write that "above an hundred families all of them rich substantial farmers" lived in Welsh Anglican Caernarvon and that "kind opulant [sic] people descended from Ireland" resided in Salisbury Township, observers undoubtedly were correct in their assessment of the material well-being of sectarian groups.[6]

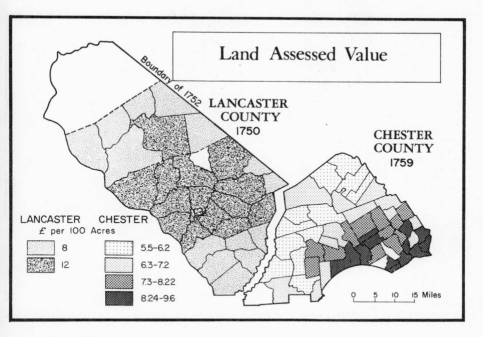

Figure 42

Land quality may have contributed to some regional distinctions in status and productivity. Since the land throughout most of southeastern Pennsylvania was fertile, the differences were not highly significant in determining wealth. But farmers on the Lancaster Plain and the Chester Valley, which is largely gently sloping limestone land, may have achieved higher yields than those farming on soils derived from crystalline rocks and especially shale (figures 6, 40, and 41; table 10). Clover probably grew better on limestone and in turn fed life-giving nitrogen into the soil. But Montgomery County, with the highest average tax in 1785, had virtually no limestone soils; much of it was derived from red shales. One is therefore led to suspect that the substantial numbers of Mennonites, Quakers, and other sectarians located there were somehow able to overcome these deficiencies (figures 6 and 14). Moreover, the lime soils of the south side of the Lehigh, Lebanon, and Cumberland valleys did not provide the means for achieving

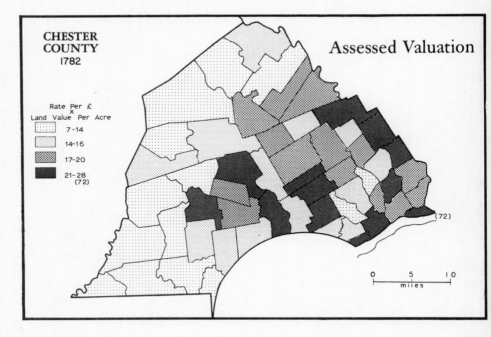

Figure 43

high average economic status, at least until 1782 (table 31 and figure 6). The adage "good soils make good people" cannot be accepted without qualification.

The influence on regional productivity of distance from Philadelphia, the Delaware River, Baltimore, and county towns is not easy to measure. The lower average taxes for the counties most distant from Philadelphia—Northampton, Berks, York, Cumberland, and the Lebanon Valley in Lancaster County—suggests that higher transport costs may have reduced farming profits (table 31 and figure 1). Assuming that farmers would tolerate transport expenses of up to 50 per cent of the value of wheat or flour, in 1772 all of these areas fell within range of Philadelphia or Baltimore (86 miles for wheat and 106 miles for flour; see figure 44).[7] Yet the Lebanon Valley in particular, was apparently close to the limit.[8] On the other hand, Northampton County had the advantage of cheaper downstream costs on the Delaware but was ranked the lowest of all counties. At the township level, conclusions are hard to draw. Tinicum, the township nearest Philadelphia in Chester County, paid an extremely high average tax, but assessors evaluated some adjacent townships quite low (figures 41, 43, and 2). Townships near the town of Lancaster appear to have been more affluent than those farther away, but these were strongly Mennonite. Distance and transport costs, like land quality, were obviously less important to prosperity than membership in denominational groups. Areas dominated by Quakers and Mennonites seem to have been the most successful.

* * *

Specialized types of agriculture developed, if only faintly, in certain areas. These are considered in terms of the hypothetical von Thünen rings (figure 44) rather than in the sequence of crops and livestock discussed in the previous chapter. In general, Penn-

Figure 44

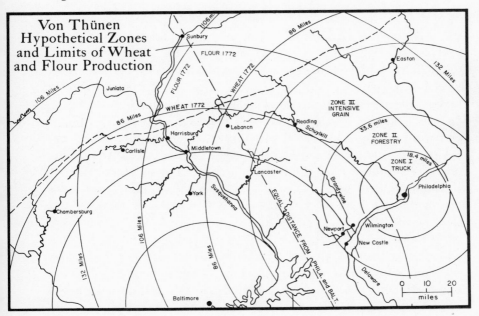

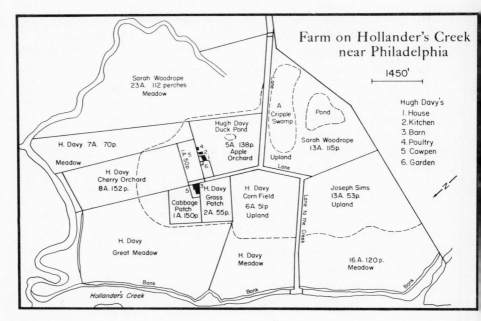

Figure 45

sylvania's mixed agriculture was more of a conglomeration than a system, so, with the exception of wheat, the earlier discussion might have followed any order. Specialization resulted from more attention to land qualities and the market, and it demanded more rationality in crop and livestock combinations and rotations.

In von Thünen's scheme, farmers involved in market gardening and fluid milk production would locate very near the market. The perishability of these commodities, the greater amounts of labor per acre required, and the higher value of land would contribute to intensive land use.[9] Returns would be higher; more food value was produced over a life span by one dairy cow than by one steer.[10]

Since tax lists of early Pennsylvania do not specify land in truck crops or milk cows, our understanding of the location of market gardening and fluid milk production is inconclusive. Advertisements of land near the city specified truck farms, and a draft of

Hugh Davy's farm of about fifty-five acres (and parts of adjacent holdings) near Philadelphia (figure 45) indicates that he had nearly fifteen acres in fruit.[11] Farms of small size near the city suggest intensive use of the land (figures 28 and 29). Nurseries were found near the city and near other towns such as Lancaster.[12] In 1804, a nursery near Burlington, New Jersey advertised 122 varieties of peaches, 97 of pears, 85 of apples, including the best-known Newton Pippin and Spitzbergen, 52 of cherries, 30 of plums, 24 of nectarines, 18 of apricots, almonds, and quince.[13] Other advertisements mentioned English walnuts, pears, Lombardy poplars, and weeping willows (the last two were becoming widespread as aesthetic landmarks). The array of varieties suggests considerable concern for fruit production. Although cider making was apparently universal, the areas around Marcus Hook on the Delaware and Reading had reputations for their cider.[14]

Figure 46

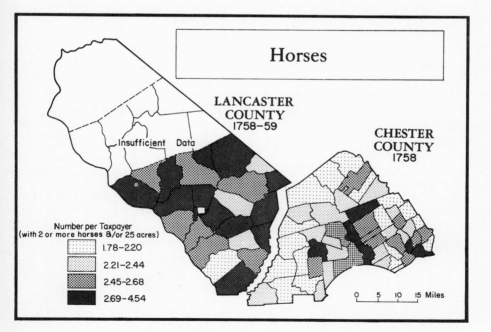

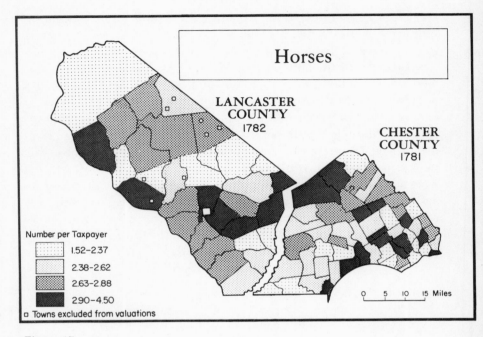

Figure 47

The relatively large number of cattle in eastern Chester County (figures 48 and 49) may indicate more fluid milk production here than elsewhere; but most of this perishable commodity consumed in cities and towns was probably produced very near them or indeed right in them, for many inhabitants kept a cow or two.[15] The number of cattle in Chester County, most definitely along the Delaware near Philadelphia in 1781, rather points to an emphasis on fattening (figure 49 and table 33).[16] By 1760 five of the six farmers in Chester County with more than 20 cattle (or perhaps 40, including those under three years) resided on or owned diked meadow land along the Delaware, where yields of hay could reach 4½ tons per acre, about three times the upland average.[17] In 1782 one herd in Tinicum Township, the most obvious example on the map, numbered 90. In 1774 one taxpayer nearby was listed as owning 100 cattle, and another grazed 1,000 on as many acres of

Carpenter's Island near Philadelphia.[18] Farmers around New Castle on the Delaware also fattened cattle. Many of the store cattle driven from western Virginia, the Carolinas, and even New England were fed for the market in these areas. The location of the fattening of cattle thus conforms to von Thünen's model.[19]

Fattening in areas beyond the Delaware was not as clear-cut. The fairly high ratio of cattle in 1772 (table 33) in Lancaster County, the presence of more large barns there than elsewhere after the Revolution, and the establishment of stockyards in the town of Lancaster in the 1790s all suggest some emphasis on fattening on the Lancaster Plain. Unfortunately the tax data of 1782 do not make this obvious (figure 49).[20] Since soils derived from limestone probably produced clover more abundantly than others (table 10 and figure 6), these possibly were becoming fattening regions. The postrevolutionary rotation schemes involving

Figure 48

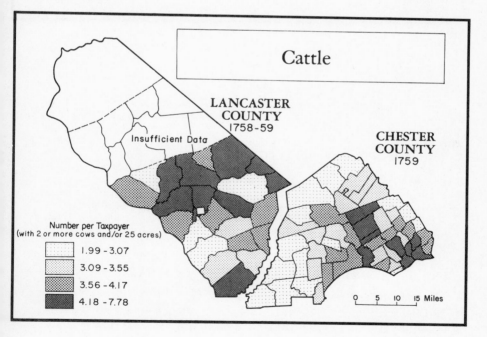

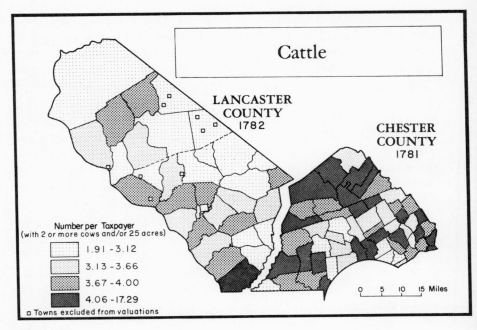

Figure 49

Table 33

Average Number of Cattle per 100 Persons, 1773

Bucks	40.5	Berks	25.0
Philadelphia		York	24.2
(excluding city)	36.9	Cumberland	19.9
Chester	30.3	Northampton	17.3
Lancaster	30.3	Southeastern Pennsylvania	
Bedford	25.1	(excluding Philadelphia city)	29.0

Source: Sutherland, *Population Distribution in Colonial America* (New York: Columbia University Press, 1936), p. 168, and fig. 11.

clover and grass cited for the Lancaster Plain and Chester County (table 30) also suggest that farmers were connecting cattle and crop production more closely.[21] In 1797 one farmer said that he was committing his operation entirely to the production of livestock.[22]

Cheese and butter making, according to von Thünen, would occur more than ninety miles from the market. The evidence from early Pennsylvania does not support this conclusion. By 1800 Chester County, mostly within forty miles of the city, had established a reputation for its cheese.[23] The relatively greater densities of cattle in 1781 in the eastern part of the county and in the Chester Valley may indicate this (figure 49). Some cheese and butter were sold in the Philadelphia market; by 1790 farmers living more than forty miles from the city in Chester, Bucks, and Montgomery counties took their produce there once a week, even though an overnight stay was necessary because of the distance involved.[24] They naturally carried out other business there, and as noted in chapter 5 this activity helped to maintain the economic power of the metropolis over adjacent counties, weakening their county towns and the incentive to establish other towns.[25]

In von Thünen's framework of the static state, silviculture, particularly lumber and firewood production, should take place in zone II near the city, closer than grain cultivation areas (figure 44). The urgent need of city dwellers for wood, low inputs of labor, and high transport costs for such a bulky commodity help to explain the proximity of this zone to the center.[26] Too little evidence is available, however, to show the situation in Pennsylvania clearly. By 1750 wood was becoming scarce within twenty-five miles of Philadelphia and was shipped from greater distances down the Delaware and Schuylkill, suggesting that the forests near the city had been too hastily cut.[27] Yet in the early 1780s, sawmills were not concentrated in any particular area of Chester and Lancaster counties (table 34 and figure 51), suggesting that lumbering was still widespread. Farmers sold surpluses of staves and lumber, as they did hay and meat, but specialization occurred toward the end of the century only beyond southeastern Pennsylvania up the Susquehanna and Delaware rivers.[28] Furnace and forge operators demanded large quantities of charcoal, and they held large tracts of forests in the hill lands of South Mountain and its various parts, such as Furnace Ridge (figures 5, 51, and 52). Baron Stiegel, for example, owned more than 12,000 acres in the 1760s.[29] These operations occurred in rough lands and so did not compete with agriculture; rather, ironmaking complemented the

Table 34

Processing Firms by Township, 1759 and 1781–82

Townships	Mills Unspecified		Grist (Flour) Mills		Saw Mills		Fulling Mills		Oil Mills	
	1759	1781–82	1759	1781–82	1759	1781–82	1759	1781–82	1759	1781–82
Chester Co.										
Astown			2	2	1	1	1	3		
Bethel										
Birmingham			1	1		4	1	1		
Bradford, E.			3	4	1	4		1		1
Bradford, W.			2	1	2	2	1	2	1	
Caln, E.	2			5		7		2		1
Caln, W.			3	3	2	2				
Charlestown			1	3		4		2		
Chester			2	3	1	1				
Chichester, L.			1	1	1	1				
Chichester, U.										
Concord				2		3				
Coventry			2	2						
Darby, L.			1	1				1		
Darby, U.			3	3	2	4		2		1
Easttown										
Edgemont										
Fallowfield, E.			1	3		2		1		
Fallowfield, W.				2		3		1		
Goshen			2	3	1	3	1	1		
Haverford			2	3		2	1	1		
Kennet			4	3	2	4	2	1		
London Britain			1		1		1	1		
Londonderry										
London Grove	4			8		4		4		
Marlborough, E.			2	3	2	2				
Marlborough, W.			2	2	2	2				
Marple				1		1				
Middletown			1	3	2	3	1			
Nantmeal, E.				4		4				1
Nantmeal, W.	6			5		6				
New Garden			1	2	2	2				
Newlin			1	1	1	1				
New London			3	3	1	1				
Newtown					1	1				

Hemp Mills		Paper Mills		Snuff Mills		Distilleries		Breweries (or Maltsters)		Tanneries		Ironworks	
1759	1781-82	1759	1781-82	1759	1781-82	1759	1781-82	1759	1781-82	1759	1781-82	1759	1781-82
						1					1		1
											1		1
											1		
	2						4						
							1						
							1				1		
									1				
											1		
											2		
													2
											1		
			2										
							2				1		
							4						
							3				1		
							1				1		
											1		
							2				1		
							1						
							1				1		
											1		
							1				1		
							1				1		
							1				1		4
							9				1		1
											1		
											1		
											1		

Table 34 *(Continued)*

Townships	Mills Unspecified		Grist (Flour) Mills		Saw Mills		Fulling Mills		Oil Mills	
	1759	1781-82	1759	1781-82	1759	1781-82	1759	1781-82	1759	1781-82
Nottingham, E.			2	3	1		3	1		
Nottingham, W.			6	4	2	3		2		
Oxford				5		2				
Pennsbury				1						
Pikeland			4	5	3	1				
Providence, L.			1		1					
Providence, U.			2	2	1	1				
Radnor			1	2	1	1				
Ridley			1	2	1	1				
Sadsbury	9			5		2				
Springfield			1	1	1	2				
Thornbury						2		1		
Tinicum										
Tredyffrin			2	3	1	3	1			
Uwchlan			2	3	1	3	1			
Vincent			4	7	1	3				1
Westtown			1	1	1					
Whiteland, E.			3	1	1	2				1
Whiteland, W.				2		1				
Willistown			1	3	3	3	1	1		
Lancaster Co.										
Bart	3	1								
Bethel		6								
Brecknock		2	3		1		1			
Caernarvon		5	1		2					
Cocalico		8	7		5				1	
Colerain		1								
Conestoga		2								
Derry		8								
Donegal		9	4		2				1	
Drumore		6	2				1			
Earl		13	9		5				1	
Elizabeth		3	1							
Hanover, E. ⎫ Hanover, W. ⎭		10								
Heidelberg		4								

Hemp Mills		Paper Mills		Snuff Mills		Distilleries		Breweries (or Maltsters)		Tanneries		Ironworks	
1759	1781-82	1759	1781-82	1759	1781-82	1759	1781-82	1759	1781-82	1759	1781-82	1759	1781-82
			1										
							4				2		
							1						
					1							1	
											1		
							2						
							1						
	1						2			1			
							2			1			
							1			1			
							1				2		
							1						
								1					
										1		2	
1		1											
							2						
											1		
											1		
						4	1						
													1

203

Table 34 *(Continued)*

Townships	Mills Unspecified		Grist (Flour) Mills		Saw Mills		Fulling Mills		Oil Mills	
	1759	1781–82	1759	1781–82	1759	1781–82	1759	1781–82	1759	1781–82
Lancaster Co.										
Hempfield		4		3		3				
Lampeter		10		4		6		1		
Lancaster		2		2		1				
Lancaster Boro.										
Leacock		6		2		2				
Lebanon		11								
Little Britain		8		2		2		1		
Londonderry		6								
Manheim		5		2		3				
Manor		10		3		3				
Martick		5								
Mt. Joy		4		1						
Paxton, L.		8								
Paxton, U.		11								
Rapho		13		3		6				
Sadsbury	1							1		
Salisbury		5		6		2				
Strasburg	2	11		2		3		1		
Warwick		9		6		5				3

Source: Ches. and Lanc. Co. MSS tax returns, 1759, 1781, 1782; 1782, *Pa. Arch.*, 3d ser., vol. 17.

commercial agriculture sector of Pennsylvania's economy. With this exception, silviculture apparently was not restricted to any particular area.

According to von Thünen's theory, commercial grain production would be located beyond 33.6 miles from the market in zones of decreasing intensity of land use (figure 44).[30] But in early Pennsylvania no such defined regions were marked out, nor apparently did production vary over the long run. All grains were produced throughout the area, and the average farmer in Chester, Lancaster, Northampton, and Franklin counties sowed eight to ten acres of winter grain, particularly wheat, and reaped about ten bushels per acre.[31] In Chester and Lancaster counties flour mills

Hemp Mills		Paper Mills		Snuff Mills		Distilleries		Breweries (or Maltsters)		Tanneries		Ironworks	
1759	1781-82	1759	1781-82	1759	1781-82	1759	1781-82	1759	1781-82	1759	1781-82	1759	1781-82
							1			1			
						3	3	2	2	6			
						3	1						
							1						
							1						
							1						
											1		
											1		
											1		
							(1783) 13					1	

and gristmills were spread around (figures 50 and 51; table 34). Even though the number of mills in Chester County increased between 1759 and 1782 from 78 to 123 and the number of persons per mill decreased from 358 to 285, no long-term changes in wheat acreage seem to have taken place.[32] The smaller population served by mills could conceivably indicate higher yields per acre, but this is not likely. The lower ratio might mean that more persons found milling worthwhile, or it might simply point to incomplete data. More conclusively, by the early 1780s average acres sown in twenty Chester townships had changed by only a half-acre from an average of ten in 1759. Changes of one acre or more occurred in only three of the twenty townships.[33] Although acre-

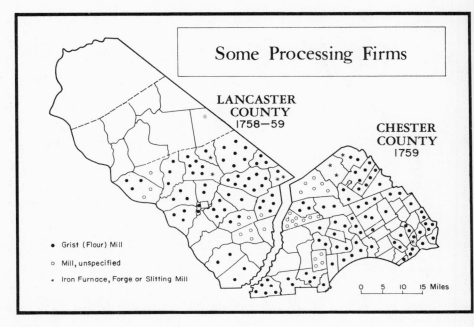

Figure 50

ages increased in response to excellent overseas market conditions, as in the early 1770s and 1790s, persistence and uniformity of winter grain production were hallmarks of early agriculture.

At a smaller scale some regional variations in winter grain production did arise, however, and these can be compared with distance from markets, soil conditions, degree of affluence, and cultural groups. Unfortunately some of the patterns are contradictory. In 1758–59, the time for which the most complete data on winter grain, particularly wheat, are available, on the Lancaster Plain more farmers sowed more acres and used more of the cleared land than elsewhere in the county (figures 52, 53, and 54, summed up in figure 55). Mills were also more concentrated on the plain (figures 50 and 51). In Chester County farmers in the south-central and north-central townships sowed more acres, although a higher proportion of taxpayers on the western side of the county sowed winter grain. However, somewhat fewer mills were located in south-central Chester than in the south-western, northern, and

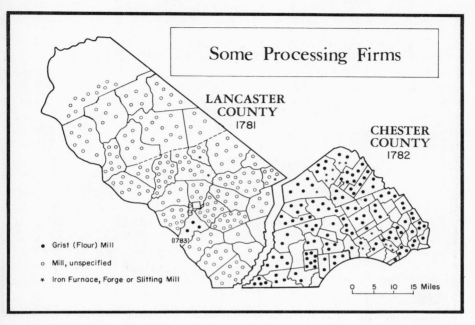

Figure 51

eastern sectors of the county. In 1762 a miller asserted in an advertisement that East Nottingham Township in southwestern Chester was an "extraordinary" wheat area.[34] Patterns in Chester were thus less definite than in Lancaster.

Distance from markets seems to have had little bearing on areas of wheat production in these two counties. The concentration of farmers producing wheat in southwestern Chester and of acreages in the south-central part and the lower density of mills in the latter area may have been a consequence of their proximity to the agglomeration of mills on the Brandywine near Wilmington. Here were eight mills in 1772 and thirteen in 1795, the largest of which had twelve millstones (figure 34).[35] Even so, in Thornbury Township (figure 2) less than twenty miles from Wilmington the average acreage fell from over fifteen in 1726 to thirteen in 1760 and to eleven in 1784.[36] Again, conclusions are hard to draw. The firmest statement is a vague one: most wheat was milled locally and mills were plentiful.

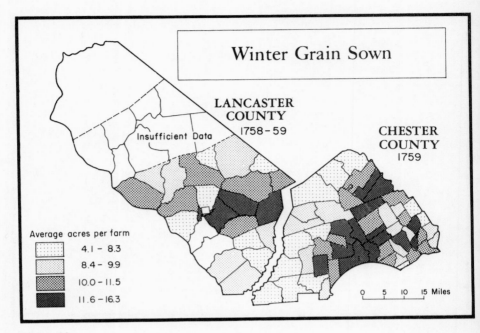

Figure 52

Varying soil conditions and affluence correlated to some degree with production. We have seen that wheat growing in Lancaster was more concentrated on the plain. This was also the area of the richest soils, the greatest extent of gentle slopes (table 10), and the area with the greatest average wealth (figures 40 and 41). The thirty-six farmers who sowed more than thirty acres in 1758–59, most of whom were located on the southern part of the plain, were among the richest taxpayers in the county. Good soils may have given them an initial lead over farmers outside the plain. Some of them were also as likely as any farmer to have tried such innovations as clover in rotation and dunging of grain fields.[37] In south-central Chester, fertile soils derived from crystalline rocks similarly had relatively large wheat acreages and corresponded to higher average taxes paid. In one of the townships there, farmers applied gypsum in the 1790s.[38]

But other data only partially support these observations. In the 1790s, according to a correspondent of George Washington, re-

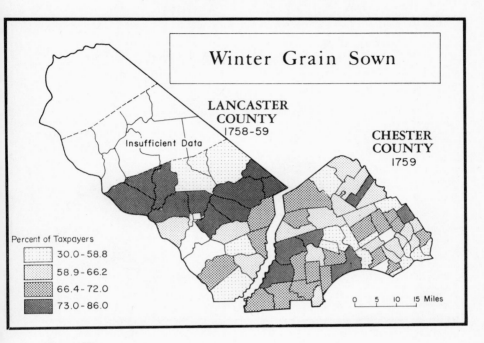

Figure 53

turns of wheat per acre in York and Franklin counties were usually 15 bushels on limestone soils and 10 to 12 on the poorer "barrens" in southern York. Yet the estimated yield was 12 to 17 bushels on red shales, which by estimates of the 1950s should have produced only 75 per cent as much wheat as limestone soils.[39] One other set of data obscures the issue: in 1759, in strongly German Cocalico Township in Lancaster, the average acreage of winter grain on "good," presumably limestone, soil was 9.8 per farm; on "middling," 10.6; and on "poor", 6.3.[40] Higher acreages on "middling" land may indicate that farmers were compensating for lower yields with larger acreages. Even if these last two sets of figures do not clearly support the view that good soils, greater affluence, possibly better practices, and greater production went hand in hand, I hypothesize they were positively correlated.

The relationship between the degree of winter grain production and cultural groups is not certain. The more prosperous Mennonites in Lancaster and the Quakers in Chester were large pro-

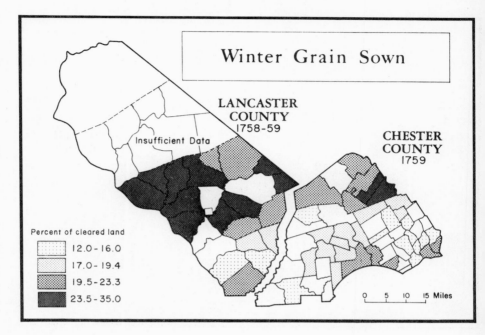

Figure 54

ducers of wheat, as we might expect from groups in tune with market conditions and improved practices.[41] Among the thirty-six Lancaster Plain farmers who sowed more than thirty acres of winter grain in 1758–59, however, were twelve Scotch-Irish, when as a group they composed only 23 per cent of the county's population (table 14). These large acreages may suggest that they and the other twenty-four, including fifteen Germans, were exploitative rather than careful farmers. We do not know; but at least we are certain that these men paid high taxes, and this is another sign that the attitudes of some Scotch-Irish may not have been very different from those of a lot of Germans.

The breeding of cattle and horses, the production of wool, and the growing of industrial crops, according to von Thünen, should occupy areas farthest from the market. We have been accustomed to thinking that breeding would be found in the frontier areas in America and Britain.[42] The evidence, however, is not clear. Calcu-

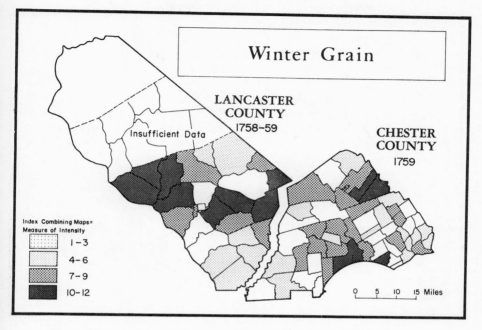

Figure 55

lations at the county level suggest that average farmers in the back-country counties of Berks, York, Cumberland, and North-ampton were less inclined to raise livestock than those nearer Philadelphia (table 33). Yet in the 1720s horse and cattle breeders held large acreages on the frontier adjacent to the Susquehanna in what became York and Lancaster counties. Later, two sites in Northampton and one in Bethel Township, Berks County, on or over Blue Mountain were described as range lands.[43] The apparent contradiction between the average figures and these other com-ments can be resolved: in frontier areas it is likely that average numbers were low because a majority of settlers were poor, but some breeders with large herds operated over many acres. The slightly higher figure for Bedford than for the Great Valley and other trans-Susquehanna counties shown in table 33 may reflect this. Unfortunately tax returns for the years between 1771 and 1782 for sparsely settled northern parts of Lancaster County

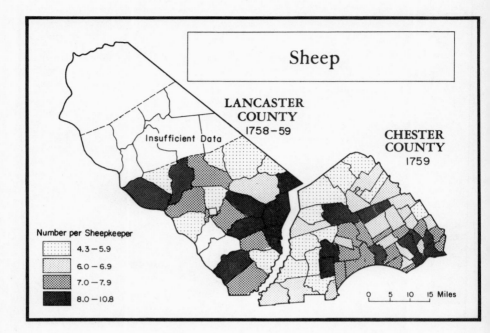

Figure 56

(Upper Paxton Township, now in Dauphin County) do not offer any evidence of large herds and extensive grazing.

Graziers and farmers nearer Philadelphia probably continued to breed cattle and horses, notably in the rougher parts of older settled counties. The relatively greater numbers in what is now Lancaster County than in Chester in 1758–59 may indicate this, and especially those in Little Britain Township in the southern end and the townships along the range of hills between the Lancaster Plain and the Lebanon Valley (figures 46 and 48). At that time in Cocalico Township two farmers owned sixty-four and sixty-five cattle each, and in 1760 the inventory of the latter listed seventy-four cattle.[44] In 1781 the large numbers of cattle and somewhat larger holdings (figures 49 and 29) in northern and southern Chester, which had more steep slopes and greater relief than other parts of the county, may indicate breeding. However, cheese and butter production and even fattening may also have been impor-

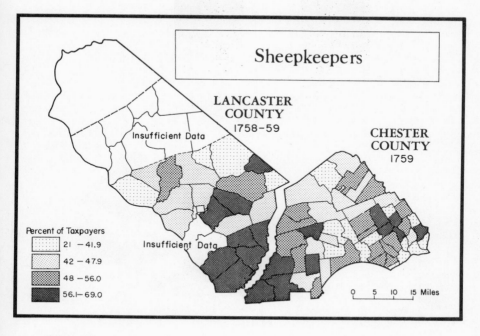

Figure 57

tant. Greater affluence among farmers and the need to haul grain to the Brandywine and flour to the east probably contributed to the relatively large number of horses on the Lancaster Plain. The "Conestoga" horse breed may have developed in Lancaster County, but a definite conclusion will never likely be reached. Even so, the area seems to have had a reputation: in 1790, George Washington ordered eleven horses from Paul Zantzinger, merchant in the town of Lancaster.[45]

Farmers in some areas may have produced more wool than those elsewhere. On the diked marsh meadows along the Delaware a few large flocks of sheep grazed. In 1782, for example, on Tinicum Island (figure 58), flocks of forty-two, fifty-five, and sixty-two presumably supplied wool to the textile manufacturers in Philadelphia.[46] Uplands in Chester and Lancaster counties and more affluent areas such as the eastern end of the Lancaster Plain tended to carry more sheep per farm than elsewhere, possibly

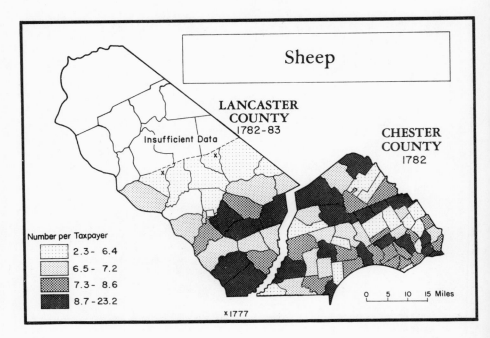

Figure 58

because persons of British ancestry were concentrated there (figures 56 and 58). More of the English and Scotch-Irish farmers in relatively poorer southern Lancaster and adjacent southwestern Chester also kept sheep than others. More people in this area did weaving, possibly to raise their incomes on these less fertile soils. A putting-out system may have been operating.[47] As noted above, at least in 1758–59, these areas produced less grain and had fewer cattle than other townships in these counties. Conclusions would be firmer if the 1782 data were less equivocal; the percentage of sheepkeepers was high on most of the Lancaster Plain and in northern Chester as well as in southern Lancaster and south-western Chester (figures 57 and 59). Moreover, if it could be shown that Germans grew more flax and hemp than the British, we might conclude that British persons used more wool. But widows of Mennonites received wool more frequently than hemp and flax (table 28), and so no final decisions can be made.

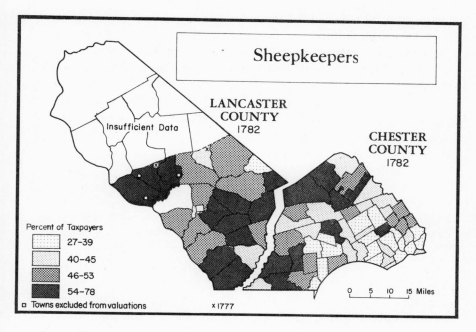

Figure 59

The two "industrial" crops, flax and hemp, showed contrasting regional patterns. Flax production, including seed for export, was probably ubiquitous, even though in 1782 there were too few oil mills to allow a definite conclusion to be drawn (table 34). Commercial hemp production seems to have been localized. In Lancaster County the rich alluvial soils on the flood plain of the Susquehanna and tributary small streams supported this nutrient-demanding crop.[48] As early as 1720 farmers imported indentured servants to work on Lancaster hemp.[49] In 1769 Bartram Galbraith grew no fewer than twenty-six acres in Donegal Township, possibly in response to the demands for self-sufficiency brought on by the nonimportation crisis. But even before this, between April 1766 and March 1767, William McCord, a Lancaster merchant, bought 18,000 pounds from eighteen farmers in flood plain areas, two-thirds of them German. Lancaster hemp was advertised in Philadelphia.[50] As indications of the long-term importance of hemp from the Susquehanna flood plain, in 1753 Philadelphians held Lancaster hemp in high repute, and Charles Norris wrote to James Wright in Hempfield Township on the Susquehanna speculating on the reasons for the success of hemp production there. He thought that the longer growing season in the valley was responsible.[51] If so, the extensive reaches of rich bottom lands, which one report said were cropped for twelve consecutive years, was a critical factor. Whether hemp production continued on a large scale after the Revolution is uncertain.[52]

* * *

Early Pennsylvania farmers and their families, with few exceptions, ate heartily, were well-clothed, and sold a surplus of goods. They were able to live comfortably even though they only scratched the soil and their system of farming was woefully inadequate in the eyes of reformers. The contentedness of working farmers made them scorn attempts to stir them to improve efficiency and intensify land use. Among the various national and denominational groups in Pennsylvania, members of sectarian groups, notably the Quakers and Mennonites, seemed more anxious to seek higher yields per acre by more astute practices. This was reflected in their generally higher economic status. Yet even these "plain folk" showed little interest in specialization, even though they sowed more acres of wheat and possessed more livestock on the average than other groups. The regionalization of agricultural types was not strongly discernible, as the theorist von Thünen might have expected, as a consequence of either distance from market or land quality. Most farmers grew wheat, other grains, fiber crops, garden crops, and fruit; raised cattle, hogs, sheep for wool; and kept draft horses to plow their land and pull their wheat-laden wagons. The only signs of specialization as a consequence of distance from the market were truck farming, dairying, and fattening near Philadelphia. Soil and topographic conditions influenced the concentration of livestock on low-lying drained meadows along the Delaware and the production of hemp on alluvial soils along the Susquehanna. Wheat and clover yields possibly were higher on limestone than other soils, and livestock breeding took place in hill lands. For the rest, regional patterns were not clear, and so distance from market, soil quality, and even denominational affiliations were secondary considerations in determining the agricultural system in any one place in the area. In the 1790s most farmers were involved in general mixed farming, with an emphasis on wheat for the export trade, as their predecessors were in 1700, and many were content with the degree of prosperity they had achieved.

CHAPTER EIGHT

The Development of
Early Southeastern Pennsylvania

By the last decade of the eighteenth century the European occupation had dramatically transformed the southeastern Pennsylvania landscape. In 1680 the area was lightly populated by Indians and a few Europeans along the Delaware. In 1800 there were more than 300,000 persons of European descent here, and many others had moved on to other areas. In this 120 years the people organized the space into farms, arrayed their social and political institutions and physical facilities over the area, built towns that became the centers of regional and local activity, and exploited the land's resources for forestry, mining, and especially agriculture.

Yet in spite of the marked alteration of the surface of the land the Pennsylvanians' mode of living had changed very little. Though their average standard of living had risen, the prosperity, paradoxically, had been achieved through traditional ways. There were few technological advances. Pennsylvanians were perhaps the most liberal people in the world—they believed implicitly, some even explicitly, in individual material success. Yet because many were successful, liberalism (in the traditional sense) became enshrined as a style of life. Many of those who were not so fortunate or were dissatisfied repeated the original movement across the Atlantic by moving to the frontier. They, too, shared the hope of achieving success. Vast resources lay out beyond the settled area, and few persons felt actually limited. (The least stable and successful were sustained by another variation: individual immortality on another

218

frontier.) The openness contributed to making these people conservative, not in the sense of espousing community but in preserving their freedom and privacy. What structures there were, and they were minimal by today's standards, existed for the individual and his family. This can be said even for the more disciplined Quakers and Mennonites. And so the paradox deepens. Their authoritarianism and ideology of hard work existed to prove not only that their groups were viable but that they as individuals were justified in seeking perfection. In this resource-rich environment, what better way could they achieve this than through exploitation of the land?

* * *

To sum up how the people related to the land, the century can be divided into four periods: establishment, 1681–1700; stagnation, 1700–1730; expansion, 1730–1760; and consolidation, disruption, and reestablishment, 1760–1800.[1]

In the years before 1700 the foundations were laid. Quakers especially, but also some German-speaking sectarians and even Anglicans, were committed to building a liberal society open to the persecuted and to the philosophy of material success through exploitation of the soil and commerce. Most of the first settlers were of "middling" means, and by 1693 little differentiation of wealth had occurred (table 1). The population grew quickly to more than 20,000 as the settlers filled the area on and near the Delaware River in the three original counties of Philadelphia, Chester, and Bucks and the three counties that soon became Delaware. Although the Quakers agreed with some of the goals of William Penn, such as fee simple tenure, they refused to follow his plan for townships with agricultural villages and meeting houses in the center. Unlike first-generation settlers in New England, they preferred to live on their own farms, and they wanted their farms to be relatively compact parcels, not scattered fields or strips. As a result, rural settlement was dispersed. Not surprisingly, the people were following a trend toward enclosure and the spatial consolidation of fields already under way in most of Britain and apparently even among the Swedes on the Delaware. Most obviously in Pennsylvania, the day of the individual and the family farm had arrived for western European society. The Quakers firmly established the pattern for all who followed in the eighteenth century, indeed well into the twentieth century. Even while small, neatly platted townships were being surveyed, rural communities had no clearly defined boundaries or centers. The "indiscriminate location" and the "metes-and-bounds" survey system, which became the norm after 1700, made any different system impossible. Counties rather than townships became the chief unit of local government, and before large numbers of settlers of many denominations and national groups arrived no semblance of the parish as a spatial unit existed. Pennsylvania thus provided the clearest antecedent in America for the open-country neighborhoods of the nineteenth century Middle West.

The early settlers recognized that they could not farm commercially and establish order without mechanisms for trade. The people and Penn were in agreement on this, and they enthusiastically supported the development of urban places, particularly Philadelphia. To promote the "holy experiment" Penn granted city lots to some purchasers of farmland. This incentive was hardly needed, however; by 1700 the metropolis was populated by 6,000 persons (figure 36). Philadelphia easily outstripped other county towns such as Chester and Bristol, inhibited promoters from laying out others, and became the center of most aspects of the province's life—government, commerce, and social activity.

Philadelphia's rapid growth was the result of good fortune as well as the commercial spirit of the people. The founding of the colony coincided with the opening of new markets, particularly in the West Indies. In these early years the agricultural system and its pattern of land use became firmly established. Because most agricultural production was for home consumption, farmers produced a wide range of crops and livestock. Nevertheless the external trading sector, the provisioning trade, and the high percentage of urban dwellers in the total population contributed to the development of a small degree of specialization. Wheat and flour were the major exports throughout the period, followed by beef, fattened near the city to provision ships. William Penn believed that the first generation of the colony had failed to live up to his somewhat ambiguous goals for the "holy experiment"; they had not taken his advice on community living, they had failed to pay quitrents promptly, they had even squatted on his land, and they had achieved power in the assembly and had passed laws in their favor. By the standards of the time, however, the province had not come to nothing; it had already established firm trading patterns, its land produced bountifully, and its people had taken up family farms in communities of their own making.

The next generation of Pennsylvanians, between 1700 and 1730, did not sustain the rapid growth of the years before. During this period of relative stagnation, population growth was considerably slower (table 7 and figure 11) and fewer migrants, in proportion to the population, arrived from Europe. By 1710 enough Scotch-Irish Presbyterians had begun to appear to rouse James Logan's fears that they would take over the province, and the arrivals of these reputedly less capable people swelled toward the end of the second decade. Shortly before 1710 and for a few years thereafter German-speaking Mennonites also arrived in substantial numbers, but the overwhelming majority of German church folk, Lutheran and Reformed, came after 1725.

Most of the people who came during this period settled together in areas and communities defined by nationality or denomination, but for the most part these were adjacent to previously occupied settlements. A few groups, such as the Mennonites of the Lancaster area, went several miles beyond the "line" of occupation (figures 7 and 8). Language and creed thus exerted considerable influence on the whereabouts of people. Yet groups were mixed in several areas, for example on the Lancaster Plain, where the soil was somewhat more fertile than in most other parts. Before 1730 all farmers in all groups set up their plantations according to the Quaker model: farms under one operator, in most cases under one owner, and farmsteads placed amidst contiguous fields.

The slower pace of development between 1700 and 1730 was apparent in several areas of life. First, no one showed interest in laying out new towns. Presumably people recognized that the metropolis was capable of handling not only provincial but also many local matters. Second, even Philadelphia did not grow as quickly; by 1725 urban population in the province had dropped to

17 per cent from 25 per cent in 1700 (figure 36). Third, trade was indifferent. In 1725 imports per capita only began to surpass the level of 1700; in 1700 they were 17 shillings and in 1725, 20 shillings (figures 4 and 11). At the same time stratification of wealth became more marked, at least in Chester County. The share of the poor there fell from over 17 per cent in 1693 to less than 10 per cent and the most prosperous held 5 per cent more. The average and somewhat better rural dwellers managed to improve their situation in this stagnant period, however, according to samples of estate inventories approximately fifteen years apart (table 17).

Between 1730 and 1760 considerable expansion occurred that was obvious in population growth, the rate of occupation of the area, the movements of people, the organization of new counties and towns, and trade. Large numbers of Germans, mostly Lutheran and Reformed, and of Scotch-Irish arrived between 1725 and 1755. This influx added to the mélange of groups in pluralistic Pennsylvania and contributed to an extremely rapid growth of population (table 7). Together with movements of older groups, such as Mennonites and Quakers (figure 14), the new settlers filled the area except the rough uplands. Some people began to filter into the "ridge and valley" area, and many, including some members of sectarian groups, went on to Maryland, Virginia, and North Carolina. Persons in all national and denominational groups sought locations on the frontier. Movements seem to have been most pronounced during the years of strongest economic growth.

Pennsylvanians in the back country brought sufficient pressure to bear on the assembly to divide the original three counties into a total of eight by 1752, beginning with Lancaster in 1729. In response to and even in anticipation of these developments, James Hamilton and the sons of William Penn laid out county seats. They expected that these county towns would assume a significant role in expediting governmental, legal, and commercial activities within their trading areas—the counties. Their assumptions were correct; Lancaster (founded by Hamilton), York, Reading, and Carlisle grew rapidly (figure 36) and became functionally important as high-ranking places within the urban system. The foresight of the founders to set them far enough from Philadelphia and from one another and generally in the accessible centers of counties was rewarded. After 1745, and especially between 1755 and 1765, many other entrepreneurs sought to emulate the Penns and to capitalize on the urban spurt by laying out towns, particularly in the new counties. Very few of these new places grew to 300 by 1800. By 1765, when economic growth had clearly slackened, the town-founding vogue had died.

This wave of urbanization occurred in response to improved economic conditions after 1725, and the new county towns in turn provided the mechanisms for growth by improving trade connections within the area. Development was also stimulated by an increased confidence of British creditors in the area, by the larger and more rapid growth of population (table 7) permitting larger bulk shipments of imported goods, by new demands in Ireland for flaxseed, by iron exports to England after 1750, and, on the production side, by expanded grain acreages for the production of crops on the longer established farms. Despite fluctuations, exports of wheat, flour, and flaxseed from Philadelphia rose more than 50 per cent per capita between 1731 and the middle 1760s. The value of imports increased even more dramatically. Although wars and depressions slowed the movement of goods, from 1749 onward per capita imports were usually double and sometimes treble those of the years around 1730.[2]

Thus during the colony's third generation the area achieved a very prominent position in the preindustrial world. Despite practices on the land that by modern standards were virtually antediluvian, farmers increased production and reached a higher standard of living. Average inventory values increased by 20 per cent in Chester County and doubled in Lancaster, and land values rose even more rapidly (tables 17 and 13). Philadelphia was rapidly moving toward a position of preeminence among urban centers on the Atlantic seaboard. Ben Franklin's arrival just before 1730 symbolized the beginning of its drive to success. His exhortations to hard work and frugality may have contributed to growth, but the skill of merchants in organizing trade and the availability of markets were also major factors. And without the recognition by Penn's sons that county towns would expedite trade, development probably would not have occurred as rapidly.

As in the previous period, however, the 1730–1760 period witnessed an increasing differentation of wealth. In Chester County the bottom 30 per cent paid 6 per cent of the taxes while the richest tenth paid 30 per cent (table 1). The Quakers in south-central Chester County and the Mennonites on the Lancaster Plain were the most affluent of the denominational groups, though individuals identified with other theological positions also became wealthy. The "sectarians" had become richer through the discipline of hard work and mutual help. They produced more wheat than others, owned more horses (figures 14, 41, 47, and 55), and probably were more inclined to try new techniques to improve yields. Their success does not seem to have been the result of occupying the best soils. In upper Philadelphia County these sectarians had settled on soils derived from red shales that were somewhat inferior to the limestone and crystalline soils in other places (tables 31 and 10; figure 6). Distinctions in wealth among national groups were not apparent in 1760.

The period between 1760 and the 1790s was troubled. Consolidation, then disruption and reestablishment of the pre-Revolutionary economy marked the period, rather than expansion. Some persons were experimenting with new ways that after 1800 would take the people beyond preindustrial practices.[3] Immigration from Germany ceased after 1755, and the flow from the British Isles, although revived by 1768, was choked off between 1775 and 1783 and was not as heavy thereafter as before 1755. Population growth generally was slower after 1760. Movements of people within the area may have been slacker, at least until the 1780s.

The decreased rate of population growth was paralleled by slower developments in other aspects of life during the decade or so after 1760. Urban populations grew at an even slower pace than previously. After 1765 few new towns were founded for two decades. Britain became a customer for Pennsylvania's wheat and flour by the middle 1760s and in 1771 and 1772, and the colonial high for imports and exports was reached. Yet the per capita yearly value of imports between 1761 and 1772 amounted to only 34 shillings compared with 42 shillings in the previous twelve years (figures 4 and 11). Although data are almost too scarce to make a judgment, exports per person seemed to rise only slightly. The ebullient days between 1748 and 1760 were replaced by times in which the economy leveled off or even weakened, if imports are the standard. Colonials began to harbor doubts about their participation in the Atlantic trading system, as evidenced by the nonimportation agreements in 1769.

Economic uncertainties of the years before 1775 contributed to the War of Independence. Between 1775 and 1783 external trade was stifled and internal markets were altered. Merchants, shopkeepers, and other persons involved in exports and imports suffered more than farmers unless they changed their activities. In 1777 a British prisoner noted that Lancaster was

now in a state of supineness, the shopkeepers lolling and smoking at their doors, their shops which were overflowing with all sorts of commodities, scarcely contain more than Shakespeare's Apothecary's "a beggarly account of empty boxes" unless indeed, some French frippery, which the inhabitants will not purchase.[4]

Many farmers sold their goods to both the British and American armies, though in 1778 farmers in York County sold their wheat for whisky rather than for flour to supply the army. Because farmers continued to produce a large share of goods for home consumption, they were better able to survive the disruption of the economy. In fact, the more successful seemed to have flourished during the period. In 1783 the average values of a sample of inventories was considerably higher than in 1760, and the upper 10 per cent of the taxpayers, in Chester County at least, paid a higher proportion of taxes (tables 17 and 1).

After the Revolution the economy did not fully revive until after 1789. The average value of exports in 1784, 1787, and 1789 was only 40 shillings, compared with 59 shillings in 1771, 1772, and 1773 (figures 4 and 11). In the early 1790s exports increased. Even so, between 1780 and 1800 the population of the area did not grow any more rapidly than during the 1760s. To be sure, Philadelphia grew more quickly than earlier (figure 36), but not as fast as New York or Baltimore; merchants in the Pennsylvania metropolis apparently did not see new opportunities as clearly as other merchants. For example, Oliver Evans' milling techniques found more favor in the Baltimore area than in Philadelphia. In the back country most county seats except Easton and Harrisburg increased more slowly. These two towns advanced chiefly because of newly developed areas along the Delaware and Susquehanna rivers beyond southeastern Pennsylvania rather than because of activities within the area itself. Despite the spectacular growth of Harrisburg, the establishment of new counties, the choice of new seats from among towns already existing, and the founding of new villages in the 1780s, the urban pattern retained much the same form as in the early 1760s. The parallel population growth rates of county towns in the back country suggests that major changes in the types of activities of these places did not occur before 1800 or even 1820.

If the trend of urbanization did not change direction during the period of the Revolution, neither did the economy and land use. Wheat continued to be the major crop as European markets expanded in the early 1790s. Gentlemen farmers wrote voluminously on how to improve the care of land and livestock (yet surprisingly little on how to conserve labor). But everyday life only hinted that major changes in farming practices might be in the offing. Certainly some more prosperous farmers saw advantages in feeding livestock, improving yields through more fertilizing, and tightening rotation schemes. These tendencies toward more intensive use of the land may have been encouraged by the weak wheat markets of the 1780s. The large number of cattle per farm in Chester County suggests that farmers there at least showed more interest in reforms (table 33 and figure 49). Farmers possibly were showing more concern for different commodities in recognition of the comparative advantage of distance from markets, notably Philadelphia. Nevertheless the system generally remained in a state of stability; most farmers still produced a diversity of goods for their own use and wheat to trade for other goods. They continued to use the soil extensively and only superficially.

Although a century of great activity had left agricultural practices much the same, the returns from farming and other pursuits were now less equally shared. The average and more prosperous farmers and craftsmen, notably millers, flourished and were satisfied with what they were earning from the system, as indicated by inventory values (table 17). However, the evidence in Chester

County shows that by 1800 the differentiation of wealth was much greater than in 1693 or even 1782. The top 10 per cent now controlled 38 per cent of the wealth (if the ratio of taxes paid is a reliable guide) and the bottom 60 per cent held only 17 per cent (table 1). Whether this means that proportionately more on the bottom were now destitute is not clear. Nevertheless, even though the vast majority may have had as much as before, many were probably dissatisfied with what they were getting, as the ancestors of the Pennsylvanians had been in western Europe. Opportunities within the region were not expanding rapidly enough. During the period of expansion before 1760, towns provided openings just as Philadelphia had at the outset; but now towns were not growing any more quickly than the whole population. By 1760 many farmers, 25 per cent or more, had become tenants on the best lands such as the Lancaster Plain. Some of these tenants were prosperous and were able to build up capital to buy farms. But in 1782 the number of landless was the same as in 1760, and possibly they had less chance to buy farms nearby (figure 30). Opportunity lay in the cheaper land to the west, so following good economic periods, which permitted a building up of capital, tenants and small owners moved. Even Quakers and Mennonites, after two or three decades during which their holdings did not expand, felt the pressure and established new colonies elsewhere. In the more expansive early 1790s movement was considerable.

A century of development brought prosperity to many southeastern Pennsylvanians. Quite possibly for the time more of them lived better than any other population of similar size in the world. Although the people followed fairly well-established European ways of organizing their lives and using the land, their individualistic drives and the richness of the land contributed greatly to their success. Here were western Europeans, many of whom, despite their various nationalities and denominations and differences in wealth, felt they had fulfilled their goals of freedom from institutional constraints and of individual and family autonomy and success. Even for those who did not win, the system was open. If land became scarce and expensive, the west was seen as a place to try again, a place to conquer. Resources were there in abundance, or so they thought.

Today, as we look back over two centuries, that society seems stable and idyllic compared to our own industrialized, bureaucratized, and urbanized scene. Even if there was conflict and conformity then, we seem more enclosed, our resources and space appear decidedly limited. Liberal individualism could work then as it cannot today. Many now preach individualistic competition as though we still lived in the eighteenth century, but now their words are destructive. Sam Warner has described privatism and its consequences in Philadelphia from the 1770s to the 1930s that has brought us decayed central cities.[5] We could add consumerism and the greed of producers that has polluted streams and has turned the "Dutch" country into a tourist trap. The legacy of individualism passed to us from Frederick Brown and his neighbors (and my ancestors) is not good enough today. Under our technological empire and in our closed environment our task is to search for community in a much more profound way than they would ever have been able to foresee. Today "Penn's woods" is anything but the best poor man's country in the world.[6]

Notes

The locations of MSS collections are cited throughout the notes, with the exception of MSS collections in the Historical Society of Pennsylvania, MSS tax assessments and returns in the Lancaster County Historical Society and Chester County Historical Society, and wills, deeds, and inventories in the Lancaster County Courthouse and Chester County Courthouse; for these, locations are noted only in their first citation. A description of the materials in these depositories may be found in the Bibliographical Note. The names of depositories and journals have been abbreviated after their first occurrence. The citations of books contain publication data only when each book is first mentioned.

PREFACE

1. This phrase or variations on it were frequently used—e.g., Christopher Sauer, "An Early Description of Pennsylvania: Letter of Christopher Sauer Written in 1724, Describing Conditions in Philadelphia and Vicinity, and the Sea Voyage from Europe," ed. Rayner W. Kelsey, trans. Adolph Gerber, *Pennsylvania Magazine of History and Biography*, 45 (1921): 249; William Moraley, *The Unfortunate: or, the Voyage and Adventures of William Moraley ... Gent. ... Containing Whatever Is Curious and Remarkable in the Provinces of Pennsylvania and New Jersey ...* (Newcastle, Eng., 1743), p. 9; Patrick M'Roberts, "Patrick M'Roberts' Tour Through a Part of the Northern Provinces of America," ed. Carl Bridenbaugh, *Pa. Mag. Hist. Biog.*, 59 (1935): 136; Joseph Poultney to Robert Dixon, Dec. 15, 1783, "A Letter of Joseph Poultney," *ibid.*, 52 (1928): 95.

2. Harry Roy Merrens, "Historical Geography and Early American History," *William and Mary Quarterly*, 3d ser., 22 (1965): 529–48.

3. Benjamin Franklin, *The Papers of Benjamin Franklin*, ed. Leonard W. Labaree *et al.* (New Haven, Conn.: Yale University Press, 1959–), 4: 120, 479–86; 5: 158–60. See also George Thomas to the Bishop of Exeter, April 23, 1748, in William Stevens Perry, ed., *Historical Collections Relating to the American Colonial Church* (Hartford, 1871), 2: 256.

4. [Benjamin Rush], "An Account of the Manners of the German Inhabitants of Pennsylvania," *Columbian Magazine, or Monthly Miscellany*, 3 (August 1789): 25. (Title varies—also *Universal Asylum and Columbian Magazine*; hereafter cited as *Colum. Mag.*) This tract was published again: ed. Israel D. Rupp (Philadelphia, 1875), and ed. Theodore E. Schmauk, *Proceedings of the Pennsylvania German Society 1908*, 19 (1910): 1–128. An editorial comment in Benjamin Rush, *Letters of Benjamin Rush*, ed.

Lyman H. Butterfield, Memoirs of the American Philosophical Society no. 30, pts. i–ii (Princeton, N.J.: Princeton University Press, 1951), 4: 368n., discusses Rush's work as a political tract. Oliver Wendell Holmes gave Rush little due: he was "observing, rather than a sound observer"; quoted in Lyman H. Butterfield, "The Reputation of Benjamin Rush," *Pennsylvania History*, 17 (1950): 12.

5. Richard H. Shryock, "British versus German Traditions in Colonial Agriculture," *Mississippi Valley Historical Review*, 26 (1939–40): 39–54. See also references under n. 39, chap. 1.

6. Douglas E. Leach, *The Northern Colonial Frontier, 1607–1763* (New York: Holt, Rinehart & Winston, 1966), p. 137; Wayland F. Dunaway, *The Scotch-Irish in Colonial Pennsylvania* (Chapel Hill: University of North Carolina Press, 1944), p. 65; Estyn E. Evans, "The Scotch-Irish in the New World: An Atlantic Heritage," *Journal of the Royal Antiquaries of Ireland*, 95 (1965): 39–49, esp. 44–47; T. W. Moody, "The Ulster Scots in Colonial and Revolutionary America," *Studies, an Irish Quarterly Review*, 34 (1945): 86. But see Theodore Huebner, *The Germans in America* (Philadelphia and New York: Chilton, 1962), p. 81.

7. "English versus Germans: Extracts Translated from the Letter of a German Gentleman Visiting Relatives in Philadelphia in the Autumn of 1747," *Pa. Mag. Hist. Biog.*, 16 (1892): 120. See discussion in James T. Lemon, "The Agricultural Practices of National Groups in Eighteenth-Century Southeastern Pennsylvania," *Geographical Review*, 56 (1966): 493–96.

8. Boston and New York: Houghton Mifflin.

9. A classic statement of liberalism and its effects is found in Karl Polanyi, *The Great Transformation: The Political and Economic Origins of Our Time* (New York: Farrar & Rinehart, 1944). The "purest" period of laissez faire capitalism was between 1830 and 1850. A more recent discussion is George P. Grant, *Technology and Empire: Perspectives on North America* (Toronto: House of Anansi, 1969).

10. See Sam B. Warner, *The Private City: Philadelphia in Three Periods of Its Growth* (Philadelphia: University of Pennsylvania Press, 1968) for a similar view. Louis Hartz, *The Founding of New Societies: Studies in the History of the United States, Latin America, South Africa, Canada, and Australia* (New York: Harcourt, Brace and World, 1964), is worth consideration in this regard.

CHAPTER 1

1. A Quaker, a Mennonite, or a Scotch-Irish Presbyterian could have been used, but as will appear shortly the Germans were the largest group and the Lutherans the largest German denomination. Hence the choice of a German Lutheran as a typical person.

2. Bernard H. Slicher van Bath, *The Agrarian History of Europe, A.D. 500–1850*, trans. Olive Ordish (London: Edward Arnold, 1963), p. 324. The discussion on Europe is based on this and the following works: papers from a symposium on the "Morphogenesis of the Agrarian Cultural Landscape," *Geografiska Annaler*, vol. 42, nos. 1–2 (1961), esp. Glanville R. Jones, "Early Territorial Organization in England and Wales," pp. 174–81; James H. Johnson, "The Development of the Rural Settlement Pattern of Ireland," pp. 165–73; and Harald Uhlig, "Old Hamlets with Infield and Outfield Systems in Western and Central Europe," pp. 285–312; James M. Houston, *A Social Geography of Europe*, rev. ed. (London: Gerald Duckworth, 1963), chaps. 4, 5; Gottfried Pfeifer, "The Quality of Peasant Living in Central Europe," in *Man's Role in Changing the Face of the Earth*, ed. William L. Thomas (Chicago: University of Chicago Press, 1956), pp. 240–77.

For a review of demographic changes, see Emmanuel Le Roy Ladurie, "From Waterloo to Colyton," *Times Literary Supplement*, 65 (Sept. 8, 1966): 791–92; and also D. V. Glass and D. E. C. Eversley, eds., *Population in History: Essays in Historical Demography* (London: Edward Arnold; Chicago: Aldine, 1965), and *Daedalus*, 90

(1968), issue on "Historical Population Studies." More particularly, see the following studies of areas: Eric L. Jones, ed., *Agriculture and Economic Growth in England, 1650–1815* (London: Methuen, 1967), which has brought together many important papers—see introduction; William G. Hoskins, *The Making of the English Landscape* (London: Hodder & Stoughton, 1955), p. 159; Gordon E. Mingay, *English Landed Society in the Eighteenth Century* (London: Routledge & Kegan Paul; Toronto: University of Toronto Press, 1963), pp. 45–47, 233; Eric Kerridge, *The Agricultural Revolution* (London: Allen & Unwin, 1967), p. 15, which supports the view that the 16th and early 17th centuries were a time of major changes; James G. Leyburn, *The Scotch-Irish: A Social History* (Chapel Hill: University of North Carolina Press, 1962), pp. 12–13, 160–64; Ingeborg Leister, "Landwirtschaft und Agrarräumliche Gliederung Irlands zur Zeit A. Youngs," *Zeitschrifts für Agrargeschichte und Agrarsoziologie*, 10 (1962): 9–44; Gilbert Camblin, *The Town in Ulster: An Account of the Origin and Building of Towns of the Province and the Development of their Rural Setting* (Belfast: W. Mullan, 1951), pp. 59–62; R. J. Dickson, *Ulster Emigration to Colonial America, 1718–1775*, Ulster-Scot Historical Series, no. 1 (London: Routledge & Kegan Paul, 1966); Friedrich Lütge, *Deutsche Sozial- und Wirtschafts-Geschichte* (Berlin, Göttingen, Heidelberg: Springer, 1952), pp. 249–51; Friedrich K. Riemann, *Ackerbau und Viehhaltung in Vorindustriellen Deutschland* (Kitzingen am Main: Holzner, 1953), p. 100; W. H. Bruford, *Germany in the Eighteenth Century: The Social Background to the Literary Revival* (Cambridge: At the University Press, 1935), p. 122; Diedrich Saalfeld, *Bauernwirtschaft und Gutsbetrieb in der Vorindustriellen Zeit* (Stuttgart: G. Fischer, 1960), esp. pp. 150–51; Wilhelm Abel, *Geschichte der deutschen Landwirtschaft vom frühen Mittelalter bis zum 19. Jahrhundert* (Stuttgart: E. Ulmer, 1962); Friedrich Lütge, *Geschichte der deutschen Agrarverfassung vom frühen Mittelalter bis zum 19. Jahrhundert* (Stuttgart: E. Ulmer, 1963). See a fuller discussion in James Thomas Lemon, "A Rural Geography of Southeastern Pennsylvania: The Contributions of Cultural Inheritance, Social Structure, Economic Conditions and Physical Resources" (Ph.D. diss., University of Wisconsin, 1964), chap. 2.

3. Alexander Thomson, "Franklin County One Hundred Years Ago: A Settler's Experience told in a Letter . . . ," ed. T. W. J. Wylie, *Pa. Mag. Hist. Biog.*, 8 (1884): 319.

4. On promotion of the region, see Hope F. Kane, "Notes on Early Pennsylvania Promotion Literature," *Pa. Mag. Hist. Biog.*, 63 (1939): 144–68; William Penn, ed., "A Letter from Doctor More, with Passages out of Several Letters from Persons of Good Credit, Relating to the State and Improvement of Early Pennsylvania. Published to Prevent False Reports . . . ," *ibid.*, 4 (1880): 452. On Mennonites' impressions, see Thomas Chalkley, *A Collection of the Works of . . . Thomas Chalkley in Two Parts* (Philadelphia, 1749), p. 73, and Samuel Guldin, "Diary of the Rev. Samuel Guldin, Relating to his Journey to Pennsylvania . . . 1710," ed. William J. Hinke, *Journal of the Presbyterian Historical Society*, 14 (1930): 66.

5. Most early works cited "push" factors, but recent studies are more open to "pull" through promotion. Edward R. R. Green, "Scotch-Irish Emigration, an Imperial Problem," *Western Pennsylvania Historical Magazine*, 35 (1952), esp. p. 196; George R. Mellor, "Emigration from the British Isles to the New World, 1765–1775," *History*, n.s., 40 (1955), esp. p. 68; Moody, "Ulster Scots," pp. 85–94, 211–21, esp. p. 90; Mingay, *English Landed Society*, pp. 94–99; Otto Langguth, "Pennsylvania German Pioneers from the County of Wertheim," ed. Donald H. Yoder, *Pennsylvania German Folklore Society* (Yearbook), 12 (1947): 172, 195, which stresses promotion; Erna Risch, "Encouragement of Immigration as Revealed in Colonial Legislation," *Virginia Magazine of History and Biography*, 65 (1937): 8; Kane, "Pennsylvania Promotion Literature," pp. 144–68; Michael Kraus, "America and the Utopian Ideal in the Eighteenth Century," *Miss. Vall. Hist. Rev.*, 22 (1936): 503.

6. Pastorius, "Positive Information from America," in *Narratives of Early Pennsylvania, West New Jersey and Delaware, 1630–1707*, ed. Albert C. Myers (New York: Scribner's, 1913), p. 397.

7. John J. Stoudt, comp., *Ordeal at Valley Forge: A Day-by-Day Chronicle from December 17, 1777 to June 18, 1778* (Philadelphia: University of Pennsylvania Press, 1963), p. 126 and *passim*. Several references, including names of some who were flogged, are noted.

8. Alexander Teamwell to Captain Chambers, Mar. 18, 1778, William Henry MSS, 1759-1812, p. 24a, Historical Society of Pennsylvania, Philadelphia.

9. Rodney C. Loehr, "Self Sufficiency on the Farm, 1759-1819," *Agricultural History*, 26 (1952): 37-42. On the earlier view, see Percy W. Bidwell and John I. Falconer, *History of Agriculture in the Northern United States, 1620-1860*, Carnegie Institution of Washington, Publication no. 358 (Washington, 1925), pp. 126-27, 133-35, 137-44.

10. July 12, 1799, Diary, 1795-1801, Hist. Soc. Pa.

11. On psychological influences, see David C. McClelland, *The Achieving Society* (Princeton, N.J.: Van Nostrand, 1961); Everett C. Hagen, *On the Theory of Social Change: How Economic Development Begins* (Homewood, Ill.: Dorsey, 1962), esp. pp. 261-309 on England; Julian Wolpert, "The Decision Process in Spatial Context," *Annals of the Association of American Geographers*, 54 (1964): 537-58, who deals with maximizers and "satisficers."

12. David Shultze, *Journals and Papers of David Shultze*, ed. and trans. Andrew S. Berky (Pennsburg, Pa.: Schwenkfelder Library, 1952-53), 1: 92.

13. Mildred L. Campbell, "Social Origins of Some Early Americans," in *Seventeenth-Century America: Essays in Colonial History*, ed. James M. Smith (Chapel Hill: University of North Carolina Press, 1959), pp. 72-73; Mildred L. Campbell, "English Emigration on the Eve of the American Revolution," *American Historical Review*, 61 (1955): 5.

14. Campbell, "English Emigration," p. 6; Abbot Smith, *Colonists in Bondage: White Servitude and Convict Labor in America, 1607-1776* (Chapel Hill: University of North Carolina Press, 1947), pp. 51-52.

15. Donald H. Yoder, ed., "Emigrants from Wuerttemberg; The Adolf Gerber Lists," *Pa. Ger. Folklore Soc.* (Yearbook), 10 (1945): 103-327, lists only 3 day laborers among the first 80 names. See also Otto Langguth, "Pennsylvania German Pioneers," *ibid.*, 12 (1947): 147-289; Green, "Scotch-Irish Emigration," p. 204; Arthur Young, *Arthur Young's Tour in Ireland (1776-1779)*, ed. Arthur W. Hutton (London and New York, 1892), 1: 145.

16. John E. Pomfret, "The First Purchasers of Pennsylvania, 1681-1700," *Pa. Mag. Hist. Biog.*, 80 (1956): 150-53; Gary B. Nash, "The Free Society of Traders and the Early Politics of Pennsylvania," *ibid.*, 89 (1965): 149-50.

17. Campbell, "Social Origins," p. 71; Pomfret, "First Purchasers," p. 153; Pastorius, "Positive Information," p. 399; Yoder, "Emigrants from Wuerttemberg," p. 128; see also editor's note in [Rush], "Manners of the German Inhabitants," ed. Rupp, pp. 10-11, on Germans in England; Campbell, "English Emigration," p. 7; Mellor, "Emigration from the British Isles," p. 72.

18. Franklin, *The Writings of Benjamin Franklin*, ed. Albert H. Smyth (New York: Macmillan, 1907), 10: 117-18; Tench Coxe, *A View of the United States of America in a Series of Papers Written at Various Times Between the Years 1787 and 1794*... (Philadelphia, 1794), p. 6.

19. In 1789 Delaware County was separated from Chester, in 1785 Dauphin from Lancaster, and in 1813 Lebanon from Dauphin. MSS tax returns for Chester for December, 1759, are found in Chester County Historical Society, West Chester, and in Shippen Family Papers, 1701-1856, Hist. Soc. Pa. Lancaster returns for 1758-59 are in the Lancaster County Historical Society, Lancaster. Single freemen are excluded from calculations.

For tables and maps throughout this discussion, these and other MSS returns and assessments from these collections are used. Some provincial tax lists for Chester and

Lancaster appear in *Pennsylvania Archives* (Philadelphia, Harrisburg, 1852–1935), 3d ser., vols. 11, 12, and 17. Much of the 1781 and 1782 data used in maps and tables were taken from these. John S. Futhey and Gilbert Cope, *History of Chester County, Pennsylvania* (Philadelphia, 1881), pp. 32, 434, reproduced some assessment lists beginning in 1693. For table 1, 1802 lists in the Delaware County Court House, Media, Pa., were also used. For some Lancaster lists see Franklin Ellis and Samuel Evans, *History of Lancaster County, Pennsylvania . . .* (Philadelphia, 1883), pp. 20–21 and *passim*; H. Frank Eshleman, ed., "Assessment Lists and Other Manuscript Documents of Lancaster County Prior to 1729," *Papers and Addresses of the Lancaster County Historical Society*, 20 (1916): 153–94 (later *Journal of . . .* ; cited hereafter as *Jour. Lanc. Co. Hist. Soc.*). See also William H. Egle, *Histories of the Counties of Dauphin and Lebanon* (Philadelphia, 1883), pp. 21–41, and other county histories. Post-1785 lists for Dauphin (and Lebanon) are in the County Courthouse in Harrisburg. The Genealogical Society of the Church of Jesus Christ of the Latter Day Saints has microfilmed many but not all extant lists. Although some were photographed neatly, such as Chester's, others were not, such as those for the Lebanon Valley in the period before the Revolution. These are impossible to use and unfortunately the originals are now missing.

Laws defining the assessable categories of wealth were passed throughout the 18th century. The most important are found in Staughton George *et al.*, eds., *Charter to William Penn, and Laws of the Province of Pennsylvania . . .* (Harrisburg, 1879), pp. 221–25 (1693), 280–82 (1699); James T. Mitchell and Henry Flanders, eds., *The Statutes at Large of Pennsylvania from 1682 to 1801* (Harrisburg, 1896–1915), 4: 10–26, chap. 284 (1724–25); 5: 201–12, chap. 406 (1755–56); 5: 337–52, chap. 431 (1757–58); 6:344–67, chap. 513 (1763–64); 8: 178–82, chap. 692 (1773–74); 9: 443–48, chap. 866 (1779); 11: 454–86, chap. 1137 (1782). The tendency over the course of a century was (*a*) to refine real property assessments by differentiating land according to its quality and use, (*b*) to extend the tax to nonlanded wealth such as plate, carriages, and income derived from trade, professions, salaries, and lucrative offices, and (*c*) to increase the tax on single freemen. Between 1757 and 1779 assessments were laid on the "clear *yearly* value of estates" which was defined as the rent they brought or, if not rented, what they would have brought in the estimate of the assessor (italics added; George *et al.*, *Charter and Laws*, 5: 340; 6: 345, etc.). Before and after this period the value of estates was assessed. In 1782 certain professions were exempted (11: 470).

20. See table 23 for urban occupations. Warwick, Elizabeth, Caernarvon, East Nantmeal, Coventry, and Vincent had forges or furnaces (figs. 2, 3).

21. Gary Nash, *Quakers and Politics: Pennsylvania, 1681–1726* (Princeton, N.J.: Princeton University Press, 1968), p. 50. By 1685 nearly half of the adult males arriving were indentured. Cheesman A. Herrick, *White Servitude in Pennsylvania* (Philadelphia: J. J. McVey, 1926), p. 35, noted 193 servants among 530 persons who arrived between 1682 and 1686, or almost 40 per cent. More went to the city than the country; Pomfret, "First Purchasers," pp. 150–51; Frederick B. Tolles, *Meeting House and Counting House: the Quaker Merchants of Colonial Philadelphia, 1682–1763* (Chapel Hill: University of North Carolina Press, for the Institute of Early American History and Culture, 1948), pp. 29–32, 34, 38, 40; John C. Wenger, *History of the Mennonites of the Franconia Conference* (Telford, Pa.: Franconia Mennonite Historical Society, 1937), pp. 10–11; Martin C. Weaver, *Mennonites of Lancaster Conference* (Scottsdale, Pa.: Mennonite Publishing House, 1931), p. 9; Arthur H. Dodd, *The Character of Early Welsh Emigration to the United States* (Cardiff: University of Wales Press, 1953), pp. 13–14; Israel D. Rupp, *History of Lancaster and York Counties . . .* (Lancaster, 1845), p. 102. James Steel to Isaac Taylor, Nov. 20, 1719, commented on affluent Scotch-Irish in Donegal Township; Logan Papers, 1664–1871, James Steel Letter Books, 1715–41, 1: 33, Hist. Soc. Pa.; James Logan, "Letter of Instructions of James Logan to James Steel, on Proprietary Affairs, 1727 [1729]," *Pa. Mag. Hist. Biog.*, 24 (1900): 495.

22. James Logan to William Penn, Nov. 8, 1713, quoted in Wilson Armistead, *Memoirs of James Logan . . . including Several of His Letters and Those of His Correspondents . . .* (London, 1851), p. 48.

23. Gottlieb Mittelberger, *Journey to Pennsylvania*, ed. and trans. Oscar Handlin and John L. Clive (Cambridge, Mass.: Harvard University Press, Belknap Press, 1960), p. 90, described the woeful condition of many of these people.

24. "List of Servants Belonging to the Inhabitants of Pennsylvania and taken into His Majesty's Service, For Whom Satisfaction has not been made by the Officers, according to an Act of Parliament, Philadelphia, Apr. 21, 1757," in Servants and Apprentice Records, Hist. Soc. Pa. More strictly 4 years was the modal number, 176 in a total of 583 persons; the average was 5.1 years. Terms ranged from 1 to 17 years; presumably children served the higher number of years. A. Smith, *Colonists in Bondage*, 21-22; Otto Pollak, "German Immigrant Problems in the Eighteenth Century as Reflected in Trouble Advertisements," *American Sociological Review*, 8 (1943): 674-84.

There were few slaves in Pennsylvania. The 1782 MS Chester County tax return listed 100 slaves, or a third of the servants recorded. In 1759 they were 289 of 483 servants listed, or 1.15 per cent of the total population. Quakers and Germans held fewer than Scotch-Irish and other British, but the small number of Negroes undercuts possible generalizations. On the slave trade of Pennsylvania see Darold D. Wax, "Quaker Merchants and the Slave Trade in Colonial Pennsylvania," *Pa. Mag. Hist. Biog.*, 86 (1962): 143-59.

25. A. Smith, *Colonists in Bondage*, p. 285, and Herrick, *White Servitude in Pennsylvania*, pp. 177-78, conclude that half the migrants to America were indentured; M. Campbell, "English Emigration," p. 4. Few hired servants and no indentured servants as such were recorded on tax lists. Those cited may refer to "hired" servants, of which we would expect few because of the high cost of labor. In 1759 in Chester the servants totaled less than 1 per cent of the population. Interestingly, many advertisements for runaway servants from Maryland appears in Pennsylvania papers, but few from Pennsylvania in the *Maryland Gazette* (Annapolis), suggesting that many more unmarried indentured persons immigrated to Maryland. Smith's study was based on Maryland data.

26. James T. Lemon and Gary B. Nash, "The Distribution of Wealth in Eighteenth-Century America: A Century of Change in Chester County, Pennsylvania, 1693-1802," *Journal of Social History*, 2 (1968): 1-24, discuss this more completely. In a society in which material achievement was highly rated, increasingly greater inequalities might be expected, given that the economic system did not change markedly. See Joseph J. Spengler, "Changes in Income Distribution and Social Stratification: A Note," *American Journal of Sociology*, 59 (1953-54): 258. See also the recent study by Donald W. Koch, "Income Distribution and Political Structure in Seventeenth-Century Salem, Massachusetts," *Essex Institute Historical Collections*, 105 (1969): 50-71.

27. Lanc. Co. MS tax list.

28. Jackson Turner Main, *The Social Structure of Revolutionary America* (Princeton, N.J.: Princeton University Press, 1965), pp. 33, 181, equates inmates with indentured persons. Arguments against this view are: (*a*) according to the 1759 and other tax lists, bound servants and slaves were listed by number whereas inmates were listed by name; and (*b*) inmates as indentured persons would probably not have been taxed, but they were. On MSS lists tenants who worked land are usually distinguishable because of their livestock holdings, and sometimes by the specification of the landlords' share of the tax. The 1758 Salisbury Township list differentiated sharecroppers. Occasionally, probably to upset twentieth century classifications, inmates had a few acres, some even sown. In 1759, to complicate matters, the London Grove, Chester Co., assessor cited some "Sojourners."

29. Christopher Sauer, "Early Description of Pennsylvania," p. 247; Francis Baily, *Journals of a Tour in Unsettled Parts of North America in 1796 and 1797*, ed. A. De Morgan (London, 1856), p. 135.

30. John Smith, *Hannah Logan's Courtship; a True Narrative: The Wooing of the Daughter of James Logan, Colonial Governor of Pennsylvania, and Divers Other Matters, as Related in the Diary of Her Lover, the Honourable John Smith, Assemblyman of Pennsylvania and King's Councillor of New Jersey, 1736–1752,* ed. Albert C. Myers (Philadelphia: Ferris & Leach, 1904), p. 152. See also Kenneth A. Lockridge, "Land, Population and the Evolution of New England Society, 1630–1790," *Past and Present,* no. 39 (April 1968): 62–80, and Aubrey C. Land, "Economic Base and Social Structure: The Northern Chesapeake in the Eighteenth Century," *Journal of Economic History,* 25 (1965): 639–54.

31. Minutes and Accounts of the County Commissioners of Lancaster, May 1751, p. 101, Lanc. Co. Courthouse.

32. Henry M. Muhlenberg, *The Journals of Henry Melchior Muhlenberg,* ed. and trans. Theodore G. Tappert and John W. Doberstein (Philadelphia: Evangelical Lutheran Ministerium of Pennsylvania and Adjacent States, 1942–58), 2: 121.

33. Edward Shippen to James Hamilton, Nov. 23, 1767, Aug. 28, 1773, Edward Shippen Letter Book, 1753–81, pp. 276, 350, Am. Phil. Soc., Phila.; Jasper Yeates to William Hamilton, Mar. 22, 1788, Hamilton Family Lancaster Estate Letter Book, 1781–89, p. 63, Hist. Soc. Pa.; François Alexandre Frédéric de la Rochefoucault-Liancourt, *Travels through the United States of North America, the Country of the Iroquois, and Upper Canada, in the Years 1795, 1796, and 1797; with an Authentic Account of Lower Canada,* trans. H. Neuman (London, 1799), 2: 354.

34. Sarah to James Burd, Mar. 3, 1764, Shippen Family Papers, vol. 11, Shippen-Burd Correspondence, p. 62.

35. Richard Parkinson, *A Tour of America in 1798, 1799, and 1800; Exhibiting Sketches of Society and Manners, American System of Agriculture with Its Recent Improvements* (London, 1805), 2: 620. Cf. Andrew Burnaby, *Travels through the Middle Settlements in North America in the Years 1759 and 1760, with Observations Upon the State of the Colonies,* 2d ed. of 1775 (Ithaca, N.Y.: Cornell University Press, 1960), p. 110, who found no cases of charity. Also see "An Act to Provide for the Erection of Houses for the Employment and Support of the Poor, in the Counties of Chester and Lancaster," 1798, in Mitchell and Flanders, *Statutes at Large, Pa.,* 16: 15–21.

36. Richard B. Morris, *Government and Labor in Early America* (New York: Columbia University Press, 1946), pp. 4–5, 44–45. Also see [Robert Parke] to his sister Mary Valentine, "Interesting Letter from Delaware County in 1725," *Pa. Mag. Hist. Biog.,* 5 (1881): 350; E. Shippen, Lancaster, to Colonel Bouquet, Sept. 3, 1759, E. Shippen Letter Book, p. 196, Am. Phil. Soc.

37. East Caln Township, Book for the Poor, 1735–53, Ches. Co. Hist. Soc.; la Rochefoucault-Liancourt, *Travels,* 2: 8, 14.

38. In 1959 there was one county with between 35 and 50 per cent of its families earning less than $3,000, 19 with 25–35 per cent, 32 with 15–25 per cent, and 15 with 2.1–15 per cent. Among all counties in the United States the average was 21.4 per cent. U.S., Bureau of Census, "Families with Incomes under $3,000 in 1959, by Counties of the United States," ser. GE-50, map 6 (Washington, 1965).

39. Among those supporting the superiority of Germans are the following: Oscar Handlin, *The Americans: A New History of the People of the United States* (Boston and Toronto: Little, Brown, 1963), pp. 92–93; Robert F. Berkhofer, Jr., "Space, Time, Culture and the New Frontier," *Agricultural History,* 38 (1964): 21–30. Frederick B. Tolles, *Quakers and the Atlantic Culture* (New York: Macmillan, 1960), p. 128, applies Redfield's comments on peasant values to the Germans but fails to indicate that Redfield had referred to many groups other than Germans; see Robert Redfield, *Peasant Society and Culture* (Chicago: University of Chicago Press, 1956), p. 66, where he discusses the common rural values of French-Canadians, Bulgarians, English, and Irish often attributed to Germans. See also Bernard C. Hennessy, "Psycho-cultural Studies of National Char-

acter: Relevances for International Relations," *Background: Journal of the International Studies Association*, 6 (1962): 27–49.

Few have questioned the presumed differences, but see esp. Alfred L. Shoemaker, "The Pennsylvania Barn," in *The Pennsylvania Barn*, ed. Alfred L. Shoemaker (Lancaster: Pennsylvania Dutch Folklore Center, 1955), p. 8. Hallock F. Raup, "The Pennsylvania Dutch at the Forks of the Delaware, Northampton County, Pennsylvania" (Ph.D. diss., University of California, Berkeley, 1935), had some doubts that Germans differed from others, but he tended to be contradictory; see esp. abstract and pp. 4, 17, 31, 73, 75, 83, 243. See also references in nn. 3–7, preface, this study.

40. Barker (see table 2) gave Scots 8.1 per cent, Ulster Irish 11.0, South Irish 3.5, Dutch 1.8, French 1.8, Swedes 0.8, and unassigned 3.9. He overstressed the number of Scots compared to Scotch-Irish. See Leyburn, *Scotch-Irish*, pp. 182–83, 186, for a discussion of Barker's calculations. Barker accepts 18th-century estimates of Germans because there are no comparative surname analyses for 19th-century Germany as in the British Isles. The figures for southeastern Pennsylvania are based on my estimates using data cited in nn. 50 and 71 below.

41. German immigration virtually ceased about 1755. Governor Thomas in 1747 estimated the Germans at 60 per cent, noted among estimates by Frank R. Diffenderffer, "The German Immigration into Pennsylvania through the Port of Philadelphia from 1700 to 1775," *Proc. Pa. Ger. Soc. 1899*, 10 (1900): 100–105. Diffenderffer, pp. 43–45, lists ship arrivals, and Levi Oscar Kuhns, *The German and Swiss Settlement of Colonial Pennsylvania: A Study of the So-Called Pennsylvania Dutch* (New York: Holt, 1901), p. 57, taking these and using an average of 200 per ship, suggested that 69,000 German-speaking persons arrived between 1726 and 1775. Perhaps there were 20,000 before 1725. Ralph B. Strassburger, *Pennsylvania German Pioneers: A Publication of the Original Lists of Arrivals in the Port of Philadelphia from 1727 to 1808*, ed. William J. Hinke (Norristown, Pa.; Pennsylvania German Society, 1934), 1: xxxi, estimates 65,040, and Abbot Smith, "Some New Facts about Eighteenth Century German Immigration," *Pa. Hist.*, 10 (1943): 117, estimates 75,000 between 1726 and 1775. Strassburger, 3: ix, says that only 1,530 came between 1785 and 1790. Some 12,000 Hessian mercenaries remained at the end of the Revolutionary War; Carl F. Wittke, *We Who Built America: The Saga of the Immigrant* (New York: Prentice-Hall, 1939), pp. 95–96. Migration from the British Isles virtually ceased between 1755 and 1768 but was quite heavy in the early 1770s and again after 1782. The numbers involved are uncertain. Leyburn, *Scotch-Irish*, p. 180, suggests that 200,000 left Ulster for America before 1775. This would be double the number of Germans and so seems excessive. On the English see Wayland F. Dunaway, "The English Settlers in Colonial Pennsylvania," *Pa. Mag. Hist. Biog.*, 52 (1928): 317–41. The Welsh came almost entirely before 1700; Dodd, *Welsh Emigration*, pp. 14–15. Most Scots came after 1768 and went beyond southeastern Pennsylvania; Ian C. Graham, *Colonists from Scotland: Emigration to North America* (Ithaca, N.Y.: Cornell University Press, 1956), pp. 185–89.

42. The rise of German newspapers might be considered a manifestation of a "third generation" reaction in search of cultural roots, especially after the Revolution weakened previous ideological stability. On this presumed phenomenon, see Marcus L. Hansen, "The Problems of the Third Generation Immigrant," *Augustana Historical Society Publications*, no. 8, pt. i (1938), pp. 5–20.

43. On charity schools, see Dietmar Rothermund, *The Layman's Progress: Religious and Political Experience in Colonial Pennsylvania, 1740–1770* (Philadelphia: University of Pennsylvania Press, 1961), pp. 88–90.

44. *Pennsylvania Gazette* (Philadelphia), Feb. 15, 1770, Jan. 21, 1789.

45. Other information supports the affluence of the Welsh persons; Sarah Barton to Miss Louisa de Normandie, 1776, in "The Bartons in Lancaster in 1776," *Jour. Lanc. Co. Hist. Soc.*, 52 (1948): 216.

46. Benjamin Marshall to Barnaby Egan, June 7, 1766, in "Extracts from the Letterbook of Benjamin Marshall, 1763–1766," ed. Thomas Stevenson, *Pa. Mag. Hist. Biog.*,

20 (1896): 212; Joseph Shippen to Edward Burd, Sept. 3, 1790, Shippen Family Papers, vol. 13, Shippen-Burd Corr., p. 185; Henry to Levi Hollingsworth, Head of Elk, Jan. 9, 1773, Hollingsworth Collection, 1748–1887, Correspondence, Hist. Soc. Pa.

47. Johann David Schoepf, *Travels in the Confederation, 1783–1784*, ed. and trans. Alfred J. Morrison (Philadelphia: W. J. Campbell, 1911), 1: 165; 2: 5–6.

48. Mrs. Eleanor Campbell to Mrs. Ewings and Mrs. Yeates, Shippensburg, Oct. 14, 1769, quoted in D. W. Thompson *et al., Two Hundred Years in Cumberland County* (Carlisle, Pa.: Hamilton Library and Historical Association, 1951), pp. 48–49.

49. *Pennsylvania Herald* (York), Oct. 3, 1792, quoted in part by Shoemaker, "Pennsylvania Barn," p. 8.

50. Calculations are based on the number of congregations and varied multipliers for different congregations derived from various estimates by observers and subsequent commentators. For a more complete discussion see Lemon, "Rural Geography," table 4. VII, p. 96, and app. 3, pp. 445–52. Major sources used were Frederick L. Weis, *The Colonial Churches and Colonial Clergy of the Middle and Southern Colonies, 1607–1776* (Lancaster, Mass.: Society of the Descendants of the Colonial Clergy, 1938), esp. p. 18, summary. Hunter Rineer, "List of Churches Founded in Pennsylvania before 1800," typewritten MS, private; Edwin S. Gaustad, *Historical Atlas of Religion in America* (New York and Evanston: Harper & Row, 1962), pp. 18, 26, 35, 50; Joseph Scott, *A Geographical Description of Pennsylvania; also the Counties with an Alphabetical List of the Townships of Each County, and their Population in 1805* (Philadelphia, 1806), p. 39; William Smith (1759), quoted by Theodore E. Schmauk, "The Lutheran Church in Pennsylvania, 1638–1800," *Proc. Pa. Ger. Soc. 1900 and 1901*, vols. 11 and 12, 11 (1902): 227; William J. Hinke and James I. Good, eds., *Minutes and Letters of the Coetus of the German Reformed Congregations in Pennsylvania, 1747–1792, together with Three Preliminary Reports of Rev. John Philip Boehm, 1734–1744* (Philadelphia: Reformed Church Publishing Board, 1903), tables *passim*, pp. 320, 386; Henry Harbaugh, *The Life of Rev. Michael Schlatter . . . his Travels and Labors among the Germans in Pennsylvania . . . 1716 to 1790* (Philadelphia, 1857), p. 37; Jonathan Oswald, ed., *Reports of the United German Lutheran Congregation in North America, especially in Pennsylvania,* "Hallische Nachrichten" (Philadelphia, 1881), 2: 242; D. C. Reber *et al., History of the Church of the Brethren of the Eastern District of Pennsylvania* (Lancaster, Pa.: Press of the New Era Publishing Co., 1915), p. 79; C. Henry Smith, "The Mennonite Immigration to Pennsylvania in the Eighteenth Century," *Proc. Pa. Ger. Soc. 1924*, 35 (1929): 158, 196; Christian Funk *et al.,* "The 1773 Letter to the Holland Mennonites," in Wenger, *Mennonites of Franconia*, pp. 395–404; Dunaway, "English Settlers in Pennsylvania," pp. 335–36. Guy S. Klett, *Presbyterians in Colonial Pennsylvania* (Philadelphia: University of Pennsylvania Press, 1937); George Ross to Secretary, Society for the Propagation of the Gospel, Dec. 30, 1712; George Craig, Sept. 3, 1764; Thomas Barton, 1761 and 1764, in Perry, *Collections Relating to the Church*, 2: 68, 328, 361, 369–70.

51. Rothermund, *Layman's Progress*, chaps. 3, 4, 7; Sidney E. Mead, *The Lively Experiment: The Shaping of Christianity in America* (New York: Harper & Row, 1963), pp. 33–37; Timothy L. Smith, "Congregation, State, and Denomination: The Forming of the American Religious Structure," *Wm. and Mary Qtly.*, 3d ser., 25 (1968): 155–76.

52. Edmund de S. Brunner, "The Country Church of the Pennsylvania German," *The Survey*, 35 (January 1916): 513, uses a sectarian-"credal" church dichotomy. H. Richard Niebuhr, *The Social Sources of Denominationalism* (New York: Holt, 1929), has adapted the concepts from Ernst Troeltsch and Max Weber to the American scene. But see Mead's comments, *Lively Experiment*, pp. 33–37.

53. Mennonites probably composed a quarter of Lancaster's population and Quakers nearly a third of Chester's; Lemon, "Rural Geography," p. 445.

54. Moravians and the "Baptists" at Ephrata were more radical. For a time they lived in communities, but these eventually broke down. The Amish, a European offshoot of Mennonites, first appeared in 1727 in Berks County, then in Lancaster. Although prom-

inent today to tourists as the chief representatives of the "quaint" Pennsylvania Dutch, they were hard to distinguish in the eighteenth century; John A. Hostetler, *Amish Society* (Baltimore: Johns Hopkins Press, 1963), p. 71. See also Gillian L. Gollin's fine study, *Moravians in Two Worlds: A Study of Changing Communities* (New York and London: Columbia University Press, 1967), esp. pp. 222-23. The rather rapid breakdown of the communitarian structure in Pennsylvania was the result of the lack of an aristocratic group. In Herrnhut, Germany, the presence of such leadership helped to maintain the choirs for a long time. The missionary zeal of Moravians, lacking in the Quakers and the Mennonites, also exposed them more easily to worldly influences and led to a weakening of religious values.

55. On the transformation of sectarian values such as other-worldliness, apocalyptic expectations, voluntarism, and democracy to their opposites, see Rothermund, *Layman's Progress*, pp. 5, 130. The Quaker principle of service to the world originally tended to set it off from other sectarian groups. Comments on the Quakers are from Sydney V. James, *A People among Peoples: Quaker Benevolence in Eighteenth-Century America* (Cambridge, Mass.: Harvard University Press, 1963), pp. ix, 1-22, 70-71, 74-75, 198, 281; Tolles, *Quakers and the Atlantic Culture*, pp. vii, 114-31; Tolles, *Meeting House and Counting House*, chap. 1; and Frederick B. Tolles, "1652 in History: Changing Perspectives on the Founding of Quakerism," in *Then and Now: Quaker Essays, Historical and Contemporary* . . . , ed. Anna Brinton (Philadelphia: University of Pennsylvania Press, 1960), pp. 73-94. Also see the romantic novel by Bayard Taylor, *The Story of Kennett* (New York, 1866), which attacks but then supports the customs and exclusiveness of rural Quakers in the 1790s. On Mennonites: Ernst Correll, "The Sociological and Economic Significance of the Mennonites as a Culture Group in History," *Mennonite Quarterly Review*, 16 (1942): 161-66; Paul Peachey, "Social Background and Social Philosophy of the Swiss Anabaptists, 1525-1540," *ibid.*, 28 (1954): 102-27; C. Henry Smith, *The Story of the Mennonites*, 4th ed., rev. by Cornelius Krahn (Newton, Kan.: Mennonite Publication Office, 1957), pp. 530-63, 584-95; John C. Wenger, *Glimpses of Mennonite History and Doctrine*, 2d ed. (Scottsdale, Pa.: Herald Press, 1947), pp. 129-30, 144, 168-69, 186, 188, 194-96; Weaver, *Mennonites of Lancaster*; Peter J. Klassen, "Mutual Aid among the Anabaptists: Doctrine and Practice," *Menn. Qtly. Rev.*, 37 (1963): 78-95.

56. Tolles, *Meeting House and Counting House*, pp. 29-32, 34, 38, 40; Wenger, *Mennonites of Franconia*, pp. 10-11; Weaver, *Mennonites of Lancaster*, p. 9.

57. Calculated in part from table 5. Miss Elizabeth Kieffer of Lancaster and the Reverend Ira Landis of Manheim Township kindly aided in determining Mennonites and others from names on tax lists.

58. I wish to thank Miss Dorothy Lapp of West Chester for her aid on Quaker genealogy.

59. W. Smith, *A Brief State of the Province of Pennsylvania . . . (1755)*, 2d ed. (New York, 1865), p. 36; August Wilhelm Du Roi, *Journal of Du Roi the Elder, Lieutenant and Adjutant, in the Service of the Duke of Brunswick, 1776-1778*, trans. Charlotte S. J. Epping (Philadelphia: University of Pennsylvania; New York: Appleton, agents, 1911), p. 144; Thomas Cheyney letter in Futhey and Cope, *Chester County*, p. 339. Tench Coxe, *View of the United States*, p. 442, noted that few Quakers were laborers. Muhlenberg, in Oswald, *Reports of the Lutheran Congregation*, 2: 55, noted that all sectarians were rich. See the activities of the Quaker Richard Barnard in his Farm Diary, 1774-92, Hist. Soc. Pa. (Hereafter Barnard Diary).

60. On Mennonite poor, see gifts specified in wills; Will Books, Lancaster County, 1A, 97; 1B, 130, 257, 464, 658; Y2, 40, Lanc. Co. Courthouse.

61. Leyburn, *Scotch-Irish*, pp. 278-82; Leonard J. Trinterud, *The Forming of an American Tradition: A Reexamination of Colonial Presbyterianism* (Philadelphia: Westminster Press, 1949), p. 134; Rothermund, *Layman's Progress*, pp. 22-24, 51, 106; Muhlenberg, *Journals*, 2: 181. Some Scottish Covenanters remained orthodox Calvinists.

62. They were not as well organized. See chap. 4 on local communities. General references: Schmauk, *Lutheran Church in Pennsylvania*; Abdel R. Wentz, *A Basic History of Lutheranism in America* (Philadelphia: Muhlenberg Press, 1955); Richard C. Wolf, "The Americanization of the German Lutherans, 1683 to 1829" (Ph.D. diss., Yale University, 1947); Harry M. J. Klein, *The History of the Eastern Synod of the Reformed Church in the United States* (Lancaster, Pa.: Eastern Synod, 1943); Rothermund, *Layman's Progress*, pp. 33–36, 45–49, 91–94, 101–5, 130.

63. Rothermund, *Layman's Progress*, pp. 49–51, 105–6, 130; W. Smith to Secretary, Soc. Prop. Gospel, May 3, 1771, in Perry, *Collections Relating to the Church*, 2: 417–19, 452; Richard Peters to Messrs. Hockley and Physick, appended to a letter of T. Barton to James Hamilton, May 9, 1768, Penn-Bailey Collection, Hist. Soc. Pa.

64. Reber *et al.*, *Church of the Brethren*; Morgan Edwards, *Materials toward a History of the Baptist Church in Pennsylvania* (Philadelphia, 1770); Gaustad, *Atlas of Religion*, pp. 11–12.

65. Burnaby, *Travels*, p. 112.

66. James McMichael, "Diary of Lieut. James McMichael of the Pennsylvania Line, 1776–1778," ed. William P. McMichael, *Pa. Mag. Hist. Biog.*, 16 (1892): 145–46. He left America in the 1790s, unassimilated it seems.

67. For example, he said the Roman Catholic priest was much esteemed. Shultze, *Journals*, 2: 193.

68. Durs Thommen letter to Basel, Switzerland, Oct. 3, 1737, in Albert B. Faust, ed., "Documents in Swiss Archives Relating to Emigration to American Colonies in the Eighteenth Century," *Am. Hist. Rev.*, 22 (1916–17): 117.

69. "Extracts from Pastor Handschuch's Diary . . . 1748 . . . 1750," in Oswald, *Reports of the Lutheran Congregation*, 2: 428.

70. On these concepts see Milton M. Gordon, *Assimilation in American Life: the Role of Race, Religion and National Origins* (New York: Oxford University Press, 1964).

71. See fig. 11. Population data were assembled from tax lists (see n. 19 above) and the following: U.S. Bureau of the Census, *Heads of Families of the First Census of the United States Taken . . . 1790; Pennsylvania* (Washington, 1908), pp. 9–11; citations in Evarts V. Greene and Virginia D. Harrington, *American Population before the Federal Census of 1790* (New York: Columbia University Press, 1932), pp. xiii, 113–17; Stella H. Sutherland, *Population Distribution in Colonial America* (New York: Columbia University Press, 1936), pp. 124–34; Herman R. Friis, "A Series of Population Maps of the Colonies and the United States, 1625–1790," *Geogr. Rev.*, 30 (1940): 463–70. Also see sources cited in Lemon, "Rural Geography," app. 1, pp. 440–42, and in nn. 40, 41, 50 above. The conversion rate from taxpayers to population used is 5.5, except that single freemen were taken as 1. Cf. William S. Rossiter, *A Century of Population Growth from the First Census to the Twelfth, 1790–1900* (Washington: U.S., Bureau of the Census, 1909), p. 224, who uses 5.7; Sutherland, who uses 5 in her *Population Distribution*, pp. 124–34; and U.S., Bureau of the Census, *Historical Statistics of the United States, Colonial Times to 1957* (Washington, 1960), p. 743, which uses 5.8. In 1693 Swedish families averaged 5.7; John H. Martin, *Chester (and its Vicinity) Delaware County, in Pennsylvania . . .* (Philadelphia, 1877), pp. 17–18. For the population growth of Pennsylvania as a whole, compare fig. 11 with Rossiter, *Century of Population Growth*, pp. 6, 10, and J. Potter, "The Growth of Population in America, 1700–1860," in Glass and Eversley, *Population in History*, pp. 638–39, who uses combined Pennsylvania-Delaware figures and cites higher figures before 1760. Also see the study by James H. Cassedy, *Demography in Early America: Beginnings of the Statistical Mind, 1600–1800* (Cambridge, Mass.: Harvard University Press, 1969).

72. Potter, "Growth of Population," pp. 646, 658, 662–63. The following discussions also deal with growth, natural increase, and birth and death rates. Benjamin Franklin, "Observations Concerning the Increase of Mankind and Peopling of Countries," in Franklin, *Papers*, 4: 225–34; William Barton, *Observations on the Progress of*

Population, and the Probabilities of the Duration of Human Life, in the United States of America ... (Philadelphia, 1791), pp. 6-14; Alfred J. Lotka, "The Size of American Families in the Eighteenth Century and the Significance of the Empirical Constants in the Pearl-Reed Law of Population Growth," *Journal of the American Statistical Association*, 22 (1927): 154-70; Alfred O. Aldridge, "Franklin as Demographer," *Jour. Ec. Hist.*, 9 (1949): 25-44; Conway Zirkle, "Benjamin Franklin, Thomas Malthus and the United States Census," *Isis*, 48 (1957): 58-62; Philip J. Greven, Jr., "Family Structure in Seventeenth-Century Andover, Massachusetts," *Wm. and Mary Qtly.*, 3d ser., 23 (1966): 234-56. Greven's estimates of death rates are much lower than some Pennsylvania data suggest. See also his *Four Generations: Population, Land, and Family in Colonial Andover, Massachusetts* (Ithaca, N.Y.: Cornell University Press, 1970); Kenneth A. Lockridge, *A New England Town the First Hundred Years: Dedham, Massachusetts, 1636-1736* (New York: Norton, 1970); and John Demos, *A Little Commonwealth: Family Life in Plymouth Colony* (New York: Oxford University Press, 1970). The records of two churches indicate that half the children were dead at 5 and two-thirds by 13; Matthew Whitehead and William Young, clerks, "An Account of the Births and Burials in the United Churches of Christ and St. Peter's, in Philadelphia ... 1772 ... 1773," Stauffer Collection, Steinman MSS (interpaged with Christopher Marshall, *Extracts from the Diary of Christopher Marshall Kept in Philadelphia and Lancaster during the American Revolution, 1774-1781*, ed. William Duane [Albany, 1877]), with p. 112, Hist. Soc. Pa.; and S. C. Albright, "Graves that Tell a Tale [Moravian Church, Lebanon]," *Papers of the Lebanon County Historical Society*, 7 (1921-24): 43-86. According to Lotka, if a mother bore 7.8 children, then about 2.3 of these would reproduce, and from the above gravestone data the figure would be 2.6. Potter, "Growth of Population," p. 646, suggests a high birth rate of 45 per 1,000 persons annually and a death rate of only 21/1,000, roughly corresponding to William Barton's ratio. In older settled areas and cities birth rates were lower.

73. See chap. 3.

74. William R. Shepherd, *History of Proprietary Government in Pennsylvania* (New York, 1896) is the standard work. Also see the recent studies by Joseph E. Illick, *William Penn the Politician: His Relations with the English Government* (Ithaca, N.Y.: Cornell University Press, 1965); Nash, *Quakers and Politics*; and Russell S. Nelson, Jr., "Backcountry (1709-1774): The Ideals of William Penn in Practice" (Ph.D. diss., University of Wisconsin, 1968), chaps. 6, 7, 8.

75. Shepherd, *Proprietary Government*, pp. 501-4; Illick, *William Penn*, pp. 28-35.

76. Illick, *William Penn*, chap. 4; Gary B. Nash, "The Framing of Government in Pennsylvania: Ideas in Conflict with Reality," *Wm. and Mary Qtly.*, 3d ser., 23 (1966): 194-209; Roy N. Lokken, *David Lloyd, Colonial Lawmaker* (Seattle: University of Washington Press, 1959), chap. 9.

77. Rothermund, *Layman's Progress*, chap. 5.

78. Sylvester K. Stevens and Donald H. Kent, eds., *County Government and Archives in Pennsylvania* (Harrisburg: Pennsylvania Historical and Museum Commission, 1947), pp. 1-14, 25, 90-92; Nelson, "Backcountry," chap. 6.

79. Stevens and Kent, *County Government*, p. 7.

80. *Ibid.*, pp. 3-5. See chap. 4 below.

81. A review of issues is found in Douglas C. North, *Growth and Welfare in the American Past: A New Economic History* (Englewood Cliffs, N.J.: Prentice-Hall, 1966), pp. 43-49.

82. Rothermund, *Layman's Progress*, p. 94.

83. See Lancaster Corporation Book ... September the 15th, Annoque Domini 1742, Feb. 8, 1743 and *passim*, Lancaster City Hall; York, Minutes and Ordinances, e.g. Nov. 22, 1790, York City Hall.

84. See calculations in James T. Lemon, "Household Consumption in Eighteenth-Century America and its Relationship to Production and Trade: The Situation Among Farmers in Southeastern Pennsylvania," *Ag. Hist.*, 41 (1967): 59-70, and chap. 6 below.

85. The structure of commerce is discussed by Arthur L. Jensen, *The Maritime Commerce of Colonial Philadelphia* (Madison: State Historical Society of Wisconsin, 1963), chaps. 2, 3; William S. Sachs, "Agricultural Conditions in the Northern Colonies before the Revolution," *Jour. Ec. Hist.*, 13 (1953): 274–90; Stuart Bruchey, *The Roots of American Economic Growth, 1607–1861: An Essay in Social Causation* (New York and Evanston: Harper & Row, 1965), chap. 3.

86. A. Jensen, *Maritime Commerce*, pp. 98–101. See discussions in chaps. 6, 8.

87. Clarence P. Gould, "The Economic Causes of the Rise of Baltimore," in *Essays in Colonial History Presented to Charles McLean Andrews* (New Haven: Yale University Press, 1931), pp. 225–51. See chaps. 5, 7 below.

88. A. Jensen, *Maritime Commerce*, chap. 1; Gordon C. Bjork, "The Weaning of the American Economy: Independence, Market Changes, and Economic Development," *Jour. Ec. Hist.*, 24 (1964): 545.

89. A. Jensen, *Maritime Commerce*, pp. 8–9, 36.

90. Charles O. Paullin, *Atlas of the Historical Geography of the United States*, ed. John K. Wright (Washington: Carnegie Institution of Washington; New York: American Geographical Society of New York, 1932), plate 138A.

91. *Pa. Arch.*, 8th ser., 7: 6304, notes that in 1769 a day's journey over the hills was about 18 to 20 miles. See discussions of costs of travel in Max G. Schumaker, "The Northern Farmer and His Markets" (Ph.D. diss., University of California, Berkeley, 1948), p. 64, and in chap. 7 below. See also John F. Walzer, "Transportation in the Philadelphia Trading Area" (Ph.D. diss., University of Wisconsin, 1968).

92. Richmond E. Myers, "The River to Be Crossed Rather Than to Be Followed," *Jour. Lanc. Co. Hist. Soc.*, 57 (1953): 133–54; George R. Prowell, "Rival Ferries over the Susquehanna in 1787—Wright's and Anderson's," *ibid.*, 27 (1923): 143–44; James W. Livingood, *The Philadelphia-Baltimore Trade Rivalry, 1780–1860* (Harrisburg: Pennsylvania Historical and Museum Commission, 1947), pp. 27–28.

93. Douglas C. North, *Economic Growth of the United States, 1790–1860* (Englewood Cliffs, N.J.: Prentice-Hall, 1961), chap. 12.

94. Harvey S. Perloff *et al.*, *Regions, Resources, and Economic Growth* (Baltimore: Johns Hopkins Press, for Resources for the Future, 1960), p. 110.

95. This is discussed more fully under the agricultural system in chap. 6 below. On material culture generally, including implements, house types, etc., see Henry Glassie, *Pattern in the Material Folk Culture of the Eastern United States*, University of Pennsylvania Monographs in Folklore and Folklife no. 1 (Philadelphia: University of Pennsylvania Press, 1968).

96. See Paul A. W. Wallace, *Indians of Pennsylvania* (Harrisburg: Pennsylvania Historical and Museum Commission, 1961), esp. pp. 140–59 on relationships with whites.

97. *Ibid.*, pp. 31, 32, 43. Also see maps and discussion in Harold E. Driver, *Indians of North America* (Chicago: University of Chicago Press, 1961); Paul A. W. Wallace, "Historic Indian Paths of Pennsylvania," *Pa. Mag. Hist. Biog.*, 76 (1952): 411–39.

98. Guldin, "Diary 1710," p. 69. See citations in n. 1 to Preface.

99. Carl O. Sauer, "The Settlement of the Humid East," in U.S., Department of Agriculture, *Climate and Man: Yearbook of Agriculture* (Washington, 1941), pp. 157–66.

100. There were numerous references to climate and weather in contemporary accounts. On late frosts, for example, see Shultze, *Journals*, May 4, 1774, 2: 67–69, and on drought, Anne Bezanson *et al.*, *Prices in Colonial Pennsylvania* (Philadelphia: University of Pennsylvania Press, 1935), p. 11. Merchants may have overstressed the effects of weather conditions on prices. The length of the growing season at Middletown (fig. 34), where the wide Susquehanna more than offsets the air drainage problem, is 200 days; at Coatesville, 175; at Ephrata, 173; and at Lebanon, 168. Data assembled by Joseph W. Glass, "Agricultural Regions of Lancaster County, Pennsylvania" (M.S. thesis, Pennsylvania State University, 1959), p. 48. See discussion of hemp production, chap. 7 below.

101. Raymond E. Murphy and Marion Murphy, *Pennsylvania: a Regional Geography* (Harrisburg: Pennsylvania Book Service, 1937), pp. 11–79, esp. p. 18; Armin K. Lobeck, "Physiographic Diagram of Pennsylvania," map (New York, 1951); Charles F. Shaw, *The Soils of Pennsylvania*, Pennsylvania State College Agricultural Experiment Station Bulletin no. 132 (State College, Pa., 1915), pp. 224–25.

102. Chester Co. Planning Commission, "Chester County; Slope," map (West Chester, Pa., 1963); Lancaster Co. Planning Comm., *A Report on the Physical Features and Natural Resources of Lancaster County, Pennsylvania* (Lancaster, Pa., 1960), p. 12.

103. U.S., Department of Agriculture, Soil Conservation Service, "Reconnaissance Erosion Survey of the State of Pennsylvania," map (Washington, 1935).

104. Livingood, *Philadelphia-Baltimore Rivalry*, pp. 27–28.

105. Shultze, *Journals*, p. 44. "Drylands" noted by Schoepf, *Travels in the Confederation*, 1: 184; Joshua Gilpin, "Journey to Bethlehem," *Pa. Mag. Hist. Biog.*, 46 (1922): 26; Raup, "Pennsylvania Dutch at the Forks of the Delaware," p. 35; and John Armstrong to Gov. Penn, June 20, 1770, Penn-Bailey Collection, Box A–W, p. 28. See George M. Hall, *Ground Water in Southeastern Pennsylvania*, Pennsylvania Geological Survey Bulletin W2 (Harrisburg: Pennsylvania, Department of Internal Affairs, Topographic and Geologic Survey, 1934), pp. 126–48, 178–95. See also Chester Co. Planning Comm., "Ground Water Capabilities," map (West Chester, 1962).

106. A. Thomson, "Franklin County," p. 317; Joseph Scott, *Geographical Description*, pp. 59, 62. But see Schoepf, *Travels in the Confederation*, 2: 9, and Parkinson, *Tour of America*, 2: 71. On bottom lands, see, e.g., J. Burd to E. Burd, July 30, 1785, Shippen Family Papers, vol. 13, Shippen-Burd Corr., pp. 53, 55, and Norris MSS, Real Estate, p. 76, Hist. Soc. Pa. Trees were used as indicators. See Christopher Sauer, "Early Description of Pennsylvania," p. 249; William Priest, *Travels in the United States of America . . . 1793–1797* (London, 1802), p. 35; and Ferdinand-M. Bayard, *Travels of a Frenchman in Maryland and Virginia with a Description of Philadelphia and Baltimore . . .*, ed. and trans. Ben C. McCary (Williamsburg, Va.: Privately printed, 1950), p. 34.

107. John B. Carey, *Soil Survey of Lancaster County, Pennsylvania*, Soil Survey, ser. 1956, no. 4 (Washington: U.S., Department of Agriculture, Soil Conservation Service, 1959), pp. 8, 85–98; W. Merrill Kunkle, *Soil Survey of Chester and Delaware Counties, Pennsylvania*, Soil Survey, ser. 1959, no. 19 (Washington: U.S., Department of Agriculture, Soil Conservation Service, 1963), map after p. 124. In table 10 values for Lancaster County only are used because Carey and Kunkle have not used equivalent data. One notable difference is that Carey specifies only a small area of Glenelg channery soils, whereas Kunkle makes this by far the largest category in Chester. In Lancaster, Chester soils occupy the largest area derived from crystalline rocks. The distinctions among Chester, Glenelg, and Manor soils are chiefly one of depth, with Chester the deepest. It would seem that Kunkle was overly cautious in his assessment of Chester soils in Chester.

108. Carey, *Soil Survey of Lancaster*, p. 121.

109. Penn Papers, 1629–1834, vol. 9, Pennsylvania Land Grants, 1681–1806, p. 301 (13), Hist. Soc. Pa. Schoepf, *Travels in the Confederation*, 1: 128, 135, suggested that red soils were good if turned up but also said that in Bucks they were not as good as others.

110. E. Lucy Braun, *Deciduous Forests of Eastern Northern America* (Philadelphia: Blakiston, 1950); J. Logan to Isaac Taylor, May 31, 1723, Taylor Papers, 14: 2987, Hist. Soc. Pa. (also, e.g., 13: 2563, 2565); Kunkle, *Soil Survey of Chester and Delaware Counties*, pp. 71–72, on the serpentine barrens that were not extensive.

111. W. Penn to the Duke of Ormond, Jan. 9, 1683 in Martin, *Chester*, p. 67, and James Logan, "Letter of James Logan to Isaac Taylor, Philadelphia, 1714–1715," *Pa. Mag. Hist. Biog.*, 22 (1898): 385, mention old fields. Gabriel Thomas, "A Historical and Geographical Account of Pennsylvania and West New Jersey . . . 1698," in Myers, *Narratives*, p. 319, and Thomas Budd, *Good Order Established in Pennsylvania and New*

Jersey . . . 1685, ed. Edward Armstrong (New York, 1865), p. 36, noted thin woods. On sapling land: Edward Shippen Holdings in Cumberland, Society Miscellaneous Collection, Surveys Box 5A, Hist. Soc. Pa.; Ellis and S. Evans, *Lancaster County*, p. 545. John M. Cooper, "The Tradition Concerning Our Limestone Lands," *Papers of the Kittochtinny Historical Society*, 2 (1899–1901): 74–92, forcefully denied that Franklin County had been a prairie grassland. Apparently the tradition was strong.

112. Andreas Hesselius, Journal, 1711–22, Mar. 10, 1714/5, typewritten copy, Ches. Co. Hist. Soc.; *Pa. Gaz.* (Phila.), Apr. 3, 1740; Peter Kalm, *The America of 1750, Peter Kalm's Travels in North America; the English Version of 1770 . . .*, ed. Adolph B. Benson (New York: Wilson-Erickson, 1937), 1: 279; Schoepf, *Travels in the Confederation*, 1: 131; Barnard Diary, Sept. 2, 1775; La Rochefoucault-Liancourt, *Travels*, 1: 46; John Pearson, "John Pearson's Description of Lancaster and Columbia in 1801," ed. James H. Mast, *Jour. Lanc. Co. Hist. Soc.*, 61 (1957): 55.

113. Taylor Papers, *passim*. Drafts in 16: 2344–2480 and 2559–2642 indicate: Black oak used by surveyors 559 times, red oak 3, white oak 509, hickory 401, chestnut 40, Spanish oak (southern red) 38, chestnut oak 16, poplar (tulip) 14, beech 14, elm 14, ash 14, walnut 14, etc. See also George Churchman Papers, 1720–1850, and Lightfoot Papers, Lanc. Co. Surveys, both in Hist. Soc. Pa. Taylor covered the Lancaster Plain and Churchman mostly the southern end of the county. The latter's drafts show a much higher incidence of chestnut than Taylor's. But preferences for various trees may have been involved. On the vegetation of the area see Braun, *Deciduous Forests*, pp. 233–48, and William C. Grimm, *The Trees of Pennsylvania* (New York and Harrisburg: Stackpole and Neck, 1950).

114. Gail M. Gibson, "Historical Evidence of the Buffalo in Pennsylvania," *Pa. Mag. Hist. Biog.*, 93 (1969): 151–60. Inventory of Richard McAllister, Hanover, York Co., 1775, McAllister Papers, box 1, carton 1, folder 2, Hist. Soc. Pa., lists 3 buffalo. Wild turkeys had disappeared from the Middletown area by 1769; J. Burd to E. Shippen, Feb. 25, 1769, Shippen Family Papers, vol. 11, Shippen-Burd Corr., p. 96.

115. Minutes and Accounts of County Commissioners of Lancaster, 10–182 (1729–72), Lanc. Co. Courthouse; Mitchell and Flanders, *Statutes at Large, Pa.*, 4: 15; 9: 403; 11: 460–61.

116. See the concluding chapter of Jane Jacobs, *The Death and Life of Great American Cities* (New York: Random House, 1961), where she discusses the city as a problem in "organized complexity." Rural Pennsylvania as a region can be regarded in the same way.

CHAPTER 2

1. The founding dates of churches were the chief source for delimiting areas occupied, even though a time lag was involved. Weis, *Colonial Churches*, and Rineer, "List of Churches." Data from county histories were also used. See also the detailed decade-by-decade isochronic map and technical discussion on simulation models in John Florin, "The Advance of Frontier Settlement in Pennsylvania, 1638–1850: A Geographic Interpretation" (M.S. thesis, Pennsylvania State University, 1966). This discussion is more detailed than mine. In some places we are in disagreement, which is not surprising, considering the lack of clarity in sources. See n. 71, chap. 1 for sources on population numbers. Areas were modified from C. E. Batchelat, ed., *Areas of the United States, 1940*, 16th Census (Washington: U.S. Bureau of the Census, 1942), pp. 14, 232–41. See the sophisticated estimates of densities by counties calculated in the late eighteenth century by Coxe, *View of the United States*, p. 483.

2. See nn. 50 and 71, chap. 1, and n. 1 above for sources.

3. The few Huguenots were Reformed, and after 1760 more "English" became Presbyterians.

4. On the Welsh see Pomfret, "First Purchasers," p. 157, and Robert Weyman to Secretary, Soc. Prop. Gospel, July 26, 1725, in Perry, *Collections Relating to the Church*, 2: 144.

5. Thomas Garrett reserved 600 acres for friends coming from Ireland; I. Taylor, Thornbury, to J. Logan, Dec. 15, 1713, Soc. Misc. Coll. Andrew Coffman wanted land for his brother expected from Germany; J. Steel to John Taylor, Mar. 18, 1737/8, Logan Papers, Steel Letter Books, 2: 173. See also T. Smith, "Congregation, State and Denomination," pp. 161, 163.

6. Muhlenberg, *Journals*, 1: 141–42.

7. Letter to his uncles Thomas and Joshua in England, Jan. 27, 1735/6, William Pim Letters and Account Book, Ches. Co. Hist. Soc.

8. Diffenderffer, "German Immigration through Philadelphia," *Proc. Pa.-Ger. Soc. 1899*, 10 (1900): 93; Nelson, "Backcountry," p. 18. On Scotch-Irish: J. Logan, "Letter of Instructions to Steel," p. 495; [James MacSparran], *America Dissected; being a Full and True Account of All the American Colonies* ... (1753), appendix in William Updike, *History of the Episcopal Church in Narragansett, Rhode Island* (New York, 1847), p. 495; *Pa. Gaz.* (Phila.), July 19, 1770.

9. Walter A. Knittle, *The Early Eighteenth Century Palatine Emigration; a British Government Redemptioner Project to Manufacture Naval Stores* (Philadelphia: Dorrance, 1937), pp. 205–7.

10. H. Frank Eshleman *et al.*, "Report on the True Character, Time and Place of the First Regular Settlement in Lancaster County," *Jour. Lanc. Co. Hist. Soc.*, 14 (1910): 21–71.

11. Abdel R. Wentz, "The Beginnings of the German Element in York County, Pennsylvania," *Proc. Pa.-Ger. Soc. 1913*, 24 (1916): 131.

12. Group settlement is suggested by the request of one person for 400 warrants; J. Logan to John Penn, Nov. 25, 1727, James Logan Letter Books, 4: 154, Hist. Soc. Pa. Names of places, e.g., "Conococheague Settlement," also suggest groups; John Reynolds to E. Shippen, June 28, 1742, Lamberton Scotch-Irish Collection, 1: 97, Hist. Soc. Pa.

13. Barton, *Progress of Population*, p. 13.

14. To Thomas Penn, Nov. 5, 1759, Penn Papers, Official Correspondence, 9: 122.

15. W. Penn, "A Further Account of the Province of Pennsylvania, 1685," and Pastorius, "Positive Information," in A. Myers, *Narratives*, pp. 263, 380.

16. Pomfret, "First Purchasers," p. 148.

17. On instructions to surveyors see J. Steel to I. Taylor, April 15, 1717, Logan Papers, Steel Letter Books, 1: 10.

18. Lokken, *David Lloyd*, pp. 12–13, dates Holme's map in 1696, although versions appeared from 1686 to 1730. Henry G. Ashmead, *History of Delaware County, Pennsylvania* (Philadelphia, 1884), *passim*, gives dates of settlement in part of area covered by Holme. On Holme see Oliver Hough, "Captain Thomas Holme, Surveyor-General of Pennsylvania and Provincial Councillor," *Pa. Mag. Hist. Biog.*, 19 (1895): 413–27.

19. In this area few township boundaries were altered after 1700; compare figs. 18 and 19 with fig. 2.

20. [W. Penn], "Penn's Proposals for a Second Settlement in the Province of Pennsylvania," *Pa. Mag. Hist. Biog.*, 28 (1904): 60–61. A list of subscribers is found in Penn Papers, vol. 9, Pa. Land Grants, p. 3. See also Frank R. Diffenderffer, "Early History as Revealed in an Old Document," *Jour. Lanc. Co. Hist. Soc.*, 2 (1897): 1–27; Gary B. Nash, "The Quest for the Susquehanna Valley: New York, Pennsylvania, and the Seventeenth Century Fur Trade," *New York History*, 48 (1967): 19–23.

21. Shepherd, *Proprietary Government*, p. 18.

22. Penn Papers, Philadelphia Land Grants, 89–95; Fretwell to W. Penn, Dec. 15, 1684, May 11, 1685, May 23, 1685, and other letters in Albert C. Myers Collection, Box 2, Ches. Co. Hist. Soc. In 1684 a grant was made to Ralph Fretwell of 40,000 acres, but it was not surveyed; *Pa. Arch.*, 3d ser., 2: 700. I am indebted to Professor Gary Nash for

these references. See also Pomfret, "First Purchasers," pp. 154-58, and John Lukens, "A List of London Company's Land Surveys," Soc. Misc. Coll., Box 5A.

23. H. Frank Eshleman, "Four Great Surveys in Lancaster County," *Jour. Lanc. Co. Hist. Soc.*, 28 (1924): 8-12.

24. *Ibid.*; Francis Jennings, "The Indian Trade of the Susquehanna Valley," *Proc. Am. Phil. Soc.*, 110 (1966): 406-24.

25. Futhey and Cope, *Chester County*, pp. 195-97; Wenger, *Mennonites of Franconia*, p. 96.

26. H. Frank Eshleman, "Two Centuries of Caernarvon History," *Jour. Lanc. Co. Hist. Soc.*, 26 (1922): 147.

27. On conservation, see Marshall D. Harris, *Origin of the Land Tenure System in the United States* (Ames: Iowa State College Press, 1953), p. 221; Gilbert Chinard, "The American Philosophical Society and the Early History of Forestry in America," *Proc. Am. Phil. Soc.*, 89 (1945): 444-88, and n. 91, chap. 6 below.

28. Edmund Physick, "Pennsylvania Cash Accounts . . . .1701-1778," pp. 365-70, Penn Papers. This detailed account of the Penn lands, both common and private "reserves," was written to ensure a fair compensation to the Penns from the state in 1779, but they received only £140,000. Nelson has calculated some of the figures; "Backcountry," pp. 102-3. See list in *Pa. Arch.*, 3d ser., 4, *passim*. Also see William A. Kain, "The Penn Manorial System and the Manors of Springettsbury and Maske," *Pa. Hist.*, 10 (1942): 225-42.

29. Lokken, *David Lloyd*, p. 202; J. Lukens to T. and Richard Penn, Apr. 23, 1763, John Lukens Surveyor General's Letter Book, 1762-64, Hist. Soc. Pa.

30. Warrant Registers, 1684-1864 (copies), Division of Public Records, Harrisburg; George Churchman Papers, *passim*.

31. Data for other townships are not available. At the time non-Germans dominated Salisbury and Caernarvon and Germans, including Mennonites, were preponderant in Earl, Manor, and Elizabeth. In 1782, total warranted land in some townships of Lancaster County was: Brecknock, 28 per cent of taxed land; Cocalico, 22; Conestoga, 5.5; and Earl, 3. These were almost entirely German. *Pa. Arch.*, 3d ser., vol. 17 *passim*, and Lanc. Co. MSS returns.

32. J. Steel to Kundigg and Herr, Oct. 20, 1732, Logan Papers, Steel Letter Books, 2: 47. Squatting by Germans was noted by J. Logan on his own land; he stated that not one in twenty intended to pay. J. Logan to James Mitchell and Andrew Galbraith, Sept. 2, 1728, J. Logan Letter Books, 3: 119-20, and J. Steel to J. Pots, Nov. 26, 1722, Logan Papers, Steel Letter Books, 1: 52. Scotch-Irish squatters were noted by J. Logan to Elisha Gatchell, Aug. 30, 1728, Logan Letter Books, 3: 119.

33. Penn, London, To Friends in Pennsylvania, June 29, 1710, Gratz Collection, Governors of Pennsylvania, Hist. Soc. Pa.

34. Thomas Sergeant, *View of the Land Laws of Pennsylvania with Notices of its Early History and Legislation* (Philadelphia and Pittsburgh, 1838), p. 40, states that the office was open, but the lack of correspondence between the office and I. Taylor suggests otherwise. See J. Steel Letter Book, vol. 1, and Taylor Papers. James Logan pleaded with Thomas Penn to come to the province and solve the problems. J. Logan to J. Penn, Sept. 11, 1728, Logan Papers, 1: 90.

35. Sergeant, *Land Laws*, p. 137. His estimate of warranted lands was 50 per cent or more short; compare with lists in *Pa. Arch.*, 3d ser., vol. 24, from which York County is missing.

36. See exchange on threats by settlers and mismanagement of surveyors in William Webb, "William Webb's Account of His Journey to the Conoys," *Pa. Mag. Hist. Biog.*, 34 (1910): 251-53; Samuel Blunston to T. Penn, June 22, 1733, Lancaster County MSS, 1: 1, Hist. Soc. Pa.; and J. Steel to J. Taylor, June 5, 1734, Logan Papers, Steel Letter Books, 2: 70. On the widespread belief that the Scotch-Irish were more prone to squatting, see Dunaway, *Scotch-Irish*, p. 58. Martin H. Brackbill, "The Manor of Conestoga in

the Colonial Period," *Jour. Lanc. Co. Hist. Soc.*, 42 (1938): 24, noted that some Scotch-Irish were ejected to make way for Germans. But Steel makes it clear that some Scotch-Irish had formally requested land. The Scotch-Irish "squatters" on the Manor of Maske in the Gettysburg area gave the proprietors' agents a difficult time; George Stevenson to Richard Peters, Oct. 26, 1754, Cadwallader Collection, Thomas Cadwallader Section, Coates List 27, Hist. Soc. Pa. From the correspondence it is clear that many Germans gave the land office and surveyors problems; e.g., "if that double faced Dutchman Whistler, or any ot his restless neighbours should apply to you for any overplus [of land]," E. Shippen to William Logan, Jan. 15, 1770, E. Shippen Letter Book, p. 311, Am. Phil. Soc. See also Benjamin Eastburn to J. Taylor, Apr. 20, 1736, in William H. Egle, ed., *Notes and Queries: Historical, Biographical and Genealogical, Chiefly Relating to Interior Pennsylvania*, 3d ser. (Harrisburg, 1895–96), 1: 9, and Joseph Swift to J. Yeates, Jan. 14, 1773, interpaged with Marshall, *Diary*, in Stauffer Coll., Steinman MSS, with p. 68.

    37. Sergeant, *Land Laws*, pp. 157–58. Complaints over earlier and lower quitrents had been expressed previously; Shepherd, *Proprietary Government*, p. 70.

    38. Nelson, "Backcountry," pp. 108–10.

    39. J. Steel to John Farrer, Jan. 30, 1730/1, to S. Blunston, Jan. 21, 1731/2, to John Ross, Feb. 14, 1737/8, etc., Logan Papers, Steel Letter Books, 2: 14, 40, 173; T. Penn to R. Peters, Aug. 22, 1743, Penn Papers, Penn Letter Books, 2: 48–49. The frustration of the Penns and their agents is apparent throughout these collections of correspondence.

    40. June 12, 1752, Penn Papers, Offic. Corr., 5: 211.

    41. E.g., J. Steel to I. Taylor, Oct. 8, 1725, Logan Papers, Steel Letter Books, 1: 63. Undeeded land was sold and willed to children, e.g., *Pa. Gaz.* (Phila.), Oct. 23, 1760, and Lanc. Co. Will Book, 1A: 16. The legislature clearly had accepted the situation by 1755; for squatters were recognized but taxed; Mitchell and Flanders, *Statutes at Large, Pa.*, 5: 206.

    42. To T. Penn, May 3, 1753, Penn Papers, Offic. Corr., 6: 49. Orphans' Courts ruled variously on warranted land; see deed books, Lanc. Co. Courthouse.

    43. "Trustees for the Pennsylvania Land Company in London v. Christian Stover" regarding a tract of 340 acres, Penn Papers, vol. 9, Pa. Land Grants, pp. 213, 215.

    44. Shepherd, *Proprietary Government*, pp. 48–50; Sergeant, *Land Laws*, pp. 51–60.

    45. Instructions from T. and R. Penn, Oct. 9, 1762, James Hamilton Papers, 1732–83, Folder 14, Hist. Soc. Pa.; Shepherd, *Proprietary Government*, pp. 87–88, on revenue; Nelson, "Backcountry," p. 89.

    46. A recent review of the disputes is William H. Bayliff, *The Maryland-Pennsylvania and the Maryland-Delaware Boundaries*, 2d ed. (Annapolis: Maryland Board of Natural Resources, 1959). See also J. Logan, "Letter of Instructions to Steel," p. 497, and E. Gatchell to T. Penn, Aug. 25, 1750, Penn Papers, Offic. Corr., 5: 45.

    47. The 1738 line ran westward 15 1/4 miles south of an imaginary line through the southern extremity of Philadelphia. West of the Susquehanna the boundary was a half mile farther north than it was east of the river.

    48. Until 1774 people south of the Mason-Dixon line in Nottingham Lots were taxed in Chester County. See Ches. Co. MSS tax lists.

    49. J. Logan to J. Penn, Nov. 25, 1727, J. Logan Letter Books, 4: 160; J. Steel to J. Penn *et al.*, Aug. 2, 1731, and J. Steel to the Proprietors, Apr. 1, 1737, Logan Papers, Steel Letter Books, 2: 25, 144–45; T. Penn to R. Peters, Feb. 24, 1750/1, Penn Papers, Penn Letter Books, 3: 37.

    50. T. Penn to R. Peters, Feb. 24, 1750/1, Penn Papers, Penn Letter Books, 3: 37; Sergeant, *Land Laws*, p. 46; Wentz, "German Element in York County," pp. 55, 62. George P. Donehoo, *A History of the Cumberland Valley in Pennsylvania* (Harrisburg: Susquehanna History Association, 1930), 1: 39–72, lists sites.

51. Pomfret, "First Purchasers," p. 157; Charles H. Browning, *Welsh Settlement of Pennsylvania* (Philadelphia: W. J. Campbell, 1912), pp. 33–35. Another Welsh tract was located in New Castle County.

52. J. Logan, "Letter of Instructions to Steel," p. 495; Jennings, "Indian Trade of Susquehanna Valley," p. 422.

53. Rupp, *Lancaster and York Counties*, pp. 288–89, mentions movement across Susquehanna, but without documentation. Governor Ogle of Maryland tried to encourage Scotch-Irish from Chester and New Castle to push out Germans on the west side of the Susquehanna, but the Penns worked to keep Scotch-Irish from moving; S. Blunston to T. Penn, Oct. 21, 1736, Lanc. Co. MSS, 1: 27.

54. Shepherd, *Proprietary Government*, p. 111.

55. J. Taylor to I. Taylor, Oct. 18, 1716, Taylor Papers, 14: 2847; J. Logan to Andrew Galbraith, Apr. 26, 1729, J. Logan Letter Books, 3: 125.

56. Success was ephemeral. T. Penn to R. Peters, July 18, Aug. 27, 1750, July 3, 1755, Penn Papers, Penn Letter Books, 3: 8, 16; 4: 108.

57. Joseph E. Johnson, "A Quaker Imperialist's View of the British Colonies in America: 1732," *Pa. Mag. Hist. Biog.*, 60 (1936): 108.

58. See n. 50 above.

59. See list of purchases in Penn Papers, Penn-Physick Papers, 4: 151–79, and Harris, *Origin of the Land Tenure System*, pp. 166–67. Several reserves were laid out in Chester and Lancaster, but apparently the Indians feared to remain. Taylor Papers, 11: 2319–20; Wallace, *Indians of Pennsylvania*, pp. 140–59.

60. Semple, *American History and its Geographic Conditions*, pp. 36–51, 59, stressed the Appalachians as a barrier to settlement. Cf. Merrens, "Historical Geography," p. 533.

61. Taylor Papers, 9: 1797.

62. Wentz, "German Element in York County," p. 14, suggested that a certain Lewis Michell sought land for Mennonites. Cf. C. Smith, "Mennonite Immigration," p. 150. Miss Elizabeth Kieffer of Lancaster suggested to the writer that a certain Franciscus may have been an agent. See draft of Mennonite tract in Eshleman *et al.*, "Report on First Settlement," after p. 75. A Mennonite named Michael Baughman took up large holdings, probably for others. Much of the land was divided among his children; Lanc. Co. Will Book, 1B: 141 (1755).

63. See nn. 22 and 23 above.

64. Surveyor's instructions, e.g., R. Peters to Benjamin Lightfoot, Sept. 27, 1749, Lightfoot Papers, Papers on Lancaster, etc. Thomas Story relayed an order from Joseph Pike to I. Taylor, Jan. 17, 1705/6, to assess land quality, water availability, accessibility to market, etc. Pike's land was not particularly good and was settled by Germans; Taylor Papers, 14: 2287. On Swedes in 1748, Muhlenberg, *Journals*, 1: 186.

65. Benjamin H. Smith, *Atlas of Delaware County, Pennsylvania, Containing Nineteen Maps Exhibiting the Early Grants and Patents Compiled from Official Sources; Together with a History of the Land Titles in the County* (Philadelphia, 1880), *passim*; "Letter of Thomas Paschall to J. J. of Chippenham, January 1682/3," in A. Myers, *Narratives*, p. 251; Witham Marshe, "Marshe's Journal: of the Treaty of the Six Nations, held in Lancaster in 1744," in Egle, *Notes and Queries*, 1: 276, noted houses near streams.

66. Eshleman, "Two Centuries of Caernarvon," p. 147; Lightfoot Papers, box 3, Lancaster Co. Unnavigable streams belonged to the owner of the land; Sergeant, *Land Laws*, p. 193.

67. Taylor Papers, 4: 578.

68. Christopher Sauer, "Early Description of Pennsylvania," p. 249; Priest, *Travels*, p. 35; Bayard, *Travels*, p. 34.

69. Ellis and Evans, *Lancaster County*, 345; Sylvanus Stall, "The Relation of the Lutheran Church in the United States to the Limestone Districts," *Lutheran Quarterly*, new ser., 13 (1883): 509; ed. note in Rush, *Manners of the German Inhabitants*, ed.

Rupp, p. 57; Stevenson W. Fletcher, *Pennsylvania Agriculture and Country Life,
1640–1840* (Harrisburg: Pennsylvania Historical and Museum Commission, 1950), pp.
49–50, 53; Moody, "Ulster Scots," p. 93.

70. Ellis and Evans, *Lancaster County*, p. 989. There are three Mennonite churches
on these soils.

71. Lanc. Co. MSS tax returns. The evaluation was probably based on soils and
slope. Muhlenberg, *Journals*, 1: 141, noted Lutherans on poor land.

72. Turner quoted by Fletcher, *Pennsylvania Agriculture*, p. 49. For the recent
distribution of Mennonite churches and limestone soils see map in Meynen, "Das Penn-
sylvaniendeutsche Bauernland," *Deutsches Archiv für Landes-und Volksforschung*, 3
(1939): 269.

73. See chap. 1.

74. For example, see John Taylor's "Account of Lands in Chester County," covering
grants in present day Lancaster between 1707 and 1723, Penn Papers, Warrants and
Surveys, p. 32. These are categorized in Lemon, "Rural Geography," table 7. III, p. 214.

75. Jonathan Dickinson to Joshua Crosby, Dec. 14, 1715, Dickinson Letter Book,
62, Hist. Soc. Pa.

76. J. Steel to Thomas Ewens, July 7, 1737, and J. Steel to Proprietors, Nov. 24,
1737, Logan Papers, Steel Letter Books, 2: 152, 166.

77. J. and R. Penn to T. Penn, Mar. 20, 1739/40, Penn Papers, Penn Letter Books,
1: 328–30; R. Peters to T. Penn, June 25, 1745, Peters Papers, 2: 36 (part of Letter
Book 3), Hist. Soc. Pa.; T. Cookson to J. Logan, Oct. 24, 1749, Logan Papers, 10: 95.

78. These figures are underestimated for some areas, especially Chester. Unfortunately a note at the end of the MSS copy of Chester returns for 1759 says the totals are
not accurate. As will be shown in chap. 7, assessors' counts of livestock, too, were
erratic. Interestingly, Jedediah Morse, *The American Geography* (London, 1792), p. 303,
estimated that the three oldest counties and Lancaster were completely settled, that
Dauphin, Berks, and Northampton were three-quarters occupied, and that York and
Cumberland were one-half full.

79. The assembly instructed them not to tax the poor at full rates; Mitchell and
Flanders, *Statutes at Large, Pa.*, 4: 14 (1724/5).

80. Jennings, "Indian Trade of the Susquehanna Valley," p. 422.

81. J. Steel to J. Taylor, Nov. 4, 1735, Logan Papers, Steel Letter Books, 2: 107.

82. *Pa. Arch.*, 2d ser., 19: 22; Nelson, "Backcountry," pp. 58, 108–10. See also
chaps. 4 and 6 below.

83. Brackbill, "Manor of Conestoga," pp. 17–46; George Wheeler, "Richard Penn's
Manor of Andolhea," *Pa. Mag. Hist. Biog.*, 53 (1934): 200–201. Some information on
the disposal of proprietary lands is given in *Pa. Arch.*, 3d ser., 3: 215–93, and Kain,
"Penn Manorial System," pp. 225–42.

84. [Parke], "Interesting Letter 1725," p. 349.

85. See discussion in chap. 7 on distribution of wealth.

86. Shepherd, *Proprietary Government*, pp. 34–35; *Colonial Records; Minutes of the
Provincial Council and Supreme Executive Council of Pennsylvania* (Philadelphia and
Harrisburg, 1852–53), 5: 452–53, in 1750.

87. Muhlenberg, *Journals*, 1: 141–42, in 1747; Lokken, *David Lloyd*, p. 202 (1719);
David Seibt to his brother in Silesia, Dec. 20, 1734, in Shultze, *Journals*, 1: 52; Arent
Hassert, Jr. to Deputy van Ostade in the Netherlands, Jan. 9, 1733, from the Hague
Archives 74. I. 13, in "Letters and Documents Relating to the Reformed Church of
Pennsylvania, 1699–1752" (typewritten), comp. and trans. William J. Hinke, Reformed
Church Library, Lancaster; John Woolman, *The Journal and Essays of John Woolman*,
ed. Amelia M. Gummere (New York: Macmillan, 1922), p. 165; T. Barton to Secretary,
Soc. Prop. Gospel, Nov. 8, 1756, in Perry, *Collections Relating to the Church*, 2: 277.

88. Nash, "Framing of Government," p. 187; Wenger, *Mennonites of Franconia*, pp.
10–11; Weaver, *Mennonites of Lancaster*, p. 9. See discussion in chap. 1.

89. Expressed, among others, by J. G. Rosengarten, trans., "Ackenwall's Observations in North America, 1767," *Pa. Mag. Hist. Biog.*, 27 (1903): 4; the idea came from Franklin. Theophile Cazenove, *Cazenove Journal 1794: A Record of the Journey of Theophile Cazenove through New Jersey and Pennsylvania*, ed. and trans. Rayner W. Kelsey (Haverford: Pennsylvania History Press, 1922), p. 81, noted four layers: Quakers; Germans; Irish and Scots; and Irish, Scots, and New Englanders in western Pennsylvania. See Tolles, *Quakers and the Atlantic Culture*, p. 128-29. Moody, "Ulster Scots," p. 91, suggests that availability of land was the key.

CHAPTER 3

1. Lawrence Stone, "Social Mobility in England, 1500-1700: Conference Paper," *Past and Present*, no. 33 (April 1966): 29-32, suggests that movement was very great between 1540 and 1640, resembling "nothing so much as Los Angeles in the mid-twentieth century." It slowed down considerably after 1640. Peter Laslett and John Harrison, "Clayworth and Cogenhoe," in *Historical Essays, 1600-1750: Presented to David Ogg*, ed. Henry E. Bell and R. L. Ollard (London: A. and C. Black, 1963), p. 174, have determined that mobility in late eighteenth-century rural England was considerable. Between 1676 and 1688 61.8 per cent died or left Clayworth. Subtracting removals by death, the percentage who departed was still 36.2, or about 3 per cent yearly. On New England, see Kenneth A. Lockridge, "The Population of Dedham, Massachusetts, 1636-1736," *Ec. Hist. Rev.*, 2d ser., 19 (1966): 322-23; Greven, *Four Generations*; and Edward S. Perzel, "Landholding in Ipswich," *Essex Inst. Hist. Coll.*, 104 (1968): 303-28, esp. pp. 314-22.

2. See the review by John M. Bumsted and James T. Lemon, "New Approaches in Early American Studies: The Local Community in New England," *Histoire Sociale/Social History: A Canadian Review*, no. 2 (November 1968): 98-112. See methodological discussions in E. Anthony Wrigley, ed., *An Introduction to English Historical Demography* (London: Weidenfeld & Nicolson, 1966).

3. Main, *Social Structure*, p. 193. If the latter was true, this rate was considerably less than the 3 per cent in Clayworth (n. 1) or in Pennsylvania (n. 4).

4. These rates of 50 and 30 per cent are round figures, calculated on a township basis. The 50 per cent was reduced to 30 as follows. Between 1774 and 1785 in Chester County 62 per cent of the persons listed in 1774 disappeared. Converting these 11 years to a decade and removing 10 per cent assumed to be nonresidents, 50 per cent of the actual residents disappeared. Since *surnames* that disappeared equaled about 40 per cent, we can assume that sons replacing deceased fathers totaled 10 per cent (50 – 40). To reduce the figure to 30 per cent, probably closer to the actual percentage of those who actually moved, a further 10 per cent is removed to account for persons who died without replacement. Thus 20 per cent of all persons listed in 1774 died over the decade—roughly 2 per cent a year. Potter, "Growth of Population in America," p. 646, suggests a crude annual death of 21/1000. Admittedly these calculations are gross and conjectural. On nonresidents see Lemon and Nash, "Distribution of Wealth," pp. 9-10.

5. Oswald, *Reports of the Lutheran Congregation*, 2: 52.

6. Wheeler, "Richard Penn's Manor of Andolhea," pp. 200-201.

7. Thomas H. Robinson, *Historical Sketch of Old Hanover Church* . . . (Harrisburg, 1878), p. 19.

8. Apr. 7, 1758, Penn Papers, Offic. Corr., 9: 21.

9. Shultze, *Journals*, 1: 135, 180, 200, 217, recorded sales of land by German neighbors averaging 3.4 per year in 10 different years between 1750 and 1795. In 1786 there were six. Also see John Logan Diary, Apr. 1, 1793, Ches. Co. Hist. Soc.

10. Lockridge, "Population of Dedham," pp. 341–42.

11. Wayland F. Dunaway, "Pennsylvania as an Early Distributing Center of Population," *Pa. Mag. Hist. Biog.*, 55 (1931): 134–69; Shultze, *Journals*, 2: 48, 80, 144, 183, 221.

12. John M. Cooper, *Some Information Respecting America*, 2d ed. (London, 1795), p. 135.

13. *View of the United States*, p. 483.

14. *Pa. Arch.*, 3d ser., 17: 194–96, 833–37, *passim*; vol. 12, *passim*. Similarly in Manheim Township (*ibid.*, 17: 219–23, 771–74, and *passim*) for the same period, of 60 persons who disappeared, possibly 13 sons replaced fathers and 6 others went to nearby townships, leaving 41 unaccounted for. Between 1774 and 1785 in Edgemont Township, Chester County (*ibid.*, 12: 33–34, 713–15, and *passim*), perhaps 10 sons replaced fathers and 2 went to other townships in the county. These account for one-third of those who disappeared. Because of the low numbers "discovered" elsewhere, I wonder how Main, *Social Structure*, pp. 183, 280, can conclude so firmly that most persons moved to nearby townships. Edgemont was one of his sample townships.

15. Leach, *Northern Colonial Frontier*, p. 137, and others. Runaway servant advertisements in *Pa. Gaz.* (Phila.) and other English-language newspapers show a large proportion of Scotch-Irish, possibly because more single indentured persons were of this group. German-language papers, such as *Germantauner Zeitung* and Miller's *Wochentliche Philadelphische Staatsbote*, carried advertisements on runaway Germans. See Pollak, "German Immigrant Problems," p. 677, and n. 25, chap. 1.

16. Robinson, *Old Hanover Church*, p. 19.

17. *Ibid.*; Oswald, *Reports of the Lutheran Congregation*, 2: 52.

18. Huebener, *Germans in America*, p. 81.

19. William Currie to Secretary, Soc. Prop. Gospel, Sept. 29, 1763, in Perry, *Collections Relating to the Church*, 2: 352, and Lanc. Co. Deed Books, A, 111, 115; B, 143; F, 178; Q, 388, etc.

20. See n. 40, chap. 1.

21. See locations on fig. 34. They have been included within townships on fig. 22 because single freemen in the towns were not separated from those in townships.

22. Note that the time span is 11 years for Chester and 10 for Lancaster. In 1920 an analysis of surnames in Lancaster County showed almost exactly the same percentage of persons of German ancestry as in 1782 (66 per cent). Whether the percentage was accurate or remained constant during the century and a half between these dates is uncertain. Heinz Kloss, *Das Volksgruppensrecht in den Vereinigten Staaten von Amerika* (Essen: Essener Verlagenstalt, 1940), p. 219.

23. See fig. 14, based on the distribution of congregations, and chap. 1.

24. Pim Letter and Account Book, 1730–42, Ches. Co. Hist. Soc.

25. Because Franklin feared the influx of Germans at the time, this statement was politically inspired. Franklin to James Parker, Mar. 20, 1750/1, Franklin, *Papers*, 4: 120.

26. Lanc. Co. Will Book, 1B: 141 (1755).

27. Dorothy B. Lapp, "Union Hall and Graveyard," *Chester County Collections*, 8 (1937): 291–92; Cazenove, *Journal*, p. 23.

28. Calculated from the number of churches. See n. 50, chap. 1.

29. Albert C. Myers, *Immigration of Irish Quakers into Pennsylvania, 1682–1850* (Swarthmore, Pa.: Albert C. Myers, 1902).

30. See n. 14 above.

31. "Letters of Phineas Bond, British Consul at Philadelphia to the Foreign Office of Great Britain, 1787, 1788, 1789," Am. Hist. Assoc., *Ann. Rep. 1896* (Washington, 1897), 619–20. Also see Rhoda Barber, "Journal of Settlement at Wright's Ferry on the Susquehanna River," written *ca.* 1830, Hist. Soc. Pa.

32. *Travels in the Confederation*, 2: 5–6.

33. For example, Drumore Township, Lanc. Co., 1759.

34. Lockridge, "Evolution of New England Society," p. 74.

35. T. Barton to T. Penn, Lancaster, Apr. 7, 1758, Penn Papers, Offic. Corr., 9: 21.
36. Robinson, *Old Hanover Church*, p. 19.
37. John Logan Diary, Apr. 1, 1793, Ches. Co. Hist. Soc.; William K. Kavenagh, "Economic History of Suffolk County, New York" (Ph.D. diss., New York University, 1966), p. 67.
38. Joseph Shippen, Lancaster, to Edward Shippen, Jr., Sept. 1, 1788, Shippen Family Papers, box of correspondence for Edward-Joseph and others.
39. See chap. 6 on pests.
40. Shultze, *Journals*, 1: 116, 122–23, 124, 130; 2: 92, 95–103. See also the case of Bebber's Township Mennonites who had not paid quitrents for 30 years in J. Steel to Michael Ziegler, Mar. 8, 1734/5, Logan Papers, Steel Letter Books, 2: 93.
41. *Pa. Arch.*, 3d ser., 1: 349 (1696); 2: 1165 (1716), 1680 (1725); 4: 2827 (bill finally passed in 1742 to guarantee rights). The German settlers were concerned about and petitioned for naturalization; May 15, 1706, *Col. Rec. Pa.*, 2: 241–42.
42. Lanc. Co. Deed Book, P, 155; Shepherd, *Proprietary Government*, p. 65.
43. E.g., S. Blunston to T. Penn, Oct. 19, 1737, Lanc. Co. MSS, 1: 33; draft of 511 acres of T. Penn, 1773 and other overlapping surveys, Penn Papers, Warrants and Surveys, 78.
44. Nelson, "Backcountry," 106; Physick, "Pennsylvania Cash Accounts," pp. 1–9, Penn Papers. About one-tenth of their gross income from land was received in 1774.
45. Sergeant, *Land Laws*, pp. 157–58; Shepherd, *Proprietary Government*, p. 70.
46. Shepherd, *Proprietary Government*, pp. 34–35; Nelson, "Backcountry," p. 80.
47. Shepherd, *Proprietary Government*, pp. 48–50; Sergeant, *Land Laws*, pp. 51–60; R. Peters to T. Penn, Mar. 16, 1752, Penn Papers, Offic. Corr., 5: 217; R. Peters to T. Penn, Oct. 30, 1756, Gratz Coll., Reverend Richard Peters Letters to the Proprietors, 1755–57, pp. 106–7.
48. From 20 to 40 cases from each period were used to reach the values. See also Penn Papers, vol. 9, Pa. Land Grants, p. 275, and Cazenove, *Journal, passim*.
49. Poor persons were less likely to have their estates evaluated. See Kenneth A. Lockridge, "A Communication," *Wm. and Mary Qtly.*, 3d ser., 25 (1968): 516–17.
50. The modal size of grants to "First Purchasers" was 500 acres. *Pa. Arch.*, 1st ser., 1: 40–46; Shepherd, *Proprietary Government*, p. 23.
51. Eleven towns were specified in returns in 1782; *Pa. Arch.*, 3d ser., 17: 687–898, *passim*. But in the county on that date about 30 towns existed. See fig. 35.
52. Mitchell and Flanders, *Statutes at Large, Pa.*, 4: 14 (1724/5).
53. Lanc. Co. Deed Books, KK, 27, 32, 38, 74, 89. 155; EE, 381; P, 269. These occurred late in the century. The first cited notes that an income of £100 was needed for a viable operation. Shultze, *Journals*, 2: 64, records divisions.
54. Lockridge, "Evolution of New England Society," pp. 67–68. Others commented on reasonable sizes in Pennsylvania: R. Peters to J. Taylor, Oct. 26, 1739, Taylor Papers, 15: 3264, on the division of Springton Manor; Henry Wilmot, "The Penns and the Taxation of their Estates by the Provincial Assembly: Mr. Wilmot's Brief in Behalf of the Proprietaries in Opposition to the Approval of Certain Acts of Assembly [*ca.* 1760]," *Pa. Mag. Hist. Biog.*, 24 (1900): 165, said "the common run of grants do not one with another exceed 200 acres (which is a good farm) each." Under the 1765 "Application System" 300 acres were permitted, but these were in more remote areas; Sergeant, *Land Laws*, p. 143.
55. William Strickland, *Observation on the Agriculture of the United States* (London, 1801), pp. 18, 52–54; M'Roberts, "Tour," p. 168 (1774–75). Both authors, biased in favor of primogeniture, blamed the practice of division.
56. See chap. 7.
57. Pfeifer, "Quality of Peasant Living," pp. 256–57. This map shows some diversity in Germany, but in the southwest, whence most immigrants had come, division is most common. H. J. Habakkuk, "Family Structure and Economic Change in Nineteenth Century Europe," *Jour. Ec. Hist.*, 15 (1955): 1–12.

58. William M. Williams, *Gosforth: The Sociology of an English Village* (Glencoe, Ill.: Free Press, 1956), pp. 49–50.

59. E.g., Bart Tp., 2 Cunkles, 100 acres; Leacock, 3 Johnsons, 150; Manor, 3 Neafs, 100; Strasburg, 2 Frees (Feree), 160; and others. *Pa. Arch.*, 3d ser., 17: 834, 826, 745, 708. Sometimes one son, presumably the eldest, received a double share. [William Penn], "Information and Direction to Such Persons as are inclined to America, more Especially Those related to the Province of Pennsylvania," *Pa. Mag. Hist. Biog.*, 4 (1880): 341. He had suggested division of grants of 500 acres into farms of 100 acres.

60. Mitchell and Flanders, *Statutes at Large, Pa.*, 2: 31–34; 3: 14–22. On New England see Donald S. Pitkin, "Partible Inheritance and the Open Fields," *Ag. Hist.*, 35 (1961): 65–69.

61. For examples of double shares: Orphans' Court Miscellaneous Book, Lanc. Co. Courthouse, vol. 1 (1742–60), pt. i, 4, 5, 7; pt. ii, 13; pt. iii, 116; vol. 2 (1772–76), 19, 72; vol. 3 (1784–87), 154, 492. Equal shares: vol. 1, pt. ii, 11; vol. 2, 75, 109; vol. 3, 204.

62. Michel-Guilliame Jean de Crèvecoeur, *Eighteenth Century Travels in Pennsylvania and New York [1801]*, ed. and trans. Percy S. Adams (Lexington: University of Kentucky Press, 1961), p. 32.

63. In Edgemont Township, of 23 landless in 1774 possibly only 3 became owners by 1785, all presumably sons of owners. *Pa. Arch.*, 3d ser., 12: 33–34, 713–15. On the 1785 list, owners are not specified as such, though three groups—owners and tenants, inmates, and single freemen—can be distinguished. Main (*Social Structure*, p. 194), using Edgemont and seven other nearby townships, asserted that perhaps 60 per cent of nonlandowners acquired land within 20 years. This seems highly unlikely, given the sample of three I have used; most persons are nearly impossible to trace (n. 14 above). Moreover, most of the nonowners who became owners were sons of owners—hardly landless persons!

64. See chaps. 5, 6.

65. On Europe, see Etienne van de Walle, "Marriage and Marital Fertility," *Daedalus*, 97 (1968): 486–501.

66. E. Shippen to Thomas Edwards, Oct. 13, 1753, to E. Shippen, Jr., Oct. 18, 1753, E. Shippen Letter Book, 52, 53, Am. Phil. Soc. In 1774 a sample of 509 shows 116 Germans, 249 English, and 101 Scotch-Irish mortgagors; General Loan Office of 1773, Mortgage Book, 1: 1774, Division of Public Records, Harrisburg.

67. Because the Loan Office was very cautious in providing mortgages, opportunities in older farming areas may have been reduced. See Paton Wesley Yoder, "Paper Currency in Colonial Pennsylvania" (Ph.D. diss., Indiana University, 1942), chap. 6, esp. p. 253.

68. John Armstrong to T. Penn, Nov. 5, 1759, Penn Papers, Offic. Corr., 9: 122; Nelson, "Backcountry," pp. 108–10.

69. At least in Salisbury Township in 1758, when about half the tenants were croppers; Lanc. Co. MS tax list. No other lists made this distinction. Single freemen have been excluded. Tenants as distinguished from inmates appeared in the main body of lists. On MSS returns usually the tenants were clearly specified; often landlords were noted. In the printed lists in *Pa. Arch.*, 3d ser., vols. 11, 12, 17, however, tenants are distinguishable only by the omission of land beside their names. No other clues are provided.

70. Fort Ligonier, Nov. 5, 1759, Penn Papers, Offic. Corr., 9: 122.

71. See n. 63.

72. Lanc. Co. MSS returns. Not all MSS returns and few printed ones in *Pa. Arch.* show occupations. The years cited were exceptionally fine. Even then, laborers were a residual category—that is, they were landless persons without any occupation listed. Older persons turned to linen making, according to William Pollard to Benjamin and John Brown, Apr. 6, 1773, Pollard Letter Book, 1772–74, pp. 185–86, Hist. Soc. Pa.

73. See chap. 5 and fig. 34; Main, *Social Structure*, pp. 194–95, 275, 278–97.

74. E. Shippen to J. Hamilton, Nov. 23, 1767, Aug. 28, 1773, E. Shippen Letter Book, pp. 276, 350, Am. Phil. Soc.; J. Yeates to W. Hamilton, Mar. 22, 1788, Hamilton Family Lancaster Estate Letter Book, p. 63.

75. *Pa. Arch.*, 3d ser., vol. 17; H. Frank Eshleman, "Lancaster County's Provincial and County Tax in 1774," *Jour. Lanc. Co. Hist. Soc.*, 28 (1924): 5.

76. *Pa. Arch.*, 3d ser., 17: 730–31, 739–40, 789–90, 842–43, 861–62, 879–81.

77. Also see discussion in chap. 5.

CHAPTER 4

1. Francis Daniel Pastorius, "Circumstantial Geographical Description of Pennsylvania," in A. Myers, *Narratives*, p. 380, and "Positive Information," p. 407. A brief but useful discussion of Penn's grant, the process of settlement of townships, and the form of Philadelphia is found in Anthony N. B. Garvan, "Proprietary Philadelphia as an Artifact," in *The Historian and the City*, ed. Oscar Handlin and John Burchard (Cambridge, Mass.: M.I.T. Press and Harvard University Press, 1963), pp. 177–201. His interpretation varies from mine.

2. Slicher van Bath, *Agrarian History of Europe*, pp. 55–57; Houston, *Social Geography*, chaps. 4, 5.

3. George *et al.*, *Charters and Laws*, pp. 83–99; Shepherd, *Proprietary Government*, p. 16; Harris, *Origin of the Land Tenure System*, p. 149.

4. Shepherd, *Proprietary Government*, p. 18.

5. W. Penn, "Further Account," p. 263.

6. *Ibid.* Fig. 31 is an actual draft generally conforming to this idea.

7. *Ibid.*, p. 263; Budd, *Good Order Established*, esp. p. 50.

8. Browning, *Welsh Settlement of Pennsylvania*, p. 259, citing the minutes of the Board of Property, Nov. 26, 1701, noted that Penn wanted a separate township for servants. The term "headland" was used, but not as prominently as in the South.

9. Pomfret, "First Purchasers," p. 148; *Pa. Arch.*, 1st ser., 1: 40–46; Shepherd, *Proprietary Government*, p. 23.

10. "Articles of Agreement between the Members of the Frankfort Company . . . 1686," *Pa. Mag. Hist. Biog.*, 15 (1891): 205–11.

11. Shepherd, *Proprietary Government*, p. 18.

12. See n. 18, chap. 2. Of 53 townships in Chester County in 1760, 14 were of about 10,000 acres and 17 of 5,000; the 22 others, mostly distant from the Delaware were of irregular size and shape.

13. Eshleman, "Four Great Surveys," pp. 9–12.

14. W. Penn to Marquis of Halifax, Mar. 9, 1683/4, quoted in Futhey and Cope, *Chester County*, p. 155; W. Penn, "Further Account," p. 263.

15. See n. 20, chap. 2.

16. Pastorius, "Circumstantial Geographical Description," p. 376.

17. See n. 7 above.

18. Isaac Weld, Jr., *Travels through the United States of North America and the Provinces of Upper and Lower Canada during the years 1795, 1796, and 1797*, 3d ed. (London, 1800), 1: 111; 2: 358–59, 363; Joseph M. Levering, *A History of Bethlehem, Pennsylvania, 1741–1892* . . . (Bethlehem: Times Publishing Company, 1903); Gilpin, "Journey to Bethlehem," p. 140 (on Nazareth); Spencer Bonsall, "Historical Map of the Barony of Nazareth" (Philadelphia, 1878)—the copy in Hist. Soc. Pa. has an inset of Nazareth village and of agricultural lands; H. A. Brickenstein, "Sketch of the Early History of Lititz, 1742–1775," *Transactions of the Moravian Historical Society*, 2 (1886): 341–74, esp. 351; Gollin, *Moravians in Two Worlds*.

19. See nn. 29, 34, chap. 2.

20. R. Peters to T. Penn, June 12, 1752, Penn Papers, Offic. Corr., 5: 211.

21. Sergeant, *Land Laws*, pp. 37, 270, on instructions to surveyors in 1701 and 1765; J. Logan to I. Taylor, Nov. 4, 1719, Taylor Papers, 14: 2931, on surveyors' right to determine form.

22. See, e.g., draft of surveyor G. Churchman's land of 251 acres with 30 points in Little Britain Township, George Churchman Papers.

23. A. Hamilton to J. Taylor, June 7, 1733, Taylor Papers, 15: 3085; J. Lukens to T. and R. Penn, Apr. 23, 1763, July 5, 1763, Lukens Surveyor General's Letter Book.

24. Taylor Papers, 12: 2399, 2401, 2402, 2404, 2418, 2421, 2424, etc.

25. *Travels in the Confederation*, p. 9. Also see William Eyre, "Colonel Eyre's Journal of his Trip from New York to Pittsburgh, 1762," ed. Francis R. Reece, *West. Pa. Hist. Mag.*, 27 (1944): 40. See location of houses on fig. 32. Usually houses and out-buildings were separated, but in 1810 there was one report of a dwelling, a weaver's shop, and a stable under one roof; Catherine Fritsch, "Notes of a visit to Philadelphia, made by a Moravian Sister in 1810," trans. A. R. Beck, *Pa. Mag. Hist. Biog.*, 36 (1912): 346.

26. See figs. 15, 31.

27. T. Penn to the Secretary, Dec. 10, 1762, *Pa. Arch.*, 2d ser., 7: 266, advocated townships in the west of 5,000 acres with proprietary reserves of one-tenth "as was the practice in the first settlement of the country." Amelia C. Ford, *Colonial Precedents of our National Land System as it Existed in 1800* (Madison: University of Wisconsin, 1910), p. 24; Shepherd, *Proprietary Government*, p. 48.

28. W. Penn, "Further Account," p. 263.

29. Sumner C. Powell, *Puritan Village: The Formation of a New England Town* (Middletown, Conn.: Wesleyan University Press, 1963), pp. 81, 83 -85; Philip J. Greven, Jr., "Old Patterns in the New World: the Distribution of Land in 17th Century Andover," *Essex Institute Historical Collections*, 101 (1965): 133 -48.

30. Lokken, *David Lloyd*, pp. 110 -13.

31. *Ibid.*, pp. 114, 116.

32. See nn. 42, 43, 44, chap. 2.

33. R. Peters to T. Penn, Mar. 16, 1752, Penn Papers, Offic. Corr., 5: 217.

34. The recorded 21.5 million acres sold by the Penns should have brought them between £1.3 million and £2.2 million sterling; Physick, "Pennsylvania Cash Accounts," p. 376. The Penns received only £140,000 from the commonwealth.

35. Harris, *Origin of the Land Tenure System*, pp. 116, 403 -5.

36. See summary in Houston, *Social Geography*, pp. 85 -102.

37. Conrad M. Arensberg, "American Communities," *American Anthropologist*, 17 (1955): 1155.

38. Hallock F. Raup, "The Pennsylvania Dutch of Northampton County: Settlement Forms and Culture Patterns," *Bulletin of the Geographical Society of Philadelphia*, 36 (1938): 8. Cf. his "Pennsylvania Dutch at the Forks of the Delaware," p. 76, where he identifies dispersal with all groups.

39. Pfeifer, "Quality of Peasant Living," p. 264; J. Johnson, "Rural Settlement Pattern of Ireland," p. 165 -67.

40. See chap. 3, including nn. 57 -61.

41. See Houston, *Social Geography*, pp. 97 -99.

42. E.g., Bidwell and Falconer, *History of Agriculture*, p. 66.

43. Chisholm, *Rural Settlement and Land Use: An Essay on Location* (London: Hutchinson University Library, 1962), p. 148.

44. See chap. 6 below.

45. Powell, *Puritan Village*, pp. 133 -38; Greven, "Old Patterns in the New World," p. 140.

46. The need for defense is a traditional explanation. See Houston, *Social Geography*, p. 101, and Edna Scofield, "The Origin of Settlement Patterns in Rural New England," *Geogr. Rev.*, 28 (1938): 652 -63.

47. Slicher van Bath, *Agrarian History of Europe*, pp. 40 -53.

48. *Ibid.*; Mingay, *English Landed Society in the Eighteenth Century*, chap. 4; Saal-

feld, *Bauernwirtschaft und Gutsbetrieb*, pp. 150–51; Riemann, *Ackerbau und Viehhaltung*, p. 100.

49. Slicher van Bath, *Agrarian History of Europe*, p. 324; Mingay, *English Landed Society*, p. 98.

50. See chap. 3 and fig. 30.

51. Burnaby, *Travels*, p. 112. Even Pastorius found Germantown life too restrictive; cited in William E. Linglebach, "William Penn and City Planning," *Pa. Mag. Hist. Biog.*, 68 (1944): 408. The Swedes had been living in dispersed patterns; Kalm, *America of 1750*, 1: 265; and Edward Jones to John Thomas, Oct. 26, 1682, in James J. Levick, "John *Ap* Thomas and his Friends: a Contribution to the Early History of Merion, near Philadelphia," *Pa. Mag. Hist. Biog.*, 4 (1880): 315–16.

52. Charles Grant, *Democracy in the Connecticut Frontier Town of Kent* (New York: Columbia University Press, 1961), chap. 3 ("The Drive for Profits"). See review of New England literature in Bumsted and Lemon, "Early American Studies," pp. 98–112, and new books listed in n. 72, chap. 1. Schoepf, *Travels in the Confederation*, 2: 23, spoke favorably of the isolated farm, chiefly because of separation from neighbors and the village "tap-house."

53. Main, *Social Structure*, p. 245.

54. "Township Map of Chester County, Pennsylvania, 1785," *Pa. Arch.*, 3d ser., vol. 12, end, clearly shows the location of churches. Churches in the Cumberland Valley and elsewhere were placed in a regular fashion. The pattern became confused when split-off churches appeared in the 1740s.

55. "Circumstantial Geographical Description," p. 406. See also Daniel Falckner, "*Curieuse Nachricht from Pennsylvania*—The Book that Stimulated the Great German Emigration to Pennsylvania in the Early Years of the XVIII Century [1702]," ed. and trans. Julius F. Sachse, *Proc. Pa.-Ger. Soc. 1903*, 14 (1905): 98–99, on the general desire for a "distinct" German colony in 1702.

56. William I. Hull, *William Penn and the Dutch Emigration to Pennsylvania* (Swarthmore, Pa.: Swarthmore College, 1935), p. 237.

57. Browning, *Welsh Settlement*, pp. 327–75, esp. pp. 337, 345. Penn also granted a Welsh tract in New Castle County.

58. Hull, *Penn and the Dutch Emigration*, p. 237.

59. Samuel W. Pennypacker, "The Settlement of Germantown, Pennsylvania and the Beginning of the German Immigration to North America," *Proc. Pa.-Ger. Soc.1898*, 9 (1899): 307.

60. The issue was not settled conclusively until 1722. It appears that Thomas Holme was first responsible for dividing the tract by drawing a line on an early draft of his map (fig. 15); *Col. Rec. Pa.*, 1: 126, 263–66; 3: 144–45, 159; Browning, *Welsh Settlement*, pp. 337, 345.

61. Stevens and Kent, *County Government*, p. 7; law for county levies, 1700, Mitchell and Flanders, *Statutes at Large, Pa.*, 2: 34–39. Election and judicial districts laid down by county government were ephemeral. There were 8 election districts in Chester in 1739, 3 in 1776, and 4 in 1785; Futhey and Cope, *Chester County*, pp. 224–25. Lancaster County was divided into 8 judicial districts under justices of peace in 1739 and 11 districts in 1787; Ellis and S. Evans, *Lancaster County*, pp. 217–18.

62. George *et al.*, *Charter and Laws*, pp. 83–99, to 1700, and the "Charter of Privileges" of 1701 abstracted in Wilmot, "Penns and Taxation," pp. 421–28.

63. Rothermund, *Layman's Progress*, p. 69; Nelson, "Backcountry," chaps. 6, 7.

64. Stevens and Kent, *County Government*, p. 7.

65. Sergeant, *Land Laws*, p. 34.

66. To T. Penn, Aug. 13, 1734, Lanc. Co. MSS, 1: 7. Garvan, "Proprietary Philadelphia," p. 199, suggests democracy and weakened structures came only in 1776.

67. Stevens and Kent, *County Government*, p. 7; Nelson, "Backcountry," p. 222.

68. County courts of quarter sessions had power to lay out townships, and residents could petition for them. Stevens and Kent, *County Government*, pp. 3-5; Shultze, *Journals*, 1: 138-39.

69. E.g., the maps of William Scull, "A Map of the Province of Pennsylvania" (1770), and Reading Howell, "A Map of the State of Pennsylvania" (1792), *Pa. Arch.*, 3d ser., app. to vols. 1-10.

70. Muhlenberg, *Journals*, 1: 67; Mittelberger, *Journey to Pennsylvania*, p. 48. Charles H. Glatfelder, "The Eighteenth Century German Lutheran and Reformed Clergymen in the Susquehanna Valley," *Pa. Hist.*, 20 (1953): 61, has computed that the ratio of churches to ministers was 4½ to 1 among these groups compared with 2 to 1 among Presbyterians. Also see Rothermund, *Layman's Progress*, pp. 37, 58; T. Smith, "Congregation, State, and Denomination," pp. 172-75.

71. Oswald, *Reports of the Lutheran Congregation*, 2: 52; Rothermund, *Layman's Progress*, chaps. on "The Great Awakening" and "The New Denominational Consciousness."

72. See chap. 2. The Amish today at least have "church districts." There are 36 in Lancaster County and average 4.3 square miles. Not all boundaries are clearly defined, although roads, creeks, power lines, and hills serve in this capacity. Hostetler, *Amish Society*, pp. 71-74.

73. Lemon, "Rural Geography," app. 3, tables I and II, pp. 451-52, lists numbers of congregations and churches.

74. Carlisle is an exception among county seats. In the countryside churches were often situated on hills as if to symbolize light to the world. In some instances they stood on steep slopes.

75. Rowland Jones to the Secretary, Soc. Prop. Gospel; Chester, June 17, 1730, in Perry, *Collections Relating to the Church*, 2: 169; T. Smith, "Congregation, State, and Denomination," p. 168.

76. Mead, *Lively Experiment*, pp. 14, 20.

77. *Ibid.*, p. 20; Rothermund, *Layman's Progress*, chap. 3.

78. See n. 55, chap. 1, on Quakers.

79. Mennonites apparently did not avoid politics entirely. In 1749 one was elected commissioner; Ellis and S. Evans, *Lancaster County*, p. 26 (identified by Miss E. Kieffer). The Moravians in Northampton County ran a slate of candidates in 1756; R. Peters to T. Penn, Oct. 30, 1756, Gratz Coll., Peters Letters to Proprietors, p. 104.

80. Roland L. Warren, *The Community in America* (Chicago: Rand McNally, 1963), chap. 6, specifies the functions relevant to localities as socialization, social control, social participation, mutual support, and the more clearly economic functions of production, distribution, and consumption.

81. T. Smith, "Congregation, State, and Denomination," p. 172.

82. *Pa. Gaz.* (Phila.), Feb. 15, 1770. See also advertisement Jan. 21, 1789 by four Germans regarding S. N. Johnson. Fletcher, *Pennsylvania Agriculture*, pp. 481-84, discusses church and neighborhood schools.

83. Jacob Carpenter of Lampeter Township asserted in his will that John Eastwood should remain as master of the schoolhouse at the end of the lane (1772); Lanc. Co. Will Book, 1C, 1357. See n. 77 above. See also Muhlenberg, *Journals, passim.*

84. Schoepf, *Travels in the Confederation*, 2: 9.

85. On peddlers and their regulation, see Shultze, *Journals, passim*; Futhey and Cope, *Chester County*, p. 432; Lancaster Corporation Book, Feb. 8, 1743, and *passim*, Lanc. City Hall; King of Prussia Tavern Book, Hist. Soc. Pa.

86. See Lanc. Co. tax returns, table 34, and Pollard to Benjamin and John Brown, Apr. 6, 1773, Pollard Letter Book, pp. 185-86.

87. Some tax lists specify weavers, most of whom were poor. There is no certainty of a putting-out system except in Philadelphia; Sam B. Warner, "Innovation and the Industrialization of Philadelphia, 1800-1850," in *The Historian and the City*, ed. Handlin and Burchard, pp. 63-69.

88. Coxe, *View of the United States*, p. 442, observed that manufacturing was scattered.

89. E.g., inventories of Patrick Campbell, Donegal, September 1772; Jonas Chamberlain, Sadsbury, December 1772; Chr. Hare, Lanc. Tp., September 1772; Chr. Wenger, Earl, October 1772; Isaac Shaver (store), February 1750; Lanc. Co. Courthouse.

90. H. Frank Eshleman, "History of Lancaster County's Highway System (From 1714-1760)," *Jour. Lanc. Co. Hist. Soc.*, 26 (1922): 37.

91. Arensberg, "American Communities," pp. 1153-55; T. Smith, "Congregation, State, and Denomination," pp. 175-76.

92. Greven, "Family Structure in Andover," p. 255, describes the family in New England as a "modified extended family." But in *Four Generations*, chap. 9, he speaks of more variation, suggesting that the extended family is more prominent today than through part of the period he studied. In Pennsylvania family ties were strong, and generations overlapped under the same roofs. Yet mobility was great, as we saw in the previous chapter.

93. See King of Prussia Tavern Book. I suspect that conditions were not much different from those of England in the 1740s described by Henry Fielding.

94. Burd, Tinian, nr. Middletown, to E. Shippen, June 17, June 23, 1769, Shippen Family Papers, vol. 11, Shippen-Burd Corr., pp. 99, 100, and Apr. 1, 1773, Elise Willing Balch Collection, Shippen-Balch Papers, 2: 17, Hist. Soc. Pa.

95. E.g., *Pa. Gaz.* (Phila.), Dec. 3, 1761, for Leacock Presbyterian lottery list of managers. See also *ibid.*, Mar. 5 and Apr. 30, and T. Barton to Secretary, Soc. Prop. Gospel, Nov. 16, 1764, in Perry, *Collections Relating to the Church*, 2: 367. William F. Worner, "The Church of England in Lancaster County," *Jour. Lanc. Co. Hist. Soc.*, 40 (1936): 87, noted the participation of Mennonites. Incidentally, lotteries were very popular in the early 1760s and after the Revolution for raising funds for many public structures. Advertisements in 1763 issues of the *Pa. Gaz.* (Phila.) indicate that they were not always successful. There were other specific instances of interaction among people of different groups. For example, witnesses to wills often were members of other groups.

96. Frederick Jackson Turner thought cooperation was a mark of the frontier; *The Frontier in American History* (New York: Holt, 1921), pp. 165, 258. See Stanley Elkins and Eric McKittrick, "A Meaning for Turner's Frontier, Part I: Democracy in the Old Northwest," *Political Science Quarterly*, 69 (1954): 323-39.

CHAPTER 5

1. Eric E. Lampard, "Historical Aspects of Urbanization," in *The Study of Urbanization*, ed. Philip M. Hauser and Leo F. Schnore (New York, London, Sydney: Wiley, 1965), pp. 519-54, recognizes that urbanization is a complex process involving more variables than size, space, and economic functions. Cities often are the organizing center over the whole range of a society's activities. Also see Julius Rubin, "Urban Growth and Regional Development," in *The Growth of Seaport Cities, 1790-1825*, ed. David T. Gilchrist, Proceedings of a Conference Sponsored by Eleutherian Mills-Hagley Foundation, 1966 (Charlottesville: University Press of Virginia, 1967), pp. 1-21.

2. Much of the data for fig. 33-37 and tables 20-22 are taken from county and other local histories and travel accounts, several of which are cited below, and especially Joseph Scott, *A Geographical Dictionary of the United States . . .* (Philadelphia, 1805) and *Geographical Description of Pennsylvania*; Jedediah Morse, *The American Gazetteer*, 2d ed. (Boston, 1804); Lewis Evans, "Map of Pennsylvania, New Jersey, New York and the Three Delaware Counties" (1749); Scull, "Map of the Province of Pennsylvania" (1770); and Howell, "Map of the State of Pennsylvania" (1792), all in *Pa. Arch.*, 3d ser., app. to vols. 1-10; Matthew Seutterum, "Pennsylvania Nova Jersey et Nova York cum Regionibus ad Fluvium Delaware in America . . . ," map (n.p., *ca.* 1748) in Div. Pub.

Rec., Harrisburg; and Pennsylvania, Bureau of Land Records, "Genealogical Map of Counties," 4th ed. (Harrisburg, 1959). Calculations of population and occupations shown in figs. 35 – 37 and tables 23 – 26 are based on data from Scott, Morse, and travel accounts; MSS tax returns in the Lancaster, Chester, York, and Berks county historical societies; tax lists printed in various volumes of *Pa. Arch.*, 3d ser.; Sutherland, *Population Distribution*, pp. 124 – 34; Greene and Harrington, *American Population 1790*, pp. xiii, 113 – 17; and various publications of U.S., Bureau of the Census, including *Heads of Families: First Census 1790: Pennsylvania*, pp. 9 – 11; *Return of the Whole Number of Persons within the Several Districts of the United States . . .* (Washington, 1801), pp. 2A – 2G; *Aggregate Amount of Persons within the United States in the Year 1810* (Washington, 1811), pp. 33 – 52a; *Census for 1820* (Washington, 1821), pp. 17 – 21; Rossiter, *Century of Population Growth*, pp. 142 – 43; and *Historical Statistics*, pp. 743 – 44. See nn. 24, 79, 83, 93, 94 below; 19, 71, 72, chap. 1; and 1, chap. 2, for further details on calculations of population and occupations.

3. Weld, *Travels*. 1: 53.

4. The extensive technical literature on central places is listed and annotated in Brian J. L. Berry and Allen R. Pred, *Central Place Studies: A Bibliography of Theory and Applications*, Regional Science Research Institute Bibliography Series, no. 2 (Philadelphia, 1961). Also see Walter Christaller, *Central Places in Southern Germany*, trans. Carlisle W. Baskin (Englewood Cliffs, N.J.: Prentice-Hall, 1966), and Brian J. L. Berry, *Geography of Market Centers and Retail Distribution* (Englewood Cliffs, N.J.: Prentice-Hall, 1967), who utilizes many empirical studies. In classical central place theory, central places are evenly distributed over space with their hinterlands falling into hexagonal patterns of differing sizes corresponding to levels in the hierarchy. All places at the same level in the hierarchy have about the same population and their hinterlands are of equal size and population. Differences between levels are at some constant factor. In Christaller's scheme 1 town is at the highest level, 2 at the next, then 6, 18, 54, and so on. Because some towns are located at the points of the market area hexagon of the next higher order place, the progression of market areas runs 1, 3, 9, 27, 81, etc. Various modifications have been made to the classical view, but the idea of thresholds remains critical.

5. Transport centers in theory should fall into linear patterns. Berry and Pred, *Central Place Studies*, pp. 16 – 17; Charles F. J. Whebell, "Corridors: A Theory of Urban Systems," *Annals Assoc. Am. Geogr.*, 59 (1969): 1 – 26.

6. A large literature exists on "external or agglomeration economies." An example is Allen R. Pred, *The Spatial Dynamics of U.S. Urban-Industrial Growth, 1800 – 1914: Interpretive and Theoretical Essays* (Cambridge, Mass.: M.I.T. Press, 1966), pp. 178, 195 – 96.

7. The early rapid growth of Philadelphia and back-country county seats seems to indicate that many people were ready to move in when the towns were founded (fig. 36). See the discussion below on laborers and the cultural activities of Philadelphia and county towns.

8. North, *Economic Growth*, pp. 157 – 59.

9. Jeannette Eckman, "Life among the Early Dutch at New Castle," *Delaware History*, 4 (1951): 258; Martin, *Chester*, p. 14.

10. On Philadelphia's early internal development see Gary B. Nash, "City Planning and Political Tension in the Seventeenth Century: The Case of Philadelphia," *Proc. Am. Phil. Soc.*, 112 (1968): 54 – 73; Hannah Benner Roach, "The Planting of Philadelphia, a Seventeenth-Century Real Estate Development," *Pa. Mag. Hist. Biog.*, 92 (1968): 3 – 47, 143 – 94.

11. This figure of 20 per cent, including suburbs, may distort the urban-hinterland relationship somewhat because half of New Jersey, most of Delaware, and a small part of Maryland looked to Philadelphia. On the other hand, Baltimore had considerable commercial control over the trans-Susquehanna area, which balances the figure somewhat. Hinterlands undoubtedly overlapped; unfortunately measures are unavailable. See fig. 44. On life and internal patterns in Philadelphia, see Warner, *Private City*, chaps. 1, 2.

12. George *et al., Charter and Laws*, pp. 85 - 86.

13. [W. Penn], "Penn's Proposals," pp. 60 - 61; Diffenderffer, "Early History," pp. 3 - 27.

14. A primate city is usually defined as being more than twice as large as cities in the next rank; Brian J. L. Berry, "City Size Distributions and Economic Development," *Economic Development and Cultural Change*, 9 (1961): 573 - 87.

15. See Jensen, *Maritime Commerce*; William Sachs and Ari Hoogenboom, *The Enterprising Colonials: Society on the Eve of the Revolution* (Chicago: Argonaut, 1965), esp. chaps. 7, 8.

16. The figures are in sterling. See discussion on currency in Bezanson *et al., Prices in Colonial Pennsylvania*, chap. 13.

17. Bjork, "Weaning of the American Economy," p. 545.

18. Matthias Slough, "Letters of Col. Matthias Slough to Robert Morris," ed. Charles I. Landis, *Jour. Lanc. Co. Hist. Soc.*, 24 (1920): 59 - 65. For shipments by shallops, John Thompson, Christiana Bridge, to Hollingsworth and Rudolph, Dec. 2, 1765, Hollingsworth Coll., Corr.

19. Reported in Rosengarten, "Ackenwall's Observations," p. 14. Franklin actually took the low year of 1723 and the high year of 1757 for his calculations. As a result he derived too favorable a figure.

20. Fig. 4 and, for the late 1780s, Bjork, "Weaning of the American Economy," p. 558.

21. Stuart Bruchey, ed., *The Colonial Merchant: Sources and Readings* (New York: Harcourt, Brace & World, 1966), pp. 119 - 25, and Calvin B. Coulter, Jr., "The Virginia Merchant" (Ph.D. diss., Princeton University, 1944), pp. 14 - 15.

22. Gould, "Economic Causes of the Rise of Baltimore," p. 231.

23. Sachs and Hoogenboom, *Enterprising Colonials*, p. 110.

24. As indicated by the top two lines of table 23, the occupations of many taxables were not specified. The closer the lower figure to the upper, the greater the likelihood of accuracy. Percentages (not shown) vary from 77 to 92 per cent. Single freemen without occupations have been entirely excluded. Some estimates have been made regarding laborers. With Lancaster as the norm, where the lists were most complete, most persons with low taxes in other towns were assumed to have been laborers. Except for Carlisle, the estimates seem reasonable. Variations from year to year even in Lancaster's figures indicate that assessors, too, had trouble assigning occupations to people. See n. 2 above for sources.

25. Arthur P. Middleton, *Tobacco Coast: A Maritime History of Chesapeake Bay in the Colonial Era* (Newport News, Va.: Mariners' Museum, 1953), pp. 353, 428, argues that the existence of estuaries inhibited the growth of towns. Coulter, "Virginia Merchant," pp. 7 - 8, 28 - 62, discussed reasons for the failure of large towns to materialize. Tobacco inspection warehousing induced some urbanization after 1730. Also see Bruchey, *Colonial Merchant*, pp. 135 - 39, and on urban settlements see Harry Roy Merrens, *Colonial North Carolina in the Eighteenth Century: A Study in Historical Geography* (Chapel Hill: University of North Carolina Press, 1964), pp. 142 - 72.

26. Barnard Diary records visits to Philadelphia, Chester, and Wilmington. He resided 30 miles west of the city.

27. *Pa. Arch.*, 8th ser., 7: 6304, notes that a day's journey over hills was 18 or 20 miles. On flat land near Philadelphia it would have been greater. Schumaker, "Northern Farmer and His Markets," pp. 63 - 64, discusses distances involved in trading wheat and flour. Also see William Gregory, "William Gregory's Journal, from Fredericksburg, Va., to Philadelphia, 30th of Sept., 1765, to 16th Oct., 1765," *Wm. and Mary Qtly.*, 1st ser., 8 (1904 - 5): 227 - 28.

28. Anna T. Lincoln, *Wilmington, Delaware: Three Centuries under Four Flags, 1607 - 1937* (Rutland, Vt.: Tuttle, 1937), p. 181. See also Warner, "Innovation and the Industrialization of Philadelphia," p. 68.

29. Livingood, *Philadelphia-Baltimore Rivalry*, pp. 15, 26, 30, 161. Mills were established after 1800 by Baltimore merchants at York Haven across from Middletown.

30. Sanford W. Higginbotham, *The Keystone in the Democratic Arch: Pennsylvania Politics, 1800–1816* (Harrisburg: Pennsylvania Historical and Museum Commission, 1952), p. 334.

31. Robert Albion, *The Rise of New York Port* (New York: Scribner's, 1939), p. 8; Livingood, *Philadelphia-Baltimore Rivalry*, pp. 11–12, 16.

32. *Col. Rec. Pa.*, 1: 513–14; George MacReynolds, *Place Names in Bucks County, Pennsylvania* (Doylestown, Pa.: Bucks County Historical Society, 1942), pp. 33, 294.

33. Martin, *Chester*, pp. 14, 87, and Henry G. Ashmead, *Historical Sketch of Chester, on Delaware* (Chester, Pa., 1883), p. 23, plan opp. p. 176, p. 300.

34. Eckman, "Life at New Castle," p. 258.

35. Lewis Evans, "A Brief Account of Pennsylvania . . . ," in Lawrence H. Gipson, *Lewis Evans* . . . (Philadelphia: Historical Society of Pennsylvania, 1939), p. 101. Alexander Graydon, *Memoirs of a Life, Chiefly Passed in Pennsylvania* . . . (Harrisburg, 1811), p. 5, commented on Bristol's stagnancy.

36. Joshua Hempstead, *Diary of Joshua Hempstead of New London, Connecticut . . . from September, 1711, to November, 1758 . . . with an Account of a Journey made by the Writer from New London to Maryland*, New London Historical Collections, no. 1 (New London, Conn.: New London County Historical Society, 1901), p. 525; James Birket, *Some Cursory Remarks made by James Birket in his Voyage to North America, 1750–1751* (New Haven, Conn.: Yale University Press, 1916), p. 53; Thomas Twining, *Travels in America 100 years Ago, being Notes and Reminiscences* . . . (New York, 1894), p. 64.

37. Barnard Diary, *passim*.

38. *Col. Rec. Pa.*, 2: 111, Nov. 16, 1703; 3: 111, Mar. 22, 1720/1.

39. W. Roy Smith, "Sectionalism in Pennsylvania," *Pol. Sci. Qtly.*, 24 (1909): 212; Rothermund, *Layman's Progress*, p. 69. Even though new counties were formed they were underrepresented.

40. J. Logan, I. Norris, and Thomas Griffith to J. Taylor, Feb. 14, 1729/30, and draft of Lancaster Townstead Surveyed for Propty 26 Feb. 1729/30, Taylor Papers, 15: 3058, 2599. The land originally thought to belong to the Penns actually was held by Andrew Hamilton. In 1734 the land passed to James Hamilton, who made a more concerted effort to plat the land. See Ellis and S. Evans, *Lancaster County*, pp. 360–68, and H. Frank Eshleman, "The Political History and Development of Lancaster County's First Twenty Years, 1729–1749," *Jour. Lanc. Co. Hist. Soc.*, 20 (1916): 37–68.

41. On York: T. Cookson to T. Penn, Nov. 13, 1742, Cadwallader Coll., Thos. Cadwallader Section, Coates List 28. On Reading: correspondence cited by J. Bennett Nolan, *The Foundation of the Town of Reading in Pennsylvania* (Reading, 1929), pp. 52–54, 58–59; idem., *Early Maps of Our Town* (Reading, 1928). On Carlisle: T. Cookson to T. Penn, Mar. 1, 1749, quoted in Samuel P. Bates *et al., History of Cumberland and Adams Counties, Pennsylvania* (Chicago, 1886), pp. 68–70; T. Penn to R. Peters, May 30, 1750, Feb. 24, 1750/1, Penn Papers, Penn Letter Books, 2: 306; 3: 37; R. Peters to T. Penn, Mar. 16, 1752, Penn Papers, Offic. Corr., 5: 219. On Easton: Andrew D. Chidsey, Jr., *A Frontier Village: Pre-Revolutionary Easton* (Easton, Pa.: Northampton County Historical and Genealogical Society, 1940), pp. 9–10. See also discussion on the Penns' towns in Nelson, "Backcountry," pp. 111–26.

42. Berry, "Remarks on Central Place Studies Conducted in the United States and Canada," in *Urban Systems and Economic Development*, ed. Forrest R. Pitts (Eugene: University of Oregon Press, 1962), p. 90, notes two of these principles in general terms.

43. "The Petition of the Inhabitants of the North East Side of the County of Lancaster," Berks and Montgomery Miscellaneous MSS, 27, Hist. Soc. Pa.; *Col. Rec. Pa.*, 3: 343, 4: 317, 15: 14; Ellis and S. Evans, *Lancaster County*, p. 24. Note also the movement in 1724 of the Bucks County seat from Bristol to Newtown. Jerome H. Wood, "Conestoga Crossroads: The Rise of Lancaster, Pennsylvania, 1730–1789" (Ph.D. diss., Brown University, 1969), deals chiefly with politics but also with the town's growth and functions.

44. From Lancaster, Dec. 4, 1749, Lancaster County MSS, 1: 65.
45. The site of Easton had been viewed by Thomas and John Penn in 1734 or 1735 but was not laid out until 1752. Chidsey, *Easton*, pp. 9-10.
46. T. Cookson to T. Penn, Nov. 13, 1742, Cadwallader Coll., Thos. Cadwallader Section, Coates List 28; Gould, "Economic Causes of the Rise of Baltimore," p. 231.
47. Thirty-eight of Pennsylvania's 67 counties were created between 1781 and 1813. Possibly Bucks was not divided because Newtown became the seat rather than off-center Bristol.
48. Egle, *Dauphin and Lebanon*, pp. 294-95.
49. La Rochefoucault-Liancourt, *Travels*, 1: 50. Compare Edouard C. V. Colbert Maulevrier, *Voyage dans l'Interieur des Etats-Unis et au Canada*, ed. Gilbert Chinard (Baltimore: The Johns Hopkins Press, 1935), p. 6, who thought Middletown's better natural site at the mouth of Swatara Creek would permit it to overtake Harrisburg.
50. Egle, *Dauphin and Lebanon*, pp. 294-95, 374, and esp. "Remonstrance and Petition" by J. Yeates of Lancaster, p. 110. See petition on behalf of Middletown, "The Petition of the Inhabitants of Lancaster County to the honourable Representatives . . . " Mar. 2, 1784, John A. McAllister Gift Collection, Hist. Soc. Pa.; J. Burd, Philadelphia, to J. Yeates, Mar. 9, 1784, Yeates Papers, 1718-1876, Correspondence, 1781-1788, Hist. Soc. Pa.; J. Yeates to W. Hamilton, Apr. 10, 1784, Hamilton Family Lancaster Estate Letter Book, p. 7.
51. There was much enthusiasm over Harrisburg especially; see Erkuries Beatty, Philadelphia, to Reading Beatty, Mar. 12, 1784, in Joseph M. Beatty, Jr., ed., "Letters of the Four Beatty Brothers of the Continental Army, 1774-1794," *Pa. Mag. Hist. Biog.*, 44 (1920): 239; John Kean, *Autobiography of Captain John Kean of Harrisburg*, ed. A. Boyd Hamilton (Harrisburg, 1888), p. 4; Egle, *Dauphin and Lebanon*, pp. 307-8.
52. See n. 24 above.
53. E.g., T. Cookson to T. Penn, June 8, 1752, Soc. Misc. Coll.
54. E.g., "Lancaster and Columbia," p. 51. See lotteries for public buildings collected from the *Pa. Gaz.* (Phila.) in early 1760s by H. Frank Eshleman, "Items of Local Interest from the Pennsylvania Gazette, 1761 to 1770," *Jour. Lanc. Co. Hist. Soc.*, 24 (1920): 6-8.
55. Schoepf, *Travels*, 2: 23; Robert Honyman, *Colonial Panorama, 1775: Dr. Robert Honyman's Journal for March and April*, ed. Philip Padelford (San Marino, Calif.: Huntington Library, 1939), p. 11; Thomas Hughes, *A Journal by Thos. Hughes for his Amusement . . .* , ed. R. W. David (Cambridge: At the University Press, 1947), pp. 66-67.
56. E.g., David McClure, *Diary of David McClure, 1748-1820*, ed. Franklin B. Dexter (New York, 1899), p. 32; John F. D. Smyth, *A Tour in the United States of America* (Dublin, 1784), 2: 161, in 1776. Estimates were often plagiarized.
57. Cazenove, *Journal 1794*, p. 51; Kean, *Autobiography*, p. 4.
58. "Petition of the Inhabitants of the North East Side of the County of Lancaster," p. 27; *Col. Rec. Pa.*, 3: 343; 4: 317.
59. Marshe, "Journal 1744," 1: 278; Ellis and S. Evans, *Lancaster County*, p. 18, 362; A. T. Volwiler, "George Croghan and the Westward Movement, 1741-1782," *Pa. Mag. Hist. Biog.*, 46 (1922): 284.
60. Luther M. Heisey, "A Biography of Paul Zantzinger," *Jour. Lanc. Co. Hist. Soc.*, 47 (1943): 113-19; Slough, "Letters," pp. 59-65.
61. E.g., Jacob Eicholtz, Lancaster Borough, 1760; John Ashbridge, Lancaster Borough, 1772; "Inventory of the Goods and Chattels, Rights and Credits which were of the Estate of George Ross deceased . . . [1786]," *Pa. Mag. Hist. Biog.*, 31 (1907): 375-76.
62. See William P. Holcomb, *Pennsylvania Boroughs*, Johns Hopkins University Studies in History and Political Science, 4th ser., no. 4 (Baltimore, 1886). On York fairs and markets without borough status, see John Gibson, *History of York County, Pennsylvania . . .* (Chicago, 1886), p. 516. Marcus Hook, a very small place, advertised its fairs;

Pa. Gaz. (Phila.), Aug. 16, 1750. See lists of fairs in, e.g., Abraham Weatherwise, *Father Abraham's Almanac . . . 1761* (Philadelphia, 1760).

63. The boroughs' lack of political significance and the open society made separate status for towns less important than in medieval England. J. Penn was opposed to the election of assembly members from boroughs; to T. Penn, Feb. 14, 1738/9, Penn Papers, Penn Letter Books, 1: 283.

64. Lancaster Corporation Book, Feb. 8, 1743, and *passim*, Lanc. City Hall; York, Minutes and Ordinances, Nov. 22, 1790, York City Hall; Luther M. Heisey, "The Famed Markets of Lancaster," *Jour. Lanc. Co. Hist. Soc.*, 53 (1949): 1-32.

65. Gibson, *York County*, p. 516.

66. Lancaster Corporation Book, July 4, 1772, 104 stalls; July 15, 1784, 53; Sept. 12, 1791, 32 (all were June fairs), Lanc. City Hall.

67. Holcomb, *Boroughs*, p. 41; J. Andrew Frantz, "History of Cattle and Stock Yards in Lancaster County Prior to 1800," *Jour. Lanc. Co. Hist. Soc.*, 28 (1924): 41-46.

68. Lemon, "Rural Geography," pp. 390-93.

69. Cazenove, *Journal 1794*, pp. 52-53, and others were impressed.

70. La Rouchefoucault-Liancourt, *Travels*, 1: 53; Worner, "Public-House Keepers in Lancaster County in 1772," *Jour. Lanc. Co. Hist. Soc.*, 35 (1931): 21-22.

71. Pownall, "Governor Thomas Pownall's Description of the Streets and the Main Roads about Philadelphia, 1754," *Pa. Mag. Hist. Biog.*, 38 (1894): 214.

72. *Pa. Gaz.* (Phila.), June 14, 1770; Carlton O. Wittlinger, "Early Manufacturing in Lancaster County, Pennsylvania, 1710-1840," *Jour. Lanc. Co. Hist. Soc.*, 61 (1957): 112.

73. Cazenove, *Journal 1794*, pp. 37, 52; Colbert Maulevrier, *Voyage*, p. 7.

74. North, *Economic Growth*, pp. 157-59.

75. See chap. 4 above; Jacob Hubley, Reading, to E. Burd, Aug. 30, 1795, Shippen Family Papers, vol. 14, Shippen-Burd Corr., 31. Hubley said the German-language Reading paper was read widely in Dauphin County.

76. Marshe, "Journal 1744," p. 278.

77. See, e.g., *Pa. Gaz.* (Phila.), Feb. 19, 1750/1. On churches, see, e.g., Henry M. Muhlenberg in Oswald, *Reports of the Lutheran Congregation*, vol. 2, *passim*. However, in 1793 Lancaster's German newspaper, *Neue Unpartheyische Zeitung*, circulated widely. Each week 50 copies went to Hagerstown, Md., according to Henry Wansey, *An Excursion to the United States of America in the Summer of 1794*, 2d ed. (Salisbury, Eng., 1798), p. 168.

78. For a discussion of social life in Lancaster, see Elizabeth C. Kieffer, "Social Life in Lancaster Borough," *Jour. Lanc. Co. Hist. Soc.*, 45 (1941): 105-23.

79. In 1774 the average tax per capita for the county was about 25s. 4d. and for the town of Lancaster 25s. 2d.; Eshleman, "Lancaster County's Tax," p. 5.

80. Chidsey, *Easton*, p. 235, map reconstruction of Easton, 1776; Christopher Marshall Diaries, 1774-85, D-F, *passim*, on Lancaster, Hist. Soc. Pa.

81. E.g., three cases from Lanc. Co. Deed Books: (1) KK, 106-14; (2) KK, 182-96; (3) KK, 77; F, 167; G, 356; M, 211; R, 323, 325. The third case indicates a decline in 1776, the first two in 1789, from previous highs.

82. See n. 24 above; J. Yeates, Lancaster, to W. Hamilton, June 19, 1784, Hamilton Family Lancaster Estate Letter Book, pp. 10-11.

83. This is admittedly a tenuous set of calculations, based as it is on table 23. The assertion is founded on the assumption that the greater the complexity of functions, the greater the occupational specialization.

84. Data from figs. 36, 11.

85. Schoepf, *Travels*, 2: 23; Hughes, *Journal*, pp. 66-67; Joshua Gilpin, "Journal of a Tour from Philadelphia through the Western Counties of Pennsylvania in the Months of September and October, 1809," *Pa. Mag. Hist. Biog.*, 50 (1926): 164; Le Chevalier Félix de Beaujour (1814), quoted in Charles H. Sherrill, *French Memories of Eighteenth Century America* (New York: Scribner's, 1915), p. 201.

86. Adam's, Bethel's, and Musser's Towns were laid out because of high prices in Lancaster proper; J. Yeates to W. Hamilton, July 17, 1784, Hamilton Family Lancaster Estate Letter Book, p. 15.

87. La Rochefoucault-Liancourt, *Travels*, 2: 47, on Maytown.

88. Baily, *Journal*, p. 130, in 1796 noted towns and villages every 7 to 8 miles between Georgetown and Frederick, Md.

89. Muhlenberg, *Journals*, 2: 391; advertisements in *Pa. Gaz.* (Phila.), Dec. 17, 1761, Apr. 29, 1762, Feb. 15, 1770. Only a few towns were advertised, and not all of these were successful. On lotteries, used very extensively for public works in the early 1760s, see S. M. Sener, "Millersville and Other Early Towns Established by Lotteries," *Jour. Lanc. Co. Hist. Soc.*, 4 (1899): 28–29. Another round of town building occurred in 1813. The Middle Atlantic area in the twentieth century has had a greater concentration of villages than other areas of the United States and consequently have smaller areas to service. But manufacturing has been important in these places. See Edmund de S. Brunner, *Village Communities* (New York: George H. Doran, 1927), pp. 28–29.

90. See table 10 and figs. 6, 35, 36.

91. Gibson, *York County*, p. 574.

92. See advertisements for planned towns in Chester County, *Pa. Gaz.* (Phila.), Feb. 18, Apr. 29, 1762. Unfortunately few town platters advertised their intentions. There were probably some ghost towns, and "Smithburg" was mentioned as one of the "lost" towns for which lottery tickets were sold; Samuel Evans, "Some Early County Mills, etc.: a Fulling Mill in 1714," *Jour. Lanc. Co. Hist. Soc.*, 1 (1896): 170.

93. Scott, *Geographical Dictionary*, and Morse, *Gazetteer*, and travelers frequently gave numbers of houses. Hypothetically the number of people can be calculated by multiplying the houses by 6, because in a sample of 39 cases in which both the population and houses were listed the average was 6.04 and the range between 5 and 7. In the few cases where the census data are available, however, many house estimates can be recognized as exaggerated. The distortions and conflicting estimates among various persons mean that compromises had to be reached. For many places an arbitrary figure of 100 was given. As a consequence of the conjectural character of data shown in table 26, a graph of the same data, normally advisable, would be stretching accuracy too far. Graphs on figs. 36 and 37 show the growth of some places for which the information is firmer than for others.

94. Tax lists are limited sources on occupations; in most lists only larger towns are differentiated in township returns. See Cazenove, *Journal 1794*, p. 31, for a census of Kutztown, a place of 50 houses and something less than 300 persons. He found 23 occupations and firms, including 2 stores, 5 taverns, 5 mill spinners, 1 tan yard, 1 tobacco factory, 1 minister, 1 schoolmaster, and 16 persons in 14 other crafts. These occupations would account for only 35 families. Some of the others would have worked in the factories or as day laborers. Kutztown was probably typical of lower third-order places with its 2 stores and was characteristic of places on main roads with 5 taverns. Also see Kean, *Autobiography*, p. 4, whose work in Hummelstown as a store clerk and conveyancer illustrates the lack of specialization in small places; Cooper, *Some Information Respecting America*, p. 50; nn. 24 and 82 above.

95. See lot holders in Earl J. Topper, *McSherrystown, Pa., Bicentennial, 1763–1963* (McSherrystown: privately printed, 1963); see assessments 1782, *Pa. Arch.*, 3d ser., vol. 17 *passim.*

96. Ellis and S. Evans, *Lancaster County*, pp. 303, 608–10; *Pa. Gaz.* (Phila.), Oct. 5, 1775; S. Evans, "Early Mills," p. 170.

97. See store at Hopewell Forge reconstruction, Berks County, and Lanc. Co. MSS taxlists, Elizabeth Township.

98. Howell, "Map of Pennsylvania."

99. Harry M. J. Klein, ed., *Lancaster County Pennsylvania: A History* (New York and Chicago: Lewis Historical Publishing Co., 1924), 2: 527.

100. Lancaster County Misc. MSS, 2: 5. See fig. 11 for population data.

101. See, e.g., James Hindman, "Map of Chester County" (Philadelphia, n.d. [ca.

1821-25]); a hamlet described in *Pa. Gaz.* (Phila.), Apr. 4, 1750. On Chester County post offices. see Scott, *Description of Pennsylvania*, pp. 58-61.

102. E.g., Delaware Co. MSS tax lists, 1802, Del. Co. Courthouse, Media.

103. Colbert Maulevrier, *Voyage*, p. 20.

104. *Pa. Gaz.* (Phila.), Feb. 20, 1749/50, Apr. 30, 1761.

105. Lincoln, *Wilmington*, map, end papers; Weld, *Travels*, 1: 34; Victor S. Clark, *History of Manufacturers in the United States* (New York: McGraw-Hill, for Carnegie Institution of Washington, 1929), 1: 185.

106. Lincoln, *Wilmington*, pp. 143-44, 181. Oliver Evans's innovations of elevators and conveyors were noted by several European travelers.

107. Médéric L. E. Moreau de Saint-Méry, *Moreau de Saint-Méry's American Journey*, ed. and trans. Kenneth and Anna M. Roberts (Garden City, N.Y.: Doubleday, 1947), p. 97.

108. Pastorius, "Positive Information," p. 399; Shoepf, *Travels*, 1: 122; Harrold E. Gillingham, "Calico and Linen Printing in Philadelphia," *Pa. Mag. Hist. Biog.*, 52 (1928): 109; Clark, *Manufacturers*, 1: 186.

109. See n. 18, chap. 4.

110. See chap. 1, Lanc. Co. MSS tax returns, 1758, 1759, 1782.

111. North, *Economic Growth*, chap. 12.

112. Weld, *Travels*, 1: 53.

113. Christaller, *Central Places*, pp. 66-67.

114. See n. 15 above and table 26.

115. Berry, "City Size Distributions," p. 575. The spatial distribution of cities today is obvious on many maps of the country. Whether eventually more equitable regional distributions will occur remains to be seen.

116. George R. Taylor, "American Economic Growth before 1840: An Exploratory Essay," *Jour. Ec. Hist.*, 24 (1964): 437; Bruchey, *Roots of American Economic Growth*, pp. 16-23.

117. See n. 49, chap. 1.

118. Lockridge, "Population of Dedham," p. 322; and "Evolution of New England Society," pp. 62-80.

119. Livingood, *Philadelphia-Baltimore Rivalry*, pp. 11, 16.

CHAPTER 6

1. Strickland, *Observations on Agriculture*, p. 3; *American Husbandry*, ed. Harry J. Carman (New York: Columbia University Press, 1939), p. 125.

2. Weld, *Travels*, 1: 112, while praising Pennsylvania, said that a farm of 50 acres in England made a better living than one of 200 acres in Pennsylvania. This may have understated the case for Pennsylvania. See Gordon E. Mingay, "The Size of Farms in the Eighteenth Century," *Ec. Hist. Rev.*, 2d ser., 14 (1962): 469-70. Burnaby, *Travels*, p. 61, said that Pennsylvanians "are by far the most enterprising people in the Continent"; and John Adams wrote Abigail that he was overcome by shame for New England farming on seeing farms near Philadelphia; May 25, 1777, *Adams Family Correspondence*, ed. Lyman H. Butterfield *et al.* (Cambridge, Mass.: Harvard University Press, Belknap Press, 1963), 2: 247.

3. George Washington, *Letters on Agriculture from his Excellency George Washington . . . to Arthur Young, Esq., F.R.S., and Sir John Sinclair, Bart., M.P. . . .*, ed. Franklin Knight (Washington, 1847), p. 36; Job Roberts, *The Pennsylvania Farmer; Being a Selection from the Most Approved Treatises on Husbandry, Interspersed with Observations and Experiments* (Philadelphia, 1804), preface.

4. For English categories see R. A. Butlin, "Some Terms Used in Agrarian History: A Glossary," *Agricultural Historical Review*, 9, pt. 2 (1961): 98-104.

5. *American Husbandry*, ed. Carman, p. 113. According to MSS tax lists, in 1759 26,837 acres of winter grain (wheat and rye) were sown in Chester and 24,247 in Lancaster. In 1898 farmers sowed 42,639 of wheat, 1,158 of rye, and 45,206 of corn. Hay acreages on the latter date exceeded 100,000. W. W. Thomson, *Chester County and Its People* (Chicago, 1898), p. 82.

6. J. Logan to W. Penn, Mar. 14, 1703/4, J. Logan Letter Books, 1: 136; "Diary of a Voyage from Rotterdam to Philadelphia in 1728," trans. Julius F. Sachse, *Proc. Pa. Ger. Soc.1907*, 18 (1909): 23.

7. Data for 1781 are from MSS lists and for 1784 from Futhey and Cope, *Chester County*, p. 336. These figures represent "winter grain," because tax returns usually did not separate wheat and rye. The only list noted that specifies "wheat" was for Earl Township, 1750.

8. Jensen, *Maritime Commerce*, p. 8.

9. U.S. production in 1950 averaged 16.6 bu. per acre; U.S., Bureau of the Census, *Historical Statistics*, p. 281. In 1898 Chester County yields averaged 20 bu. per acre; W. Thomson, *Chester County*, p. 82.

10. Leaming Diaries, 1770–77, vol. 1, July 6, 1750, Hist. Soc. Pa.; Shultze, *Journals*, *passim*, where records are fairly clear for yields in 1757, 1759, 1774, and 1786; Richard Buffington, Arithmetic and Farm Book, 1770–76, Ches. Co. Hist. Soc.

11. Losses are listed in Futhey and Cope, *Chester County*, p. 434.

12. Washington, *Letters on Agriculture*, pp. 83, 72, 38. Yields of spelt, now considered a different species, were supposedly 20 to 35 bu. per acre, but it was not mentioned frequently as most persons considered it a wheat. Both *Triticum spelta* and *T. sativa*, which includes most of our winter and spring wheat, have 42 chromosomes. Schoepf, *Travels in the Confederation*, 1: 305, noted its use among Germans and Scotch-Irish in Path Valley.

13. Cazenove, *Journal 1794, passim*, gave various estimates but none for Lancaster; La Rochefoucault-Liancourt, *Travels*, 1: 42, 31; Cooper, *Some Information Respecting America*, p. 114. Strickland, *Observations on Agriculture*, p. 44, said he found yields of 18, even 30, bu. per acre in Lancaster.

14. [John Beale Bordley], *Sketches on Rotation of Crops* (Philadelphia, 1792), p. 9; Parkinson, *Tour of America*, 1: 201–2, thought they were as low as one bu. where the Hessian fly attacked. But Bond to Lord Carmarthen, Oct. 1, 1788, "Letters of Bond, 1787–1789," p. 572, thought Pennsylvania had been spared the attacks of the fly until then. See Fletcher, *Pennsylvania Agriculture*, pp. 146–47.

15. Tax returns showing "sown" land were made in December, when wheat and rye were the only grains in the ground. If farms averaged about 10 acres of winter grain and if 2 were in rye (see below), then there were 8 of wheat. So if yields were 8 to 10 bu. per acre, an average farm would produce 64 to 80 bu. See figs. 52–55. In other counties acreages were similar. See David G. Williams, *The Lower Jordan Valley Pennsylvania German Settlement* (Allentown, Pa.: Lehigh County Historical Society, 1950), p. 71, where 10 was the average and the range 8 to 15. In Antrim Township, Cumberland County, 1763, the average was 8.5 acres; Lamberton Scotch-Irish Coll., p. 41.

16. W. Penn, "Further Account," p. 264; see below on efforts to improve agriculture.

17. "Diary of a Voyage 1728," p. 23; Bond to the Duke of Leeds, Mar. 1, 1790, "Letters of Phineas Bond, British Consul at Philadelphia to the Foreign Office of Great Britain, 1790-1794," Am. Hist. Assoc., *Ann. Rep. 1897* (Washington, 1898), p. 457. Sometimes wheat and rye were sown together as maslin; Fletcher, *Pennsylvania Agriculture*, p. 151, says this was done frequently.

18. See calculations in Table 8.I in Lemon, "Rural Geography," p. 242; Futhey and Cope, *Chester County*, p. 108.

19. Bond to Duke of Leeds, Mar. 1, 1790, "Letters of Bond, 1790-1794," p. 457. For table 28, a sample of 159 wills from the period 1740 to 1790 were used. The wills were written by what were average or better than average farmers, most of them German "plain folk." About one-third were written by English and Scotch-Irish, especially

Quakers, and one-eighth by Lutheran and Reformed Germans. Sectarians showed a greater propensity to specify goods than others. The sample as an indicator of diets may be skewed because older widows usually were the recipients. They may have eaten less than the average person and received some special concessions because of their age. But I assume that widows approximated the mean of a family of 5 or 6. See Lemon, "Household Consumption," pp. 60-61, 63-64.

20. Three-fifths of the names on a petition in 1733 from Lancaster County asking exemption from excise tax on liquor were German; *Pa. Arch.*, 8th ser., 3: 2196. Also see William Douglas, *Summary, Historical and Political of the First Planting, Progressive Improvements, and the Present State of British Settlements in North America* (London, 1755), 2: 333; Archibald Steel to Edward Hand, Nov. 6, 1791, Major General Hand Papers, 1771-1807, 2: 75, Hist. Soc. Pa.; L. Evans, "Brief Account" (1753), p. 116. Compare Benjamin Rush, "Dr. Benjamin Rush's Journal of a Trip to Carlisle in 1784," ed. Lyman H. Butterfield, *Pa. Mag. Hist. Biog.*, 74 (1950): 456.

21. Futhey and Cope, *Chester County*, p. 434; John Sugar Diary, 1794, Ches. Co. Hist. Soc.; James Tilton, "Answers to Queries on the Present Status of Husbandry and Agriculture in the Delaware State," *Colum. Mag.*, 3 (April 1789): 217; Parkinson, *Tour of America*, 1: 192; 2: 332, 325; Shultze, *Journals, passim.*

22. See below on horses. Washington, *Letters on Agriculture*, p. 39; Cooper, *Some Information Respecting America*, p. 121. Compare Philadelphia Society for Promoting Agriculture, *Memoirs* (Philadelphia, 1808), 1: xxxii.

23. Fletcher, *Pennsylvania Agriculture*, p. 152, has claimed that Germans "gave impetus" to barley production. Tax lists of urban centers cite breweries, but beer was so uncommon that reformers sought to promote its use to reduce whisky consumption. Lemon, "Household Consumption," pp. 65-66.

24. Bond to Duke of Leeds, Mar. 1, 1970, "Letters of Bond, 1790-1794," p. 457; Parkinson, *Tour of America*, 2: 356; Shultze, *Journals*, 2: 74 and *passim*; Scott, *Geographical Description of Pennsylvania*, p. 69; Tilton, "Answers on Agriculture in Delaware," p. 217; Cazenove, *Journal 1794*, p. 41; Muhlenberg, *Journals*, 3: 613.

25. "Peter Kalm's Description of Maize, How It is Planted and Cultivated in North America, Together with the Many Uses of This Crop Plant," ed. and trans. Esther L. Larsen, *Ag. Hist.*, 9 (1935): 98-117. Charles Varlo, *Nature Display'd, A New Work* (London, 1793) contains a discussion "On Indian Corn or Maize, Its Perfection and How to Raise It," p. 285. Also see W. Thompson, *Chester County*, p. 82.

26. Kalm, *America of 1750*, 1: 80; *American Husbandry*, ed. Carman, p. 116; Futhey and Cope, *Chester County*, p. 434; Washington, *Letters on Agriculture*, p. 83.

27. "Interesting Letter of Morgan Evan, 1714," *Pa. Mag. Hist. Biog.*, 42 (1918): 176-77; Cazenove, *Journal 1794*, pp. 41, 53; La Rochefoucault-Liancourt, *Travels*, 1: 6; 2: 261, 286, noting as low as 8 bu.; Morse, *American Geography*, p. 351; Scott, *Geographical Descriptions of Pennsylvania*, p. 69, saying 100 bu. was known in 1805.

28. Observers occasionally noted corn planted in rows. Moraley, *The Unfortunate*, p. 9; Kalm's "Description of Maize," pp. 105-6; Cooper, *Some Information Respecting America*, p. 137; Parkinson, *Tour of America*, 2: 326; [John Beale Bordley,] *A Summary View of the Courses of Crops, in the Husbandry of England and Maryland* . . . (Philadelphia, 1784), pp. 11, 15; Judge Richard Peters, *Agriculture Enquiries on Plaister of Paris, also Facts, Observations and Conjectures on that Subtance* [sic], *when Applied as Manure* . . . (Philadelphia, 1797), p. 51.

29. Lanc. Co. Commissioners' Book, pp. 91-103, Lanc. Co. Courthouse.

30. Edward Brinton Account Book, Ches. Co. Hist. Soc.; John Beale Bordley, *Essays and Notes on Husbandry and Rural Affairs*, 2d ed. (Philadelphia, 1801), pp. 310-11; Moraley, *The Unfortunate*, p. 9; Kalm, "Description of Maize," p. 111; La Rochefoucault-Liancourt, *Travels*, 1: 17-18; 2: 393.

31. See below for hogs. Andrew Hershy will, 1754, Lanc. Co. Will Book, 1B: 74; Moraley, *The Unfortunate*, p. 9 (1743); Johann C. Buettner, *Narrative of Johann Carl*

Buettner in the American Revolution (New York: printed for C. F. Heartman, 1915), p. 32; George R. Stewart, *American Ways of Life* (Garden City, N.Y.: Doubleday, 1954), p. 88; Richard O. Cummings, *The American and His Food: A History of Food Habits in the United States*, rev. ed. (Chicago: University of Chicago Press, 1941), pp. 14, 22.

32. Franklin to Jared Eliot, July 16, 1747, in Franklin, *Papers*, 3: 148; A. Jensen, *Maritime Commerce*, p. 86; George Logan, "On the Culture of Flax," *Colum. Mag.*, 8 (September 1792): 151.

33. E.g., Shultze, *Journals, passim*; Barnard Diary, Feb. 27, 1774. In 1787 one acre seeded with 1 bu. produced 80 to 200 lb. hackled and 4 to 10 bu. seed; George Morgan to Society, Mar. 1, 1787, Phila. Soc. Prom. Agric. Collections, George Morgan MSS, pp. 44-45, University of Pennsylvania Library.

34. Budd, *Good Order Established*, p. 47; *American Weekly Mercury* (Philadelphia), Oct. 12, 1721; Edward Antill, "An Essay on the Cultivation of the Vine . . . ," *Trans. Am. Phil. Soc.*, 1 (1769): 180-267. See chap. 7 on the regionalizing of hemp.

35. [Parke], "Interesting Letter, 1725," p. 350; "Diary of a Voyage 1728," p. 18; Cooper, *Some Information Respecting America*, p. 51. Fletcher, *Pennsylvania Agriculture*, p. 205, suggested that horticulture played a minor role in agriculture, but see his chap. 9.

36. Buettner, *Narrative*, p. 29; A. Thomson, "Franklin County," p. 318.

37. G. Thomas, "Historical and Geographical Account, 1698," p. 320; *Am. Wkly. Merc.* (Phila.), Mar. 22, 1722/3; *Pa. Gaz.* (Phila.), Apr. 3, 1729, Dec. 4, 1740; T. Barton, "The Farm of the Conestoga Indians" (Letter from Rev. Thos. Barton, Lancaster, to Edmund Physick, Dec. 18, 1770), *Pa. Mag. Hist. Biog.*, 4 (1880): 119.

38. Cazenove, *Journal 1794*, p. 11; Cooper, *Some Information Respecting America*, p. 129; *Pa. Gaz.* (Phila.), Mar. 4, 25, 1762; Christopher Sauer, "Description of Pennsylvania," p. 232. On wine production see E. Shippen to Edward, Jr., Apr. 19, 1771, E. Shippen Letter Book, p. 323, Am. Phil. Soc.

39. Slicher van Bath, *Agrarian History of Europe*, pp. 267, 278; Fletcher, *Pennsylvania Agriculture*, pp. 163-66.

40. W. Penn, "Information and Direction," pp. 332-33, and others; John G. Kasebier letter, 1724, in "Two Early Letters from Germantown," trans. Donald F. Durnbaugh, *Pa. Mag. Hist. Biog.*, 84 (1960): 225; Bishop John C. Cammerhoff, "Journal," in Egle, *Dauphin and Lebanon Counties*, p. 22; Hassert to van Ostade in the Netherlands, Jan. 9, 1733 (from the Hague Archives 74.I.13), in "Letters and Documents Relating to the Reformed Church," trans. William J. Hinke, Ref. Ch. Lib., Lancaster.

41. James Magraw letter, May 21, 1733, in Bates *et al.*, *Cumberland and Adams Counties*, p. 257; *Pa. Gaz.* (Phila.), May 24, 1750; and Cornwall Ledger G, 1774-76, p. 216, Hist. Soc. Pa., mention seed potatoes. Also see Scott, *Geographical Dictionary*, n.p., art. on Pennsylvania.

42. Cazenove, *Journal 1794*, p. 24; Futhey and Cope, *Chester County*, p. 434; [Parke], "Interesting Letter 1725," p. 350; Shultze, *Journals*, 1: 94; Tilton, "Answers on Agriculture in Delaware," p. 217; Parkinson, *Tour of America*, 2: 374, 336.

43. "Philadelphia in 1698," ed. Howard W. Lloyd, *Pa. Mag. Hist. Biog.*, 18 (1894): 247; Budd, *Good Order Established*, p. 36. On forage crops, see Bidwell and Falconer, *History of Agriculture*, pp. 102-5; Lyman Carrier, *The Beginnings of Agriculture in America* (New York: McGraw-Hill, 1923), pp. 26-29 and chap. 19; William A. Wheeler, *Forage and Pasture Crops* (New York, Toronto, London: Van Nostrand, 1950); and Henry E. Muhlenberg's list in Rupp, *Lancaster and York Counties*, app. Muhlenberg, son of the Lutheran "patriarch," was a noted minister and botanist in Lancaster. His papers are in the library of the American Philosophical Society.

44. Dickinson to Richard Champion, July 9, 1717, Dickinson Letter Book, p. 126; Burnaby, *Travels*, p. 88; Strickland, *Observations on Agriculture*, pp. 11-12.

45. *Am. Wkly. Merc.* (Phila.), Oct. 19, 1721, Mar. 22, 1722/3, June 13, 1723; Ches. Co. inventory, 1731, showing Susanna McCain with 24 lb. of clover seed, whether white

or red is not clear; *Pa. Gaz.* (Phila.), May 29, 1740; Cooper, *Some Information Respecting America*, p. 138; Washington, *Letters on Agriculture*, p. 38. See table 10.

46. *Am. Wkly. Merc.* (Phila.), Mar. 7, 1723; Futhey and Cope, *Chester County*, p. 336; Logan to Eliot, Oct. 14, 1755, in Jared Eliot, *Essays on Field-Husbandry in New England and Other Papers*, ed. Harry J. Carman and Rexford G. Tugwell (New York: Columbia University Press, 1934), p. 233; E. Shippen to Logan, Apr. 9, 1760, E. Shippen Letter Book, p. 212, Am. Phil. Soc.; Tilton, "Answers on Agriculture in Delaware," p. 217; Cazenove, *Journal 1794*, pp. 24, 58, 77.

47. Thomas Hill, "Journey on Horseback from New Brunswick, New Jersey, to Lycoming County, Pennsylvania, in 1799," *Pa. Mag. Hist. Biog.*, 14 (1890): 190; Cazenove, *Journal 1794*, p. 77; *Pa. Herald* (York), 1792, quoted in Gibson, *York County*, p. 352.

48. Judge R. Peters, *Agricultural Enquiries on Plaister of Paris*, pp. 19, 48, 92. See discussion of fertilizer below.

49. Franklin to Eliot, July 16, 1747, in Eliot, *Essays*, p. 221; *Pa. Gaz.* (Phila.), May 29, 1740. Timothy was probably domesticated in Europe rather than in New England, as Eliot (p. 61) claimed. Compare Charles V. Piper and K. Bort, "The Early Agricultural History of Timothy," *Journal of the American Society of Agronomy*, 7 (1915): 1–14.

50. Pollard to Thomas Swaine, Apr. 30, 1774, Pollard Letter Book, p. 402; Buffington and Marshall Papers, 4: 1435, Ches. Co. Hist. Soc.

51. La Rochefoucault-Liancourt, *Travels*, 2: 346; 1: 6; Jacques P. Brissot de Warville, *New Travels in the United States of America* (1788), trans. from French, 1792 ed. (Bowling Green, O.: Historical Publications Co., 1919), p. 150; Washington, *Letters on Agriculture*, p. 38. Meadows along the Delaware yielded 3½ to 4½ tons per acre, according to Michel-Guillaume Jean de Crèvecoeur, *Journey into Northern Pennsylvania and the State of New York*, trans. Clarissa S. Bostelmann (Ann Arbor: University of Michigan Press, 1964), pp. 573–74.

52. This amount of hay would probably result in one-third dry weight. On New England, see Bidwell and Falconer, *History of Agriculture*, p. 105.

53. Kalm, *America of 1750*, 1: 75. Black, brown, red, red and white, red with white faces (Hereford), and brindle were noted.

54. *Pa. Gaz.* (Phila.), Jan. 11, 1770; Bordley, *Essays*, pp. 162, 164; Parkinson, *Tour of America*, 1: 284–85; Fletcher, *Pennsylvania Agriculture*, p. 176; Rodney C. Loehr, "The Influence of English Agriculture, 1775–1825," *Ag. Hist.*, 11 (1937): 3–15; Charles T. Leavitt, "Attempts to Improve Cattle Breeds in the United States, 1790–1860," *ibid.*, 7 (1933): 51–67.

55. *Col. Rec. Pa.*, 2: 27, Sept. 1, 1701; John Jones, "Letter of John Jones, 1725," in Myers, *Narratives*, p. 458; Chester Co. inventories, 1730; George Stevenson letter, 1752, in Gibson, *York County*, p. 523; *Pa. Gaz.* (Phila.), Feb. 20, 1749/50, June 11, Dec. 17, 1761; Pollard to Swaine, Mar. 4, 1773, Pollard Letter Book, p. 167; G. Thomas, "Historical and Geographical Account, 1698," p. 319.

56. In 1701 cattle were imported from New Jersey and farmers were encouraged to raise sheep and to limit slaughtering of cattle; *Col. Rec. Pa.*, 2: 27.

57. *Pa. Arch.*, 8th ser., 4: 3126–27. Residents of Bucks County also complained of horses from New England; *ibid.*, p. 3238. See also John Reynell to brother, Feb. 28, 1771, John Reynell Letter Book, November 1770–April 1774, Hist. Soc. Pa.

58. Schoepf, *Travels in the Confederation*, 1: 213. A. Thomson, "Franklin County," p. 323, in 1773 mentioned the possibilities of raising cattle in the Ohio country to be driven east.

59. See regional distinctions in next chapter, especially n. 16.

60. Schumaker, "Northern Farmer and His Markets," p. 46. Numbers compiled for 16 places in New England by Mrs. Marga Stone yield average figures ranging from 2.2 to 10.1 of cattle over one year, plus oxen, 0.53 to 2.4; personal communication, Mar. 18, 1966. Mrs. Stone, assistant to Professor Lawrence Harper at the University of California,

Berkeley, has collected considerable data and contributed many perceptive comments. Also see Merrens, *Colonial North Carolina*, pp. 136–37; Jackson T. Main, "The Distribution of Property in Post-Revolutionary Virginia," *Miss. Vall. Hist. Rev.*, 41 (1954): 251.

61. Kalm, *America of 1750*, 1: 308; Thomas Jefferson, *Notes on the State of Virginia*, introduced by Thomas Abernethy (New York: Harper Torchbooks, 1964), p. 53.

62. Pim Letter and Account Book, Ches. Co. Hist. Soc. Cattle were slaughtered at 7 years according to [Bordley], *Sketches on Rotation of Crops*, p. 42, at 4 years according to *Letters on Emigration, by a Gent Lately Returned from America* (London, 1794), p. 34.

63. Bordley, *Essays*, pp. 162–63; Jacob Hiltzheimer, "Extracts from the Diary of Jacob Hiltzheimer, 1768–1798," *Pa. Mag. Hist. Biog.*, 16 (1892): 97, 166; Jefferson, *Notes on Virginia*, p. 53; Parkinson, *Tour of America*, 1: 285. Other sizes noted: Christopher Sauer, "Early Description of Pennsylvania," p. 251, a fat ox of 500–600 lb.; and Shultze, *Journals*, 1: 215, 310 lb. from a steer.

64. C. Marshall, *Diary*, pp. 213, 225; Washington, *Letters on Agriculture*, p. 74; Carl R. Woodward, ed., *Ploughs and Politics: Charles Read of New Jersey and His Notes on Agriculture, 1715–1774* (New Brunswick, N.J.: Rutgers University Press, 1941), p. 80. Cf. production in Frank B. Morrison *et al.*, *Feeds and Feeding; A Handbook for the Student and Stockman*, 22d ed. (Ithaca, N.Y.: Morrison Publishing Co., 1956), pp. 192, 225, who says a "fairly good cow" will yield 8,000 lb. milk, or 930 gallons.

65. Parkinson, *Tour of America*, 1: 87; Guldin, "Diary 1710," p. 68; Andreas Rudman, letter in "Two Swedish Pastors Describe Philadelphia, 1700 and 1702," ed. Ruth L. Springer and Louise Wallman, *Pa. Mag. Hist. Biog.*, 84 (1960): 206; Pastorius, "Postive Information," p. 397; Christopher Sauer, "Early Description of Pennsylvania," p. 251.

66. On stables: *Pa. Gaz.* (Phila.), Dec. 6, 1739, Dec. 4, 1740, Apr. 4, 1750, Mar. 1, Sept. 27, 1770; Shultze, *Journals*, vol. 1 *passim*, in 1750 hauled manure from stables; J. Burd to E. Shippen, Dec. 12, 1768, Shippen Family Papers, vol. 11, Shippen-Burd Corr., p. 87. On stall-feeding: Feree inventory, 1760, Lanc. Co., Hopewell Forge Journal A: 224, Hist. Soc. Pa., and R. L. Hooper to Edward Hand, Dec. 25, 1778, General Hand Papers, 1: 53. The quotation is from E. Shippen to [J. Hamilton], Mar. 9, 1769, E. Shippen Letter Book, p. 301, Am. Phil. Soc. See also *Col. Rec. Pa.*, 2: 27 (1701); Fletcher, *Pennsylvania Agriculture*, p. 169.

67. See n. 86 below on sources for proportions of land.

68. Washington, *Letters on Agriculture*, p. 40. Inventories also indicate this. Slicher van Bath, *Agrarian History of Europe*, p. 289, suggests that horses were more prevalent where cultivated crops were more important than livestock because of the need for transportation. This fits the Pennsylvania scene.

69. Schumaker, "Northern Farmer and His Markets," p. 46; Slicher van Bath, *Agrarian History of Europe*, pp. 290–93; Main, "Property in Virginia," p. 251; Mitchell and Flanders, eds., *Statutes at Large, Pa.*, 3: 422–24, also 5: 65–68.

70. Barnard Diary; *Pennsylvania Packet* (Philadelphia), Apr. 15, 1778. See also Pollard to Swaine, Apr. 30, 1774, Pollard Letter Book, pp. 400–401. Pollard hoped to breed 40 to 50 mares in the Carlisle area.

71. Fletcher, *Pennsylvania Agriculture*, p. 200.

72. Parkinson, *Tour of America*, 1: 250; Schoepf, *Travels in the Confederation*, 1: 204. M'Roberts, "Tour of America," p. 167, was more complimentary than others. Among European observers Parkinson was the most critical of American agriculture. Unlike most travelers, he actually farmed for a time near Baltimore. On sizes, see *Pa. Gaz.* (Phila.) advertisements. Most were 13 to 14 hands, but I suspect many of these were riding horses.

73. [Rush], "Manners of German Inhabitants," *Colum. Mag.*, pp. 23–24; Fletcher, *Pennsylvania Agriculture*, pp. 198–99, most of whose evidence is hearsay; Evelyn A. Benson, "The Earliest Use of the Term—'Conestoga Wagon'," *Jour. Lanc. Co. Hist. Soc.*,

57 (1953): 109-19. "Dutch" cited in 1728 petition for road, Futhey and Cope, *Chester County*, p. 167; "Irish" by W. Logan to John Smith, Nov. 30, 1762, Smith MSS, 6: 33, Hist. Soc. Pa.; "English," *Pa. Gaz.* (Phila.), June 5, 1760; "great," Andrew Feree inventory 1735, cited in Kuhns, *German and Swiss Settlements*, p. 87; "Philadelphia" in inventories, e.g., Peter Bricker, 1760, Lanc. Co.

74. In 1771, according to tax lists, 73 per cent of taxpayers in Lancaster Co. (not including single freemen) owned horses; 80 to 90 per cent had at least one cow, *Pa. Arch.*, 3d ser., 17: 3-165.

75. E.g., inventory of Wilkins of Donegal, *ca.* 1732, Lanc. Co., 30 horses.

76. Fletcher, *Pennsylvania Agriculture*, p. 260; Burnaby, *Travels*, p. 62. See n. 86 below.

77. Sarah Burd to Mrs. E. Shippen, Nov. 20, 1774, Shippen Family Papers, vol. 12, Shippen-Burd Corr., p. 28; Joseph Leonard Account Book, 1783-98, Ches. Co. Hist. Soc.; *Pa. Gaz.* (Phila.), Aug. 19, 1789 (G. Logan); Bordley, *Essays*, p. 186; Roberts, *Pennsylvania Farmer*, p. 199; Fletcher, *Pennsylvania Agriculture*, p. 190; Parkinson, *Tour of America*, 2: 290.

78. Shultze, *Journals*, *passim*; Leonard Account Book, folio 35, Ches. Co. Hist. Soc.; C. Marshall, *Diary*, pp. 236, 266; Parkinson, *Tour of America*, 2: 292; Jefferson, *Notes on Virginia*, p. 53; Bordley, *Essays*, pp. 180, 185, 187.

79. See n. 31 above; Lamech and Agrippa, *Chronicon Ephratense: A History of the Community of Seventh Day Baptists at Ephrata, Lancaster County, Penna.*, trans. J. Max Hark (Lancaster, 1889), pp. 221-22.

80. Schumaker, "Northern Farmer and His Markets," p. 46. Romney Marsh held a large number, but other places were little different from Pennsylvania, according to list compiled by Mrs. Marga Stone.

81. Numbers returned by assessors in December undoubtedly underestimated the spring stock. See n. 16, chap. 7.

82. John Buffington Arithmetic and Shoemaker Account Book, 1771-73, Ches. Co. Hist. Soc.; Parkinson, *Tour of America*, 1: 293. The longest discussion on sheep is Judge Richard Peters to John Sinclair through George Washington, n.d., in Captain Richard Peters Papers, 1687-1871, Correspondence Relating to Agriculture, 1772-1815, Hist. Soc. Pa. Arthur Young and Judge Peters debated climate and prejudice against sheep; Washington, *Letters on Agriculture*, pp. 86-87, 99, 109-12. See also Parkinson, *Tour of America*, 1: 75; La Rochefoucault-Liancourt, *Travels*, 4: 214; Franklin to Eliot, Dec. 10, 1751, in Franklin, *Papers*, 4: 214; M'Roberts, "Tour of America," p. 167; John Beale Bordley, "Directions for Obtaining a Good Stock of Sheep," *Colum. Mag.*, 9 (August 1792): 90.

83. On sizes of sheep and fleeces (tables 27, 28), see: Parkinson, *Tour of America*, 1: 6-7; Tilton, "Answers on Agriculture in Delaware," p. 219; Jefferson, *Notes on Virginia*, p. 54; John Beale Bordley, "Purport of a Letter on Sheep," *Colum. Mag.*, 4 (January 1790): 36; Shultze, *Journals*, 1: 94, 187. See n. 86 below.

84. *Pa. Gaz.* (Phila.), Mar. 20, 1760; Futhey and Cope, *Chester County*, p. 148; Parkinson, *Tour of America*, 1: 299; Christopher Marshall Diaries, Book D, Dec. 25, 1777.

85. G. Thomas, "Historical and Geographical Description, 1698," p. 324; Thomas Anburey, *Travels through the Interior Parts of America* (Boston and New York: Houghton Mifflin, 1923), 2: 164; Shultze, *Journals*, 1: 239-40; 2: 18, 20, 22, 186, 193.

86. On the average size of farms, see chap. 3. See collected list of advertisements in Lemon, "Rural Geography," p. 303, table 9.I. Other sources on proportions: a typical farm in Bucks County and pasture data from York County, Washington, *Letters on Agriculture*, pp. 83, 35-36; farms along the Delaware River, with more meadow than usual, Taylor Papers, 16: 3445; 7: 1312; and fig. 45. Several travel accounts, farm diaries, and the like also provided data, e.g., Cazenove, *Journal 1794*, and Shultze, *Journals*. See specific references above and below. Cf. on New England, Charles S. Grant,

"A History of Kent, 1738-1796" (Ph.D. diss., Columbia Univ., 1957), pp. 62-69, 323-28. Beef was calculated at 55 per cent of live weight and pork at 72 per cent by Marga Stone, "Caloric Values of Colonial Foodstuffs," MS, University of California, Berkeley.

87. See figs. 52-55 in Lemon, "Rural Geography," and fig. 54, this volume.

88. Return in Cope, "Historical Sketch of Chester County Agriculture," in Pennsylvania Board of Agriculture, *Report 1880* (Harrisburg, 1881), p. 209. Unfortunately interpolation using adjacent townships was necessary because for 1759 Thornbury data are lacking.

89. Muhlenberg, *Journals*, 3: 48; T. Penn to R. Peters, Jan. 9, 1753, Penn Papers, Penn Letter Books, 3: 181; W. Davy, "Mr. Davy's Diary 1794," ed. Norman B. Wilkinson, *Pa. Hist.*, 20 (1953): 132.

90. J. Steel to Michael Atkinson, Aug. 26, 1738, Logan Papers, Steel Letter Books, 2: 188; E. Shippen to Colonel Alford, Dec. 11, 1753, E. Shippen Letter Book, p. 65, Am. Phil. Soc; Washington, *Letters on Agriculture*, p. 83.

91. La Rochefoucault-Liancourt, *Travels*, 1: 9; Weld, *Travels*, 1: 32; *Pa. Gaz.* (Phila.), Jan. 7, 1762; Chinard, "Early History of Forestry," p. 451, citing Franklin in 1742; E. Shippen to [J. Hamilton], Mar. 9, 1769, E. Shippen Letter Book, p. 301, Am. Phil. Soc. Near Reading, John Penn, "John Penn's Journal of a Visit to Reading, Harrisburg, Carlisle, and Lancaster, in 1788," *Pa. Mag. Hist. Biog.*, 3 (1879): 289. Peter Miller of Ephrata, "Scheme of Floating Firewood on Creeks," n.d., in Stauffer Coll., Steinman MSS, interpaged with C. Marshall, *Diary*, with p. 130, complained that German farmers in Cocalico Township were destroying a lot of timber.

92. Cope, "Sketch of Chester Agriculture," p. 209.

93. Pearson, "Description of Lancaster and Columbia in 1801," p. 55.

94. Tilton, "Answers on Agriculture in Delaware," p. 219; Cooper, *Some Information Respecting America*, p. 114; La Rochefoucault-Liancourt, *Travels*, 1: 30; Scott, *Geographical Description of Pennsylvania*, p. 23.

95. Thomas Cheyney letter, 1796, quoted in Futhey and Cope, *Chester County*, p. 339.

96. Pastorius, "Positive Information," p. 405; E. Shippen to his children at Shippensburg, Feb. 4, 1754, E. Shippen Letter Book, p. 85, Am. Phil. Soc.; L. Evans to Pownall, Mar. 25, 1754, Etting Collection, Miscellaneous MSS, 1: 80, Hist. Soc. Pa.; Brissot de Warville, *New Travels*, p. 260; Magraw letter, May 21, 1733, in Bates *et al.*, *Cumberland and Adams Counties*, p. 257.

97. John Mair, "Journal of John Mair, 1791," *Am. Hist. Rev.*, 12 (1906): 81; Judge R. Peters, *Agricultural Enquiries on Plaister of Paris*, p. 81; "A Twelve Month Tour of Observation through America," in Varlo, *Nature Display'd*, p. 97.

98. Cheyney letter in Futhey and Cope, *Chester County*, p. 339.

99. T. Penn to R. Peters, July 17, 1752, Jan. 9, 1753, Penn Papers, Penn Letter Books, 3: 181; Taylor Papers, 16: 3402½, 3445; Penn Papers, vol. 9, Pa. Land Grants, p. 215(3); Buffington and Marshall Papers, 1: 271; 3: 1034, Ches. Co. Hist. Soc.; Hassert to Van Ostade in the Netherlands, Jan. 9, 1733 (from Hague Archives 74.I.13), in "Letters and Documents Relating to the Reformed Church," trans. Hinke, Ref. Ch. Lib., Lancaster; [Parke], "Interesting Letter, 1725," p. 349.

100. *Pa. Gaz.* (Phila.), May 17, 1759, Nov. 6, 1760, Feb. 12, 1761, Jan. 4, Dec. 27, 1770; J. Burd to E. Shippen, Feb. 25, 1769, Shippen Papers, vol. 11, Shippen-Burd Corr., p. 96; J. Shippen to E. Shippen, Jr., Feb. 7, 1789, Shippen Family Papers, Box of Edward-Joseph and others.

101. [Bordley], *Sketches on Rotation of Crops*, p. 8; Tilton, "Answers on Agriculture in Delaware," pp. 219, 157.

102. E. Jones, "Agriculture and Economic Growth in England, 1660-1750," *Jour. Ec. Hist.*, 25 (1965): 3-5 (reprinted in E. Jones, *Agriculture and Economic Growth in England, 1650-1815*, pp. 154-57); Budd, *Good Order Established*, p. 32.

103. Benjamin Hawley, Diary, 1761-63, Mar. 20, 1761, Ches. Co. Hist. Soc.; Schoepf, *Travels in the Confederation*, 1: 130; John Sellers reporting to Judge Peters in Judge R. Peters, *Agricultural Enquiries on Plaister of Paris*, p. 42.

104. Cazenove, *Journal 1794*, pp. 29, 48, 59; Cheyney letter in Futhey and Cope, *Chester County*, p. 339; Philip Price, Jr. to Judge Peters in Judge R. Peters, *Agricultural Enquiries on Plaister of Paris*, p. 22; Cooper, *Some Information Respecting America*, pp. 124, 137; [Bordley], *Sketches on Rotation of Crops*, p. 1; Mary K. Scheerer, "Development of Colonial Agriculture in Southeastern Pennsylvania" (M.A. thesis, Pennsylvania State College, 1933), p. 31, listing rotations, but without citations; Fletcher, *Pennsylvania Agriculture*, pp. 129-30.

105. Shultze, *Journals*, 2: 154; Schoepf, *Travels in the Confederation*, 1: 194; Judge R. Peters, *Agricultural Enquiries on Plaister of Paris*, pp. 170-71, 67; *Pa. Gaz.* (Phila.), June 24, 1789; *Die Germantauner Zeitung*, Feb. 22, 1785.

106. [Bordley], *Summary View of Courses of Crops*, p. 4; *American Husbandry*, ed. Carman, p. 41; George Logan, "Fourteen Agricultural Experiments, to Ascertain the Best Rotation of Crops," *Colum. Mag.*, 6 (March 1791): 162-68; Frederick B. Tolles, *George Logan of Philadelphia* (New York: Oxford University Press, 1953), chaps. 4 and 5; Lucius F. Ellsworth, "The Philadelphia Society for the Promotion of Agricultural Reform, 1785-1793," *Ag. Hist.*, 42 (1968): 189-99.

107. Cazenove, *Journal 1794*, p. 24; Bordley, *Essays*, p. 32.

108. [Bordley], *Sketches on Rotation of Crops*, p. 32; Pastorious, "Positive Information," p. 397; Hassert to van Ostade in the Netherlands, Jan. 9, 1733 (from Hague Archives 74.I.13), in "Letters and Documents Relating to the Reformed Church," trans. Hinke, Ref. Ch. Lib., Lancaster; Jan. 1, 1753, 1761, 1763, Norris MSS, Miscellaneous Large Folio, pp. 27, 37, 39, 41, Hist. Soc. Pa; Alison to Am. Phil. Soc., Apr. 2, 1773, MSS communications to the American Philosophical Society on Trade, &c., p. 6, Am. Phil. Soc.

109. Schoepf, *Travels in the Confederation*, 1: 212.

110. *Ibid.*, 1: 196; "Davy's Diary 1794," p. 137; *Die Germantauner Zeitung*, July 24, 1787; A. Thomson, "Franklin County," p. 321.

111. Adams, *Diary and Autobiography*, ed. Lyman H. Butterfield (Cambridge, Mass.: Harvard University Press, Belknap Press, 1961), 3: 225 (June 21, 1795); Cazenove, *Journal 1794*, pp. 33, 58; L. Evans to Pownall, Mar. 25, 1754, Etting Coll., Misc. MSS, 1: 80; Alison to Am. Phil. Soc., Apr. 2, 1773, Am. Phil. Soc.; Schoepf, *Travels in the Confederation*, 1: 196.

112. Cheyney letter in Futhey and Cope, *Chester County*, p. 339; La Rochefoucault-Liancourt, *Travels*, 2: 396.

113. Moraley, *The Unfortunate*, p. 9; La Rochefoucault-Liancourt, *Travels*, 1: 6; 2: 345, 390.

114. F. Morrison *et al.*, *Feeds and Feeding*, p. 568. Cf. La Rochefoucault-Liancourt, *Travels*, 1: 31, 42.

115. Slicher van Bath, *Agrarian History of Europe*, pp. 290-96, 312.

116. V., "On the Use of Oxen in Husbandry," *Colum. Mag.*, 1 (February 1787): 275; A Farmer [George Logan?], "The General Introduction of Working-Oxen, on Our Farms, a Most Desirable and Highly Beneficial Event," *ibid.*, 1 (July 1787): 521-25; Timothy Matlack, *An Oration . . . March 16, 1780 before the American Philosophical Society* (Philadelphia, 1780), p. 21; *Pa. Gaz.* (Phila.), Jan. 7, 1789; Roberts, *Pennsylvania Farmer*, pp. 189-90.

117. "Pownall's Description of the Streets and Roads," *Pa. Mag. Hist. Biog.*, 18 (1894): 213; L. Evans to Pownall, Mar. 25, 1754, Etting Coll., Misc. MSS, 1: 80; *Pa. Gaz.* (Phila.), May 17, 1759, Nov. 20, 1760, Feb. 12, 1761, Sept. 20, 1770, Feb. 20, 1772, Sept. 22, 1773; *Diary of McClure*, p. 32.

118. *Pa. Gaz.* (Phila.), Jan. 7, 1789, Feb. 20, 1772; B., "Method of Dressing Land with Lime," *Colum. Mag.*, 1 (September 1787): 632-33.

119. Woodward, *Ploughs and Politics*, pp. 189-90; Fletcher, *Pennsylvania Agriculture*, pp. 133-36; Schoepf, *Travels in the Confederation*, 1: 196; *Pa. Gaz.* (Phila.), July 29, 1789.

120. Gilpin, "Journal of a Tour 1809," p. 67; Judge R. Peters, *Agricultural Enquiries on Plaister of Paris*, pp. 19, 48, 66, 92.

121. Brinton Mill Account, folio 1977, Ches. Co. Hist. Soc.

122. Cazenove, *Journal 1794*, p. 33; Fletcher, *Pennsylvania Agriculture*, p. 136. Other manures, including potash, were mentioned infrequently.

123. John Bartram to Eliot, Feb. 4, 1752, in Eliot, *Essays*, pp. 191-92; *Pa. Gaz.* (Phila.), July 22, 1789; Judge R. Peters, *Agricultural Enquiries on Plaister of Paris*, p. 31; A Farmer, "Observations on Dr. Logan's Rotation of Crops," *Colum. Mag.*, 9 (August 1792): 89-91; Roberts, *Pennsylvania Farmer*, pp. 25-27; Cheyney letter in Futhey and Cope, *Chester County*, p. 339.

124. Schoepf, *Travels in the Confederation*, 1: 129-30; Matlack, *Oration, 1780*, p. 17; Ashmead, *Delaware County*, pp. 207-8; Fletcher, *Pennsylvania Agriculture*, pp. 91-99; L. Evans to Pownall, Mar. 25, 1754, Etting Coll., Misc. MSS, 1: 80.

125. Kalm, *America of 1750*, 1: 80, 88; Adams to Abigail Adams, May 25, 1777, in *Adams Family Correspondence*, 2: 278; Honyman, *Colonial Panorma, 1775*, p. 8; Twining, *Travels*, p. 75.

126. Warren C. Scoville, "Did Colonial Farmers 'Waste' Our Land?" *Southern Economic Journal*, 20 (1953): 178-81, has argued that they did not.

127. See table 1 and discussion of opportunity in chap. 3.

128. See draft of 112 acres between Crum and Darby creeks divided into "moieties" and 10 plots, Norris MSS, large folio, p. 67.

129. *Diary of Joshua Hempstead*, p. 523; *Pa. Gaz.* (Phila.), Feb. 8, 1770. See chap. 7 on regions.

130. Cooper, *Some Information Respecting America*, p. 131; Fletcher, *Pennsylvania Agriculture*, pp. 156-57.

131. W. Penn, "Further Account, 1685," p. 264; J. Steel to John Robinson, Feb. 10, 1734/5, Logan Papers, Steel Letter Books, 2: 87; *Am. Wkly. Merc.* (Phila.), June 13, 1723; "Pownall's Description of Streets and Roads," p. 215; Strickland, *Observations on Agriculture*, p. 68, 70; Lanc. Co. Will Book, 1B: 171, also 1A: 226, 1B: 74, 301; Shultze, *Journals*, 1: 95; E. Jones, "Agriculture and Economic Growth in England, 1660-1750," p. 4; Judge R. Peters, *Agricultural Enquiries on Plaister of Paris*, p. 66; Bordley, *Essays*, p. 31.

132. Pastorius, "Positive Information," p. 405; Mitchell and Flanders, *Statutes at Large, Pa.*, 2: 93; Shultze, *Journals*, 1: 141; *Pa. Gaz.* (Phila.), Feb. 20, 1749/50; Alison to Am. Phil. Soc., Apr. 2, 1773; Peter Kalm, "Peter Kalm's Observations on the Fences of North America," trans. Esther L. Larsen, *Ag. Hist.*, 21 (1947): 75-78.

133. Minutes and Accounts of County Commissioners of Lancaster, pp. 95, 99, Lanc. Co. Courthouse.

134. See, e.g., Schoepf, *Travels in the Confederation*, 1: 31, 209, 224; Muhlenberg, *Journals*, 3: 544, on locusts; Benjamin Jacobs [to Am. Phil. Soc.], Jan. 10, 1769, MSS Comm. on Trade, &c., p. 2, Am. Phil. Soc., on weevils south of Pennsylvania. Reports on the presence of the Hessian fly in Pennsylvania are not clearcut. J., Lancaster, to E. Shippen, Jr., Sept. 1, 1788, Shippen Papers, Edward-Joseph and others' box, noted the fly was "raging" in Bucks County, enough to force some farmers to sell out. Bond to Lord Carmarthen, Oct. 1, 1788, in "Letters of Bond, 1787-1789," p. 572, found none in the state, but later Bond to Duke of Leeds, Dec. 1, 1790, "Letters of Bond, 1790-1794," p. 466, noted its presence. Kavenagh, "Economic History of Suffolk County, New York," pp. 45-56, 161, deals with the fly in Long Island, where the problem was serious in the late 1780s. See also Cazenove, *Journal 1794*, p. 77; La Rochefoucault-Liancourt, *Travels*, 1: 31.

135. George Morgan to Society, May 20, 1787, Phila. Soc. Prom. Agric., Collection

of Letters (Typewritten), U. Pa.; *Pa. Gaz.* (Phila.), Oct. 28, 1789; John Sugar Diary, Oct. 4, 1773, Ches. Co. Hist. Soc.; Tobias Rudolph to Hollingsworth and Rudolph, Dec. 16, 1765, Hollingsworth Coll., Corr.

136. Pastorius, "Circumstantial Geographical Description," p. 376, and "Positive Information," p. 408; James Vaux and John Jacobs of Providence, Montgomery County, "Observations on the Destruction of Wheat by the Hessian Fly," *Colum. Mag.*, 2 (August 1788): 459.

137. La Rochefoucault-Liancourt, *Travels,* 1: 31; Pollard to Edward Barrett of Jamaica, July 11, 1773, Pollard Letter Book, p. 233; see n. 100, chap. 1.

138. Pastorius, "Positive Information," p. 397. See Ches. Co. inventories, 1714, and advertisements in *Am. Wkly. Merc.* (Phila.).

139. Kalm, "Description of Maize," p. 108; Barnard Diary, Jan. 5, 1789; *Pa. Gaz.* (Phila.), Dec. 4, 1740, Feb. 6, 1749/50, Jan. 29, 1761; Ross to J. Steel, June 14, 1739, Provincial Council Records, MSS, 1684–1823, Hist. Soc. Pa.

140. *Pa. Gaz.* (Phila.), Aug. 5, 1762, May 31, Sept. 27, 1770; Lanc. Co. MS tax list; [Rush], "Manners of the German Inhabitants," *Colum. Mag.*, p. 22; Cheyney letter in Futhey and Cope, *Chester County,* p. 339; Bordley, *Essays,* pp. 134–35.

141. Suggested to me by Clarence Kulp of Vernfield, a local historian who had studied records.

142. On the yearly round see Barnard Diary and Shultze, *Journals.* The timing of Shultze's sales of wheat and other grain to mills fits with seasonally high prices in Bezanson *et al., Prices in Colonial Pennsylvania.* In the late 1760s prices were high during and immediately after the harvest.

143. Chester Co. inventory, 1717 (no name); *Diary of Joshua Hempstead,* p. 522; Tilton, "Answers on Agriculture in Delaware," p. 219.

144. Shultze, *Journals, passim;* Joseph Jones Account Book, 1775–78, Ches. Co. Hist. Soc. In July 1775, 14 men were used by General Wayne; General Anthony Wayne Papers, Wayne Farm Book, Hist. Soc. Pa.

145. *Pa. Gaz.* (Phila.), Oct. 25, 1770.

146. Jacob Bare inventory, Lanc. Co.; Shultze, *Journals,* 1: 233; *Pa. Gaz.* (Phila.), July 8, 1756, Jan. 21, 1762, Oct. 23, 1760, Apr. 26, 1770; Futhey and Cope, *Chester County,* p. 337. A. Acker claimed to have made 1,660 fans; *Wochentliche Philadelphische Staatsbote,* Aug. 14, 1770. Sieves and riddles used for cleaning were noted in inventories.

147. Jacob Welshover inventory in Wentz, "York County," p. 206; Futhey and Cope, *Chester County,* p. 338.

148. Bordley, *Essays,* pp. 511–12; Bordley to Samuel Powel, June 22, 1788, Phila. Soc. Prom. Agric., MSS, 1: 22, U. Pa.

149. Bordley, *Essays,* p. 202; B. Jacobs to Am. Phil. Soc., Jan. 10, 1769, MSS Comm. to Am. Phil. Soc. on Trade, &c., p. 2, Am. Phil. Soc.

150. Matlack, *Oration, 1780,* p. 13; Schoepf, *Travels in the Confederation,* 2: 92, noting girdling in German Northampton County. Cf. Fletcher, *Pennsylvania Agriculture,* p. 64; G. Thomas, "Historical and Geographical Account, 1698," p. 319.

151. Fletcher, *Pennsylvania Agriculture,* p. 96.

152. Greville Bathe and Dorothy Bathe, *Oliver Evans: a Chronicle of Early American Engineering* (Philadelphia: Historical Society of Pennsylvania, 1935).

153. See n. 36, chap. 1; Andreas Sandel letter, June 17, 1702, in Springer and Wallman, "Two Swedish Pastors Describe Philadelphia," p. 214; [Parke], "Interesting Letter 1725," p. 350; Strickland, *Observations on Agriculture,* p. 16; La Rochefoucault-Liancourt, *Travels,* 2: 260. See also *American Husbandry,* ed. Carman, p. 127.

154. Thommen in Faust, "Documents in Swiss Archives," p. 117; Muhlenberg, *Journals,* 2: 121, noted that servants moved slowly; S. Burd to J. Burd, Mar. 3, 1764, Shippen Family Papers, vol. 11, Shippen-Burd Corr., p. 62.

155. E. Burd, Lancaster, to J. Burd, May 26, 1777, Shippen Family Papers, vol. 8, Corr., 1777-1821, p. 11; La Rochefoucault-Liancourt, *Travels*, 2: 253; Cazenove, *Journal 1794*, pp. 24, 34, 77, showing a varied picture; Bordley, *Essays*, p. 391. See chap. 4.

156. G. Thomas, "Historical and Geographical Description, 1698," p. 325; Guldin, "Diary 1710," p. 70; Seibt letter, 1734, in Shultze, *Journals* 1: 52.

157. Cf. densities in England, H. Clifford Darby, ed., *Historical Geography of England before A.D. 1800* (Cambridge: At the University Press, 1936), pp. 524-25.

158. A more complete discussion is found in Lemon, "Household Consumption," pp. 59-70, but note some changes in figures. See also n. 86 above and Russell W. Gilbert, "Pennsylvania German Wills," *Pa. Ger. Folklore Soc.* (Yearbook), 15 (1951): 5-107. On family sizes see n. 71, chap. 1.

159. Lemon, "Household Consumption," pp. 67-70. Lanc. Co. Deed Book, KK: 32, specified that a farm of 150 acres had to earn £100 a year to be viable. It was sold by the sheriff at £665.

160. Quakers were more inclined to grant a sum of money than Mennonites.

161. See n. 11, chap. 5, and tables 25 and 26.

162. Jensen, *Maritime Commerce*, pp. 15-16, 292-93. The year 1770 is chosen rather than 1772 because the latter was abnormally high. Prices used are presumably those paid to farmers, but this is not certain; Bezanson *et al.*, *Prices in Colonial Pennsylvania*, p. 3. The calculations are based on a population of about 200,000, or 36,000 to 40,000 families (table 7). Assuming that the rural population was 80 per cent of the total and that farm families were two-thirds of all rural families, farm families would have numbered roughly 20,000.

163. A. Jensen, *Maritime Commerce*, pp. 294, 296. Both products showed considerable fluctuation. Corn was sold chiefly in southern Europe but also in the West Indies and mainland colonies. The flax seed was sent to Ireland. On flax seed: Kalm, *America of 1750*, 1: 28, 255; *Pa. Gaz.* (Phila.), Nov. 8, 1770.

164. A. Jensen, *Maritime Commerce*, pp. 293, 243. Of 950 lb. of meat produced, 750 were consumed at home. Barrels contained 200 lb. Wood products were second to flour.

165. E. Jones, "Agriculture in England," pp. 3-6. See chap. 1 and nn. 57, 58 above.

166. A shortage of meat was noted in 1770, A. Jensen, *Colonial Commerce*, p. 19; Pollard to Thomas Earle, Liverpool, May 6, 1773, Pollard Letter Book, p. 208.

167. Washington, *Letters on Agriculture*, p. 36; "Address from the Philadelphia Agricultural Society," *Colum. Mag.*, 1 (September 1786): 36.

168. "Ein Bauer," in *Die Germantauner Zeitung*, May 29, Sept. 4, 1787. Strickland, *Observations on Agriculture*, p. 18, blamed the lack of tenancy for poor agriculture.

169. [Charles Thomson?], *Notes on Farming* (New York, 1787), p. 18, noted that Germans sowed clover with wheat. Most of this study was based, as the author says, on Arthur Young's tours of England.

170. Lütge, *Deutsche Sozial-und Wirtschafts Geschichte*, p. 252.

171. Bordley, *Summary View of Courses of Crops*, p. 4; n. 116 above.

CHAPTER 7

1. Peter Hall, ed., Introduction, in Johann Heinrich von Thünen, *Von Thünen's Isolated State: An English Edition of "Der Isolierte Staat,"* trans. Carla M. Wartenberg (Oxford, etc.: Pergamon, 1966), esp. pp. xx-xl. Another way to describe the logic of von Thünen is through the concept of economic rent. Like David Ricardo, von Thünen used the idea though stressing the bearing of location on rent rather than varied qualities

of land. As will be shown, the latter also bore on the regional patterns. Also see Chisholm, *Rural Settlement and Land Use*, esp. chap. 2.

2. L. Evans, "Brief Account," p. 101.

3. Main, *Social Structure*, p. 25, says that Berks County was "subsistent" rather than commercial.

4. On the basis of taxation; see n. 19, chap. 1.

5. Calculated from number of churches and table 5. See n. 50, chap. 1.

6. Barton, "Some Account of the Missions in Pennsylvania," May 2, 1760, in Perry, *Collections Relating to the Church*, 2: 315; *Germantauner Zeitung*, July 24, 1787; Cooper, *Some Information Respecting America*, p. 137; Oswald, *Reports of the Lutheran Congregations*, 2: 55; Mrs. Barton to Miss Louisa de Normandie, in "The Bartons in Lancaster in 1776," *Jour. Lanc. Co. Hist. Soc.*, 52 (1948): 216.

7. Schumaker's estimate, "The Northern Farmer and His Markets," p. 64, is based on the assumption that wheat and flour would not be shipped where the transport costs exceeded more than half the value. To ship a cwt. 100 miles cost 7s. 6d., according to Cooper, *Some Information Respecting America*, pp. 110, 133. Flour could be shipped greater distances because of value added per unit weight and the reduction of wheat by a third, although barrels added to the cost (1s. 8d. each) and weight. See also graph of costs in North, *Growth and Welfare in the American Past*, p. 111.

8. Cazenove, *Journal 1794*, pp. 54, 77, reported that by wagon the cost from Harrisburg was three times the cost from Downingtown, 8s. vs. 15–18d. per cwt. *Ibid.*, p. 60, noted that the cost of shipping a bbl. of flour from Carlisle was 10s. to Philadelphia and 7s. 6d. to Baltimore. La Rochefoucault-Liancourt, *Travels*, 1: 49, reported that the cost of shipment from Middletown was as high as from Harrisburg.

9. Von Thünen, *Isolated State*, ed. Hall, pp. xxxviii, 9–11.

10. F. Morrison *et al.*, *Feeds and Feeding*, pp. 225–27.

11. *Pa. Gaz.* (Phila.), Feb. 14, July 17, 1760, Jan. 4, 1770.

12. Moraley, *The Unfortunate*, p. 14 (1743); *Pa. Gaz.* (Phila.), Sept. 27, 1775.

13. "A Catalogue of the Fruit Trees, &c. in the Nursery of Daniel Smith and Co., Burlington, New Jersey . . . 1804," in Norris MSS, large folio, pp. 133, 135, 137. Cazenove, *Journal 1794*, p. 12, noted that a farmer in Jersey was turning from grain to apples.

14. "Pownall's Description of Streets and Roads," p. 216; James Read, Reading, to E. Shippen, Jan. 10, 1766, Shippen Family Papers, vol. 6, Corr. 1763–68, p. 139.

15. Tax lists for Philadelphia City and Lancaster, *Pa. Arch.*, 3d ser., 14: 151–220, 223–303, 471–561, 747–838; 17: 1–13, 290–99, 454–65, 602–16, 753–65.

16. I would be more definite were the data agreeable. If Chester County turned markedly to fattening, the tax returns do not show this. In 1759 there were supposedly 9,818 cattle; in 1764, 11,900; in 1773, 9,705; in 1781, 12,241; and in 1784, only 10,107. In 1800 as well there were fewer than in 1781, according to lists; excluding what was by then Delaware County, only 9 townships had higher average numbers than in 1781, and 25 showed fewer. (Officially, at least, only cattle and horses over three years of age were rated after 1764; Mitchell and Flanders, *Statutes at Large, Pa.*, 4: 358.) Similarly, horses and sheep show erratic patterns. For example, in 1764 there were supposedly 8,889 horses in Chester but only 7,260 in 1773; and 18,061 sheep were listed in 1781 but only 11,896 in 1784. The higher number in 1781 reflects a May assessment, whereas the other years were returned in December. But even assuming a 20 per cent annual slaughter rate for cattle (Marvin W. Towne and Wayne D. Rasmussen, "Farm Gross Product and Gross Investment in the Nineteenth Century," in National Bureau of Economic Research, *Trends in the American Economy in the Nineteenth Century*, Studies in Income and Wealth no. 24 [Princeton, N.J.: Princeton University Press, 1960], p. 283), the variations are great. Inability or inefficiency on the part of assessors would seem to have been responsible. Certainly it is not easy to make judgments on the basis of this data. Cf. Schumaker, "Northern Farmer and His Markets," p. 71, whose calculations differ from table 33. He probably grants Chester much too high a figure.

In figs. 46-49 the data are somewhat normalized by the removal of holders of one cow and one horse and of less than 25 acres. This deletes nonfarmers, including most inmates.

17. *Pa. Arch.*, 3d ser., 14: 402; Crèvecoeur, *Journey into Northern Pennsylvania and New York*, pp. 573-74.

18. Miss Alexander, "Social Life in Philadelphia in 1762," ed. Martha J. Lamb, *Pa. Mag. Hist. Biog.*, 10 (1886): 116.

19. *Col. Rec. Pa.*, 2: 39; 9: 4-5, 245; La Rochefoucault-Liancourt, *Travels*, 2: 263; *Pa. Arch.*, 8th ser., 4: 3126-27; Reynell to brother, Feb. 28, 1771, J. Reynell Letter Book, 1770-74; Schoepf, *Travels in the Confederation*, 1: 213; Scott, *Geographical Dictionary*, art. on Pennsylvania; Merrens, *Colonial North Carolina*, p. 135; Von Thünen, *Isolated State*, p. 155.

20. Shoemaker, *Pennsylvania Barn*, pp. 91-96, based on 1799 direct tax; Frantz, "Cattle and Stock Yards in Lancaster," pp. 41-46.

21. See references in nn. 103, 104, chap. 6.

22. B., *Order of Cultivation and of Crops* (Philadelphia, 1797), pp. 1-8 (in MSS section, Hist. Soc. Pa.). This person said he was leaving Philadelphia, which would probably mean it was not Bordley, who lived in Maryland.

23. Cazenove, *Journal 1794*, p. 78; Fletcher, *Pennsylvania Agriculture*, p. 183.

24. La Rochefoucault-Liancourt, *Travels*, 2: 396.

25. In von Thünen's scheme, butter production would be distant, over 90 English miles from the market; *Isolated State*, ed. Hall, pp. xxxvii, 149-50.

26. *Ibid.*, pp. 106-23; Chisholm, *Rural Settlement and Land Use*, p. 30.

27. Muhlenberg, *Journals*, 3: 48; Chinard, "American Philosophical Society and Forestry," p. 451; Alfred P. Muntz, "The Changing Geography of the New Jersey Woodlands, 1600-1900" (Ph.D. diss., University of Wisconsin, 1959), pp. 94-121.

28. Livingood, *Philadelphia-Baltimore Rivalry*, p. 29; Cazenove, *Journal 1794*, p. 52; Pearson, "Description of Lancaster and Columbia," p. 57.

29. Jacob H. Byrne, "Henry William Stiegel's Land Holdings," *Jour. Lanc. Co. Hist. Soc.*, 39 (1935): 13.

30. *Isolated State*, ed. Hall, pp. xxiii, 140-43. In 1830 von Thünen's 3d zone would have been under the "Belgian" system without fallow; the 4th, "Mecklenberg" with grass and clover fallows; and the 5th, "three fields." It seems fairly clear that in early Pennsylvania variations on the 4th occurred more frequently toward the end of the century, but the bare or rubbish fallow type similar to the 5th was still widespread. See discussion on rotations, chap. 6.

31. See chap. 6. In 1773 the average acreage in at least one area of Northampton County was 10, the same as in Chester and Lancaster in 1759; Williams, *Lower Jordan Valley*, p. 71. In Antrim Township, now in Franklin County, the average was 8.5 in 1763; Lamberton Scotch-Irish Coll., p. 41. Probably around 1770 and in the early 1790s acreages expanded somewhat; Pollard to Earle, May 6, 1773, Pollard Letter Book, p. 208; Bond to Duke of Leeds, Mar. 1, 1790, "Letters of Bond, 1790-1794," p. 456.

32. In 1782 Chester gristmills or flour mills composed 46 per cent of all mills. If the same ratio held in Lancaster the number of persons per mill would be 495, which undoubtedly underestimates the number of flour mills. If all mills noted in Lancaster in 1782 were flour mills, the number of persons per mill would be 228, which seems more appropriate. See lists in Sutherland, *Population Distribution in Colonial America*, p. 168 (1773), and in Scott, *Geographical Dictionary*, art. on Pennsylvania. The latter suggests that Montgomery had the greatest concentration of mills, but his data are incomplete.

33. 1781 data from MSS tax lists; 1784 from Futhey and Cope, *Chester County*, p. 336.

34. *Pa. Gaz.* (Phila.), Jan. 28, 1762. The eastern shore of Maryland was the "finest wheat district," according to Cazenove, *Journal 1794*, p. 50.

35. Lincoln, *Wilmington*, map, end papers; Weld, *Travels*, 1: 34; Crèvecoeur, *Journey into Northern Pennsylvania and New York*, p. 573.

36. Thornbury 1726 MS return, Ches. Co.

37. In general, farmers did not. See chap. 6.
38. A. Brinton Mill Account, Ches. Co. Hist. Soc.
39. Washington, *Letters on Agriculture*, p. 83.
40. Lanc. Co. MSS tax returns, 1759.
41. See above and chap. 6.
42. *Isolated State*, ed. Hall, pp. xxxviii, 149–58 (cf. Merrens, *Colonial North Carolina*, 137–40); E. Jones, "Agriculture and Economic Growth in England, 1660–1750," p. 6.
43. Lanc. Co. inventories, 1732: Wilkins, 30 horses, another 41; James Coultas to Hance Hamilton, Oct. 26, 1767, Hance Hamilton Papers, 1739–79, Hist. Soc. Pa.; *Pa. Gaz.* (Phila.), Jan. 17, Mar. 27, Dec. 4, 1760, Feb. 5, 1761.
44. Lanc. Co. MSS tax returns; inventory of Peter Bricker, Cocalico Tp., Lanc. Co.
45. Heisey, "Paul Zantzinger," p. 116. More requests for wagons for war purposes were made to Lancaster than to other counties—200 to, e.g., 60 from Chester and 60 from Berks; *Pa. Gaz.* (Phila.), May 24, 1759. Fewer than Chester might reflect the realistic assessment of a lack of willingness among Quakers. The number of 200 was supposed to be one-tenth of the total in Lancaster County; however, because the quota was not filled there, either the potential or the willingness of residents seems to have been exaggerated. Henry Bouquet to Col. Burd, June 27, 1759, to E. Shippen, Aug. 13, 1759, "Selections from the Military Correspondence of Colonel Henry Bouquet, 1757–1764," ed. Helen Jordan, *Pa. Mag. Hist. Biog.*, 33 (1909): 106, 111.
46. Warner, "Innovation and the Industrialization of Philadelphia," p. 66, notes the large number of weavers in the city.
47. Eric L. Jones, "Agricultural Origins of Industry," *Past and Present*, no. 40 (July 1968), pp. 58–71.
48. *Pa. Gaz.* (Phila.), Feb. 20, 1772.
49. *Am. Wkly. Merc.* (Phila.) Dec. 27, 1720; in Arthur Oliver's ledger, 1730, Martin Mylin was credited with 1,378 lb., Herbert H. Beck, "The Martin Mylin Anvil and Papers," *Jour. Lanc. Co. Hist. Soc.*, 53 (1949): 153.
50. Galbraith to J. Yeates, Aug. 20, 1769, in Stauf.er Coll., Steinman MSS interpaged with C. Marshall, *Diary*, with p. 87; Accounts, 1761–67, Div. Pub. Rec., Harrisburg; *Pa. Gaz.* (Phila.), May 30, 1765.
51. J. C. Wylie, ed., "Four Gossipy Letters," *Pa. Mag. Hist. Biog.*, 39 (1915): 464; Glass, "Agricultural Regions of Lancaster County," p. 48, notes a longer growing season along the Susquehanna, 200 days at Middletown, compared with 158 at Lancaster.
52. J. Bartram to Eliot, n.d., in Eliot, *Essays*, p. 205. The strict regionalizing of hemp in Lancaster or its ephemerality is supported by Parkinson, *Tour of America*, 2: 358 and a York County correspondent of Washington, *Letters on Agriculture*, p. 38, who said hemp was absent or scarce.

CHAPTER 8

1. These periods correspond roughly with those discussed in the context of urban development in chap. 5.
2. In 1730 the value of imports per capita was 20 shillings. It rose to 52 shillings in 1749 and in 1760, admittedly a year of unusually large imports following the end of the French and Indian War, to 81 shillings (figs. 4 and 11).
3. On economic growth after 1800 see the following. G. Taylor, "American Economic Growth before 1840," p. 437, does not think that conditions before 1830 were any better than in the 1790s. But Paul A. David, "The Growth of Real Product in the United States before 1840: New Evidence, Controlled Conjectures," *Jour. Ec. Hist.*, 27 (1967): 154, considers this estimate "barely more substantial than the Cheshire cat's smile." Nevertheless, Donald R. Adams, Jr., "Wage Rates in the Early National Period:

Philadelphia, 1785-1830," *ibid.*, 28 (1968): 404-26, argues that real wage rates rose in the 1790s and again between 1815 and 1830. In Pennsylvania the pattern of urban growth before 1840 hardly changed directions. By then towns in western New York and inland Massachusetts had become larger, averaging 16,500 and 8,300 respectively, compared with only 4,800 in Pennsylvania (calculated from G. Taylor, "American Urban Growth Preceding the Railway Age," *ibid.*, 27 [1967]: 311-15, and presented in my paper, "On the Regional Development of Southeastern Pennsylvania to 1830," at a conference on "Regional Economic Study: Problems, Procedures, and Priorities," Eleutherian Mills Historical Library, Greenville, Del., October 1968). Fletcher, *Pennsylvania Agriculture*, e.g. pp. 286, 338, does not recognize major changes in agriculture in Pennsylvania before 1840, although his evidence is unclear.

4. Anburey, *Travels*, 2: 176.

5. Warner, *Private City*.

6. A recent serious discussion of these issues is found in Leo Marx, "American Institutions and Ecological Ideals," *Science*, 170 (Nov. 27, 1970): 945-52.

Bibliographical Note

Vast amounts of material exist for studying the development of early Pennsylvania and the spatial consequences. Yet the record is uneven. For some questions there is a plethora of data; for others, as is apparent in the text, several months of sifting unearthed a scant record or intractable sets of information. Yet from the primary literature, both manuscript and printed, I have been able to piece together many aspects of life. Some information, notably in tax lists, deed books, wills, gazetteers, travel accounts, and farm diaries, could be quantified and mapped. I have relied on many secondary accounts, such as studies of particular institutions and places put together by local historians who were intensely interested in their ancesters' lives and times. Of course, I have not always agreed with these interpretations, nor with those of professional scholars to whom I am nevertheless indebted for explanations and hypotheses.

The Historial Society of Pennsylvania and the Chester County Historical Society were the most important sources of manuscript material. In the former, the correspondence and other papers of prominent persons such as the Penns, James Logan, James Steel, Richard Peters, the Yeateses, Hamiltons, Shippens, Burds, Pembertons, and others were useful, particularly on government participation in the process of occupation of the land but here and there on relevant economic, social, and geographical matters. The Taylor, Churchman, and Lightfoot papers of surveyors contained a great deal of material on the land and the people. Philadelphia merchants' letters, such as those of William Pollard and the Hollingsworths, provided critical insights. Miscellaneous collections on various counties held some gems. Unfortunately, too few farm records are found in the Historical Society, but Richard Barnard's, Aaron Leaming's, and General Wayne's diaries are valuable. Christopher Marshall's diaries and the King of Prussia Tavern Account Book, among other smaller items, contain some important items. In the Chester

County Historical Society, thanks to Gilbert Cope and those who have followed him, is located what seems to be the best collection of manuscript material on early Pennsylvania farm life. The Amos Brinton grinding account, ledger, and day book, Benjamin Hawley's diaries and day books, Joseph Leonard's diary, and William Pim's letter and account book, for example, certainly brought me closer to everyday life. Then, too, this society holds the most comprehensive collection of county tax assessments and returns in Pennsylvania, beginning in 1693 and consecutively after 1715. Even though the accuracy of these records can be questioned, they provide the best material for analysis.

Other depositories provided valuable data. I used the manuscript tax list collection in the Lancaster County Historical Society, and to a lesser extent those in the historical societies of York, Berks, and Bucks and in the courthouses at Harrisburg, Carlisle, and Media. In the courthouses at Lancaster and West Chester I compiled some data from wills, estate inventories, and deeds. Inventories unfortunately do not record land, nor do they represent a complete cross section of society. The poor were more likely to die intestate than the affluent. Even so, the inventories are extremely useful. Inventories and deeds could be profitably mined much more than I did for this study. In the American Philosophical Society library the letters of Edward Shippen and MSS Communications to the Society on Trade, etc., were particularly useful. The library of the Division of Public Records in Harrisburg has some important manuscripts, such as William McCord's accounts, 1761–67, and the General Loan Office accounts. The municipal records of Lancaster and York inform us of the preoccupations of the borough fathers. I utilized the collection of letters and documents translated by Willian J. Hinke and in the Reformed Church Library, Lancaster. Finally, for the end of the period under study and beyond, I used the manuscripts of the Philadelphia Society for Promoting Agriculture in the University of Pennsylvania.

A wide array of printed primary material exists. Among the several newspapers, I explored the *Pennsylvania Gazette* most intensively. A sample of farm advertisements, taken every ten years after 1729, provide unparalleled data on farms, including sizes, fields, crops, livestock, and markets. Between 1719 and 1729 advertisements in the *American Weekly Mercury* yield similar information. I also used other newspapers, notably the *Pennsylvania Journal*, *Wochentliche Philadelphische Staatsbote*, *Germantauner Zeitung*, *Neue Unpartheyische Lancaster Zeitung*, and *York Herald*. Articles by gentlemen farmers in the *Columbian Magazine*, begun in 1786, are helpful, if often wrongheaded. Benjamin Rush's "Manners of the German Inhabitants in Pennsylvania" was first published in this magazine.

Several books by inhabitants and travelers were used and criticized. The plans for agriculture by John Beale Bordley and reports sent to Richard Peters and George Washington provided key thoughts. Among the travelers I found most helpful were the anonymous author of *American Husbandry*, Andrew Burnaby, Theophile Cazenove, Thomas Cooper, Peter Kalm, William

Moraley, Thomas Parkinson, the Duc de la Rochefoucault-Liancourt, Johann Schoepf, William Strickland, and Isaac Weld. Joseph Scott's *Geographical Dictionary* and *A Geographical Description of Pennsylvania* contain a good deal of specific data on towns and other areas for the end of the period. Tench Coxe's *A View of the United States of America* (1794) had some interesting ideas. The best collection of shorter printed primary works is the *Pennsylvania Magazine of History and Biography*, particularly in its earlier years. Invaluable were the collected works and diaries of Benjamin Franklin, Henry M. Muhlenberg (including his *Journal* and the *Reports of the Lutheran Congregation*), David Shultze (a surveyor-farmer in what is now Montgomery County), Christopher Marshall, and Albert C. Myers (*Narratives of Early Pennsylvania*). The tax lists and government records in the *Colonial Records* and *Pennsylvania Archives* were also drawn on heavily. I used numerical data on population, trade, etc., brought together in the *Historical Statistics of the United States* and books on population by Evarts P. Greene and Virginia Harrington and by Stella Sutherland. The early maps by Thomas Holme, Lewis Evans, William Scull, and Reading Howell and the county maps published around 1820 provided evidence, particularly on towns and roads.

The writings since 1800 are legion. The late nineteenth century county histories, such as John S. Futhey's and Gilbert Cope's *Chester County* and Franklin Ellis's and Samuel Evans's *Lancaster County*, and the articles in the *Papers and Addresses* (more recently *Journal of the Lancaster County Historical Society*) revealed a vast store of information and some ideas. Stevenson Fletcher's *Pennsylvania Agriculture and Country Life, 1640–1840*, if not very analytical, is a gold mine of information. It is my good fortune that local historians have saved so much material.

I am in debt to professional scholars in a number of fields. The work of economic historians on Europe, for example Wilhelm Abel and his students in Germany, G. E. Mingay, E. L. Jones and others in England, and B. H. Slicher van Bath, especially in his *Agrarian History of Western Europe*, has been not only a source of data but an inspiration. Their analyses have cut through many previous misconceptions. The geographers Glanville Jones, James Johnson, and Gottfried Pfeifer, who with other scholars are assessing European rural life and settlement patterns, gave me many insights. On immigration and national and religious groups, the collection of lists gathered by Donald Yoder in the Pennsylvania German Folklore Society yearbooks were useful, as were the discussions by Mildred Campbell, James Leyburn, John Pomfret, and Abbot Smith.

On religious groups and attitudes in Pennsylvania, Dietmar Rothermund was of great use as were journals such as the *Mennonite Quarterly Review*. Frederick L. Weis's *The Colonial Churches and Colonial Clergy of the Middle and Southern Colonies* and Edwin Gaustad's *Atlas of Religion*, together with Hunter Rineer's manuscript list, kindly loaned to me, have specified dates and locations of churches. J. Potter's discussion in the Eversley and Glass *Popula-*

tion in History is the best yet on the population of the colonial period, though the new studies of New England's population are leading to a greater understanding of demographic history. The estimates of national groups by Howard F. Barker and others in the *Report of the American Historical Association 1931* were useful. Among the books on land tenure and the land systems, Marshall Harris's *Origin of the Land Tenure System in the United States* gives the best overall view. On settlement, although I disagreed with them in some basic ways, Conrad Arensberg's "American Communities," *American Anthropologist*, 57 (1955) and Glenn Trewartha's "Types of Rural Settlement in Colonial America," *Geographical Review*, 36 (1946) are the best overall surveys. On social structure, even though I have criticized it, Jackson T. Main's *Social Structure of Revolutionary America* is the basic work. On rural life generally, Max Schumaker's dissertation (University of California, 1948) on "The Northern Farmer and his Markets" was a critical source. On New England, Charles Grant's study of Kent, Connecticut; Philip Greven's on Andover, Massachusetts; Sumner C. Powell's *Puritan Village* and other new studies; Main's work on Virginia; and H. Roy Merrens's on North Carolina provided comparisons. On the economy of early America, Douglass C. North, George R. Taylor, Arthur Jensen, and William Sachs influenced my interpretations. Jerome H. Wood, in his dissertation on Lancaster, "Conestoga Crossroads" (Brown University, 1969), has done a valuable service of opening up the study of urban places at a scale other than that of large cities.

Theories from various quarters helped in the development of the framework. The spatial concepts of Walter Christaller and Heinrich von Thünen have been employed. On social theory such divergent thinkers as Talcott Parsons and C. Wright Mills, among others, have influenced my ideas. That I stress the equilibrium in Pennsylvania life may indicate the greater influence of Parsons than Mills, but the time scale and issues discussed led to this idea of stability more than an uncritical acceptance of the functionalists who see American society as fundamentally sound. The concepts used by Eric Lampard and others on economic development and urbanization have been useful. I have already acknowledged my debt to Andrew H. Clark and my fellow students in historical geography, who have contributed much to my understanding the tasks of geography in a developmental framework.

Sources for Figures

1. Pennsylvania, Bureau of Land Records, "Genealogical Map of Counties," 4th ed. (Harrisburg, 1959).

2. Various, esp. *Pennsylvania Archives*, 3d ser., vol. 12, map at end.

3. Various. Cf. John W. W. Loose, "Our Townships," *Journal of the Lancaster County Historical Society*, 66 (1962): 143–48.

4. U.S., Bureau of the Census, *Historical Statistics of the United States, Colonial Times to 1957* (Washington, 1960), p. 757; Robert Proud, *The History of Pennsylvania* (Philadelphia, 1793), 2: 264–65, 269–71; Arthur Jensen, *The Maritime Commerce of Colonial Philadelphia* (Madison: State Historical Society of Wisconsin, 1963), pp. 292–96.

5. Raymond E. Murphy and Marion Murphy, *Pennsylvania: A Regional Geography* (Harrisburg: Pennsylvania Book Service, 1937), p. 18; Armin K. Lobeck, "Physiographic Diagram of Pennsylvania," map (New York, 1951).

6. Charles E. Shaw, *The Soils of Pennsylvania*, Agricultural Experimental Station Bulletin no. 132 (State College, Pa., 1916), pp. 224–25.

7–11. See n. 71, chap. 1.

12–14. See nn. 71, 40, 50, chap. 1.

15. Photo of the original supplied by Rare Books Section, State Library of Pennsylvania, Harrisburg.

16. Fred J. Gorman, "Map of Penn's Manors" (Chester, Philadelphia, and Bucks counties), MSS, superimposed on a modern road map, Historical Society of Pennsylvania.

17. William H. Bayliff, *The Maryland-Pennsylvania and the Maryland-Delaware Boundaries*, 2d ed. (Annapolis: Maryland Board of Natural Resources, 1959); Pennsylvania, Bureau of Land Records, "Genealogical Map."

18. Chester County MSS tax assessments, Chester County Historical Society.

19. Ches. Co. and Lancaster County MSS tax assessments and returns, Ches. Co. Hist. Soc., Lancaster County Historical Society.

20. Lanc. Co. MSS tax returns.

21. *Pa. Arch.*, 3d ser., 24: 59–106, 347–568, 625–792.

22. *Pa. Arch.*, 3d ser., 17: 169–321, 689–898.

23. *Pa. Arch.*, 3d ser., 12: 3–124, 665–823.

24–25. Ches. Co. MSS tax assessments.

26. *Pa. Arch.*, 3d ser., 12: 665–823; 17: 689–898; Ches. Co. and Lanc. Co. MSS tax assessments.

27. Isaac Taylor, "Account of the Survey'd Lands in the County of Chester Deliver'd to the Justices Grand Jury and Assessors in ye Year 1710" (*ca.* 1712), and "A Supplement . . ." (*ca.* 1718), Ches. Co. Hist. Soc.

28. Ches. Co. and Lanc. Co. MSS tax returns.

29. *Pa. Arch.*. 3d ser., 12: 665–823; 17: 689–898; Ches. Co. and Lanc. Co. MSS tax returns.

30. *Ibid.* Single freemen excluded.

31. Benjamin Smith, *Atlas of Delaware County* . . . (Philadelphia, 1880).

32. Taylor Papers, 16: 3457–58, Hist. Soc. Pa. This is a draft of a proposed township, *ca.* 1710, apparently surveyed in 1682 and 1700 along the lines advocated by Penn but eventually resurveyed in a different fashion. The regular pattern of Xs denoting farmsteads is hypothetical. For a discussion of the failure of the township see Theodore W. Bean, *History of Montgomery County, Pennsylvania* (Philadelphia, 1884), pp. 1029–32. I am indebted to Mrs. Hannah Roach for bringing Plymouth to my attention.

33–37. Compiled from a wide range of sources, including local histories, travel accounts, maps, and census data. For details see n. 2, chap. 5.

38. Anne Bezanson *et al.*, *Prices in Colonial Pennsylvania* (Philadelphia: University of Pennsylvania Press, 1935), app.; *idem.*, *Wholesale Prices in Philadelphia, 1784–1861* (Philadelphia: University of Pennsylvania Press, 1936), app.; and *idem.*, *Prices and Inflation during the American Revolution, Pennsylvania, 1770–1790* (Philadelphia: University of Pennsylvania Press, 1951), app.

39. Ches. Co. MSS tax assessments.

40. Ches. Co. and Lanc. Co. MSS tax assessments.

41. *Ibid.*; *Pa. Arch.*, 3d ser., 12: 665–823; 17: 689–898.

42. Ches. Co. and Lanc. Co. MSS tax assessments and returns.

43. Ches. Co. MSS tax assessments and returns.

44. Johann Heinrich von Thünen, *Von Thünen's Isolated State: An English Edition of "Der Isolierte Staat,"* ed. Peter Hall, trans. Carla M. Wartenberg (Oxford, etc.: Pergamon, 1966); Max G. Schumaker, "The Northern Farmer and His Markets" (Ph.D. diss., University of California, Berkeley, 1948), p. 64.

45. Norris MSS, large folio, p. 91, Hist. Soc. Pa.

46. Ches. Co. and Lanc. Co. MSS tax returns.

47. *Ibid.*; *Pa. Arch.*, 3d ser., 12: 665–823; 17: 689–898.

48. Ches. Co. and Lanc. Co. MSS tax returns.

49. *Ibid.*; *Pa. Arch.*, 3d ser., 12: 665–823; 17: 689–898.

50. Ches. Co. and Lanc. Co. MSS tax returns.

51. *Ibid.*; *Pa. Arch.*, 3d ser., 12: 665–823; 17: 689–898.

52–57. Ches. Co. and Lanc. Co. MSS tax returns.

58–59. *Ibid.*; *Pa. Arch.*, 3d ser., 12: 665–823; 17: 689–898.

Index

Accessibility: centrality principle, 132-33, 222-23; to courts, 64; distance to market, 41, 64-65, 67, 207; to other areas, 29. *See also* Towns; Trade; Transportation

Adams County, 143. *See also* York County

Agriculture: change and reform of, 3, 4, 30-31, 171, 174, 175, 182, 208, 224, 226; commercialization of, 21, 31, 178; consumption of produce from, 155, 180; denominations and, 30, 160, 173, 190, 193, 209-10, 214, 224; extensive/intensive, 108, 150, 169, 177, 179, 194, 226; Indians and, 31-32; labor and, 179-80; land availability and, 180; land use types in, 151, 154, 167-69; mixed system of, 107-8, 151, 181, 216-17, 220; national groups and, xvi, 107, 165, 175, 183, 210, 214; in other colonies, 127, 161, 164, 166; regionalization of, 2, 150-51, 184-216, 226; techniques in, 30-31, 40, 169-80; territorial organization and, 107; in western Europe, 3, 4, 107-8, 174. *See also* Climate; Crops; Farms; Fertilizer; Land surface; Livestock; Soils; Towns; Trade

Alcoholic beverages, 115, 139, 147, 155, 156, 157, 195, 201, 203, 205, 225. *See also* Occupations, tavern keepers

American Revolution, 5-6, 21, 22, 26, 73, 81, 87, 125, 143, 225

Americans, reputation of, 76

Amish, 82-83, 91, 237-38. *See also* Mennonites

Anglicans, 18, 21, 47, 51, 55, 219

Animal life, native, 40, 157, 243

Area studied, xviii, xix, 41, 122

Atlantic world, 26, 27, 28, 29, 225

Back country, 28, 41, 55, 120-22, 131, 143, 222

Baptists, 18, 21

Barley, 152, 155, 156-57, 170, 171, 172

Bedford County, 198, 211

Bees, 153, 155, 167

Berks County, 43, 67, 81, 133, 174, 186-87, 192, 198, 211

Boundary disputes, 58-59

Breweries. *See* Alcoholic beverages

British (in Pennsylbania), 14, 78. *See* English; Scotch-Irish; Scots; Welsh

Bucks County, 36, 43, 55, 64, 76, 94, 130, 145, 168, 186-87, 198, 199, 219

Buckwheat, 152, 155, 157, 171, 172

Buildings: barns and outbuildings, 116, 163-64, 177, 197; church, 99, 110, 116, 140, 255; farmsteads, 102-9 *passim,* 254

Carolinas, 43, 66, 76, 86, 87, 161, 182, 197, 222

Cattle, 153, 155, 160-64, 171, 173, 194, 195-99, 211-13, 220, 268-69. *See also* Livestock

Chester County: acreages assessed in, 67; acreages warranted in, 67-68; crops in, 154, 156, 157, 158, 159, 204-11; denominations in, 19-20, 110; disputed areas in, 59; division of, xviii; fertilizing in, 174; holdings in, 52, 89-92, 104, 107-8; land cleared in, 168; land mort-

287

THE JOHNS HOPKINS PRESS

Composed in Baskerville text and display
by Jones Composition Company, Inc.

Printed on 60-lb. Sebago MF, Regular
by Universal Lithographers, Inc.

Bound in Bancroft Kennett
by L. H. Jenkins, Inc.

Binding designed by Victoria Dudley